Teaching and Researching Listening

APPLIED LINGUISTICS IN ACTION

General Editors:

Christopher N. Candlin and David R. Hall

Books published and forthcoming in this series include:

Teaching and Researching Listening

Second edition

Michael Rost

Longman
is an imprint of

Harlow, England • London • New York • Boston • San Francisco • Toronto
Sydney • Tokyo • Singapore • Hong Kong • Seoul • Taipei • New Delhi
Cape Town • Madrid • Mexico City • Amsterdam • Munich • Paris • Milan

Pearson Education Limited

Edinburgh Gate
Harlow CM20 2JE
United Kingdom
Telephone: +44 (0)1279 623623
Fax: +44 (0)1279 431059
Website: www.pearsoned.co.uk

First edition published in Great Britain 2002
Second edition published 2011

© Pearson Education Limited 2002, 2011

The right of Michael Rost to be identified as author
of this work has been asserted by him in accordance
with the Copyright, Designs and Patents Act 1988.

Pearson Education is not responsible for the content of third-party internet sites.

ISBN: 978-1-4082-0507-5

British Library Cataloguing in Publication Data
A CIP catalogue record for this book can be obtained from the British Library

Library of Congress Cataloging in Publication Data
Rost, Michael, 1952–
    Teaching and researching listening / Michael Rost. – 2nd ed.
        p. cm. – (Applied linguistics in action)
    Includes bibliographical references and index.
    ISBN 978-1-4082-0507-5 (pbk.)
    1. Listening–Study and teaching.   2. Listening–Research.
    3. Applied linguistics–Research.   I. Title.
    P95.46.R67 2011
    418.0071–dc22

                                                    2010040858

10   9   8   7   6   5   4   3   2   1
15   14   13   12   11

Typeset in 10.5/12pt Janson by Graphicraft Limited, Hong Kong
Printed and bound in Malaysia, CTP-KHL

Contents

General Editors' Preface

Applied Linguistics in Action, as its name suggests, is a series which focuses on the issues and challenges to teachers and researchers in a range of fields in Applied Linguistics and provides readers and users with the tools they need to carry out their own practice-related research.

The books in the series provide the reader with clear, up-to-date, accessible and authoritative accounts of their chosen field within applied linguistics. Starting from a map of the landscape of the field, each book provides information on its main ideas and concepts, competing issues and unsolved questions. From there, readers can explore a range of practical applications of research into those issues and questions, and then take up the challenge of undertaking their own research, guided by the detailed and explicit research guides provided. Finally, each book has a section which provides a rich array of resources, information sources and further reading, as well as a key to the principal concepts of the field.

Questions the books in this innovative series ask are those familiar to all teachers and researchers, whether very experienced, or new to the fields of applied linguistics.

- What does research tell us, what doesn't it tell us and what should it tell us about the field? How is the field mapped and landscaped? What is its geography?
- How has research been applied and what interesting research possibilities does practice raise? What are the issues we need to explore and explain?
- What are the key researchable topics that practitioners can undertake? How can the research be turned into practical action?
- Where are the important resources that teachers and researchers need? Who has the information? How can it be accessed?

Each book in the series has been carefully designed to be as accessible as possible, with built-in features to enable readers to find what they want quickly and to home in on the key issues and themes that concern them. The structure is to move from practice to theory and back to practice in a cycle of development of understanding of the field in question.

Each of the authors of books in the series is an acknowledged authority, able to bring broad knowledge and experience to engage teachers and researchers in following up their own ideas, working with them to build further on *their* own experience.

The first editions of books in this series have attracted widespread praise for their authorship, their design, and their content, and have been widely used to support practice and research. The success of the series, and the realisation that it needs to stay relevant in a world where new research is being conducted and published at a rapid rate, have prompted the commissioning of this second edition. This new edition has been thoroughly updated, with accounts of research that has appeared since the first edition and with the addition of other relevant additional material. We trust that students, teachers and researchers will continue to discover inspiration in these pages to underpin their own investigations.

Chris Candlin
David Hall

Preface

Teaching and Researching Listening is designed to be a reference source and guide for teachers and researchers who have an interest in the role of listening in language education and other areas of applied linguistics. In keeping with the intentions of the Applied Linguistics in Action series, *Teaching and Researching Listening* outlines issues of ongoing relevance to teachers and researchers of both first and second languages and suggests concepts and principles, approaches and resources for exploring these issues.

Readers may use the book as a selective reference, using only those sections that may help clarify their current teaching or research goals. Or, because of the wide range of issues introduced, the book may be used as an exploratory text that may impact the teacher's or researcher's work and interests in a broader sense and provide useful points of departure for further exploration.

M.R.

Acknowledgements

Due to the ever-expanding nature of this project on listening, I have had the good fortune of reviewing the work of a range of researchers, language specialists and teachers. Through correspondence, interviews, conferences, informal conversations and reading, I have had the privilege of contacting many individuals who have made significant contributions to this project. Without their willingness to share their ideas, this present volume would not be possible. In particular, I wish to thank: Please add and include in alphabetical order in this list: Ken Beatty, Phil Benson, Todd Beuckens, Leticia Bravo, Katharina Bremer, Jeanette Clement, David Conium, Shireen Farouk, Marc Helgesen, Ellen Kisslinger, Cynthia Lennox, Joseph McVeigh, Mario Rinvolucri, Katherine Rose, Eric Tevoedjre, Mary Underwood, Goodith White, JJ Wilson, Gillian Brown, Gary Buck, Anne Cutler, Karen Carrier, Wallace Chafe, Craig Chaudron, David Mendelsohn, Catherine Doughty, Rod Ellis, John Flowerdew, Stephen Handel, Jonathan Harrington, Greg Kearsley, Walter Kintsch, Tony Lynch, Dominic Massaro, Lindsay Miller, David Nunan, Teresa Pica, Jill Robbins, Larry Vandergrift, and Jef Verschueren. Although I have tried to do justice to their work in integrating, paraphrasing and synthesising selected portions of it, I accept responsibility for any oversimplifications, omissions, or errors of interpretation.

I would like to thank my colleagues, Julie Winter, Ruth Desmond, Steve Brown, Brett Reynolds and Leigh Stolle for their supportive work at checking out references and sources, and test-driving some of the sections. I also wish to thank my many inspiring students at Temple University and University of California, Berkeley, and participants at teaching seminars around the world, for their reviews of the teaching applications and research projects.

I especially wish to thank Chris Candlin, series editor and personal guru, for inviting me to undertake this project, for providing me with access to his broad knowledge of applied linguistic realms and for patiently guiding me through the maze of developing this work.

I would also like to thank David Hall, the series co-editor, and the staff at Pearson Education, particularly Kate Ahl, Josie O'Donoghue, Ray Offord, and Kathy Auger for shepherding this edition through development and production.

M.R.

Publisher's Acknowledgements

We are grateful to the following for permission to reproduce copyright material:

Figures

Figure 10.7 from *Official Guide to Pearson Test of English Academic (with CD-ROM)*, 1 ed. Pearson Education; Figure 10.9 from www.examenglish.com

Tables

Table 2.1 from Extending Our Understanding of Spoken Discourse, *International Handbook of English Language Teaching*, pp. 859–873 (McCarthy, M. and Slade, D. 2006); Table 10.3 from Council of Europe (2010), http://www.coe.int/T/DG4/Portfolio/?M=/main_pages/levels.html, http://www.ealta.eu.org/, © Council of Europe

Text

Box 2.3 from Grasping the nettle: The importance of perception work in listening comprehension (Caudwell, R.) 2002, www.developingteachers.com; Box on page 171 adapted from *English First Hand, Teacher's Manual*, 4 ed., Pearson Longman (Helgesen, M., Wiltshier, J., Brown, S. 2010); Box on page 285 adapted from Some self-access principles, *Independence*, Spring, pp. 20–1 (Cooker, L. 2008), IATEFL Learner Autonomy SIG; Box on pages 448–450 from http://www.joemcveigh.com

In some instances we have been unable to trace the owners of copyright material, and we would appreciate any information that would enable us to do so.

Section Introduction:
Perspectives on listening

Listening is a topic that has relevance to all of us. As one of the crucial components of spoken language processing – there is no spoken language without listening – listening is also an area that is interconnected with numerous areas of inquiry and development. Listening is quite apparently relevant in humanities and applied sciences such as linguistics, education, business and law, and in social sciences such as anthropology, political science, psychology and sociology. At the same time, the processes of listening are relevant to natural sciences such as biology and chemistry, neurology and medicine, and to the formal studies of computer sciences and systems sciences.

The relevance and prevalence of listening, however, does not make it readily knowable. Indeed, at a recent conference on spoken language processing, I heard one of the noted presenters go so far as to say, 'Spoken language is the most sophisticated behaviour of the most complex organism in the known universe.' It is not so surprising then that even after decades of study, we may just be scratching the surface of a deep understanding of the fundamental processes and mechanisms that underpin our ability to communicate with members of our own species.

In my research of listening as both a linguist and an educator, I have become curious about the ways listening is portrayed by the people I encounter in my everyday life and also by professionals various fields. Not surprisingly, both individuals and specialists tend to define listening in terms of their personal or theoretical interests in the topic. Looking at professional trends, we can see how these interests have evolved. In the early 1900s, when, due to developments in recording technology, acoustic phonetics was seen as a major breakthrough in communications research, listening was defined in terms of reliably recording acoustic signals in the brain for later use. In the 1920s and 1930s with advancing research into the human psyche, listening was defined as a largely unconscious process controlled by mysterious cognitive mechanisms. In the 1940s, when advances in telecommunications were exploding, and information processing was seen as a vast scientific frontier, listening was defined in terms of successful transmission and re-creation of messages (see for example Nichols, 1947). In the 1950s, when advances in computational science began to influence cognitive psychology, listening was defined in terms of dissecting and tagging input so that it could be stored and retrieved efficiently (see for example Cherry, 1953). In the 1960s, with the rise of transpersonal psychology, listening was defined by heuristics for understanding the inner worlds of both the speaker and listener (see for example Deutsch and Deutsch, 1963). With the renewed interest in globalism and anthropology in the 1970s, definitions of listening as invoking cultural schemata gained acceptance (see for example the historical review by Robb, 2006). In the 1980s, with growing interest in organisational behaviour, listening was defined in terms of 'people skills' and the conscious decisions a person made to be an active listener. In the 1990s, with advances in computer technology for dealing with vast quantities of data, listening came to be defined as the processing of input. In the 2000s, with the emerging ubiquity of digital networking, listening came to include the notion of keeping multiple events and people in one's accessibility network, and connecting with others quickly and efficiently. These shifts reflect changes in our expectations of what we are able to achieve through listening. I believe that our characterisations of listening, and of communication generally, will continue to evolve to reflect our changing worldview and our expectations what advances in science and technology will enable us to do.

Because listening is essentially a transient and invisible process that cannot be observed directly, we need indirect descriptions – analogies and metaphors to describe It. Here again, we find our descriptions consistent with our current perspective. A common metaphor from many people may be in terms of getting something: listening means catching what the speaker says. Among others, there is the familiar transaction allusion: listening is a type of negotiation for information or some desirable outcome.

While nearly every characterisation I hear has some unique perspective or personal tone to it, most definitions of listening I encounter seem to gravitate toward one of four orientations: receptive, constructive, collaborative and transformative. Here are some examples of definitions I have come across:

Orientation 1: receptive

Listening = receiving what the speaker actually says:

- Listening means catching what the speaker said.

- Listening means getting the speaker's idea.
- Listening means decoding the speaker's message.
- Listening means unpacking the speaker's content.
- Listening is harvesting what is in the speaker's mind.
- Listening refers to the selective process of attending to, hearing, understanding and remembering aural symbols.
- Listening is receiving the transfer of images, impressions, thoughts, beliefs, attitudes and emotions from the speaker.

Orientation 2: constructive

Listening = constructing and representing meaning:

- Listening means figuring out what is in the speaker's mind.
- Listening means finding something interesting in what the speaker is saying.
- Listening means finding out what is relevant for you.
- Listening means reframing the speaker's message in a way that's relevant to you.
- Listening means understanding why the speaker is talking to you.
- Listening means noticing what is not said.
- Listening is the process by which oral language is received, critically and purposefully attended to, recognised and interpreted in terms of past experiences and future expectancies.

Orientation 3: collaborative

Listening = negotiating meaning with the speaker and responding:

- Listening is co-ordinating with the speaker on the choice of a code and a context.
- Listening means responding to what the speaker has said.
- Listening is the process of negotiating shared information or values with the speaker.
- Listening means acting interested while the speaker is talking.
- Listening is signalling to the speaker which ideas are clear and acceptable to you.

- Listening is sharing the emotional climate of the speaker.
- Listening is the acquisition, processing, and retention of information in the interpersonal context.

Orientation 4: transformative

Listening = creating meaning through involvement, imagination and empathy:

- Listening is being involved with the speaker, without judgement.
- Listening is creating a connection between the speaker and the listener.
- Listening is showing empathy with the speaker.
- Listening is seeking synchronicity with the speaker.
- Listening is imagining a possible world for the speaker's meaning.
- Listening is the process of creating meaning in the speaker.
- Listening is the intention to complete the communication process.
- Listening is feeling the flow of consciousness as you pay attention to things.
- Listening is entering the flow created by the convergence of different media.
- Listening is the process of altering the cognitive environment of both the speaker and the listener.
- Listening is taking to heart, being moved and appreciating.

Some of these definitions and groupings may resonate with you, while others may be confusing or seem nonsensical. The purpose of this book is to examine a wide range of perspectives about listening in order to find those which are the most complete, the most inclusive, and will therefore best serve us in our teaching and in our research of spoken language.

The purpose of this book is to motivate informed teaching and research by considering listening in its broadest sense, and then by stimulating and guiding exploration of listening in teaching and research contexts. The reader is likely to find many of the topics in this book quite familiar and relevant, while others may seem somewhat tangential to their interests. My hope is that you, as the reader, will become more curious about these familiar aspects and then explore the newer aspects, with an openness to allowing ideas to cross-pollinate your own ideas for teaching and researching.

Outline of *Teaching and Researching Listening*

Section I, 'Defining listening', introduces the conceptual background of listening by highlighting a number of notions relevant to the teaching and researching of listening. Section II, 'Teaching listening', reviews principles of instructional design and methods of teaching listening, highlighting key features of various approaches and suggesting solutions to various pedagogic issues. Section III, 'Researching listening', provides a selective set of research areas involving listening that can be undertaken by teachers in the context of their own teaching, and provides action research frameworks for investigating these areas. Section IV, 'Exploring listening', provides a range of resources that can be used in pursuing questions related to defining, teaching and researching listening.

Readers can use this book in a number of ways. The book has been partitioned into sections with particular orientations and chapters with particular content focuses. Throughout the book, across sections, there is an intentional overlap of issues. This guarantees the reader exposure to the main concepts, regardless of how he or she approaches the text.

I Defining listening

Section Introduction:
The nature of processing

This section defines listening in terms of overlapping types of processing: neurological processing, linguistic processing, semantic processing, and pragmatic processing. A complete understanding of listening needs to account for all four types of processing, indicating how these processes integrate and complement each other.

Chapter 1 describes neurological processing as involving consciousness, hearing, and attention. The chapter describes the underlying universal nature of neurological processing and the way it is organised in all humans, for users of all languages. The chapter also attempts to elucidate nature of individual differences in neurological processing, to explain the individualised nature of the listening experience.

Chapter 2 describes linguistic processing, the aspect of listening that requires input from a linguistic source – what most language users would consider the fundamental aspect of listening to language. This chapter begins with a section on perceiving speech, and proceeds to describe the way in which listeners identify units of spoken language, use prosodic features to group units of speech, parse speech into grammatical units and recognise words.

Chapter 3 details semantic processing, the aspect of listening that integrates memory and prior experience into understanding events. This chapter focuses on comprehension as constructing meaning and the memory processes that are involved.

Chapter 4 introduces the broad issue of pragmatic processing. While closely related to semantic processing, pragmatic processing evolves from the notion of relevance – the idea that listeners take an active role in identifying relevant factors in verbal and non-verbal input and inject their own intentions into the process of constructing meaning.

Finally, Chapter 5 describes automatic processing – the simulation of listening by a computer. This chapter outlines the ways that natural language processing by computers emulates the linguistic, semantic, and pragmatic processing of humans.

Section I lays the groundwork for the discussion of teaching listening and researching listening that will follow in subsequent sections. Though a number of teaching and research considerations will be indicated in Section I, the primary focus of the chapters in this section is on understanding the processes themselves.

Chapter 1

Neurological processing

This chapter:

- differentiates hearing from listening and describes in detail the processes involved in hearing;
- defines the properties of consciousness that are involved in listening;
- describes attention as the initiation of the listening process.

1.1 Hearing

A natural starting point for an exploration of listening in teaching and research is to consider the basic physical and neurological systems and processes that are involved in hearing sound.

Hearing is the primary physiological system that allows for reception and conversion of sound waves. Sound waves are experienced as pressure pulses and can be measured in **pascals** (Force over an Area: $p = F/A$). The normal threshold for human hearing is about 20 micropascals – equivalent to the sound of a mosquito flying about 3 m away from the ear. These converted electrical pulses are transmitted from the **outer ear** through the **inner ear** to the **auditory cortex** of the brain. As with other sensory phenomena, auditory sensations are considered to reach **perception** only if they are received and processed by a cortical area in the brain. Although we often think of sensory perception as a passive process, the responses of neurons in the auditory cortex of the brain can be strongly modulated by attention (Fritz *et al.*, 2007; Feldman, 2003).

Beyond this conversion process of external stimuli to auditory perceptions, hearing is the sense that is often identified with our affective experience of participating in events. Unlike our other primary senses, hearing offers unique observational and monitoring capacities that allow us to perceive life's rhythms and the 'vitality contours' of events (Stern, 1999) as well as of the tempo of human interaction in real time and the 'feel' of human contact and communication (Murchie, 1999).

In physiological terms, hearing is a neurological circuitry, part of the vestibular system of the brain, which is responsible for spatial orientation (balance) and temporal orientation (timing), as well as **interoception**, the monitoring of sensate data for our internal bodily systems (Austin, 2006). Hearing also plays an important role in animating the brain, what Sollier (2005) calls cortical recharging of the sensory processing centers in the brain.

Of all our senses, hearing may be said to be the most grounded and most essential to awareness because it occurs in real time, in a temporal continuum. Hearing involves continually grouping incoming sound into pulse-like auditory events that span a period of several seconds (Handel, 2006). Sound perception is about always anticipating what is about to be heard – hearing forward – as well as retrospectively organising what has just been heard – hearing backward – in order to assemble coherent packages of sound.

While hearing provides a basis for listening, it is only a precursor for it. Though the terms **hearing** and **listening** are often used interchangeably in everyday talk, there are essential differences between them. While both hearing and listening are initiated through sound perception, the difference between them is essentially a *degree of intention*. Intention is known to involve several levels, but initially intention is an acknowledgement of a distal source and a willingness to be influenced by this source (Allwood, 2006).

In psychological terms, perception creates knowledge of these distal objects by detecting and differentiating properties in the energy field. In the case of **audition**, the energy field is the air surrounding the listener. The perceiver detects shifts in intensity, which are minute movements in the air, in the form of sound waves, and differentiates their patterns through a fusion of **temporal processing** in the left cortex of the brain and **spectral processing** in the right. The perceiver designates the patterns in the sound waves to various learned categories, which is the first stage of assigning some meaning to the sound (Zatorre *et al.*, 2002; Harnad, 2005; Kaan and Swaab, 2002).

The anatomy of hearing is elegant in its efficiency. The human auditory system consists of the outer ear, the middle ear, the inner ear, and the auditory nerves connecting to the brain stem. Several mutually dependent subsystems complete the system (see Figure 1.1).

The outer ear consists of the pinna, the part of the ear we can see, and the ear canal. The intricate funnelling patterns of the pinna filter and amplify

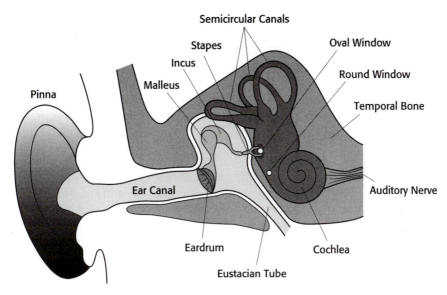

Figure 1.1 *The mechanism of hearing.* Sound waves travel down the ear canal and cause the eardrum to vibrate. These vibrations are passed along through the middle ear, which is a sensitive transformer consisting of three small bones (malleus, incus, and stapes) surrounding a small opening in the skull (the oval window). The major function of the middle ear is to ensure efficient transfer of sounds, which are still in the form of air particles, to the fluids inside the cochlea (the inner ear), where they will be converted to electrical pulses and passed along the auditory nerve to the auditory cortex in the brain for further processing.
Note The semicircular canals, which are also part of the inner ear, are used primarily for equilibrium but share the same cranial nerve (the eighth) that the auditory system uses, so hearing and balance are interrelated neurally

the incoming sound, in particular the higher frequencies, and allows us the ability to locate the source of the sound.

Sound waves travel down the canal and cause the eardrum to vibrate. These vibrations are passed along through the middle ear, which is a sensitive transformer consisting of three small bones (the ossicles) surrounding a small opening in the skull (the oval window). The major function of the middle ear is to ensure efficient transfer of sounds, which are still in the form of air particles, to the fluids inside the cochlea, where they will be converted to electrical pulses.

In addition to this transmission function, the middle ear has a vital protective function. The ossicles have tiny muscles that, by contracting reflexively, can reduce the level of sound reaching the inner ear. This reflex action occurs when we are presented with sudden loud sounds such as the thud of a dropped book or the wail of a police siren. This contraction protects the delicate hearing mechanism from damage in the event that the loudness persists. Interestingly, the same reflex action also occurs automatically when we begin to speak. In this way the ossicles reflex protects us from receiving too much feedback from our own speech and thus becoming distracted by it.

The cochlea is the focal structure of the ear in auditory perception. The cochlea is a small bony structure, about the size of an adult thumbnail, that is narrow at one end and wide at the other. The cochlea is filled with fluid, and its operation is fundamentally a kind of fluid mechanics. (Bioelectric engineers at MIT recently redesigned an ultra-broadband radio chip modelled on the fluid mechanics of the cochlea. See Trafton, 2009.)

The membranes inside in the cochlea respond mechanically to movements of the fluid, a process called **sinusoidal stimulation**. Lower frequency sounds stimulate primarily the narrower end of the membrane, and higher frequencies stimulate only the broader end. Each different sound that passes through the cochlea produces varying patterns of movement in the fluid and the membrane.

At the side of the cochlea, nearest the brain stem, are thousands of tiny hair cells, with ends both inside and outside the cochlea. The outer hair cells are connected to the auditory nerve fibres, which lead to the auditory cortex of the brain. These hair cells respond to minute movements of the fluid in the membrane and **transduce** the mechanical movements of the fluid into nerve activity.

As with other neural networks in the human body, our auditory nerves have evolved to a high degree of specialisation. There are five different types of auditory nerve cells. Each auditory nerve system has different **Characteristic Frequencies (CF)** that they respond to continuously throughout the stimulus presentation. Fibres with high CFs are found in the periphery of the nerve bundle, and there is an orderly decrease in CF toward the centre of the nerve bundle. This **tonotopic organisation** preserves the frequency spectrum from the cochlea, which is necessary for speedy, accurate processing of the incoming signal pulses. Responding to their specialised frequencies, these nerves actually create tuning curves that correspond to the actual shape of their cell and pass along very precise information about sound frequency to the **superior olivary complex** of the central auditory nervous system (Musiek *et al.*, 2007).

The distribution of the neural activity is called the **excitation pattern**. This excitation pattern is the fundamental output of the hearing mechanism. For instance, if you hear a specific sequence of sounds, there is a specific excitation pattern produced in response that is, in principle, precisely the same as the excitation pattern produced in all other hearing humans. While the excitation patterns may be identical, how the hearer interprets the signal and subsequently responds to it is, of course, subject to a wide range of individual differences, especially age and language learning background.

Concept 1.1   **Excitation patterns and hearing**

Excitation patterns in the inner ear and auditory nerve become automated through experience with familiar stimuli. Without excitation patterns, hearing cannot take place: the auditory stimulus will not reach the brain.

In a sense, this means that not everyone hears the same thing, even though the excitation pattern for a particular stimulus will be neurologically similar in all of us. On a physical level, the difference in our perception is due to the fact that the individual **neurones** that make up the nerve fibres are interactive – they are affected by the action of all the other neurones they interact with. Sometimes, the activity of one neurone is suppressed or amplified by the introduction of a second tone In addition, since these nerves are physical structures, they are affected by our general health and level of arousal or fatigue. Another fact that interferes with consistent and reliable hearing is that these nerves sometimes fire involuntary even when no hearing stimulus is present. This occurs when the **vestibular nerve**, which is intertwined with the auditory nerve and helps us keep our balance, is activated. (Musiek *et al.*, 2007; Moore, 2004).

The physiological properties of listening begin when the **auditory cortex** is stimulated. The primary auditory cortex is a small area located in the **temporal lobe** of the brain. It lies in the back half of the Superior Temporal Gyrus (STG) and also enters into the transverse temporal gyri (also called Heschl's gyri). This is the first brain structure to process incoming auditory information. Anatomically, the **transverse temporal gyri** are different from all other temporal lobe gyri in that they run mediolaterally (towards the centre of the brain) rather than dorsiventrally (front to back).

As soon as information reaches the auditory cortex, it is relayed to several other neural centres in the brain, including **Wernicke's area**, which is responsible for speech recognition, and lexical and syntactic comprehension, and **Broca's area**, which is involved in calculation and responses to language-related tasks.

Imaging studies have shown that many other brain areas are involved in language comprehension as well (see Figure 1.2). This neurological finding is consistent with language processing research indicating simultaneous **parallel processing** of different types of information.

These studies have shown that all of these areas are involved in competent language comprehension to varying degrees, with certain areas more

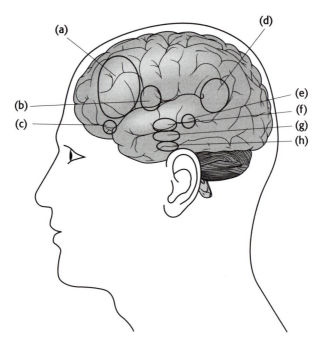

Figure 1.2 *Primary areas of the brain involved in listening.* Several areas of the brain are involved in listening, most of them in the left hemisphere. (*a*) The left prefrontal cortex is involved in processing information during speech comprehension. (*b*) The left pars triangularis is involved in syntactic processing. (*c*) The left pars orbitalis is involved in semantic processing of lexical items; the right pars orbitalis (in the right hemisphere of the brain) is involved in semantic processing of discourse. (*d*) The left superior temporal sulcus (STS) is involved in phonetic processing of sounds; the right STS is involved in processing prosody. (*e*) The left plenum temporale is involved in speech–motor interface. (*f*) The primary auditory cortex is involved in speech perception. (*g*) The secondary auditory cortex (which wraps around the primary auditory cortex) is involved in the processing of intonation and rhythm. (*h*) The left superior temporal gyrus (STG) is involved in semantic processing of lexical items; the right STG is involved in semantic processing at the discourse level

active while processing particularly complex sentences or disambiguating particularly vague references. Impairments in any one area, often defined as an **aphasia** (if acquired by way of an injury or aging process), can result in difficulties with lexical comprehension, syntactic processing, global processing of meaning and formulation of an appropriate response (Poeppel *et al.*, 2008; Harpaz *et al.*, 2009).

1.2 Consciousness

Concept 1.2 **Consciousness and listening**

Consciousness is the aspect of mind that has a self-centred point of view and orientation to the environment. Consciousness is directly related to intentionality – the intention to understand and to be understood.

Once we understand the basic physiology of hearing and listening, we realise that a complex neural architecture underlies our ability to understand language and the worlds around and within us. At the same time, through simple reflection, we realise there are non-physical aspects of processing and understanding that go well beyond the systems we have just outlined.

The concept that has been used most often to describe this neurological-cognitive bridge between individual and universal perception and experience is **consciousness** (Chafe, 2000). Consciousness is the root concept for describing the processes that initiate attention, meaning construction, memory and learning.

Just as we characterised sound perception as a neurophysical process originating from an energy pattern in air outside of us, we may think of consciousness in a similar way. Consciousness has been described as a flow of energy, emerging when two cognitive processes coincide: (1) The brain identifies an outside object or event as consisting of independent properties; and (2) The brain sets up the listener as the central agent who willingly and purposefully witnesses this object or event. Consciousness is the phenomenon of experiencing this integration as a subjective phenomenon (cf. Czikszentmihalyi, 1992; Chella and Manzotti, 2007).

Beyond this characterisation of subjective experience, it has been said that consciousness is a dynamic neurophysiological mechanism that allows a person to become active and goal-directed in both internal and external environments (Alexandrov and Sams, 2005). This means that consciousness is a continuous force that links experiences in the internal and external environments and allows the experiencer to make sense of these experiences and, to some degree, direct them.

For the purposes of describing listening, the concept of consciousness is important because it helps to define the notion of **context**. Consciousness involves the **activation** of portions of the listener's model of the surrounding world – a model that is necessarily self-referenced. The portions of this model that are activated are those that are involved in understanding the current encounter, including whatever language is associated with it. Viewed technically, this active portion of the model is constructed from perceptual contact with the external event (**external context**) and from our subjective experience (**internal context**).

The concept of consciousness is important for communication – both listening and speaking – because something must direct the individual's attention to the external world. For the speaker, consciousness influences what aspects of the person's experience to communicate – the signalling and displaying levels of communication (Holmqvist and Holsanova, 2007). For the listener, consciousness guides the person's intentions to experience the speaker's world and to attempt to construct meaning from this experience.

Concept 1.3 **The properties of consciousness**

There are five properties of consciousness that affect listening.

- Consciousness is *embedded* in a surrounding area of peripheral awareness. The active focus is surrounded by a periphery of semi-active information that provides a context for it.

- Consciousness is *dynamic*. The focus of consciousness moves constantly from one focus, or item of information, to the next. This movement is experienced by the listener as a continuous event, rather than as a discrete series of 'snapshots'.

- Consciousness has a *point of view*. One's model of the world is necessarily centred on a self. The location and needs of that self establish a point of view, which is a constant ingredient of consciousness and a guide for the selection of subsequent movements.

- Consciousness has a need for *orientation*. Peripheral awareness must include information regarding a person's location in space, time, society and ongoing activity. This orientation allows consciousness to shift from an **immediate mode**, in which the person is attending to present, tangible references, to a **distal mode**, in which the person is attending to non-present, abstract, or imaginary references and concepts.

- Consciousness can *focus* on only one thing at a time. The limited capacity of consciousness is reflected as a linguistic constraint: A speaker can produce only one focus of consciousness at a time, which is reflected in brief spurts of language, called **intonation units**.

Adapted from Chalmers (1996), Chafe (2000) and Allwood (2006)

1.3 Attention

Attention is the operational aspect of consciousness and can be discussed more concretely. Attention has identifiable physical correlates: specific areas of the brain that are activated in response to a decision to attend to a particular source or aspect of input. Attention is the focusing of consciousness on an object or train of thought, which activates parts of the cortex that are equipped to process it (Figure 1.3).

Because of the deliberate nature of attention, we can consider attention to be the beginning of **involvement**, which is the essential differentiation

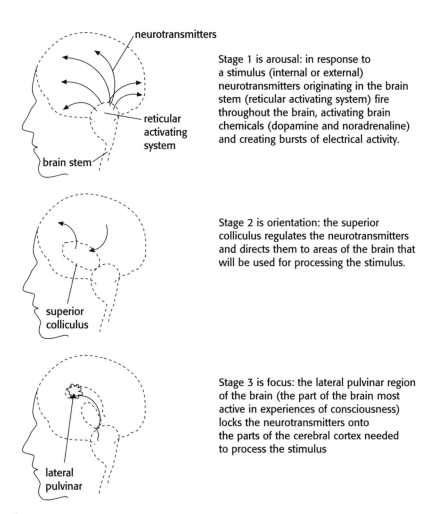

Stage 1 is arousal: in response to a stimulus (internal or external) neurotransmitters originating in the brain stem (reticular activating system) fire throughout the brain, activating brain chemicals (dopamine and noradrenaline) and creating bursts of electrical activity.

Stage 2 is orientation: the superior colliculus regulates the neurotransmitters and directs them to areas of the brain that will be used for processing the stimulus.

Stage 3 is focus: the lateral pulvinar region of the brain (the part of the brain most active in experiences of consciousness) locks the neurotransmitters onto the parts of the cerebral cortex needed to process the stimulus

Figure 1.3   *Three stages of attention*. Attention consists of three nearly simultaneous stages.

between hearing and listening. Psychologists often refer back to the original definition given by William James, considered the founder of modern experimental psychology.

> **Quote 1.1**   William James on attention
>
> Everyone knows what attention is. It is the taking possession of the mind, in clear and vivid form, of one out of what seem several simultaneously possible objects or trains of thought. *Focalisation and concentration of consciousness* are of its essences. It implies withdrawal from some things in order to deal effectively with others.
>
> William James (1890: 405)

In neurolinguistic research, attention is seen as a timed process requiring three neurological elements: **arousal, orientation** and **focus**. Arousal begins with the **Reticular Activating System (RAS)** in the brain stem becoming activated. When this happens, the RAS releases a flood of neurotransmitters to fire neurons throughout the brain. Orientation is a neural organisation process performed near the brain stem (specifically, in the superior colliculus part of the brain above the brain stem). This process engages the brain pathways that are most likely to be involved in understanding and responding to the perceived object (i.e. the external event or the internal train of thought). Activation is simultaneous on both sides of the brain – in the right hemisphere, which functions as a parallel processor, and in the left hemisphere, which functions as a serial processor. Focus is achieved in the higher cortex of the brain, the lateral pulvinar section. This process selectively locks on to the pathways that lead to the frontal lobe of the brain and are involved in processing incoming stimulus, thus allowing for more efficient use of energy (Carter, 2003).

Two notions are central to understanding how attention influences listening: **limited capacity** and **selective attention.** The notion of limited capacity is important in listening. Our consciousness can interact with only one source of information at a time, although we can readily and rapidly switch back and forth between different sources, and even bundle disparate sources into a single focus of attention. Whenever multiple sources, or streams, of information are present, **selective attention** must be used. Selective attention involves a decision, a commitment of our limited capacity process to one stream of information or one bundled set of features.

Concept 1.4   **Processes of attention**

- Attention is a limited capacity system.
- Automatic activities that require little or no attention do not interfere with each other.
- Controlled processes require attention and interfere with other control processes.
- Attention can be viewed as three separate but interrelated networks: alertness, orientation and detection.
  1 Alertness represents a general readiness to deal with incoming stimuli.
  2 Orientation refers to a specific aligning of attention.
  3 Detection is the cognitive registration of sensory stimuli.
- Detected information is available for other cognitive processing.

As we listen, our attention can be selectively directed to a rich variety of acoustic features beyond linguistic aspects, including spatial location, auditory pitch, frequency or intensity, tone duration, timbre, and characteristics of individual voices. Depending on which of the multiplicity of acoustic dimensions we choose to attend to, a different area of the brain will become active. Indeed, it has been shown that the locations of the multiple loci of attentional influence on auditory information processing are flexible and dependent not only on the nature of the input, but also on the specific demands of the behavioural task being performed. Another influence on the cortical locus of attention is the involvement of other modalities. For instance, if visual and auditory attention are activated simultaneously, different areas of the frontal-parietal network in the brain will become involved.

Concept 1.5   **Selective attention and processing breaks**

Among the best known experimental studies dealing with selective attention are **dichotic listening** studies in which subjects are presented with different messages through left and right earphones. When told to attend to one message only or shadow it, subjects can readily comply, switching attention to the second message. However, subjects can shift attention only at pauses in the attended message, which suggests that we can shift our attention only at suitable 'processing breaks' in the input.

Just as important, results from these studies show that attention is needed not only for monitoring input, but also for effectively storing and retrieving messages. A consistent finding in these experiments is that only information in the attended channel (i.e. the ear with the attended input) can be remembered.

An everyday example of this is the **cocktail party effect**. In a chaotic – inherently unpredictable – cocktail party environment, numerous streams of conversation are taking place, yet you can attend to only one at a time. It is possible to focus on a conversation taking place across the room while ignoring a conversation that is closer and louder. Attention is directional and under the control of the listener, within certain constraints. This ability is also much reduced in individuals with hearing loss, or with hearing aids and cochlear implants.

Although attention can usually be controlled, shifts in attention are not always voluntary. For example, while we are watching television, our baby starting to cry takes over the attention system momentarily whether we want it to or not. Instinctively, we respond to what is perceived to be most relevant to our needs. Beyond obvious examples of overt emergency signals (such as a baby's crying signalling a need for us to take care of it) overtaking our previous attentional focus (such as watching the news), our needs are complex and subtle and may be ordered in ways that are not fully conscious to us. Because of this complex nature of our informational and emotional needs, we may often respond to subtle distractions when we are listening and become derailed from our original focus.

1.4   Individual differences in neurological processes

Among linguists, psychologists, and philosophers, language is regarded as the most complex of all human behaviours. And within the modalities of language use, speech processing may be the most intricate. At any given moment during language processing, we may be engaged simultaneously in speaking, hearing, reading, formulation and comprehension. Each of these individual component skills requires the involvement of large areas of the brain and a complex interplay of neural health, attentional readiness, local neural processing, coordination of functional neural circuits, and high-level strategic organisation. As we have seen in earlier sections of this chapter, work in cognitive neuropsychology has helped identify the basic functions of brain areas in terms of language processing. New scanning techniques also are leading to a fuller understanding of these interactions and how they are linked together into functional neural circuits for language processing. In spite of these common capacities for language processing, not all humans process language in the same way. As in other areas of neural processing, individuals display a great range of differences across these functions. This section outlines six critical differences among individuals:

- *Local processing*. In terms of basic-level processing, individuals show marked differences in basic attributes such as speed of neural transmission, activation of neural transmitters, involvement of the thalamus (relay centre for all neural impulses) and hippocampus (part of the limbic system involved in orientation), memory and attention, and patterns of neural connectivity.

- *Commitment and plasticity.* As basic linguistic functions develop, they become confined to progressively smaller areas of neural tissue, a process called **neural commitment**. This leads to a beneficial increase in automaticity and speed of processing, but it also results inevitably in a decline in plasticity. (There is also some loss in the potential to function if brain injury occurs in an adjacent area). It appears that the process of neural commitment leads to a neural separation between different languages in bilinguals and second language learners. The plasticity or neural flexibility required for language reorganisation declines progressively through childhood and adolescence and may be the primary cause of some of the difficulties that adults face in second language learning (Gitterman and Datta, 2007; Van Den Noort *et al.*, 2010).

- *Integrative circuits.* Current models of the formation and consolidation of episodic memories focus on the role played by the hippocampus in forming integrated representations (MacWhinney, 2005a; Kroll and Tokowitz, 2005). In terms of language learning and use, these neural connections allow a variety of local areas of the brain to form a series of impressions of sensory and conceptual aspects of an utterance, which are then linked into a new grammatical form or syntactic construction. (All mammals use connections between the hippocampus and local areas to form memories. However, humans are unique in using those connections to support language learning.) In addition to this central memory consolidation circuit, a variety of local circuits are likely used in analysing and breaking apart local memories through a process called **resonance** (Grossberg, 2003). Resonant circuits copy successfully detected linguistic forms to temporary local buffers so that the system can focus on incoming, unprocessed material while still retaining the recognised material in local memory. As with all neural mechanisms, differences in the efficiency of these individual circuits can be assumed.

- *Functional neural circuits.* The types of local integration supported by the episodic memory system are complemented by a variety of other functional neural circuits that integrate across wider areas of the brain. A prime example of such a circuit is the **phonological rehearsal loop** (Lopez *et al.*, 2009), which links the auditory processing in the temporal lobe with motor processing from the prefrontal cortex. We use this loop to store and repeat a series of words or to speed the learning of new words. Differences in the abilities of listeners to store items in this loop have been shown to correlate strongly with relative success in both L1 and L2 learning (Aboitiz *et al.*, 2010; Gathercole *et al.*, 1994).

- *Strategic control*. Brain functioning can be readily modified, amplified, integrated and controlled by higher-level strategic processes. These higher-level processes include mood control, attentional control, motivational control as well as learning strategies and applications of cognitive maps and scripts. The degree to which the listener can activate and apply these higher-level processes will determine relative success and failure in language comprehension in specific instances and in long-term acquisition (Van Heuven and Dijkstra, 2010).

- *Level of attention*. Some listeners pay more attention to overall conceptual structure, attempting to process incoming language more through top-down inferential, whereas other learners focus more on bottom-up detail (Bransford, 2003). This individual difference is also likely to be important in determining the relative success of listeners in language comprehension to specific texts and in longer-term acquisition of the language.

Summary: organisation of neurological processing

This chapter has surveyed the neurological processes that are involved in listening. Though the processes are wired through complex electro-chemical circuitry, these processes are far from mechanist and robotic. We humans are a meaning-oriented species, and our neurobiology is geared not only to process information and make sense of the external world, but also to understand and find meaning in both the external world and our internal world.

Philosophers have long argued that the deepest sources of human understanding lie not in external information sources or information processing, but in feelings, emotions, qualities and patterns of bodily perception and motion. Images, qualities, emotions and metaphors are rooted in our physical encounters with the world and provide the basis for our most profound feats of abstract understanding. As Johnson (2007) emphasises, though the contemporary study of neurolinguistics often focuses on the more scientific aspects of information processing and meaning building, we should not lose touch with the understanding that meaning-making is also fundamentally human, interactive, and aesthetic.

Chapter 2

Linguistic processing

This chapter focuses on the linguistic decoding processes that are the basis of listening. The chapter:

- outlines the phonological procedures involved in perceiving speech;
- outlines the process of word recognition;
- outlines the kind of phonotactic rules that a listener must acquire;
- explains the process of parsing, or applying grammatical rules, while listening;
- describes the basic unit of speech processing – the pause unit – and shows how it helps the listener manage incoming speech;
- shows how prosodic features assist the listener in understanding speech;
- outlines the non-verbal cues available to the listener.

2.1 **Perceiving speech**

The goal of speech production is to maximise communication, putting as many bits of retrievable information into every second of speech as possible (Boersma, 1998). Languages evolve in congruence with this **efficiency principle**. To this end, the most frequently used words tend to be the shortest ones in a language, and communication patterns develop to allow for a maximum of **ellipsis** – omissions of what is presumed to be understood by the listener. Zipf (1949) first summarised this evolutionary tendency as the **principle of least effort** – speakers want to minimise articulatory effort and hence encourage brevity and **phonological reduction**.

In the same way, the listener has to adopt an efficient principle for understanding speech. This means processing language as efficiently as possible in order to keep up with the speaker. At a perception level, two fundamental heuristics are needed to do this:

- *Maximisation of recognition.* Because the speaker is reducing effort in production, the listener will try to make maximum use of the available acoustic information in order to reconstruct the meaning of the utterance.
- *Minimisation of categorisation.* Because there are large variations between speakers, the listener must tolerate ambiguity and create as few perceptual classes as possible into which the acoustic input can be grouped.

In order to maximise recognition of what has been spoken, the listener uses three types of perceptual experience. The first type is the experience of **articulatory causes** for the sounds that strike the ear. For spoken language, the perceptual objects are the effects of particular vocal configurations in the speaker (the lip, tongue and vocal tract movements that cause the proximal stimulation in the ear). The second type is through **psychoacoustic effects**. The perceptual objects are identified as auditory qualities (the frequency, timbre and duration of sounds that reach the ear). The third type is the listener's construction of a model of the speaker's **linguistic intentions**. The perceived sounds are drawn from a matrix of **contrasts** at multiple levels of a language (phonemic, morphological, lexical, semantic, pragmatic). The listener's knowledge of and experience with these three systems – **articulatory causes** of sounds, the psychoacoustic effects of sounds, and the likely linguistic intentions of a speaker – all maximise the efficiency of speech perception. At the same time, if the listener's knowledge or experience is incomplete or flawed, use of these systems will limit or distort perception.

Concept 2.1   **Complementary sources in speech perception**

Four **psychoacoustic elements** are available to the listener in the speech signal. By identifying the unique combinations of these elements, the listener differentiates sounds.

- *Frequency*, measured in hertz (Hz). Humans are capable of hearing sounds from 20 Hz to 20,000 Hz, but human languages typically draw upon sounds in the 100–3,000 Hz range. Detecting movements in the fundamental frequency of sound is an important element in speech perception.
- *Tone*, measured in sine wave forms. Every configuration of the vocal tract produces its own set of characteristics, which are represented as sound pressure variations and mapped as sine waves. Further, each sound will have a simultaneous set of overtones or harmonic tones or frequencies, above the fundamental frequency. The relation of the fundamental frequency to the overtone frequencies (i.e. the sound formants) assists the hearer in identifying particular speakers.

- *Duration*, measured in milliseconds (ms). Languages differ in the average length of both phonemes and syllables; for instance, in American English, syllables average about 75 ms; in French, syllables average about 50 ms. Duration between sounds in a language can vary widely.

- *Intensity*, measured in decibels (dB). Whispered language at one metre is about 20 dB, while normal speech at 1 m is about 60 dB. (For reference, measurements at rock concerts and sports matches often reach 120 dB. The loudest possible sound is 194 dB.) However, there is a normal fluctuation of up to 30 dB in a single utterance of any speaker in a typical conversation. Intensity is particularly important for detecting prominences in an utterance (i.e. what the speaker considers focal information).

Concept 2.2   **Perception and sampling**

Humans perceive speech through the **sampling** of sound characteristics in the speech signal – frequency, duration and amplitude. The redundant nature of the speech signal allows for selective sampling. The listener does not need to attend to the speech signal continuously to assure accurate perception.

Because of the inherent nature of sound, whenever we create a speech sound, we simultaneously create that sound in several harmonic ranges. The ratio between the frequencies in these harmonic ranges vitally affects our differentiation of the sound from other similar sounds. In other words, each individual phoneme of a language has a unique identity in terms of frequency ratios between the fundamental frequency of a sound (f_0) and the frequency of the sound in other harmonic ranges (f_1, f_2, f_3). This is called the **perceptual goodness** of the sound (Pickett and Morris, 2000). When we learn to articulate the sounds of a language, we learn to manipulate these frequencies, without conscious attention (Kuhl, 2000). Although there is an ideal prototype for each phoneme of a language, there is also a relatively broad acceptable range of ratios between frequencies, that is, sound variations, within a given phoneme that makes it **intelligible** to us and allows us to distinguish one phoneme from another (Lachmann and van Leeuwen, 2007).

2.2   Identifying units of spoken language

In order to manage speech in real time, it is essential for the listener to group the speech into a small number of constituents that can be worked easily within short-term memory. The metaphor of a sausage machine is sometimes used to describe the nature of the listener's task: taking the language as it comes out and separating it into constituents. However, this metaphor is misleading unless we add two factors: the listener would also need to know what the ingredients are in the sausage mixture and how to package and where to deliver the sausages once they have been produced.

To understand the perceptual process fully, we need to understand pre-perceptual and post-perceptual states of the listener. Spoken language has evolved in a way that allows a listener to parse speech in real time, in the most effective manner given the specific resources of our short-term memory. Based on examinations of multiple corpora of language spoken in naturally occurring contexts (**unplanned discourse**), researchers have found a number of characteristics to be representative of spontaneously spoken English (see Table 2.1).

Many of these features of speech are considered by the layperson to be signs of careless use of language, particularly when viewed from the perspective of written standards. However, it is now widely established that written and spoken language, while based on the same underlying conceptual, grammatical, lexical and phonological systems, simply follow different realisation rules and standards of well-formedness (Chafe and Tannen, 1987; Houston, 2004; Carter and McCarthy, 2004). The reason is that the conventions and standards for spoken language have evolved interactively: they allow speaker and listener to co-ordinate on the time, timing and conditions needed to communicate in an oral medium.

A specific cause for the surface-level differences in speech and writing is the difference in planning time. Brazil (1995) was among the first to describe in detail how speakers put their speech together in real time. He characterised spoken language construction as taking place in a piecemeal fashion, in short bursts of planning time, in part because of the speaker's need to adjust messages based on listener response and on the listener 'need to know', and in part because of the speakers' own need to adjust their message based on their own assessment about what they are saying and how they are getting their messages across to the listener. As Brazil suggested, we get much closer to an understanding of what spoken language is like for the users – both the speakers and the listeners – if we take this piecemeal planning into account in describing a grammar of the spoken language. Because speakers and listeners typically operate in the context of a need to meet specific communicative goals, they are more likely (than writers and readers) to use time-sensitive and context-sensitive strategies to compose and understand language. Speakers and listeners are also likely to abandon and reformulate strategies, even in the middle of utterances, when the strategies seem to be unsuccessful. To an outsider or **overhearer**, these adjustments may seem to make the resultant language 'sloppy', but these shifts in strategies and devices actually improve comprehension for the actual participants.

Table 2.1 Features of spoken language

FEATURE	EXAMPLE
Speakers speak in **short bursts of speech**	*The next time I saw him/ he wasn't as friendly/ I don't know why.*
Spoken language contains more **topic-comment structures** and uses more topic restatement	*The people in this town – they're not as friendly as they used to be.*
Speakers frequently use additive (**paratactic**) ordering with *and, then, so, but*	*He came home/ and then he just turned on the TV/ but he didn't say anything/ so I didn't think much about it/*
Speech is marked by a high ratio of **function** (or **grammatical**) **words** (particles, preposition, pro-forms, articles, *be* verbs, auxiliary verbs, conjunctions) to **content words** (nouns, verbs, adjectives, adverbs, question words)	Written version: *The court declared that the deadline must be honoured.* (Content words, 4; function words, 5) Spoken version: *The court said that the deadline was going to have to be kept.* (Content words, 4; function words, 9)
Speech is marked by incomplete grammatical units, **false starts**, **incomplete/abandoned structures**	*I was wondering if . . . Do you want to go together?* *It's not that I . . . I mean, I don't want to imply . . .*
Speakers frequently use **ellipsis** – omitting known grammatical elements	*(Are you) Coming (to dinner)?* *(I'll be there) In a minute.*
Speakers use the most frequent words of the language, leading to more loosely packed, often imprecise language	*the way it's put together* (v. *its structure*)
Topics may not be stated explicitly	*That's not a good idea.* (The topic is *that*, the action referred to earlier, but never explicitly mentioned)
Speakers use a lot of **fillers, interactive markers** and **evocative expressions**	*And, well, um, you know, there was, like, a bunch of people . . .* *And I'm thinking, like, what the hell's that got to do with it?*
Speakers employ frequent **exophoric reference**, and rely on gesture and non-verbal cues	*that guy over there* *this thing* *why are you wearing that?*
Speakers use variable speeds, accents, **paralinguistic features** and gestures	

Source. Based on McCarthy and Slade (2006), Roland *et al.* (2007).

2.3   Using prosodic features in processing speech

Because planning constraints are central to speaking, it is important for the grammar of spoken language to take the effects of online planning into account. Speech is typically uttered not in a continuous stream but in short bursts. (In addition to whatever communicative function short bursts of speech may have, speaking in this manner is a biological necessity: It allows the speaker periodically to replace air in the lungs efficiently.) These units of speech have been identified by various terms, but the term **intonation units** may be preferable. This term indicates that an intonational contour is constructed by the speaker to indicate a **focal centre of attention**.

Intonation units typically consist of phrases or clauses and average two or three seconds in length. Bound by pauses, these temporal units mark the speaker's rhythm for composing and presenting ideas. Some anthropologists have argued that, from an evolutionary perspective, it makes sense that the duration of phonological short-term memory generally coincides with the length of the unit of articulation (Chafe, 2000). Because these units are bound by perceptible pauses, linguists sometimes refer to them as **pause units**.

Quote 2.1   Chafe on studying spoken language

Researchers are always pleased when the phenomena they are studying allow them to identify units ... It would be convenient if linguistic units could be identified unambiguously from phonetic properties: if, for example, phonemes could be recognised from spectrograms, or intonation units from tracings of pitch. For good or bad, however, the physical manifestations of psychologically relevant units are always going to be messy and inconsistent.

Chafe (1994)

Although the speaker has choices as to which words to stress, the language itself presents constraints about how this stress can be articulated. All content words typically receive some stress (contrastive duration and loudness), and the last new content word in a phonological phrase usually receives the primary stress (**tonic prominence**) in an intonation unit. By 'new word' we mean a word that has not occurred in the previous discourse or a word that is not closely related lexically to a word in the previous discourse.

Even though the peak of tonic prominence can usually be identified on a single syllable in a pause unit, the onset of the stress and the decline of the stress are usually spread over several syllables, almost always encompassing more than one word. What is identified as prominent or focal in a pause unit then will usually be a **clitic group** – a lexical item that consists of one core word and other grammaticalising words.

Concept 2.3   **Pause units and prominence**

Speech is best described in intonation units or pause units. By characterising a spoken text as phonological units, we can better recreate the sense of the listener hearing it for the first time. Syllables in CAPITAL letters indicate **prominence**, where stress occurs. Double slashes (///) indicate boundaries of the unit, the pauses between bursts of speech. Arrows indicate the pitch direction: r = rising (or 'referring'), l = level, f = falling.

1 // (r) WHILE i was at uniVERsity //

2 // (l) i was VEry inVOLVED //

3 // (l) with THE //

4 // (l) STUdents //

5 // (f) ARTS society //

6 // (f) which was CALLED the ARTS umBRELla //

Example from Cauldwell (2002)

We can readily identify differences between the spoken realisation and what the written version might be. Although the first and third clauses occur in tone units much as we would expect, the main clause is broken up into four tone units (units 2–5). The speaker uses level tone in speech units 2, 3 and 4 to allow time to decide what to say next; the speaker uses two falling tones (units 5 and 6) instead of just one, showing how additional pause units can be added to a 'final' proposition.

The choice of tones is constructed in the incremental (or 'piecemeal') fashion referred to by Brazil (1995). The choice of tones is related in part to the speaker's ongoing assessment of the listener's current state of knowledge, that is, what the speaker considers 'shared with the audience' or 'new to the audience' at the time of the utterance. The choice of tones is also related in part to the speaker's style and competence. Rising tones (r) at the end of a pause unit are most often used to indicate common ground, or information that the speaker considers already shared with the listener. (For this reason, they are sometimes called 'referring' tones.) Shared information may be either through assumed prior knowledge of the listener, or through reactivation of information that has been previously mentioned. Level tones (l) are used to indicate that additional information is coming and that the speaker wishes to keep the floor. Falling intonation (f) is used to identify focal or new information. For this reason, these tones are sometimes called 'proclaiming' tones. Falling intonation often also fills a turn-taking function, showing that the speaker may be interrupted or the floor may be ceded.

Most sequences in any connected turn by one speaker will consist of a set of pause units with a typical two (referring) to one (proclaiming) – a 2:1 ratio – although this varies by speaker and topic. It is reasonable to assume from this observation that competent speakers in conversation seek to maintain a balance of new versus shared information as they speak, in relation to their audience's information requirements. For example, speakers will often backtrack to shared information (using referring tones), whether previously referred to in the current discourse or previously known by their interlocutors in their own experience, when they see that their audience is not responding to new information. (As we will see in Chapter 8, a key component of simplified speech for language learning purposes is a high density of referring tones signalling shared information, as the speaker attempts to control the amount of new information the listener needs to understand.)

A third type of information available in sequences of pause units is related to connectivity. Speakers signal through **intonational bracketing** which pause units are to be interpreted as closely related. Sequences of connected pause units will end with a falling, proclaiming tone, and although a speaker may add on other units with falling tones, as in the example above, there is usually only one final falling tone. When the speaker starts again on a high rise, he or she indicates the start of a new group of tone units.

Listeners who are 'in tune' with the speaker will readily process pauses in conjunction with this tonic bracketing, which corresponds to the speaker's planning of what to say. Relatively short pauses before the next pause unit will typically be intended to link pause units, while relatively long pauses before the next pause unit may indicate the speaker is beginning a new topic.

In addition to the purpose of indicating tonic prominence in an utterance, intonation can help the speaker express various nuances of meaning. Roach (2000), following the pioneering work of Brown (1977), has elaborated a framework of paralinguistic features that speakers can use to shade linguistic meaning of an utterance: pitch span, placing of voice in the voice range, tempo, loudness, voice setting (breathy–creaky), articulatory setting (unmarked–tense), articulatory precision (precise–slurred), lip setting (smiling–pursed), timing and pause. Through combinations of features, a speaker can create a range of emotional tones including warmth, thoughtfulness, anger, and sexiness (see Table 2.2).

Another way of viewing the role of intonation is in the framework of relevance theory, which considers all communication to be an **ostensive-inferential process** (Sperber and Wilson, 1995; Moeschler, 2004). In this system, the speaker is continually offering **ostensive signals** – both

Table 2.2 Voice modulations correlating to emotion: references from American, British English

ARTICULATORY SETTING	REPLIED ANSWERED SAID	RETORTED EXCLAIMED	IMPORTANT POMPOUS RESPONSIBLE	DEPRESSED MISERABLY SADLY	EXCITED	ANXIOUS WORRIED NERVOUS	SHRILL SHRIEK SCREAM	WARMLY	COLDLY	THOUGHTFULLY	SEXILY	CROSSLY ANGRILY	QUERIED ECHOED
Pitch span		Extended		Restricted	Extended		Extended	Extended	Restricted		Extended	Extended	Extended
Placing in voice range			Lowered	Lowered	Raised	Raised	Raised	Lowered			Lowered	Raised	Raised
Tempo		Rapid	Slow		Rapid	Rapid	Rapid			Slow	Slow	Rapid	
Loudness				Soft	Loud		Loud				Soft	Loud	Loud
Articulatory setting					Breathy	Tense	Tense		Tense			Tense	
Articulatory precision				Slurred					Precise		Slurred		
Lip setting								Smiling			Smiling		
Timing			Extended				Extended		Extended		Extended		

Note. The table shows the choices of articulatory settings that a speaker has to modulate speech: pitch span may be extended or restricted; tempo may be show or rapid; loudness may be soft or loud; articulatory setting may be breathy or tense; articulatory precision may be precise or slurred; lip setting may be smiling or pursed; timing may be extended or restricted. All settings may also be 'neutral' that is, unmarked (tinted cells) for additional meaning.

Sources. Based on Brown (1977); Rost (1990); Yanushevskaya *et al.* (2008).

linguistic and paralinguistic signals – from which the listener derives inferences. Although there is never a guarantee that the listener will be able to infer the intention of the speaker, paralinguistic signals, including voice modulations, can provide an additional layer of cues (Mozziconacci, 2001; Gobl and Chasaide, 2010).

Concept 2.4   **Types of information available in speech signal**

Six types of information have been noted in the paralinguistic signals of speakers in all languages. These are:

- *Emotional.* The intonation is used to express speaker's attitudinal meaning, such as enthusiasm, doubt, or distaste for the topic (Ohala, 1996).
- *Grammatical.* Intonation can be used to mark the grammatical structure of an utterance, like punctuation does in written language (Brazil, 1995).
- *Informational.* Intonational peaks indicate the salient parts of an utterance that a speaker wishes to draw attention to for both self and listener (Chafe, 1994).
- *Textual.* The intonation is used to help large chunks of discourse contrast or cohere, rather like paragraphs in written language.
- *Psychological.* Intonation involving a rhythm of vowel sounds is used to chunk complex information into units which are easier to deal with. For example, lists of words, or telephone or credit card numbers are grouped into units to make them easier to hold in short-term memory. (Cheng *et al.*, 2005).
- *Indexical.* Intonation and speech melody are used as a sort of social group identifier, often as a conscious or habitual 'speech strategy' (Eckert and McConnell-Ginet, 2003). For example, preachers and newscasters often use a recognisable intonation pattern; gays or lesbians are often identified through intonational and melodic features in their speech (Livia and Hall, 1997).

2.4   Recognising words

Recognition of units of spoken language is a fluid process which can accommodate a fluctuating range of units in the input. What provides stability is its essential focus on **word recognition**. Recognising words in fluent speech is the basis of spoken language comprehension, and the development of automaticity of word recognition is considered to be a critical aspect of both L1 and L2 acquisition (Segalowitz *et al.*, 2008). Although all aspects of speech recognition are important contributors to comprehension, under conditions of noise or other perceptual stress, or when sounds are ambiguous or degraded and marginally intelligible (or especially for L2 listeners, when syntax is indecipherable), listeners will tend to focus on and rely on lexical information alone (Mattys *et al.*, 2009).

The two main synchronous tasks of the listener in word recognition are (1) identifying words and **lexical phrases** and (2) activating knowledge associated with those words and phrases.

If we want to understand spoken word recognition, it is important to note that the concept of a word itself is different for the spoken and written versions of any language. The concept of a word in spoken language can be understood best as part of a **phonological hierarchy**. A phonological hierarchy starts with the largest **psychologically valid** unit (that which typical users acknowledge in planning their language use). It then describes a series of increasingly smaller regions of a phonological utterance, which may indeed not be units that a typical user acknowledges. From larger to smaller units, this hierarchy is generally described as follows:

- *Utterance*, a grammatical unit, consisting of an intonation unit, plus surrounding grammatical elements needed for its interpretation.
- *Intonation Unit (IU)/phonological phrase (P-phrase)*, a phonological unit consisting of a lexically stressed item plus supporting grammatical elements, uttered in a single pause.
- *Lexical phrase*, a formulaic element consisting of frequently used clitic groups and phonological words, e.g. try as one might.
- *Phonological word* (P-word), a word or set of words uttered and interpreted as a single item, e.g. in the house.
- *Clitic group*, a focal item plus grammaticalising elements: e.g. an apple.
- *Foot* (F), 'strong–weak' syllable sequences such as ladder, button, eat it.
- *Syllable* (σ), e.g. cat (1), ladder (2); syllables themselves consist of parts: onset (optional), nucleus (required), coda (optional).
- *Mora* (μ), half-syllable or unit of syllable weight, used in some languages, such as Japanese and Hawaiian.
- *Segment* (phoneme), e.g. [k], [æ] and [t] in cat.
- *Feature*, glides, obstruents, sonorants, etc.

Identification of phonological words then is a process involving a process of estimating lexical units and boundaries within larger phonological groupings (Cutler and Broersma, 2005). In listening to continuous speech there is no direct auditory equivalent to the white spaces between words encountered when reading continuous text. Because there are no reliable cues marking every word boundary, word recognition is initially an approximating process marked by continual uncertainty.

There are several simultaneous processes that increase the reliability of word recognition:

- Words are recognised through the interaction of perceived sound and the understood likelihood of a word being uttered in a given context.
- Speech is processed primarily in a sequential fashion, word by word. Recognition of a word achieves two goals:
  - It locates the onset of the immediately following word.
  - It provides syntactic and semantic constraints that are used for predicting a number of following words.
- Words are accessed by various clues:
  - The sounds that begin the word.
  - Lexical stress.
- Speech is processed in part retrospectively, by the listener holding unrecognised word forms for a few seconds in a **phonological loop** in **Short-Term Memory** (STM) while subsequent cues are being processed (Baddeley and Larsen, 2007).
- A word has been recognised when the analysis of its acoustic structure eliminates all candidates but one – in other words, when the listener identifies the most likely or most relevant candidate.

Word recognition does not always succeed, of course. Spoken language comprehension can usually continue successfully even if all words are not recognised because the listener can make inferences about the meaning of an utterance through other sources of information, including the pragmatic context. Successful listeners must often tolerate ambiguity, and wait for later utterances to decide what was intended before – what Cicourel refers to as the **et cetera principle** (Cicourel, 1999).

Concept 2.5   **Segmentation and variation**

Any model of word recognition needs to account for two characteristics of fluent speech: segmentation and variation.

Segmentation refers to the problem of locating word boundaries in a continuous signal in which physical cues are rarely present.

Each language has preferred strategies for locating word boundaries. In English, the preferred **lexical segmentation strategy** is identifying stressed syllables and organising word identification around those stressed syllables. Since 90 per cent of all content words in English have stress on the first syllable (many are monosyllabic, of course), and since non-content words are generally not stressed, the proficient listener to English can use stress as an indicator of the start of a new word (Indefrey and Cutler, 2004; Altenberg, 2005).

Variation refers to the problem of recognising words that are characterised by 'sloppy' articulation, so that words must often be recognised from partial acoustic information.

Proficient listeners hold **prototypes** of particular sounds in a language in memory, though they seldom expect to hear a pure prototype in actual speech. Rather the prototype serves as a basis from which **allophonic variations** can be interpreted.

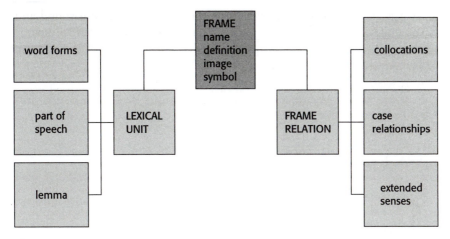

Figure 2.1   *Lexical frames activated during word recognition.* When a word is recognised, a framework associated with the word is activated. The frame includes associations of semantic meaning (its frame relationships) and syntactic expectations for its usage.
Source. Illustration adapted from FRAMENET (Lonneker-Rodman and Baker, 2009).

The notion of word recognition involves more than simply recognising a single sense of a word. According to current semantic theory, competent word recognition invokes a **frame** for the word, involving its acceptable word forms, its **lemma** (basic sense), part of speech, **frame relationships** and **collocations** with other words, in an ontology-like network (Lonneker-Rodman and Baker, 2009).

Concept 2.6   **Sources of information in word recognition**

During word recognition, the listener utilises multiple sources of information in order to recognise words. Three popular models of how this recognition takes place, involving **feature analysis, multi-time resolution**, and **analysis-by-synthesis**, are outlined here.

Feature detection models

Detection models, such as the original Logogen model proposed by Morton (1969), are based on the idea that language users have stored each word that the individual knows as a neural representation in long-term memory. To describe this representation, Morton uses the term logogen (*logos*, word; *genes*, born). Each logogen is considered to have a resting level of activity, a level that can be increased by contextual information in the input. When a logogen reaches a threshold, it 'fires', and the word is recognised. The threshold is a function of word frequency: more frequent words have a lower threshold for recognition. Word recognition requires time and effort because of the existence of competitors. For example, a word like speech has competitors (words with similar phonological forms), such as speed species and peach. The threshold level for word recognition is not reached until the competitors in the mental lexicon have been overruled by either phonological evidence, contextual evidence or both. Subsequent detector models, called Interactive Activation Models (a term originated by McClelland and Rumelhart, 1981) added the notion of feature inhibitors, which speed up recognition by ruling out competing words that would violate the phonotactic rules of the language (rules that govern allowable sequences of sound) (McQueen, 2005).

TRACE model

The TRACE model is a top-down model of speech perception that relies on predictions of likely words in context. McClelland *et al.*, (2006) have proposed that three levels of **bottom-up information** are used simultaneously in word recognition: phonetic features, phonemes and word contours. Perception of particular phonological features (such as the voicing of a /b/ or /v/) activate all phonemes that contain these features. This in turn activates words in the mental lexicon that contains those phonemes. An important feature of this kind of interactive activation model is that higher-order units also activate lower-order units.

According to the TRACE model, word recognition takes place by degrees of confidence, in successive time slices. Input processing undergoes a number of recursive cycles during which all levels simultaneously update their respective activations and levels of confidence, in an interactive fashion. For example, if the listener perceives /b/ + /r/, she will activate words that begin with these phonemes. Once additional sounds are perceived sequentially, such as /I/, words that contain this string of phonemes become active. When a subsequent phoneme /ng/ is perceived, the word /bring/ is activated with a high degree of confidence.

Fuzzy logic models

The Fuzzy Logic model of speech perception holds that word recognition proceeds through three perceptual operations: feature evaluation, feature integration and decision. Incoming speech features are continuously evaluated, weighted, integrated with other information (including visual information, such as lip movements of the speaker, if available) and matched against prototype descriptions in memory. An identification decision is made on the basis of a goodness-of-fit judgement at all levels (Massaro, 1994).

Fuzzy Logic models derive from **fuzzy set theory** (Zadeh, 1965) in order to deal with everyday reasoning, such as language comprehension, that is approximate rather than precise. In contrast with **crisp logic**, where binary sets employ only **binary logic**, the fuzzy logic variables may have a membership value of not only 0 or 1, and are not constrained to the black-or-white truth values of classic propositional logic. For example, if the listener perceives /brig/ in the context of 'would you —— me a . . . ?' the listener is likely to keep the possibility open that 'brig' was not the right target, since it does not make sense in everyday reasoning.

In a fuzzy logical model, the most informative feature in the input is always the one that has the greatest impact on the decision phase. Once this impact is calculated, selective reasoning takes over, and the influence of information from other sources is ignored. For example, if a listener clearly identifies the input *veer* on a phonological level – but the context is about things to drink, and the syntactic phrase was *bring me a* . . . – then the semantic and syntactic features of the input will outweigh the phonological features of the input, and the listener will decide that the word *beer* was uttered. At this point, all other competing logical calculations will be dropped. (When applied to multimodal processing in a computer speech recognition program, this is known as the Morton–Massaro law of information integration: Massaro, 2004.)

We have outlined these three common models of word recognition in order to highlight that they share common features. These features are activation of multiple knowledge sources, an accounting for the efficiency that is needed in rapid decoding of speech, and a focus on decision-making (McQueen, 2007).

2.5   Employing phonotactic knowledge

Effective speech recognition involves an automated knowledge of the phonotactic system of a language – that is, knowledge of its allowable sounds and sound patterns – and an acquired sensitivity to the allophonic variations of the prototypes in the system. Some speech processing researchers contend that **phonetic feature detectors** in the auditory cortex, which enable the listener to encode speech into linguistic units, atrophy during development if they are not used. This means that adults eventually retain only the phonetic feature detectors that were stimulated by their native language, and will experience perceptual difficulties with any L2 sounds that are not similar to those in their L1. According to this view, exposure to speech during childhood alters neural organisation such that individuals, born capable of learning any language, develop perceptual and cognitive processes that are specialised for their own native language. This means that, for adult L2 learners, L2 speech can be difficult to segment into words and phonemes, different phonemes in the second language can sound as if they are the same, and the motor articulations of the second language can be difficult to reproduce (Kuhl, 2000; Yuen *et al.*, 2010).

One of the interesting aspects of auditory decoding is **allophonic variation**, the alternate pronunciations of a **citation form** (pure form, uttered in isolation) of word or phrase that occur due to context. Allophonic variations (e.g. *gonna* versus *going to*) are allowed in every language because of **efficiency principles** in production. For reasons of efficiency, speakers of a language tend to use only the minimum energy (loudness and articulatory movement) required to create an acceptable phonological string, one that is likely to be recognised by the intended listener. As a result, nearly all sound phrases in a natural spoken language sample are underspecified – that is, they are always less clearly articulated than pure citation forms would be.

The variations are brought about through **co-articulation** processes of **assimilation**, vowel **reduction** and **elision**. These changes – essentially simplifications – shorten both production and reception time. In essence, they allow the speaker to be more efficient in production, and the listener to be more efficient in perception and processing (cf. Hughes, 2010). Of course, this principle tends to hold true only for native listeners of a language; non-native listeners often find the simplifications to make the spoken language more difficult to process, particularly if they have learned the written forms of the language and the citation forms of the pronunciation of words in the language before they have begun to engage in natural spoken discourse.

Concept 2.7   **Connected speech patterns**

Connected speech results in numerous allophonic variations which the listener must interpret as equivalent to their citation forms. Most allophonic variations can be described in terms of consonant assimilation, consonant cluster reduction, and vowel reduction. These changes that occur at morpheme and word boundaries are sometimes collectively referred to as **sandhi**.

2.5.1   Assimilation

Consonant assimilation takes place when the pure sound of the consonant is changed due to phonological context. (See Table 2.3 for a display of the consonants in English, in **IPA** form, organised by **phonetic features**.) The top row indicates point of primary articulation. The left column indicates the type of friction that is created. **Assimilation** occurs in several forms:

- /t/ changes to /p/ before /m/, /b/ or /p/ (labialisation):

basket maker	mixed bag
best man	mixed blessing
cat burglar	mixed marriage
cigarette paper	mixed metaphor
circuit board	pocket money
coconut butter	post mortem

Table 2.3 Consonants of English

FRICTION	BILABIAL	LABIODENTAL	DENTAL	ALVEOLAR	PALATAL-ALVEOLAR	PALATAL	VELAR	GLOTTAL
Plosive	p b			t d			k g	ʔ
Nasal	m			n			ŋ	
Fricative		f v	θ ð	s z	ʃ ʒ			h
Approximate				ɹ		j		
Lateral				l				

Note. There are twenty-two consonants in most varieties of spoken English, represented here in IPA (International Phonetic Alphabet) transcription. However, all consonants are spoken with multiple variations, depending on the variety of English spoken, and on the phonological context in which the consonants occur.

- /d/ changes to /b/ before /m/, /b/ or /p/ (labialisation):

  bad pain   good cook
  blood bank   good morning
  blood bath   grand master
  blood brother   ground plan

- /n/ changes to /m/ before /m/, /b/ or /p/ (nasalisation):

  Common Market   open prison
  con man   pen pal
  cotton belt   pin money
  button pusher

- /t/ changes to /k/ before /k/ or /g/ (velarisation):

  cigarette card   short cut
  credit card   smart card
  cut glass   street cred

- /d/ changes to /g/ before /k/ or /g/ (glottalisation):

  bad girl   hard cash
  bird call   hard copy
  closed game   hard core
  cold call   hard court

- /n/ changes to /ŋ/ before /k/ or /g/ (glottalisation):

  Golden Gate   tin can
  golden goose   tone control
  human capital   town clerk
  in camera   town crier

- /s/ changes to /ʃ/ before /ʃ/ or /j/ (palatalisation):

  bus shelter   nice yacht
  dress shop   space shuttle
  nice shoes   less yardage

- /z/ changes to /ʒ/ before /ʃ/ or /j/ (palatalisation):

  cheese shop   where's yours?
  rose show   whose yoghurt?
  these sheep

- /θ/ changes to /s/ before /s/ (palatalisation):

  bath salts   earth science
  bath seat   fifth set
  birth certificate   fourth season
  both sides   north–south divide

2.5.2 Cluster reduction and dropping

When two or more consonants, often of a similar nature, come together, there is a tendency in English to simplify such a cluster by eliding one of them. The longer the cluster, the greater the chance of elision.

Examples of cluster reduction:

Word/combination	No elision	Elision
asked	[ɑːskt]	[ɑːst]
desktop	['dɛskˌtɒp]	['dɛsˌtɒp]
hard disk	[ˌhɑːd'dɪsk]	[ˌhɑː'dɪsk]
kept quiet	[ˌkɛpt'kwaɪət]	[ˌkɛp'kwaɪət]
kept calling	[ˌkɛpt'koːlɪŋ]	[ˌkɛp'koːlɪŋ]
kept talking	[ˌkɛpt'toːkɪŋ]	[ˌkɛp'toːkɪŋ]
at least twice	[əˌtliːst'twaɪs]	[əˌtliːs'twaɪs]
straight towards	[ˌstɹeɪt'tʊwoːdz]	[ˌstɹeɪ'tʊwoːdz]
next to	['nɛkstˌtʊ]	['nɛksˌtʊ]
want to	['wɒntˌtʊ]	['wɒnˌtʊ]
seemed not to notice	['siːmdˌnɒttə'nəʊtɪs]	['siːmˌnɒtə'nəʊtɪs]
for the first time	[fəðəˌfɜːst'taɪm]	[fəðəˌfɜːs'taɪm]

Examples of dropping:

where **he** lived	where (h)e lived
comf**or**table chair	comf(or)table
goi**ng to** be here	go(i)n(gt)o be here
I'll pay for it	I('ll) pay
given to **th**em	given to (th)em
succeed **in im**agining	succeed in (i)magining
te**rror**ist attack	terr(or)ist attack
in the envir**on**ment	in the envir(on)ment

2.5.3 Vowel changes

Vowel reduction refers to various changes in the acoustic *quality* of vowels, which is related to changes in stress, sonority, duration, loudness, articulation, or position in the word, and which is perceived as **weakening**.

Examples of reduced vowels:

Chariot	Connecticut	symthesis
idiot	Iliad	harmony
Mohammed	myriad	period

Elision is another type of assimilation. It is specifically the omission of one or more sounds (such as a vowel, a consonant, or a whole syllable) in a word or phrase, producing a result that is easier for the speaker to pronounce. (Sometimes, sounds may also be elided for euphonic effect.) Elision is normally automatic and unintentional, but it may be deliberate. All languages have examples of this phonological phenomenon.

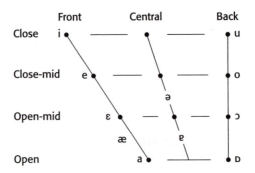

Figure 2.2 *Vowels of English*. There are eleven main vowels in most varieties of English. The vowel system is often depicted in two dimensions, corresponding to the position of tongue mass relative to the front or back of the mouth (front–central–back axis) and to the relative openness of the mouth and jaw during voicing of the vowel (close–open axis). More so than with consonants, vowel sounds will vary according to the variety of English (all front and back vowels have degrees of rounding) and by phonological context (vowels in unstressed syllables are generally reduced, or centralised for quicker articulation)

Examples of elision in English:

comfortable:	/ˈkʌmfərtəbəl/	→ /ˈkʌmftəbəl/ (British English) → /ˈkʌmftərbəl/ (American English)
fifth:	/ˈfɪfθ/	→ /ˈfɪθ/
him:	/hɪm/	→ /ɪm/
laboratory:	/læˈbɔrətɔri/	→ /ˈlæbrətɔri/ (American English), /ləˈbɔrətri/ (British English)
temperature:	/ˈtɛmpərətʃər/	→ /ˈtɛmpərtʃər/, /ˈtɛmprətʃər/
vegetable:	/ˈvɛdʒətəbəl/	→ /ˈvɛdʒtəbəl/

2.5.4 Syntactic parsing

While processing speech starts with successful chunking of sound into phonological groups, followed by word recognition, a more automated and more precise processing of the auditory input is possible if the listener can map incoming speech onto a grammatical model of the language (Baggio, 2008). This aspect of linguistic processing is called **parsing**, and like word recognition, it is also seen as involving two passes and taking place on two levels. As with phonological parsing, these two passes take place simultaneously, but operate across differing time spans and with different, though consistent, priorities. As is inferred from neural imaging studies, the first pass involves a broader time frame – typically six to eight seconds (the span of two to three pause units) – while the second pass involves a more constrained time frame – typically just the two or three seconds of a single pause unit (Schuler *et al.*, 2010).

2.6 Utilising syntactic parsing

As words in speech are recognised, processing the language for meaning requires a partial syntactic mapping of incoming speech onto a grammatical model. A number of syntactic and morphological (word form) cues influence how the listener processes meaning: word order, subject-verb (topic-comment) matching, pro-form agreement (e.g. agreement of pronouns with their antecedents), case inflections (e.g. *I* versus *me*), and contrastive stress. The listener's grammatical knowledge, and ability to utilise that knowledge in real time, is called on during syntactic processing.

Syntactic processing occurs at two levels: that of the immediate utterance, or **sentence level**, and that of the extended text, or **discourse level**. There is some evidence that syntactic processing takes place in two passes. The **first pass** identifies syntactic categories of units in the speech stream, and the **second pass** integrates syntax of the immediate utterance with syntax of the larger speech unit that is being processed. (Osterhout and Nicol, 1999).

In the first pass, syntactic processing, or parsing, accomplishes three basic goals: (1) It speeds up aural processing by using constraints to quickly assign parts of incoming utterances to inviolable syntactic categories; (2) it allows for predicting functions of incoming parts of an utterance and for disambiguating partially heard parts of an utterance; (3) and it helps the processor create a **propositional model** of the incoming speech from which **logical inferences** can be calculated for further comprehension.

Because of the redundancy in ongoing communication, a listener usually does not have to complete both levels of parsing in order to understand adequately. Indeed, from a functional perspective, because listeners have limited processing resources, they will attend primarily to the broader first pass of parsing – that is, the communicative function of the utterance and its place in the overall topical structure of the discourse. This first pass creates a syntactic **reference frame** that can be used as a kind of net for comprehension. If an automised syntactic reference frame is activated and the communicative function has been recognised, a listener will not need to attend to all of the formal (i.e. syntactic) manifestations of that function within each utterance (Baggio, 2008).

It is rarely possible, except with extremely slow speech, for a human listener to monitor a complete second pass (word-for-word) parsing of an incoming auditory signal. A complete verbal parsing would entail consciously assigning all recognised units (words and lexical phrases) into grammatical constituents (noun, verb, adjective, etc.) and computing a workable semantic relationship between these constituents. A listener needs only draw upon a reduced set of grammatical rules to assist them in interpretation of form–function mappings. Competent listeners use what is referred to in machine translation as top-down **fragment grammar**, which allows for large chunks of language to go unparsed, yet for comprehension (or translation) to still take place at a satisfactory level (O'Donnell *et al.*, 2009).

A first pass parsing uses a referential interface or reference frame to identify the discourse topic – what is being talked about generally – as superordinate to sentence topic in order to determine dependencies in an incoming utterance (Winkler, 2006).

In a first pass parsing, utterances are initially scanned for references that link to previous utterances and ultimately to a dependency on the discourse topic (Martín-Loeches *et al.*, 2009). When a fuller, second pass **parsing** is necessary, the listener assigns all words into grammatical categories (**content words**, such as noun, verb, adjective, adverb or **function words** attached to a content word) and assigns structural and semantic relations between them. The primary grammatical cues that are needed for a second pass parsing are word order, subject–verb agreement, pro-form agreement and case inflections. Selective use of these syntactic and morphological cues, along with the use of **semantic cues**, such as animacy (i.e. the logical viability of a given subject acting upon a given verb) and pragmatic cues, such as topic–comment relationship, and contrastive stress, allow the listener to utilise a referential interface between grammatical knowledge of the language and real world knowledge (Tanenhaus *et al.*, 2004).

For fluent listeners, syntactic processing at the utterance level is typically noticed only when an anomaly occurs. Perception of a syntactic anomaly produces a characteristic disruption in L1 listeners. This has been called the P-600 effect, in which electrical activity in the auditory cortex is disrupted about 600 ms after presentation of the anomaly. Interestingly, for most L2 listeners who have not reached an advanced stage of acquisition, this syntactic disruption effect typically does *not* occur, suggesting that syntactic processing is not entirely automised in beginner and intermediate level learners of a language (Rayner and Clifton, 2009).

Because the two parsing passes overlap and converge, an integration of the information they provide to the listener is what is most important. The most critical syntactic integration processes for the listener are (1) determining conjunctions between utterances, including equivalences between text items in adjoined utterances, by calculating cohesion markers for **anaphoric** (previously mentioned), **cataphoric** (to be mentioned), and **exophoric** (references external to the text) references, and (2) filling in

ellipsis (items that are left out of the utterance because they are assumed to be known by the listener, or already given in the text), and (3) calculation of logical inferences that link propositions within the discourse, which most often are not explicitly stated (Chater and Manning, 2006).

As with other phases of linguistic processing, integration of parsing is facilitated by underlying knowledge at multiple levels:

- **Pragmatic knowledge** of common **discourse functions** (e.g. apologies, invitations, complaints) and types (e.g. greeting routines, personal anecdotes). In particular, an ability to note episode boundaries, routines, or other conventional division points that bind sets of utterances together will assist in discourse (first pass) parsing (Gernsbacher and Foertsch, 1999).

- **Intertextual knowledge** of likely speaker experiences that affect the meaning of the message. Because of the pervasive intertextual nature of language – any utterance is likely to reflect the past linguistic experience of the speaker and hearer – awareness of the speaker's background experiences, including the types of metaphors he or she is apt to use and the range of cultural experiences he or she is able to draw upon, will influence speed and efficiency of linguistic processing (Flowerdew and Miller, 2010). (This aspect of processing will be discussed in Chapters 3 and 4.)

- Familiarity with common sequences of **formulaic language** that can be processed quickly. This category of formulaic language covers various types of word strings which appear to be stored whole in memory and retrieved rapidly from memory by the listener with only minimal cueing. A formulaic sequence can be a continuous or discontinuous string, of words which appears to be prefabricated: that is, stored and retrieved whole from memory at the time of use or interpretation, rather than being subject to generation or parsing by the language grammar. This would include knowledge of what Wray (2009) calls tightly idiomatic strings, such as by and large, which are immutable to change, as well as flexible ones containing slots for open class items, like NP be-TENSE sorry to keep-TENSE you waiting.

Formulaic language of this nature has been referred to by many terms, including: amalgams gambits, reassembled speech, prefabricated routines, chunks, holistic patterns, holophrases, co-ordinate constructions, high frequency collocations, composites, irregular routine formulae conventionalised forms, Lexical phrases, semi-preconstructed phrases, fixed expressions, multiword units, and unanalysed chunks of speech. All allude to the notion that such phrases are a unit of both production and comprehension that allow for increased fluency and comfort in the use of spoken language (cf. Hughes, 2010).

- Wray and Perkins (2000) organise formulaic language into six major categories:
  - Polywords, e.g. *the oldest profession; to blow up; for good.*
  - Fixed phrases, e.g. *by sheer coincidence.*
  - Meta-messages, e.g. *for that matter* . . . (message: I just thought of a better way of making my point); . . . *that's all* (message: Don't get frustrated).
  - Sentence builders, e.g. (*person A*) *gave* (*person B*) *a* (*long*) *song and dance about* (*a topic*).
  - Situational utterances, e.g. *How can I ever repay you?*
  - Verbatim texts, e.g. *better late than never; How ya gonna keep 'em down on the farm?*
- A knowledge of context-appropriate prosody, with the ability to attend to pitch levels, as episodes in discourse are often bracketed intonationally. Different pitch contours between pause units can indicate newness, separateness, connectedness, incompletion, or completion (Zubizarreta, 1998). In English, for example, completeness is achieved through closing the topic on a low tone, immediately followed by a new topic starting on a high tone (Traat, 2006).

Concept 2.8   **Propositional model as representation**

A propositional model of speech represents, in the listener's mind, text referents (lexical items in the text) and their relationship to each other.

To understand this process explicitly, we can use any functional grammar, such as **case grammar** (Fillmore, 1968), **systemic grammar** (Halliday and Webster, 2009) or a **construction grammar** (Brisard *et al.*, 2009), which focuses on the argument structure of an utterance and the link between the verb and the grammatical context it requires.

Grammatical context includes obligatory and optional **case relations** such as Agent, Object, Recipient, Instrument, Goal, Temporal, and Locative. In a construction grammar, constituents in an utterance are defined by their relationship to a theme or verb. While listening, the receiver can construct a hierarchical map of how the words recognised in speech fit into the semantic frameworks of the verbs in the utterance. For instance, if the listener identifies a verb such as *give*, he or she knows that it requires an agent, recipient, and object, and can also, optionally, entail a time and a place. Based on a map of structural-functional expectations, the listener can reconstruct the propositional meaning of an utterance.

Concept 2.9   **Semantic roles as units in parsing**

In most languages, and particularly in English, the most commonly identifiable cases in an utterance are agent, object and patient, and are typically required in a grammatical utterance. Other semantic roles occur less explicitly, but other relevant case-roles (e.g. time, location, source) still must be inferred in order for an utterance to make sense.

agent (A) (primary do-er of an action)
patient (P) (receiver of an action)
object (O) (that which is acted upon by the agent)
instrument (I) (means of doing an action)
goal (G) (destination or desired end point)
temporal (T) (when action is carried out)
locative (L) (where action is carried out)
path (P) (way of motion)
source (S) (origination, starting point)
manner (M) (way of doing)
extent (E) (how far completed)
reason (R) (motivation for action)
beneficiary (B) (for whom action is carried out)

Stated another way, if the verb, or theme, is central to parsing an utterance, a listener cannot fully complete a parsing without first identifying the verb. Once the verb is identified, the listener can then relate the other constituents to it. For example, if the listener hears *Tom and Mary took us to dinner last night*, she may parse the utterance as:

(A)   VERB (P)   (G)   (T)
Tom and Mary | took | us | to dinner | last night.

A more abstract, propositional representation would be:

THEME: took (past of 'take')
Agent = Tom and Mary
Patient = us (= speaker + someone)
Goal = to dinner
Time = last night.

Both of these views have **psychological validity** – they resonate with the experience of actual users. The linear model represents the temporal nature of parsing, though it is clear that the listener has to hold constituents in short-term memory without completely parsing them until the utterance, or the larger grammatical unit or semantic argument, is judged to be complete. Items within the units that are not understood can be held temporarily in an episodic buffer for several seconds (Baddeley, 2001). The hierarchical view may be a closer psychological representation of what the listener does in real time, because it addresses how short-term memory holds input only until it can be related to the theme of the utterance and fit into a developing hierarchical (situational or propositional) model of the text (Kintsch, 1998).

2.7   Integrating non-verbal cues into linguistic processing

A large body of research has demonstrated that listening involves integration of verbal and non-verbal cues. As an utterance unfolds, listeners take advantage of both linguistic and extra-linguistic information to arrive at interpretations more quickly than they could using the spoken language alone. For instance, listeners have been shown to use visual (**exophoric**) information about the scene (Tanenhaus *et al.*, 1995), the goals and perspectives of their partners (Hanna *et al.*, 2003), and spatial constraints about how objects in the world can be manipulated (Chambers *et al.*, 2002) during language understanding, all of which serves to restrict the set of potential interpretations that need to be considered. Similarly, information from different levels of processing, such as phonology and prosody, syntax, semantics, along with real-world reference, can be combined by listeners to constrain the set of potential interpretations that are explored.

Some of the non-verbal information available to the listener is communicated independently of the language – before or after the language is uttered, and sometimes offered by someone other than the speaker. Because of the prevalence of visual information in most live discourse situations, and particularly with advancing use of visual media and multimedia, it is useful to consider how visual information enhances linguistic input, or distorts it, or replaces it, and sometimes even contradicts it.

Visual signals must be considered as **co-text**, an integral part of the input which the listener is able to use for interpretation (Harris, 2008; Fukumura *et al.*, 2010). Visual signals are of two basic types: **exophoric** and **kinesic**. Exophoric signals, such as a speaker holding up a photograph or writing some words on the board, typically serve as references for the spoken text and are critical for text interpretation. Exophoric signals are particularly crucial in situations of high information flow, such as scientific documentaries and academic lectures.

Kinesic signals are the body movements, including eye and head movements, the speaker makes while delivering the text. There are numerous systems for describing a speaker's body movements and their role in communication (cf. Goffman, 1974; Birdwhistell, 1970; Harrigan *et al.*, 2007;

Plonka, 2007). From these sources, the most commonly occurring sets of kinesic signals are baton signals, directional gaze and guide signs.

Baton signals are hand and head movements, which are typically associated with emphasis and prosodic cadence. For instance, a speaker will often indicate with rhythmic, bounding motions of his or her hands the number of stressed syllables in a pause unit. Emphatic motions of the lips, chin, or cheeks associated with articulation are also baton signals.

Directional gaze is eye movement and focusing used to direct the listener or audience to an exophoric reference or to identify a particular moment in the discourse as relevant in some way to the listener. Even in lectures, when there is little or no direct verbal interaction between speaker and audience, lecturers will often make and maintain eye contact with several individuals intermittently throughout the lecture to amplify and personalise meaning. In all live discourse, the main function of eye contact is to maintain the sense of contact with the listeners and to allow for them to give backchannel signals to the speaker about their state of interest and understanding of the conversation or speech.

Guide signals are the systematic gestures and movements of any part of the body, such as extending one's arms or leaning forward. Many guide signals may be purely idiosyncratic, with no clear meaning, but most will have some clear role in a speaker's emphasis or shading of a particular point. For instance, speaking with one's arms outstretched may be a way for the speaker to attempt to persuade the listener to take a particular point seriously. Needless to say, guide signals will vary from culture to culture, and from speaker to speaker, and it is possible to increase comprehension by learning the guide signals of a particular speaker. However, it is difficult to formulate a systematic grammar of guide signal gestures that consistently contributes to discourse meaning across speakers. An exception to this is lip-reading, which can be considered interpreting guide signals (cf. Vendrame *et al.*, 2010).

As with paralinguistic cues, non-verbal cues are intended to confirm the speaker's linguistic meaning. However, when messages in the linguistic and paralinguistic or non-linguistic channels are detected to be inconsistent, the listener may have reason to believe that the speaker is being deceptive, and is likely to attend to the non-verbal cues (McCornack, 1997). Similarly, in intercultural communication, when the speaker uses a gesture or body language that may connote something to the listener in his or her native culture that is not intended by the speaker, it will be difficult for the listener to process the verbal message separately from the non-verbal message (cf. Arasaratnam, 2009; Scollon and Scollon, 1995; Roberts, Davies and Jupp, 1992).

Concept 2.10   **Non-verbal cues in listening**

Listening face-to-face, particularly to a familiar speaker, makes listening easier because it provides an extra layer of information: non-verbal cues. Non-verbal cues serve to amplify meaning or to confirm/disconfirm linguistic meaning.

Summary: unification of linguistic processing

This chapter has outlined the processes of linguistic decoding that are often referred to as bottom-up processes. The analogy of bottom-up processing is very useful when employed in conjunction with the notion of top-down processing in that it implies that language understanding involves parallel and complementary processes. The use of bottom-up processing (using data derived from the speech signal directly to make sense) and top-down processing (using concepts in the brain to impose meaning) in conjunction allows an acceptable measure of comprehension to take place smoothly, at least in our first language, and at least most of the time.

Bottom-up processing has its limitations. You can experience the limitations easily in your first language if you play back an audio recording at a fast speed. Most people can listen to a familiar topic at up to three or four times the normal speaking speed (180 words per minute is considered normal). But we can do this only if we sample bits of speech, make quick inferences about the meaning, and simply ignore ambiguous or inaudible (overly compressed) parts. In normal speech comprehension, we are similarly sampling the speech stream, but usually ignoring less and making more thoughtful inferences to arrive at an acceptable understanding. Bottom up language processing is not the goal of comprehension, but rather a tool we can use to unify our understanding.

Chapter 3

Semantic processing

Semantic processing encompasses the listening processes involved in comprehension, inferencing, learning, and memory formation. This chapter:

- outlines the processes of comprehension, in terms of given and new information, and updating mental models;
- discusses the concept of knowledge activation, the notions of schema and constructive memory;
- discusses the process of inference, which is central to all language understanding, and presents different systems of inferences;
- presents fundamental concepts of memory that are used during listening, including phonological loop or echoic memory, short-term memory and long-term memory;
- presents an outline of how listening relates to learning.

3.1 Comprehension: the role of knowledge structures

Comprehension is often considered to be the **first-order goal** of listening, the highest priority of the listener. Many people even consider it the sole purpose of listening. Although in the vernacular the term listening comprehension is widely used to refer to all aspects of listening, the term comprehension is used in a more specific sense in this chapter. Comprehension is the process of what Sanders and Gernsbacher (2004) called **structure building**, relating language to concepts in one's memory and to references in the real world in a way that aims to find coherence and relevance. Concepts, not words, are the fundamental units of reason and comprehension, and as such are assumed to be the result of neural activity inside the brain (Gallese and Lakoff, 2005). According to Gernsbacher's **structure building framework**, the initial goal of comprehension is to build coherent mental representations from concepts. Comprehenders (listeners or readers or observers) build a comprehension structure by first developing a map in which the concepts will fit. As they listen (or read or observe) comprehenders then place concepts representing new information into this figurative map. They can do this only if and when the new information relates to previous information already in the structure. However, when the incoming information is judged to be unrelated, comprehenders shift attention and attach a new substructure. The building blocks of mental structures are **memory nodes**, which are activated by incoming stimuli and controlled by two cognitive mechanisms: **suppression** and **enhancement**.

In terms of language processing, comprehension is the experience of understanding what the language heard refers to in one's experience or in the outside world, and sensing how any incoming burst of language enhances or suppresses one's current understanding. Complete comprehension then refers to the listener having a clear concept in memory for every **reference** used by the speaker, not necessarily the same referents in the speaker's memory.

Because comprehension involves the mapping and **updating** of references that the speaker uses, the process of comprehending occurs in an ongoing cycle, as the listener is attending to speech. A useful starting point for discussing how comprehension – the mapping and updating procedure – takes place is the notion of **given information** and **new information**.

Each intonation unit uttered by a speaker unit can be seen as including both new or **focal information** and given or **background information**. 'New' refers to the assumed status, *in the speaker's mind*, that the information is not currently active in the listener's working memory. 'New information' does not necessarily mean that the speaker believes the information itself is novel or unknown to the listener. 'Given' refers to the status, again in the speaker's mind, that information presented is already active *in the listener's memory*. (The speaker may, of course, be mistaken about either assumption.) The interplay of given and new information in spoken discourse is reflected in the prosody of speech – generally corresponding to **rising tones** (also called **referring tones**) for given information and falling tones for new information, which in turn provides overt clues to the listener in how to attend to the speech.

Concept 3.1   **The status of information in discourse: active versus accessible**

The concept of given-new is helpful in understanding the relationship between speaker and listener. This concept provides a basis for negotiation of what the speaker wants to become active or salient in the conversation.

A more accurate characterisation of 'new' is . . . 'newly activated at this point in the conversation'. Conversely, 'given' can be characterised as already active at this point in the conversation. We can add a third possibility to (these) distinctions by labelling information that has been activated for a previously **semi-active state** as accessible (Chafe, 1994: 72).

Chafe views the process of bringing inactive or semi-active information into a conversation as involving mental effort or **activation costs**. Given information is obviously least costly in this sense because the information is already active. Accessible information is more costly, and new information most costly. New information is most likely to receive prominence, in order to signal that this unit of information will require greater attention and processing. This prominence can be signalled through phonology and through syntactic placement in the utterance.

The central process in comprehension is the **integration** of the information conveyed by the text with information and concepts already known by the listener. Comprehension occurs as a modification (additions, deletions, amendments) of the internal model of the discourse by the listener, in which the explicit information in the text plays only one part. This process of integration is necessarily sensitive to whether the information conveyed by a sentence provides given information (already known to the listener) or new information (not already known to the listener, or not already known in the presented context). Without this interplay of new and given, there can be no updating, and no comprehension. The listener may already know everything that the speaker is saying, but there is no comprehension of the speaker unless the listener integrates information from the speaker's text with what is active in the listener's own memory.

The speaker conveys his or her own distinctions between given and new information through **presentation cues**. In English, presentation cues are both linguistic and paralinguistic. The paralinguistic cues are primarily intonational. The main stress or **prominence** (increased **duration, loudness**, and/or **pitch**) within an intonational unit falls on the word that is the locus of the new information. While all content words in English receive some stress according to basic phonological-lexical rules of the language, the prominent word will receive even greater stress, usually indicated by lengthening the vowel sound. For example, in the following extract the stressed syllables (often whole words) are capitalised, while the prominent words in each intonation unit are both capitalised and underlined to indicate greater volume and lengthening. These prominent syllables guide the listener to the focal information.

she'd been STANding in the CAR park
and it was FREEZing COLD
and she asked her to TAKE her round to her DAUGHTer's
so she aGREED to take her ROUND
what ELSE could she DO
she COULDn't leave her STANDing
in this CAR park

(Brazil, 1995: 100)

These prominent words guide the listener in comprehending the extract by indicating what should be processed as 'new' information. One could imagine that the listener would have significant difficulties comprehending the extract if it were delivered in a monotone without any intonational cues to provide guidance toward focal information, or if the intonational cues were misleading, as in the following composed version of the text:

she'd BEEN standing in THE car park
and IT WAS freezing cold
and she ASKED her to take her ROUND to her daughter's
so SHE agreed to take HER round
WHAT else COULD she do
she couldn't LEAVE her standing
in THIS car park

With the latter composed text, the listener may have the distinct feeling of being misled by the unconventional signalling of new information, rather than guided toward a congruent understanding of the story that requires minimal processing effort.

Presentation cues are also provided in the speaker's **manner of delivery**, including **pacing**, **pausing**, and frequency and type of **disfluency**. Disfluencies, while often considered to be signs of flawed speech, can actually improve communication through adding processing cues for the listener. For instance, in a study by Arnold *et al.* (2007), it was shown that subjects had better comprehension of task instructions when the instructions included disfluencies, such as pauses, fillers, and self-corrections. (See Figure 3.1.)

• Instruction without disfluencies: *Click on the red object. Then . . .*
• Instruction with disfluencies: *Click on thee, uh, red object. Then . . .*

Comprehension is intricately tied to memory, so it is important to consider what the listener actually takes away from a listening experience. While attending to speech over a period of several intonation units, the listener

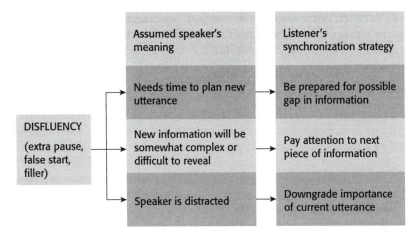

Figure 3.1 *Listener strategy for adjusting to disfluency.* When listeners hear a speaker disfluency (such as a pause or a filler or a restart) they may assume that the speaker is distracted, needs extra time to plan the next utterance or is preparing them for complex information. Based on this assumption, they can then adjust their expectations to synchronise with the speaker

has to store a **mental representation** of the discourse and continuously update the representation with new information. The listener's representation of a comprehended text is stored as sets of interrelated **propositions** (Singer, 2007). Propositions may be seen as units in memory, which are used both in encoding and retrieval of comprehended information.

3.2   Cognitive understanding: the role of schemata

Listening is primarily a cognitive activity, involving the activation and modification of concepts in the listener's mind. The conceptual knowledge that the listener brings to text comprehension needs to be co-ordinated in ways that allow him or her to activate it efficiently and continuously arrive at an acceptable cognitive understanding of the input.

As a way of referring to activated portions of conceptual knowledge, cognitive psychologists and linguists often refer to modules of knowledge as **schemata**. It is estimated that any normal adult would have hundreds of thousands of available schemas in memory, which would be interrelated in an infinite number of ways. Further, new schemata are created and existing ones are updated constantly: every time we read, listen to, or observe something new we create a new schema by relating one fact to another through logical or semiotic links (Amoretti *et al.*, 2007; Reitbauer, 2006). Comprehension researchers agree that a key to effective comprehension is activating appropriate schemata that will assist in understanding the incoming text.

A schema is a figurative description for any set of simultaneously activated connections (related nodes) in the vast frontal cortex of the brain. According to schema theory, the entire network of activation may be triggered by the individual activation of any node in the network (Rumelhart and Norman, 1981). What defines a schema is not its structure – since a schema is not a neurological structure – but rather its heuristic nature. A set of memory nodes needed to guide one through an activity, such as 'withdrawing money from an ATM' or 'dealing with phone solicitor', becomes a heuristic when it first works as a solution to a comprehension problem. Because these schemata can be interrelated and cross-referenced in a variety of ways, the connections among them is virtually infinite (Churchland, 1999). In order for schemata to be useful as heuristics for real time comprehension, new schemata are created every day and existing ones are updated constantly. Every time we read, listen to, or observe something new we create a new schema by relating one fact to another through a logical or semiotic link (Feldman, 2006).

For example, if you are listening to a news broadcast on an international conflict, you inevitably bring to mind numerous existing schemata about the countries involved, their leaders, past history, and recent relevant events. Indeed, you will need to bring relevant schemata into your short-term memory in order to stay interested in the news story and comprehend it. These schemata, built from your accumulated understandings of the world, will be networked in your mind in ways that make them accessible in real time as you listen. No special effort is involved. It is important to note that schemata are sets of activated nodal links in the brain rather than specific physical locations. Schema organisation and accessibility is influenced by a number of factors, such as their relative importance to your personal value system, as well as their frequency (how often you activate particular schemata) and their recency (how recently you have activated related schemata).

When we are in the act of listening – to a conversation, radio program, etc. – we activate the smallest number of schemata that we estimate will be relevant to understanding the text adequately. This is what has been called the **parsimony principle** (or **Occam's razor**) in language processing: a person should not increase the number of entities required to explain anything nor make more assumptions than needed (Wimmer and Dominick, 2005). In understanding a news story, for example, it is more parsimonious to update active schemata related to specific items in the news story than to attempt to comprehend the text as entirely new and unique information (Murray and Burke, 2003).

All of our schemata contain a shorthand code for our cumulative experiences, a retrieval system which will consist of both linguistic and non-linguistic aspects. Activation of multiple schemata is the basis of elaborative inferencing, as it allows us to invoke the presence of people, events, static and dynamic imagery and other sensory data that are not explicitly referred to in the text. For example, if the speaker is describing an incident at a city train station during rush hour, the listener can presume the presence of numerous people, the noise of trains, the crush of bodies, and so on. Because a schema contains fully elaborated prototypical elements, the prototypes can be used to generate default values when specifics are left unspoken.

The speaker and the listener do not need to have identical schemata relating to the conversational topics in order for adequate understanding to take place. Simply activating an appropriately related schema allows the listener to make inferences that are essential to comprehending a text. When there is a relative match or congruence of schemata in the listener's and speaker's mind, we can say an **acceptable understanding** has taken place. When there are significant **mismatches** between the speaker's and the listener's schemata, we say that a **misunderstanding** has occurred. When there are lapses and the listener is unable to activate *any* appropriate schema, we say that **non-understanding** has occurred. (See Table 3.1.)

Table 3.1   **Types of understanding and non-understanding**

TYPE	LISTENER ACTION
Non-understanding	Listener is unable to activate any appropriate schemata to understand speaker
Misunderstanding	Listener activates schemata that have significant mismatches to speaker's schemata
Partial understanding	Listener activates schema that include some overlap with speaker's active schemata
Plausible understanding	Listener activates schema that include central items in speaker's discourse, though not largely shared with speaker
Acceptable understanding	Listener activates schema that include central items in speaker's discourse, largely 'shared' with speaker
Complete understanding	Listener activates schema that are completely 'shared' with speaker

Note. This table represents a range of possible understandings in discourse. At any given time in a discourse a listener may gravitate from non-understanding to complete understanding, based on shared schemata with the speaker.

3.3   Social understanding: the role of common ground

Understanding spoken discourse goes beyond creating a **cognitive map** of the speaker's intended meaning. **Social frameworks** and **affective elements** are also involved, even with seemingly objective texts and innocuous interactions. What a listener understands depends to a large degree upon having common ground with the speaker: shared concepts and shared routines, ways of acting in and reacting to the world. Of course, it is impossible that two persons would share an identical schema or perspective for any conversational topic, for either something concrete like 'having breakfast' or for something abstract, like 'an ideal marriage'. Similarly, it is not possible for two speakers to have same **script** for sequences of action, like 'commuting to work' or 'having an argument with a spouse'. However, it is possible that two conversants will share what are known as common **activation spaces** in memory that will allow them to arrive a mutual empathy and acceptable understanding, due to their having common cultural or educational or experiential backgrounds (Bowe and Martin, 2007; Poldrack *et al.*, 2009). (This concept is essential for automatic processing by computers, as will be discussed in Chapter 5.)

Our schemata, our conceptual frameworks in memory, consist of activation patterns across the brain's neurons (estimated to be about 10^{11} or 100,000,000,000). Each **activation space** (called 'activation vector space' in neuropsychology) has a distinct weight, or **activity level**, for each neural synapse that is involved in the concept used in comprehension. Activity levels are influenced by frequency of use, but also by emotional factors. A specific configuration of synaptic weights will partition the activation space of a given neuronal pathway into distinct **prototypes** (Churchland, 1999; Geeraerts, 2006). Speakers and listeners communicate in part through activation of similar prototypes.

As we listen, prototype neural patterns get activated as we respond intellectually to certain language inputs (Rosch *et al.*, 2004). While there will be individual differences in the synaptic weights of concepts we respond to (some will be more important to one individual than to another), the actual neural space in which these differences occur is similarly partitioned in speakers and listeners of similar backgrounds. According to **prototype theory**, people may react to events in the world in similar ways not because their underlying memories (i.e. synaptic configurations in memory) are closely similar, but because their activation spaces are similarly partitioned and their concentration on particular partitions is equally energised (Haynes and Rees, 2005; Churchland, 2006; Churchland and Churchland, 2002).

While the details of these neurological processes themselves are not relevant to the listener, the outputs of the process are essential. In every listening situation, it is essential for the listener to activate knowledge from stored prototypes. When relevant knowledge is activated during comprehension, additional information in related schemata becomes available to the listener. At the same time, whenever a knowledge structure is activated, the listener also may experience an affective response associated with it – a **cognitive commitment** – which further influences connections with the speaker and her ideas, and empathic responses to what she has said (cf. Havas *et al.*, 2007; Zwaan, 2004; Firth and Firth, 2006).

> **Quote 3.1**   Bartlett on constructive memory
>
> The influence of background knowledge on comprehension has long been of interest to psychologists. Charles Bartlett, often considered the founder of cognitive psychology, notes in his book *Remembering:* 'Every social group is organised and held together by some specific psychological tendency or group of tendencies, which give the group a bias in its dealings with external circumstances. The bias constructs the special persistent features of group culture... [and this] immediate settles what the individual will observe in his environment and what he will connect from his past life with this direct response. It does this markedly in two ways. First, by providing that setting of interest, excitements, and emotion, which favors the development of specific images, and secondly, by providing a persistent framework of institutions and customs which acts as a schematic basis for constructive memory.'
>
> Bartlett (1932: 55)

3.4   The role of inference in constructing meaning

> **Quote 3.2**   George A. Miller on listening
>
> George Miller founded (with Jerome Bruner) the Center for Cognitive Studies at Harvard University in 1960, which gave rise to the study of language and memory. Miller is credited with a number of influential concepts and quotes. Here is one of his quotes concerning the psycholinguistic processes involved in understanding: 'In order to understand what another person is saying, you must assume it is true and try to imagine what it could be true of.' (This principle is now referred to as Miller's Law.

Since we do not have direct access to a speaker's intended meaning in producing an utterance or series of utterances (and since the speaker often is not fully aware of all of his or her intended meanings in any event), the listener has to rely repeatedly on the process of inference to arrive at an acceptable interpretation of each utterance and the connection between a series of utterances. One part of the process of inference by the listener is achieved through conventional inferencing involving linkages within the language used and another part is achieved through problem-solving-oriented heuristic procedures involving both logic and real-world knowledge.

When a speaker makes an utterance, she is typically adding successive bits of information about a topic or set of topics that are already 'in play'. The references for information within any one utterance and the connections between the bits of information across utterances will be signalled by the speaker through conventional use of cohesion devices, such as anaphora, lexical substitution, conjunction and ellipsis. All of these are in the domain of **text linguistics**, and a competent user of the language will acquire the ability to process them quickly via a cognitive process known as **priming**, which helps the listener anticipate and recall expected discourse structures (Hoey, 2005).

Concept 3.2   **Cohesion devices and extended discourse**

Language comprehension involves finding coherence across utterances. The listener must be able to construct coherence by following the speaker's use of cohesion devices.

- *Anaphora:* reference back to an item previously mentioned in the text. 'My brother stayed at my apartment last week. He left his dog here.'
- *Exophora:* reference to an item outside the text. (*Pointing*) 'That's his dog.'
- *Lexical substitution:* using a similar lexical item to substitute for a previous one. 'His dog . . . that animal . . .'
- *Lexical chaining:* using a related lexical item as a link to one already mentioned. 'The dog makes a mess . . . it sheds everywhere, it tears up newspapers . . .'
- *Conjunction:* using links between propositions, such as *and, but, so.* 'The dog is a bit much for me, but I promised I'd take care of it.'
- *Ellipsis:* omission of lexical items that can be recovered by the listener through conventional grammatical knowledge. 'I promised to take care of it, so I will' (take care of it).
- *Integration:* synthesising visual and aural cues.

3.5   Listener enrichment of input

Speech processing is known to be aided by consistent visual signals from the speaker, in the form of both gestures and articulatory movements (of the mouth, lips, cheeks, chin, throat, chest) that correspond to production of speech. (Conversely, speech processing is hindered by unfamiliar or inconsistent visual signals.) Because of the importance of visual cues, psycholinguists consider face-to-face and audio-visual speech perception to be bi-modal, involving both auditory and visual senses (Massaro, 2001; Ouni *et al.*, 2007). Indeed, it has been shown that children acquire speech perception in their L1 through a strong dependence on visual signals from their caretakers (Ochs and Schieffelin, 2009).

When visual and auditory signals do not coincide, there are a great number of incidences of blended mishearings, called the **McGurk Effect** (McGurk and MacDonald, 1976). This cognitive effect occurs when part of the signals taken from visual cues and auditory cues are fused and illustrates how a listener attempts to integrate information from multiple channels. (Stork and Hennecke, 1996 provide additional examples and discussion of **blended mishearings**.) Consistent with the principle of integration, when auditory cues are completely absent (as in listening on the telephone or to the radio), **acoustic mishearings** and other comprehension problems are significantly higher than in face-to-face delivery of messages (Blevins, 2007).

Understanding any extended text or an extended speaking turn involves making use of semantic knowledge or background knowledge. Although an understanding of text-level cohesion devices aids comprehension, a large part of language understanding cannot be explained in terms of conventional language knowledge. Language comprehension requires activation of stores of knowledge that are not contained in the text, and may be only indirectly signalled in it. The speaker has to leave much of this supplementing and retrieval work to the listener **(listener enrichment** in Levinson's terms) if the discourse is to proceed at a comfortable pace. The process of providing these supplements, or enrichment, in order to understand texts can be called **making inferences** or simply **inferencing**.

3.6   Problem-solving during comprehension

According to Barbey and Barsalou (2009), inferences are **problem-solving processes** that are employed only when there is *a need to draw* a relevant inference before comprehension can continue, and when evidence is available from which some conclusion can be drawn. (The authors avoid the use of the term inferencing to cover general knowledge-retrieval processes in which any piece of prior knowledge is retrieved from memory.)

Inferences involve operations on a mental model that a listener has produced while listening. Several types of inferencing algorithms have been identified in everyday language comprehension contexts:

- Estimating the sense of **ambiguous references**:

    Speaker. I talked to John today about the gophers.

    Listener inference. John, the gardener, who was working in our yard today . . .

- Supplying missing links in **ellipted propositions**:

    Speaker. He can't work next weekend. But the following weekend is good.
    Listener inference. . . . he is free to work the following weekend.

- Filling in **schematic slots**:

    Speaker. If we really need it done this weekend, Pedro can come over.
    Listener inference. Pedro is a guy who works with or for John.

- Supplying plausible **supporting grounds** for logical arguments:

    Speaker. He said his kids are in town for holiday weekend.
    Listener inference. His kids aren't in town very often, and he wants to spend as much of his time with them as he can.

- Using text genres to generate expectations about what will occur:

    Speaker. It might be best if we hire someone else to do it.
    Listener inference. Since she's creating a problem–decision type of conversation, she's likely to ask me for my opinion next.

- Supplying **plausible intentions** for the speaker:

    Speaker. Is that OK with you?
    Listener inference. She's telling me all this because she wants to assure me that she's taking care of things, and she wants to give me a face-saving choice if I need it.

Through the use of this kind of inferencing, the listener builds and updates her cognitive representation from one utterance to the next, updating both the **transactional level** (what is said and meant) and the **interactional level** (how this affects the relation between the listener and speaker). There is of course a capacity limit to how many items of new information can be added and to how quickly this kind of updating can be done. This internal updating of one's cognitive representation corresponds to the listener's flow of consciousness (Norrick, 2000; Chafe, 1980). Because of our limited working-memory capacity, the exact verbal (veridical) representation that has been processed will be quickly forgotten. All that may be available to the listener are traces to a **syntactic reference map** and a few key lexical items, related to concepts in long-term memory.

Consistent with the cognitive psychology tradition, Dietrich (2004) proposes that during cognitive processing of a text, new information chunks are integrated into higher-order chunks. These have been called **flowing chunks** since they involve processing of information in both brain hemispheres, temporal associations in the left hemisphere and holistic image-oriented associations in the right hemisphere. This integration or chunking process also increases the functional capacity of working memory. Working within the limitations of short-term memory, the listener will construct *only those inferences necessary* to maintain a coherent representation of the text. In this view of text processing, the order of presentation of propositions in a text will influence the fluency and ease of processing.

Concept 3.3   **Inference types**

The main types of inferences that have been identified are set out below. Note that more than one inference type can be used – and often is used – to represent the link between two propositions. Types of logical inference during text comprehension

- *Initiating links*. A is the reason for B. 'He was afraid to fly. He wasn't getting on that plane' (afraid → causes → not getting on).
- *Enabling links*. A makes Y possible. 'I sat down in the driver's seat. I felt something wet and spongy through my trousers' (sitting down → enables → feeling wet).
- *Schematic links*. A contains an **information framework** that is needed to interpret B. 'He's a pain in the neck to go out with. He always questions the waiter about the bill' (go out → entail → restaurant → entails → waiters, bills).
- *Classification links*. B expresses something that can be **classified** in terms of A. 'My husband eats a ton of fruit every day. I'm always finding banana peels, orange rinds and grape stems all over the kitchen' (fruit → includes → bananas, oranges, grapes → contains → outer peels).
- *Paratactic links*. B expresses something that **follows** A. 'Nela put on her raincoat. She looked at us with this disgusted expression and left' (put on → precedes in sequence → look, leave).
- *Logical links*. A and B together express a **syllogism** in logic (reasoning from multiple premises to a conclusion). 'Suzanne boasts that her children always do well in school, but her son Alex is a slacker, so that can't be true' (condition X + Y → lead to → Z).
- *Reference links*. **Anaphoric** links between items across utterances. 'I got the beer out of the car. It was very warm' (it → refers to → the beer, not the car).
- *Elaborative links*. Any inference that is made by the listener not necessary for text coherence. Such inferences are generally culturally relative, and informed by both individual experiences and values. 'Barbara was thrilled when Todd popped the big question. She was even more thrilled when he gave her the ring' (→ the speaker is almost certainly talking about a marriage proposal and an expensive, diamond ring).
- *Bridging links*. Any inference that fills in assumed facts or presupposes details in order to make a coherent representation. Like elaborative inferences, bridging inferences are culturally relative, based on cumulative experiences and personal attitudes. 'The surgeon was perspiring profusely at the completion of the heart operation. One of the attendants spoke to . . .' (→ him/her). While listening, the listener will form a representation of the surgeon, including unstated details such as whether the surgeon is male or female, by way of bridging inferences.

Based on Nix (1983), Chikalanga (1992) and van den Broek *et al.* (2005)

3.7   Reasoning during comprehension

Much of the language comprehension we do in everyday discourse situations – from watching television to talking with colleagues – involves logical and elaborative inferencing. Both of these types of inferencing processes are based on reasoning, the use of mental logic, involving **claims** and **grounds** of support (cf. Newton and de Villiers, 2007, Braine and O'Brien, 1998, Toulmin, 1987). In **real time reasoning** during discourse comprehension, we must depend on short-term memory, a calculation space in our memory. And because of limitations of short-term memory, we are apt to over-simplify complex arguments and interpretations in order to arrive more readily at an acceptable understanding.

The process of reasoning during listening is relatively straightforward, though not always easy to apply in real time. Reasoning involves five basic cognitive processes: comprehension of facts, categorisation of claims about those facts, relative assumptions of truth value in what the speaker is saying, **induction** of unknown or unknowable facts from given information, and **deduction** of a generalisation based on evidence given.

Reasoning while listening involves rapid identification and evaluation of facts, premises and claims. Listeners need to make assessments quickly in order to understand the claims that the speaker is making – directly or indirectly. Claims are the assertions (e.g. *My boss is taking advantage of me. My kids are driving me crazy. This new law will be good for the economy*, etc) that the speaker wishes us to accept in order to keep the conversation going. Behind the claims are the **grounds**: the supporting facts or ideas which supposedly lead us to accept the claim. It is an axiom of communication (the **maxim of quality** in Gricean terms) that whenever a person makes a claim, let us say of the sort, *Shanghai is the best place to live in China*, the person is accountable, if asked, to produce the data on which the claim is based.

The following are some claims recently heard in conversations:

The Mehtas are pretty good neighbours.

It's OK to cheat on exams sometimes.

If the government doubles the tax on gasoline, I'm sure it'll cut down on green house gases.

If you are engaged in a conversation in which one of these claims is made, you might be willing to accept it because you can readily understand what the **implicit grounds** of support must be and accept these grounds as true. However, if you have reason to doubt the claim, you may choose to ask for the specific underlying grounds for that claim:

You say they're good neighbours (but I've found that they're kind of nosy). Why do you think they're good neighbours?

You say it's OK sometimes to cheat on an exam (but I've been taught that cheating diminishes your character). When would it be OK to cheat in an exam?

You say an extra tax will reduce consumption (but I know I'd have to keep buying gasoline anyway). Don't you think that people who have to use gasoline will continue to buy it anyway?

This type of challenge will usually force the speaker to make *their grounds* of the claim explicit:

I say they're good neighbours because they maintain their property well.

I believe that occasional cheating in exams can sometimes be justified when a course isn't part of a student's major.

I know that, for me, the tax would force me to use gasoline only when absolutely essential.

Even after hearing the grounds explicitly, listeners may still disagree with the force of the claim. They may find the grounds irrelevant, that is, not directly related to the claim, or they may find the grounds contradictory in their own experience, leading them to reject the claim rather than accept it. Similarly, they may find the claim too strong in that there are other grounds, or counter-evidence, that would lead to an alternate claim.

The point here is that a central part of the propositional comprehension of conversation consists of initially understanding the claims that the speaker is making and then accepting, rejecting, or partially accepting or rejecting them – or not passing judgement at all. To the extent that the claims or the grounds may be culturally specific, comprehension will involve not only textual (language-based) competency, but also **intertextual** (reference-based) **competency** (cf. Duff, 2007; Chandler, 2007; Ferri, 2007).

Because successful language comprehension involves reasoning, it follows that unsuccessful language comprehension may involve **fallacies of reasoning**. Indeed, many of the reported examples of miscomprehension in all kinds of discourse, from academic lectures to daily chit-chat, are due to faulty reasoning by the listener. Because of our attention and short-term memory limitations, no one can be expected to process language perfectly in all situations. (In addition, attempting to process *all* of the language we hear around us would be quite contrary to the notion of the relevance seeking human mind!)

A number of studies over the past decades have explored the fallacies of reasoning that occur in discourse. (See Table 3.2.)

Table 3.2   Informal fallacies in everyday discourse reasoning

CATEGORY OF FALLACY DURING LISTENING	TYPE OF FALLACY	SAMPLE INPUT TO LISTENER	PARAPHRASE OF LISTENER FALLACY DURING INFERENCE PROCESS	EXPLANATION
Cognitive	False dilemma	*I thought we were friends, but all my friends came to my wedding and you weren't there*	I guess I'm not really her friend after all	A situation in which only two alternatives are considered, when in fact there are other options; also called black-and-white thinking
	Perfect solution	*These anti-drunk driving ad campaigns are not going to work. People are still going to drink and drive no matter what*	That's right. We might as well forget about trying to discourage drunk driving	The argument assumes that a perfect solution exists and/or that a solution should be rejected because some part of the problem would still exist after it were implemented
	Denying the correlative	*I would give money to the poor, but I believe the world is wonderful and abundant, so no one is really poor*	That's a really admirable attitude. I hadn't thought of it that way before	A type of argument which tries to redefine a correlative (two mutually exclusive options) so that one alternative encompasses the other, i.e. making one alternative impossible

Deductive	Misleading exceptions	*All right, but apart from the sanitation, medicine, education, wine, public order, irrigation, roads, a fresh water system and public health, what have the Romans ever done for us?* (Monty Python film *Life of Brian*)	I agree. The Roman influence on modern society is really overrated. Those so-called accomplishments aren't really so important	A generalisation which is accurate, but comes with one or more qualifications which eliminate so many cases that what remains is much less impressive than the initial statement might have led one to assume
	Hasty generalisaton	*Every American I've met is monolingual, so it must be true that all Americans are monolingual.*	He must be right. I haven't met many Americans, like he has, so I ought to take his word on this	Reaching an inductive generalisation based on insufficient evidence
Inductive	Biased sample	*All intelligent people are opposed to a public health plan – I know both of my parents are*	Maybe I'm not as intelligent as I thought. I actually thought a public health plan was a good idea	Reaching an inductive generalisation based on a sample that does not represent the larger population
	False analogy	*A university is not so different from a business. It needs a clear competitive strategy that will lead to profitable growth*	Actually, I guess treating a university more like a business would solve a lot of the problems I've seen at universities	Extending a comparison of one characteristic to reach a larger argument that covers other characteristics

Sources. Based on Risen and Gilovitch (2007), Bennett (2003) and Damer (2001).

3.8   Compensatory strategies during comprehension

Given natural limitations of memory, all listeners need to resort to compensatory strategies from time to time to perform semantic processing – to make sense of spoken language when conditions become severe. At any point during semantic processing, the listener's capacity for comprehension may be overworked or exhausted, or the listener becomes distracted, and some kind of compensation may be required.

A breakdown in semantic processing may occur when:

- the listener cannot hear what the speaker is saying;
- the listener does not know specific expressions the speaker is using;
- the information the speaker gives is incomplete;
- the listener hears a familiar word, but it is used in an unfamiliar way;
- the listener encounters an unknown word or concept, or when the speakers proceed too quickly for the listener to conduct all of the reasoning processes required, and no opportunity for clarification is available.

In these cases, some kind of compensation is required if the listener aims to maintain full participatory status in the discourse or aims for full comprehension.

Some of the commonly noted compensation strategies are:

- *Skipping:* omitting a part or a block of text from processing for comprehension.
- *Approximation:* using a superordinate concept that is likely to cover the essence of what has not been comprehended; constructing a less precise meaning for a word or concept than the speaker may have intended.
- *Filtering:* compressing a longer message or set of propositions into a more concise one. (This is different from skipping or approximation, which are 'reduction' strategies, because filtering involves active construction of a larger semantic context.)
- *Incompletion:* maintaining an incomplete proposition in memory, waiting until clarification can be obtained.
- *Substitution:* substituting a word or concept or proposition for one that is not understandable.

Table 3.3 shows examples of compensatory strategies taken from simultaneous interpreters. Simultaneous interpreters perform an additional production task that a normal listener does not have: they have to mediate the understood message into a second language. As a result, their cognitive

Table 3.3 Compensatory strategies used by listeners in an interpretation context

SOURCE LANGUAGE TEXT (ENGLISH)	TARGET LANGUAGE (ARABIC) VERSIONS

Skipping

The French Minister was greeted with jeers and violence	The French Minister was greeted with violence
They were all very glum and kept complaining that it was impossible to catch up with Western military technology	They were all very . . . and kept complaining that it was impossible to catch up with Western military technology
In the Senate today, the $15 billion appropriation Bill was approved by a vote of ninety-eight to one	In the Senate today, the $15 billion Bill was approved by a vote of ninety-eight to one
It named the missile 'the shale stone', a reference to a story in the Koran	It names the missile as a kind of stone, a reference to a story in the Koran

Approximation

Iran has embarked on a methodological campaign . . .	Iran has launched a methodological campaign
In Damascus Syrian radio said that fighting had spilled into Tikrit	In Damascus Syrian radio said that there was fighting in Tikrit
to patch up their historical hatreds	to agree among themselves
Press and public largely acquiesced in this disclosure of only selected information	Press and public welcomed this disclosure of only selected information
East European governments that once belonged to the defunct Soviet-led Warsaw Pact	East European governments that once belonged to the former Soviet-led Warsaw Pact

Filtering

There's nothing new in wartime about exaggerated claims of success, or inflammatory charges of atrocities	There's nothing new in wartime about exaggerated claims of success
Smouldering fires of tension throughout the region have been fanned as countries are drawn into the sphere of confrontation	Tension is increasing among countries drawn into confrontation in the region
The king visited front-line units of the 12th Royal Mechanised Division	The king visited an army unit

Incompletion

They don't have complete control of all lines of communication or transportation. They haven't really stonewalled us	They don't have complete control of all lines of communications or transportation. They . . .

Table 3.3   Compensatory strategies used by listeners in an interpretation context

SOURCE LANGUAGE TEXT (ENGLISH)	TARGET LANGUAGE (ARABIC) VERSIONS
Baker did not act like a tough businessman, or the duck hunter, with Israel assigned to the role of scared duck at bay	Baker did not act like a tough businessman, or the duck hunter, with Israel ...
In the bewildering thicket of rebel claims it is unclear exactly what is happening	In the ... it is unclear exactly what is happening in spite of rebel claims
Substitution	
collateral damage	a lot of damage
Soviets vote in unity showdown	Soviets vote in a unity referendum
But the gulf crisis jarred perceptions	But the Gulf crisis changed perceptions
The greatest subversion brought by the war is the thousands of satellite television dishes	The greatest problem brought by the war are the thousands of television dishes

Source. Data from Al-Khanji *et al.* (2000).

capacities are typically overloaded and even the top interpreters display more compensatory strategies than a typical, non-mediating listener will display. (Weller, 1991; Lee, 2006; Hatim, 2001).

3.9   Memory building during comprehension

When we refer to memory access during listening, we mean both the process of activating existing memories to assist in comprehension and also the process of forming new memory connections or updating or strengthening existing memories during and immediately following comprehension.

Memory is generally discussed as involving two dimensions: **long-term memory**, associated with the sum of all of a person's knowledge and experience, and **short-term memory**, associated with knowledge that is activated at a particular moment. Cowan (2000) notes that the popular term **Short-Term Memory (STM)** is often used ambiguously to refer to either (1) the set of representations from **long-term memory** stores that are currently and temporarily in a state of heightened activation, or (2) the focus of attention or content of awareness that can be held for a limited period of time. Cowan argues for a more consistent conception of STM that is hierarchical, with compound capacity constraints. The key concept is that listeners are able to focus their attention sequentially – and not simultaneously – within different subsets of the neural connections in long-term memory.

Over the past century, research on **working memory** has been dominated by the construct of memory as a structural entity. Descriptions of short-term memory have focused on storage, with the role of STM described as specialised for information maintenance for retrieval after a brief interval, such as when we try to retain a new phone number that someone is telling us before we enter it on our phone pad. There has been little emphasis on STM as a means of activating or transforming information or as a means of integrating selected portions of long-term memory with new material.

More recent models have challenged this traditional model of a single short-term store. For example, newer models posit *multiple* working memories, modules that are associated with different modalities (e.g. speech versus writing) and with different kinds of representations (e.g. spatial, serial, verbal), all of which are used during oral language processing (Ronnberg *et al.*, 2008).

Another new proposal is a computational model of working memory. Working memory is seen as a 'computation space' in which various operations, such as rehearsal, phonological looping of input, and information reductions, generalisations, and inferences occur. A computational version of working memory still has strict temporal-span limitations. Cowan (1998) has discussed two phases of short-term memory with very different properties: (1) a brief sensory unresolved **after-image** lasting up to two seconds (sometimes called **echoic memory**) and (2) a more perceptually resolved short-term memory lasting up to twenty seconds. Under this conception, the second phase of short-term memory, lasting ten to twenty seconds, is just one of a series of activated features in memory.

Short-term and long-term memory can be associated with **active information** and **inactive information** respectively. For purposes of understanding verbal communication, psychologists now consider it preferable to speak in terms of memory activation rather than in terms of memory size.

3.10   Comprehension and learning

Once a listener has participated in an event, something is likely to be retained or learned. In psychological terms, learning can be defined most simply as the *durable modification of a concept* in memory due to an experience. The degree of learning is reflected initially in the way the listener represents what he or she now knows, what new knowledge is being constructed during the event. Degree of learning is then reflected in the impact of that new knowledge on the listener's subsequent attitudes, beliefs and actions. Recent research consistently suggests that we have two types of memory systems involved in learning, and that most learning is a hybrid process involving both systems.

- *Type 1. Associative processing.* Associative processing draws on associations that are structured by similarity and contiguity in memory – they share some of the same neural connections. Increased experience with these memories leads to long-term learning, so that these associations occur automatically. Associative learning generally occurs without awareness of the steps of processing.

- *Type 2. Rule-based processing.* Rule-based processing draws on symbolically represented rules that are structured by language and logic. With rule-based processing, new information can be learned in just one or a few experiences. Rule-based learning generally occurs with conscious awareness of steps of processing.

Learning through associative principles requires activating prior knowledge, or knowledge schemata and updating them through addition, negation, generalisation, reduction, or abstraction. There are three basic types of associative learning. The most basic type of learning is a **textbase model** of memory use (Kintsch, 2007; Zwaan, 2006). This type of learning tends to be temporary, fading after even a few hours, because the new learning is not sufficiently integrated with prior knowledge and can only be retrieved by using established indexes related to the learned text.

Learning for a long-term purpose involves a **situational model** of memory that integrates prior knowledge with knowledge gained from the text. This type of learning tends to last beyond a few hours because it is better integrated, and has multiple means of being accessed.

In a cognitivist framework learning requires four elements:

- *Units of learning*: words or concepts or configurations of concepts that are represented in long-term memory. These units (words or concepts or configurations) must have **psychological reality** for the learner, that is, they must be relevant to the learner.

- *Activation values* for these units: the cognitive importance attached to a unit by the learner, and the recency of its prior activation in working memory. Importance (or salience) and recency will increase the likelihood of these new units being retained.

- *Connection weighting*: the links of a unit to other units in memory, and the strength of connection. The strength of the links of the new unit (concept or configuration, etc.) to prior experience, and to the listener's own interests, views and needs, will predict strongly a likelihood of the new learning becoming permanent. The ways in which the listener experiences the text (which modes of experience are active) will also influence the weighting of new connections.

- *Learning rules:* the ways (both innate and acquired) that the connections can be augmented or changed, or unlearned. The ways that the listener 'processes' the text – fills in the gaps in the text to achieve her own sense of continuity and completion – and the beliefs that the learner has about this processing – how his own learning can be altered – are the basic learning rules that the listener employs.

- *Emotional and motivational weighting:* conceiving of representations as reconstructed (rather than 'searched for' or 'retrieved') allows us to understand that all aspects of the person's state (e.g., mood, goals, physical location) will influence the exact details of what is reconstructed. In other words, reconstructions will differ for the same person across time and contexts. This type of context sensitivity is characteristic of human memory function during listening (Baddeley, 1997).

Because these complex principles for learning are involved in episode, it is impossible to predict what a particular listener will learn from any particular text or listening experience. First of all, the sheer number of the connections of brain circuitry involving units of representations and weights cannot be determined. Secondly, the 'drive' systems of the human brain concerned with motivation and attention influence the way the listener perceives the input and responds to it at basic visceromotor levels, which feed the interactions between perception and learning (Austin, 1998). In sum, there are numerous sources of individual differences for what is learned and retained, and subsequently recalled.

Summary: comprehension and understanding

This chapter has outlined the semantic, meaning-oriented processes involved in comprehension. This meaning level of processing that originates in the listener's memory is often called **top down processing** in contrast to characterising the linguistic level, which originates in the speech signal, as **bottom up processing**. If there is a misunderstanding during the listening process, we can often consider the 'what' is misunderstood to be the actual linguistic elements and the 'why' it is misunderstood as the semantic processing.

We have seen that semantic processing involves activating knowledge structures, which are activated from various points in the listener's brain. The skilled listener needs to enhance or suppress these structures appropriately in order to comprehend speech in terms of 'new' information (what is not active in the listener's memory at the time of hearing the input) or 'given' information (what is active in the listener's memory at the time of hearing the input). The listener also needs to activate appropriate schemata in order to fill in missing information, as no utterance in speech contains all of the information needed to understand it. In addition to the cognitive elements of comprehension, there are always social elements involved in understanding speech.

In addition to the psycholinguistic knowledge needed to understand speech, the listener needs to activate social structures as well in order to weigh the relevance of what the speaker is saying. A major aspect of this is calculating or establishing **common ground** with the speaker in order to construct the social dimensions and implications of the message. This is achieved partly through conventional inferencing (cohesion elements that can be recovered from the language itself) and partly through the listener's own enrichment of the input involving reasoning processes. In short, we can see that semantic processing involves a lot of effort by the listener. To use a term coined by Bremer *et al.* (1996), listeners must achieve understanding, it is not given to them.

An additional consideration of semantic processing concerns the memory and learning. This chapter outlines a basic connectionist model of learning, showing how the listener's memory is updated when a new listening experience has been integrated. It is important to note that what is remembered and learned from a listening experience, however, is not purely a function of textual information or information processing. Emotional and individual experiential factors play a major role in learning through listening.

Chapter 4

Pragmatic processing

This chapter:

- explains the ways we infer speaker intention through use of conversational conventions and inference;
- defines the notion of social frame and shows how the listener uses social frames and perceived social roles to construct meaning;
- defines the crucial concept of listener response and outlines the types of listener responses that can be used in conversation;
- details the concept of listener collaboration and the notions of goal-oriented communication and benchmarks.

4.1 Listening from a pragmatic perspective

As we have outlined in the previous chapters, the listener has access to multiple layers of information in the speech signal. In order to make use of this information, the listener needs to access multiple interconnections in memory when listening. Effective listening involves making use of available information in the speech signal and activating these cognitive resources. However, there is more to listening than linguistic decoding and semantic processing. There is an additional, overarching component which we will call **pragmatic competence**. This competence is essential to the social dimension of listening, including **pragmatic comprehension** (Kasper, 2006; Taguchi, 2009), **interactional competence** (Hymes, 2001), and **symbolic competence** (Kramsch and Whiteside, 2008). Discourse analysis, as a branch of pragmatics, is concerned with the ways listeners make use of linguistic information and background knowledge as they listen in a social context. The ability to understand another speaker's intended meaning, in context, can be considered a primary goal of listening and a primary objective in learning to listen in an L2.

To describe listening from a pragmatic perspective is to consider phenomena of language from the subjective point of view of the speaker and the listener, and the intersubjectivity that is co-constructed in an interaction. A pragmatic perspective includes what Verschueren (2009) refers to as the speaker's and the listener's situated presence at the time of the interaction. When we consider the listener's role in particular, it is important to emphasise that presence entails engagement in an event (see Figure 4.1). The notion of engagement encompasses the listener's relationship with the speaker, including his or her awareness of emotional shifts in the speaker's state. We refer to monitoring this engaged state of listening as pragmatic processing.

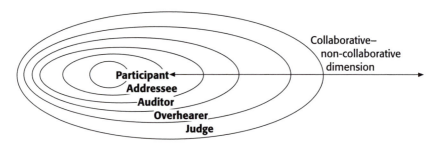

Figure 4.1 *Listener roles*. Level of engagement is an important factor in pragmatic processing. As the listener becomes a more active participant in discourse, the listener is more 'engaged'. Here are descriptions of this range of listener roles. *Participant:* a person who is being spoken to directly and who has speaking rights equal to others involved in the discourse (e.g. a conversation between two friends on a topic of mutual interest and shared background). *Addressee:* a person in a discourse who is being spoken to directly and who has limited rights to respond (e.g. a student in a traditional classroom in which the teacher is lecturing). *Auditor:* a person in a discourse who is a member of an audience that is being addressed directly and who has very limited rights to respond and is not expected to respond (e.g. a bus driver announcing the name of the next bus stop to the passengers (audience) on the bus). *Overhearer:* a person who is not being addressed, but who is within earshot of the speaker, and who has no rights or expectations to respond (e.g. hearing the conversation of a bank teller and the customer who is in front of you as you stand in line waiting)

4.2   Inferring speaker intention

> **Quote 4.1** Sperber and Wilson on inference
>
> Verbal communication is a complex form of communication. Linguistic coding and decoding are involved, but the linguistic meaning of an uttered sentence falls short of encoding what the speaker means: It merely helps the audience infer what she means.
>
> Sperber and Wilson (1995: 27)

The central aspect of pragmatic processing is deriving and building contextual meaning. Contextual meaning includes the interactional status and interpersonal relationship between the speaker and listener. Part of contextual meaning is signalled in and recoverable from the language used, and part of it is invoked by the listener, through inferring the intentions of the speaker in order to conform to – or to depart from – the norms of language for particular purposes.

From a pragmatic perspective, both the speaker and the listener have intentions in any discourse situation, and the interaction of their intentions contributes to the meaning of the discourse. In every situation, the listener has an **intention** to complete a communication process to some degree – even if the listener intends only partial participation or feigned comprehension. In order for this completion to occur, there must be engagement, in which a listener takes on an **interpreter role** (Verschueren, 1999). The implicit assumption in a pragmatic view of communication is that language resources – the listener's knowledge of phonology, morphology, syntax, lexis – *cannot* be activated until the listener takes on a pragmatic perspective.

A pragmatic perspective includes the degree of co-ordination and collaboration between speaker and listener on the **goals** of the interaction and the **rules** for conducting the interaction. In nearly all natural language use, this co-ordination is always a less than perfect heuristic: there are never guarantees of successful co-ordination, successful assumptions or inferences, or mutual understanding.

Researchers in the area of pragmatics concur that there are four key pragmatic notions that contribute to a listener's understanding of spoken language: (1) deixis, anchoring of language to a real context; (2) intention, indicating the desired force of the language used; (3) strategy; and (4) conversational meaning.

4.2.1   Deixis

Language used meaningfully in communication has to be anchored in the real world. As they interact, listener and speaker continuously point to or indicate variables of time (*then, now, today, eventually, whenever . . .*), space (*there, here, come back . . .*), objects (*that, it, those . . .*), persons (*he, she, we, they . . .*), and status (*sir, hey you, . . .* or *tu* versus *vous* distinctions in French). These **deictic** elements of an utterance can only be interpreted with respect to the physical context in which they are uttered. **Deictic reference** is a crucial notion in understanding how listening occurs in context.

In his seminal work on the topic, Hymes (1964; 2009) set forth these elements as identifiable features of context:

- **Addressor** (the speaker of the utterance), **addressee** (the intended **recipient** of the speaker's utterance), **audience** (any **overhearers**).
- **Topic** (what is being talked about).
- **Setting** (where the event is situated in place and time).
- **Code** (the linguistic features of the utterance).
- **Channel** (how the communication is maintained – by speech, writing, texting, images, etc.).
- **Event** (the social norms affecting the interaction and its interpretation).
- **Message form** (the conventional categories of speech events).
- **Key** (the tone, manner, or spirit of the event).
- **Purpose** (the intended outcome of the event).

Hymes's ethnographic features serve as a checklist that would allow an observer of a communication event to describe its various layers of potential meaning for the participants.

From a listener's perspective, we can outline the parallel situational co-ordinates or indices needed to interpret an utterance fully. Lewis (1970), in an early treatment of semantics in spoken discourse, called this the 'package of relevant factors' needed in interpreting any utterance beyond the sentence level. The listener co-ordinates and their use in understanding meaning are:

- *Possible world:* to account for references to current and possible states of affairs: 'Our financial situation is really serious, and it's not likely to get better any time soon.'
- *Time:* to account for adverbials and tenses, necessary for example, to interpret the utterance 'I'll see you next week.'

- *Place:* to account for deictic utterances such as 'I found it. Here it is.'
- *Speaker:* to account for personal reference: 'Give it to me, please.'
- *Audience:* to account for directional force of utterance: 'I need you to pick up the kids today.'
- *Indicated object:* to account for demonstrative pointers: 'This is the right room.'
- *Previous discourse:* to account for reactivation of elements in an utterance: 'The guy I told you about is . . .'
- *Assignment:* to account for ordering, inclusion, exclusion: 'The second choice is better.'

From a pragmatic perspective, if a listener can establish co-ordinates for even some of these variables, there is at least partial comprehension of what the speaker says, and often 'good enough comprehension' for the situational demands (Ferreira *et al.*, 2002).

4.2.2   Intention

A cornerstone of pragmatics is characterising the purpose of communication as an act to *influence* people with intent (Berlo, 1960). Situated speech began to be understood as succeeding or failing at two levels: by the objective truth value of the words spoken and by the subjective intention of the speaker in uttering those words. In all communicative situations, the speaker intends to exert some influence on the listener through the presentation of linguistic and non-linguistic elements.

The subsequent detailed analyses proceeded from this conception of dual levels of language. Austin (1962) soon made the distinction between **constatives** and **performatives** in speech. Constatives are the aspect of a speech act that can be evaluated in terms of their truth value. For example, the utterance *It rained yesterday* can be evaluated as true or false based on observable evidence. Performatives are the aspect of the speech act that can be evaluated in terms of **felicity**, that is, what the speech act accomplishes in the interaction. For example, the utterance, *I sent you an e-mail about it yesterday*, can be evaluated in terms of its felicity (offering an answer to a question or a defence to an accusation) as a response to the question (accusation) *Why didn't you tell me about the meeting?*

Austin later replaced the constative–performative distinction with a threefold contrast:

- *Locutions:* the act of saying something as true (e.g. *I sent you an e-mail yesterday*).
- *Illocutions:* what is done *in* saying something (e.g. denying an accusation).

- *Perlocutions:* what is done as a result of saying something (e.g. the speaker makes the listener believe that the accusation is false).

These distinctions are useful in characterising listening in that they show how the listener's comprehension of an utterance, and subsequent uptake and response, is quite often *not* precisely what was intended by the speaker. Any failure in the discourse may be at any of these three levels, and is often not due to any deficiency in linguistic competence by either the speaker or the listener.

4.2.3   Conversational maxims

Communication is generally experienced as successful when both speaker and listener have congruent strategies – when their plans of action are in alignment, and both can achieve their communicative goals simultaneously.

Within the framework of inferring speaking intention, a communication strategy can be understood as a particular use of the rules and restrictions that speaker and listener are agreeing to observe. Grice (1969) proposed that speakers create meaning with listeners on a pragmatic level through an agreement to co-operate in their use of **conversational maxims**. He outlined four basic co-operative principles of conversation, which can be understood as default strategies – the plans of action assumed to be in motion unless there is evidence to the contrary. These can be readily understood with examples of both observation and violation of the maxims.

The maxim of quantity

Make your contribution to the conversation as informative as is required. Do not make your contribution more informative than is required.

Example of observation of the maxim: appropriate amount of information:

A. What day are you leaving for Brazil?
B. Monday.

Example of violation of the maxim (by B): too much information:

A. What day are you leaving for Brazil?
B. I'm leaving on one day next week. It's not Sunday, not Tuesday, not Wednesday . . .

Example of violation of the maxim (by B): not enough information:

A. Where is the freeway entrance?
B. Not far.

Example of observation of the maxim: appropriate amount of information:

A. Where is the freeway entrance?

B. Down Main Street, just a minute or so past the Target store, on the right.

The maxim of quality

Do not say what you believe to be false. Do not say something for which you have inadequate evidence.

Example of violation of the maxim: the teacher believes the son will not be accepted based on evidence of his performance but says the contrary (for strategic purposes that go beyond engaging in this particular exchange):

Parent. Do you think my son Alex has a chance to get into Harvard?

High-school teacher A. Oh, absolutely.

Example of violation of the maxim: the teacher has no evidence of the son's performance but acts as if she does (again for strategic reasons beyond this particular exchange):

Parent. Do you think my son Alex has a chance to get into Harvard?

High-school teacher B. Oh, absolutely.

The maxim of relevance

Make your contribution relevant to the interaction. If your contribution cannot be maximally relevant, indicate any way that it may not be relevant.

Example of observation of the maxim: direct response to A's question:

A. How are you doing in school?

B. Not too well, actually. I'm failing two of my classes.

Example of observation of the maxim: B's response does have some relevance to A's question, but B is not indicating how it may be relevant:

A. How are you doing in school?

B. We'll have time to talk about this after the next report card comes out.

Example of violation of the maxim: B's response is either irrelevant to the question, or A does not indicate how it is relevant.

A. How are you doing in school?

B. My teachers this year are terrible.

The maxim of manner

Avoid obscurity and ambiguity. Be brief and orderly. Give the listener only the information that allows focus.

Example of observation of the maxim: brief and orderly response to A's question:

A. How is the sales department doing this year?

B. We're down about 10 per cent from this quarter last year, but we expect to do better in the coming quarter.

Example of violation of the maxim: adding obscurity and ambiguity:

A. How is the sales department doing this year?

B. Given the complex economy we're involved with on the demand side, the sales figures can be interpreted in various ways. For example . . .

4.3   Detecting deception

While observance of maxims generally leads to successful communication, speakers can also create specific modifications and nuances of meaning by **flouting** these maxims, that is, strategically **infringing**, ignoring, subverting, or **opting out** of a maxim for a particular effect (Thomas, 2006). Indeed, in many conversational settings, particularly those in which the speaker feels the need to modify a speaking contribution to render a specific emotional effect, flouting of maxims is quite common. Flouting is referred to as **irony** (Colston, 2007) and is used in various forms of humour. It is typically intended to evoke a particular emotional response in the listener or wider audience, when the speaker estimates that observing usual conventions, or maxims, will not be as effective (Kiesling and Johnson, 2009).

Although much of the flouting of conversational maxims and norms in daily interactions are innocuous and unintentional, it is often a form of **communicative insincerity** (Okamoto, 2008) in which a speaker is consciously manipulating the listener. Systems and strategies for violating conversational norms and intentionally deceiving listeners have been examined formally as part of **information manipulation theory** (Levine *et al.*, 2003) and **interpersonal deception theory** (Burgoon and Qin, 2006).

Within these theories of listener manipulation and deception, speakers may deliberately violate conversational maxims in order to obtain some strategic advantage (McCornack, 1997; Renkema, 2004):

- By flouting the maxim of quantity, the speaker may prevent an interlocutor from getting the floor and presenting information that may contradict the speaker's assertions or intentions.
- By flouting the maxim of quality, the speaker may gain the perception of authority without needing to provide adequate evidence for assertions.

- By flouting the maxim of relevance, the speaker may derail the interlocutor's intentions.
- By flouting the maxim of manner and creating ambiguity, the speaker may later exploit this ambiguity and turn it into a desired result.

Generally, a listener will be able to detect if and when a speaker is flouting a maxim – manipulating or playing with language in some way – and will be able to calculate the intended effect, that is, will be able to derive an **implicature**. If we can't derive an implicature to explain an apparent violation, then the effect is simply bizarreness. You, as a listener, understand that the speaker is violating any number of conversational maxims, but you don't know why.

> *A* (on a train, asking a passenger to share a seat). Excuse me, do you mind if I sit here?
>
> *B*. My name is Daphne and this is my world.

Although flouting maxims may be used for deceptive or competitive purposes, more often flouting is done in an attempt to **save face**, or to make a situation more comfortable for the speaker or listener.

4.4   Enriching speaker meaning

Inferring speaker intention through the strategic use of conversational maxims is vital to pragmatic competence. Another aspect of inferential listening involves enriching speaker input. This is achieved in two ways: through inferring speaker emotion and elaborating speaker meaning.

- *Inferring speaker emotion*. A key part of pragmatic competence is not only inferring speaker intention, but also inferring speaker emotion. Even more than with intentions, emotions are very seldom explicit, and are often not even acknowledged by the speaker (Ekman *et al.*, 1987; Pasupathi, 2003).

- *Elaborating speaker meaning*. Elaborating speaking meaning refers to making semantic inferences based on the concepts used by the speaker *and* also making pragmatic inferences based on context-dependent conditions of the current discourse (Levinson, 1983).

In order to bring the listener more centrally into the characterisation of communication, Levinson (2000) proposed that the original Gricean maxims be reduced to pragmatic principles that both the speaker and the listener invoke: what he dubbed the Q[uantity], I[nformativeness] and M[anner] principles.

4.5   Invoking social expectations

By definition, all genuine language is situated. The language is used by real speakers for a meaningful purpose, and the user desires a meaningful response from one or more listeners. As a result, all understanding of genuine language requires a conscious accounting for the **context of situation** (a term coined by Malinowski, 1923). The users must have a mutually acceptable identity of speakers, purposes, setting, relevant objects, and prior relevant action. According to this view of language, the very meaning of an utterance is seen as the function of the situational and cultural context in which it occurs.

Concept 4.1   **Use of social frames to understand speech**

There are five ways in which using social frames helps the listener understand what the speaker is saying, even if the linguistic message is unclear:

- Identify prototypical elements in the text.
- Assume through analogy that meaning is similar to other texts with these elements.
- If conventional meanings fail, evoke alternate texts with at least one related element.
- Evoke alternative interpretations by comparing analogous experiences.
- When an acceptable understanding is reached, rekey the social frame to include the new elements.

From a sociolinguistic perspective, all language comprehension is filtered through the norms of the **interpretive community** that you belong to (Denzin, 2001). An interpretive community is defined as any group that shares common contexts and experiences. In any complex situation requiring comprehension, such as watching a political debate or a town hall meeting, the listener will invariably draw upon expectations of the social group he or she most closely identifies with in interpreting the actions and the language within that event. The definition of membership is somewhat circular. As Lakoff (2000) points out, people who share the same expectations as the listener will be deemed to 'get it', while those who don't share those expectations 'just don't get it'. Much of our understanding of events, particularly complex and socially significant events, is heavily influenced by our membership, or desire for membership, in various discourse communities, and much of the progress that second language listeners experience is attributable to becoming part of a native speaker discourse community (cf. Swales, 1990; Briggs and Bauman, 2009; Duff, 2007).

> **Quote 4.2** Goffman on framing
>
> Part of what makes natural conversation of so much interest for language learning is that it is a container of culture. As Goffman (1974) says, 'Talk is like a structural midden, a refuse heap in which bits and oddments of all the ways of framing activity in culture are to be found.'

At a personal level, that of one-to-one interaction, this social phenomenon is more readily observable. Interaction takes place within social frames that influence how the speaker and listener act. The social frame for an interaction involves two interwoven aspects: the **activity frame**, which is the activity that the speaker and listener are engaged in, and the **participant frame**, which is the role that each person is playing within that activity (Tyler, 1995). From a pragmatic perspective, a good deal of conversation is, in effect, using context cues to negotiate and establish the exact nature of the activity frame and the participant frame, rather than simply exchanging information (e.g. Szymanski, 1999; Beach, 2000).

Once the frame is established, all conversational behaviour is interpreted within that particular context. Thus, the interpretation that a listener gives to any utterance is heavily dependent on the frames that he or she assigns to the interaction, and the expectations about how those frames are enacted in conversation. While activity frames can vary widely, participant frames are more simply divided into **knowledge superior** (K+), **knowledge equal** (K=), or **knowledge inferior** ($\tilde{\text{K}}$–).

The determination of the participant frame and the concomitant decisions about superiority or inferiority of knowledge involve the notions of social class, social status, and rank. Carrier (1999) notes that the societal nature of status can be predicted from knowledge of existing social mores (e.g. doctors are seen as superior in knowledge to their patients), and the situational nature of status is less predictable because it is co-constructed by both interlocutors in each particular encounter.

> Concept 4.2   **Interpretation**
>
> Different listeners understand different things from the same text. The differences in interpretation are due to:
>
> - degree of familiarity with the language;
> - degree of familiarity with the speaker;
> - amount and kind of background knowledge of the topic;
> - motives for listening;
> - what the listener finds relevant;
> - social frames enacted for understanding;
> - influence of interpretive communities.

4.6   Adjusting affective involvement

How interlocutors in a conversation define their status relative to the other – that is, how they wish to set up the participant frame – will determine a great deal about how they will communicate with each other, the style they will adopt in the conversation. Not only will the participant frame influence what is and is not said, it will also influence the **affective involvement** of both participants.

One aspect of affective involvement in an interaction is the raising or lowering of anxiety and self-confidence, and thus the motivation to participate in interactions in meaningful, open and self-revelatory ways. For listeners, greater affective involvement promotes better understanding through better connection with the speaker, while lower affective involvement typically results in less connection, less understanding and minimal efforts to evaluate and repair any misunderstandings that arise. For example, Yang (1993) found in a study of Chinese learners of English a clear negative correlation between learners' levels of anxiety and their listening performance. Aniero (1990) noted that this situational anxiety (sometimes called **receiver apprehension** or **communication apprehension**) correlated with poor listening performances in pair interactions. One implication is that receiver apprehension may indeed be triggered by social factors, such as perception of roles and status, and the sense that one's interlocutor does or does not have a parallel recognition of these roles, and may also be amplified by a **low action orientation** to listening (Villaume and Bodie, 2007), one of several personality variables that affects communication style.

One known effect of **perceived social distance** is a reduction in the amount of **Negotiation for Meaning (NfM)** that the listener is willing to undertake. NfM, the work that interlocutors do to resolve communication difficulties, is also known to accelerate language acquisition, so at face value, receiver anxiety poses a major impediment to language acquisition (Block, 2003; Bremer *et al.*, 1996).

A vital line of research relating to apprehension and listener perceptions of social role is based on **uncertainty management theory** (Gudykunst, 2003; Bradac, 2001). This theory maintains that (1) initial uncertainty and anxiety about another's attitudes and feelings in a conversation are the basic factors influencing communication, (2) language and language use itself inevitably introduces ambiguity and uncertainty into communication, and (3) the perception of uncertainty inhibits effective communication. This theory predicts that the amount of information-seeking and openness that takes place in an interaction will be determined by the degree of uncertainty.

In a study of L2 learners in a university setting, Carrier (1999) proposed the hypothesis that social status would have an effect on listening comprehension because opportunities for negotiation of meaning are likely to be limited in socially asymmetrical interactions, such as between a university student and a professor. She further conjectured that comprehension of the NNS by a NS interlocutor would also be influenced negatively by an asymmetrical status relationship because the NNS would have fewer opportunities to restate unclear information. Neither hypothesis was supported by her research. She found, for the cultural groups represented in her study, that the superior party often used politeness strategies to affect the status relationship between the NS and NNS and to allow for more negotiation of meaning and more attempts at output by the NNS.

Uncertainty itself refers primarily to lack of clarity about how one's social or situational status affects the interaction. The **equality position** of both parties in an interaction sharing common ground is considered the starting point for effective communication. The central prediction of this theory is that when equality is in doubt, or when a **superior position** is claimed by one party without the consent of the other party, communication will be strained and ineffective. In strained encounters of this type, **politeness strategies** must be used to restore **common ground** (Clark, 2006). Politeness strategies are developed in order to 'save face'. Face, as defined by Goffman (1974), refers to a self-referenced respect that a participant has, and the inherent desire to maintain that 'self-esteem' in public or private interactions. Face-threatening Acts (FTAs) are discourse acts that challenge the listener's capability to maintain this esteem and respect.

Concept 4.3   Politeness strategies in discourse

There are two categories of politeness strategies that a participant can use:

- *Negative politeness*. Make the demand on the listener less infringing, less direct, so that he or she can find ways to avoid loss of face, if necessary.
- *Positive politeness*. Make overt attempts to respect the listener through direct shows of generosity, modesty, agreement, and sympathy. (Leech, 2003; Cutting, 2002.)

However, Scollon (2008) notes that in some intercultural encounters exceeding the norms of politeness is often interpreted as more impolite than not adhering to them (cf. Spencer-Oatey and Franklin, 2009).

Concept 4.4   Gender roles in listening

The role of gender and effects of gender differences on communication has been the focus of numerous linguistic studies. Misunderstandings in male–female communication arise, it is often claimed, because men and women approach conversation differently. They may implicitly disagree on the appropriate activity frame and participant frame for a given conversation and thus proceed to develop the conversation according to different sets of rules.

Tannen (1990) reports the following incident, which suggests how expectations about the purpose of an interaction influence affective involvement. A woman is out walking on a pleasant summer evening and sees her neighbour, a man, in his yard. She comments on the number of fireflies that are out that evening: 'It looks like the Fourth of July.' The man agrees and then launches into a lengthy commentary on how the insects' lighting is part of a complex mating ritual. The woman becomes irritated with the course of the conversation, abruptly ends it, and walks on.

This incident illustrates that interlocutors sometimes have different orientations to the purpose of a conversation. The woman made her comment about the fireflies as a way to show her feeling of appreciation for the pleasantness of the evening and to share her feeling with her neighbour. The neighbour apparently took this opening as a chance to reveal his knowledge of insects and to teach his neighbour some of the things he knows. While both neighbours had the good intention of engaging in a friendly conversation, and perhaps even of opening up to each other to establish a deeper connection, they had differing expectations about the direction such a conversation should take. The man may have believed that a 'good conversation' is one with interesting, factual content that shows the speaker's knowledge, while the woman may have believed a good conversation to be one with personal content which discloses more directly our own feelings and beliefs. In cases like this, which reveal systematic differences in male–female conversational purposes, Tannen has used the term **genderlect** to denote the difference in interactional styles.

Table 4.1   **Some noted differences in male and female conversational styles**

FEMININE	MASCULINE
Facilitative perspective	Competitive perspective
Tend to give supportive feedback	Tend to interrupt
Conciliatory orientation to conflicts	Confrontational orientation to conflicts
Tend to use indirect speech acts	Tends to use direct speech acts
Seek collaborative speaking turns	Seek autonomous speaking turns
Readily cedes floor (in public)	Dominates (public) talking time
Person- and process-oriented	Task- and outcome-oriented
Affectively oriented	Referentially oriented

Sources. Based on Maltz and Borker (2007), Holmes (2006) and Sunderland (2006).

4.7   Formulating responses

Although it is often overlooked, the listener has a powerful role in conversation, shaping the meaning of the interaction in collaboration with the speaker. By examining listener response in discourse we can see how the listener contributes to the conversation and achieves meaning, and at times clarifies or even creates meaning in the speaker.

In a discourse analytic framework, conversation can be seen as organised around a series of intentions, which are originated by **initiating acts**, such as a request. A speaker initiates an act in conversation and the listener has the choice of **uptaking** the initiating move or ignoring it. Typically, the speaker intends or expects the listener to uptake the act in a specific way, in a way that is considered normal within the speaker and listener's discourse community. In discourse-analysis parlance, the speaker intends to elicit a **preferred response**. This preferred response from the listener completes the exchange.

For example, the request *Can I stay at your place for a few days?* is designed to elicit a *yes* or *no* response. In a discourse-analysis sense, either *Yes, sure* or *No, it's not such a good time* would be 'preferred' responses in that they 'comply' with the structure of the request.

> *A.* Can I stay at your place for a few days?
>
> *B.* Um, no, not this month.

This is different from the normal sense of a speaker preferring – that is, hoping – that the other person says *yes*. Responses such as *I don't know. Why do you always ask me that?* and *My name is Daphne* are all **dispreferred responses** because they do not comply – they do not complete the initiating act in the expected way (Bilmes, 1988).

In normal conversation, a listener is expected to comply with a speaker's initiating move. A listener response that expresses inability or reluctance to provide information, or a lack of capability to otherwise comply with the speaker's initiating move, creates a **challenge**. The listener, intentionally or not, is challenging the presupposition that the addressee has the information or resource the speaker needs and is willing to provide it, or it challenges the speaker's right to make the initiating move.

> *Son.* I've got this term paper due tomorrow and I was wondering if you could read over my draft tonight.
>
> *Father.* You're a busy guy.

In this case, the father issues a challenge by not responding directly to the son's request for help, by withholding the information or resource that the son is seeking. Following the tradition of Goffman's (1974) treatment of participant roles, Eckert and McConnell-Ginet (2003) would further contend that the listener here (Father) is being cast by the speaker (Son) as an **adjudicator**, a person has additional power in the transaction.

Challenges are **face-threatening** – they upset the participation frame by demoting one interlocutor's power. Of course, some challenges are less face-threatening than others. Specifically, challenging the presupposition that one is *able* to provide the information is less face-threatening than challenging the presupposition that one is *willing* to provide it. This is why in most cultures it is more polite to declare ignorance than refuse to comply with a request.

Another type of listener response is **backchannelling**, which is when the listener sends short messages back during the partner's speaking turn or immediately following the speaking turn. These messages may include brief verbal utterances (e.g. *Yeah, right*), brief **semi-verbal utterances** (e.g. *uh-huh, hmm*), laughs or chuckles (transcribed in various ways, often as *hhhh*), and postural movements, such as nods. Backchannelling, which always differs in form from culture to culture and within subcultures, is important in conversation for showing a number of listener states: **reception** of messages, **readiness** for subsequent messages, turn-taking **permissions**, **projections** (see Tanaka, 2001, for examples of projections in Japanese), and **empathy** for the speaker's emotional states and shifts in emotion during the conversation.

Backchannelling occurs more or less constantly during conversations in all languages and settings, though in some languages and in some settings, it seems more prevalent. LoCastro (1987) and later Maynard (2002) in their analyses of Japanese casual conversation note regular backchannelling on average of every two and a half seconds. Maynard terms the interplay between speaker and listener as the 'interactional dance', a key part of creating the tenor of 'emotivity' that constitutes effective interpersonal conversation. When backchannelling is withheld or disrupted, the interaction becomes perceptibly disrupted and even emotionally disturbing, and the speakers will usually seek to repair the interaction.

Quote 4.3 Maynard on listener response

In monitoring conversation we tend to notice the speaker's actions more than the listener's. It is obvious, however, that conversation cannot proceed without a listener who is minimally active through backchannelling. Backchannels, since they often do not have an easily identifiable meaning, have sometimes been considered marginal and insignificant semantically, but they are quite meaningful in conversational interaction...

Maynard provides a framework (with examples from Japanese) showing how backchannels apply to a broad range of behaviour, including:

1 *Continuer:* a signal sent by the listener to the speaker to continue the talk.

2 Displaying understanding of content.

3 Giving emotional support for the speaker's judgement (even if you don't agree with it).

4 Agreeing (at least in a *tatemae* – surface – manner).

5 Strong emotional response (including *futaku*, a class of peculiarly Japanese hyper-emotive responses, such as *ehh!* and *waa!*).

Maynard (2005)

A third class of listener response in discourse is the follow-up act. Follow-up acts are responses to a discourse exchange, and can be provided either by the listener or the speaker from the previous exchange. Follow-up acts can be **endorsements** (positive evaluations), **concessions** (negative evaluations), or **acknowledgements** (neutral evaluations). In the following extracts, we see examples of each type.

A. How long will you be staying with us?

B. Till next Sunday.

A. Great.

A. Are you joining us tonight?

B. Sorry, I can't. Too much work.

A. I understand.

A. How did he hurt himself?

B. Skateboarding.

A. Oh.

Listener responses, in the form of uptaking (accepting the force of the speaker's utterance) or challenging the speaker's initiating act, providing backchannelling, or providing follow-up acts, are an integral and active aspect of conversation. Expectations about how listeners should respond is part of the cultural knowledge that is acquired when one learns a first or second language (Lantolf and Thorne, 2006; Ohta, 2000; Ushioda, 2008).

In professional encounters (e.g. doctor–patient, manager–employer, mediator–client), the notion of listener response has received increasing attention because of the acknowledged importance of listening in various phases of problem assessment, **gatekeeping** and treatment. Increasingly, training in responsive listening has become part of many professional curricula.

Roberts and Sarangi (2005) present a framework that is used to describe and help train medical professionals in better understanding and responding to patients (see Table 4.2). A key notion in this type of listening training is metacognition. As the professional or service provider learns to monitor his or her responses to clients, those responses become more amenable to observation, control, and adjustment depending on the kinds of outcomes desired or undesired.

Table 4.2 **Framework for understanding and responding in a professional context: types of listening, empathetic and retractive (extracts from doctor–patient interactions)**

Empathetic
- Responsive listening (focusing)

  Act. That doesn't do me any harm.
  Can. You're not worried about that at all?

- Inclusiveness ('we' affect; eliciting patient awareness/perspective and aligning with it)

  Can. We obviously want to sort out your problem.
  Can. OK, seeing it is only for one day.
  Can. What do you understand about why we did the test in the first place?

- Framing (framing intention and social relationships, often conveyed as 'talk about talk')

  Can. I wanted to ask you...
  Can. Do you have any idea about...

- Hedging (acknowledging own difficulty and using softeners)

  Can. It's very difficult for us to say...
  Can. Would it be OK if I just tell you a little...

- Evaluating (may also be part of responsive listening)

  Can. OK, that's good.

- Checking understanding/commitment

  Can. OK. Anything you don't understand so far?

Retractive
- Trained empathy

  Can. I can understand.
  Can. How did the chest x-ray go?

- Labelling/high inferencing

  Can. You don't feel guilty?

- Take in/storage failure

  Can. How did your husband pass away?
  Act. I told you, he died of cancer.

Note. Act. Patient. *Can.* Candidate, professional in training.
Sources. Data from Roberts and Sarangi, 2005; Wilce, 2009; Jhangiani and Vadeboncoeur, 2010.

Concept 4.5   **Listener response**

Listeners have three types of responses in face-to-face interaction: (1) uptaking of speaker's moves; (2) backchannelling; and (3) follow-up acts. Listener response serves to guide the course and depth of the conversation, and also to shape the 'emotivity' of the interaction.

4.8   Connecting with the speaker

In early communication theory, listening is viewed as part of a transactional process – a kind of conduit – in which all participants are simultaneously sending and receiving messages. Later communication theory views speaking and listening as equal parts of a co-construction process. In both views of a communicative transaction, a listener is 'speaking' continuously through non-verbal responses as well as through periodic verbal responses. The speaker simultaneously 'listens' to these non-verbal and verbal messages and adapts his or her communicative behaviour, attitudes, and affective states according to an assessment of how he or she is being understood (Beale, 2009). Listening then becomes an interactive and co-constructive process in which the outcomes of any communication include renewed perceptions of self, other and the relationship. In this view, the goal of listening is not primarily comprehension of messages, but rather establishing interactive connections with one's interlocutors and mutually moving toward goals. These goals may be related to mutual comprehension of messages in the discourse, but they will also be related to adjustments in the 'relationship system' between the speakers.

Concept 4.6   **Connection or comprehension**

In collaborative listening, the primary purpose of listening is not comprehending messages but rather establishing an interactive connection with one's interlocutors, finding common ground, and mutually moving toward goals.

Listening can thus be studied as part of a theory of action in human behaviour. Systems theory is one theory of action that views interactions dynamically, in that each person in an interaction is seen as contributing to stated or unstated goals of the group. Each person's actions, in the form of verbal and non-verbal behaviour, are reflected in the **communicative states** of the system. The communicative states of the system – a dyad or a larger group – can be determined by examining the **disclosure patterns** and speaker boundaries formed during the interaction (Petronio, 2002).

The goals for any communicative dyad or group will of course vary, and may shift during an interaction. For instance, one dyad may have the goal of agreeing on an acceptable remedy for a problem, as in a service encounter at a complaint desk. Another dyad may have the prescribed goal of achieving empathy, as in a counselling session, in order to help the client eventually move toward solving a particular problem. In either case, what a systems theory approach seeks to invoke is a means of examining and evaluating frames of interactions as they contribute to or detract from achievement of a defined goal.

In **goal-directed communication**, the participants' success or failure depends upon a number of factors:

- the understanding each has of the situation;
- the clarity of their goals;
- their perception of and sensitivity to one another's needs;
- the strategic choices they make;
- their ability to put their choices into action;
- their ability to monitor their progress toward the goals;
- their ability to provide feedback about their perceived progress.

These last two factors are considered so vital in effective communication that they have become the cornerstone of definitions of listening in communication theory. In a study of 123 dyads involved in couple relationships, Halone and Pecchione (2001) define 'relational listening' as the process of monitoring progress toward a goal, through monitoring turn-by-turn connection, and providing feedback about one's perception of that progress.

Other communication theorists argue further that listening includes not only **monitoring** and **feedback** but also **response**. 'The response stage of listening is especially crucial for judging the success of the listening act as a whole' (Steil, Barker and Watson, 1983: 22). In this view listening includes four stages: (1) **sensing** (taking in messages); (2) **interpreting** (arriving at a degree of understanding); (3) **evaluating** (judging, weighing evidence, deciding on degree of agreement with the speaker) and (4) **response** (non-verbal feedback to show understanding, and verbal contributions, such as asking questions or paraphrasing).

The response stage is crucial for two reasons. First, it is one concrete aspect of listening from which other participants can determine whether they have been understood. Second, the speaker must incorporate these **listener messages** in order to monitor goal achievement and to select further strategies in the interaction. In short, and as noted above, pursuit of goals through communication requires effective listening, including feedback and response, on the part of the listeners.

Effective listening from a systems theory perspective requires evaluation of communication patterns in the interaction, and a way of operationalising notions such as empathy, regard, depth of understanding (Gambrill, 2006). An example is the Truax–Carkhuff scale (Truax and Carkhuff, 2007) used in relational psychotherapy:

- *Level 4.* The listener communicates his or her understanding of the speaker's expressions at a deeper level than they were expressed.
- *Level 3.* The listener seems to be listening at a depth similar to the depth intended by the speaker.
- *Level 2.* The listener subtracts noticeable affect from the communication.
- *Level 1.* The listener fails to attend and thus detracts significantly from the message the speaker is trying to get across.

Because goal orientation and maintenance of communication assume a high priority, communication research has devoted much attention to factors that promote, maintain or erode interaction. These factors are often discussed as **benchmarks,** that is, criteria against which interactions can be evaluated and through which effective listening may be modelled and learned. Benchmarking is the practice of identifying specific patterns of behaviours or attitudes or affective signals that contribute to the success or failure of an interaction.

Quote 4.4 Rhodes on listening as monitoring

...if we assume that the degree to which the participants in a goal-oriented communication event succeed or fail depends largely on whether or not their communicative choices produce a desired effect...then we need to include additional factors... [including] each participant's ability to monitor his or her progress toward the goal(s) and to provide the other person with feedback ... These processes of monitoring progress toward a goal and providing feedback about one's perception of that progress can be referred to as listening.

Rhodes (1987: 34–5)

Concept 4.7 **Benchmarks**

Various interactive behaviours and attitudes have been established as benchmarks for communicative behaviour (Greene and Burleson, 2003):

- Conversational appropriateness: patterns of responding appropriately to the speaker's message.
- Conversational effectiveness: overall effect of listening behaviour on achievement of communication goals.

- Communicative impact measure: memorability of the listener (i.e. how well the speaker recalls the listener's effect on the communication).
- Argumentativeness scale: communication patterns that indicate a tendency to approach or avoid arguments or confrontations.
- Interpersonal communication motives scale: patterns of exhibiting and discovering reasons or motives for communicating with others.
- Interpersonal **solidarity** scale: patterns of communication that demonstrate solidarity with the speaker.
- **Syntonic** adjustment measures: patterns of responses between participants (evaluative versus summative), and the use of positive versus negative affect in those responses.

Other studies of communicative behaviour patterns have concentrated on: affinity-seeking, audience activity, communication anxiety, compliance-gaining, interpersonal attraction, personal involvement, receiver apprehension and self-disclosure.

Adapted from Baxter and Braithwaite (2008), Whaley and Samter (2007), Greene and Burleson (2003) and Elgin (2000)

The focus on these patterns for purposes of training listeners is intended to counter the natural effects of **accommodation** – the tendency for both parties in an interaction to compromise toward the norms of the other (Giles, 2009) or **interaction adaptation** – the display of involvement when presented with a persuasion-seeking argument (White and Burgoon, 2006). Once an interaction is under way, the communicative intent of our interaction partner may gain potency over our own affect and cognitions as determinants of the way we communicate in the interaction, as well as the style and efficacy of our listening.

Summary: listening as co-construction of meaning

This chapter has outlined the pragmatic dimension of listening. While listening is essentially an internal cognitive process, the listener must utilise social knowledge in order to listen competently and appropriately. Pragmatic competence in listening involves understanding speaker intentions and speaker strategies for communicating, using contextual sources of information, using social conventions of language use (and knowledge of how these conventions are manipulated), enriching speaker input by supplying context and elaboration, providing a subtle array of interactive responses while the speaker is talking, and responding substantively to what the speaker is saying. Above all, pragmatic competence involves a sense of engagement with the speaker and the speech event, and a willingness to participate in co-construction of meaning.

Chapter 5

Automatic processing

Automatic Processing (AP), also known as Natural Language Processing (NLP), refers to computer interfaces that can understand and produce a natural language, such as English or Chinese. Natural language in this sense is an evolved language used by humans as opposed to synthetic or programming languages, such as C or JavaScript or Perl, that are normally used to communicate with computers.

NLP is now used for a wide range of applications such as information extraction, machine translation, automatic summarisation, and interactive dialogue systems. Automatic processing presents similar kinds of challenges to the computer that humans face in understanding language: linguistic analysis of the input (deciding what was actually said), semantic processing of the input (interpreting what the input means), pragmatic processing of the input (decisions on how to respond to the input). Because of these parallels, this chapter is included in the book. For most language teaching and research purposes, it is not essential that the reader understand AP processes in detail. These processes are outlined here to provide a further dimension to our definition of listening.

This chapter will:

- provide an overview of issues in NLP to show how they parallel issues in human processing and understanding of spoken language;
- demonstrate how NLP utilises multiple layers of meaning;
- show how NLP parallels the human processes of linguistic processing, semantic processing, and pragmatic processing.

5.1   Goals of automatic processing

The study of human communication has been accelerated and enriched by the introduction and development of new media and technology, and particularly by efforts to emulate speech communication. Earliest efforts were aimed at rudimentary tasks in very limited domains, such as the IBM 'Shoebox', showcased at the 1964 World's Fair. It was approximately the size and shape of a standard US shoebox and had a display of ten small lamp lights labelled with the digits 0 through 9 and an attached microphone. Speaking the name of a digit into the microphone – by virtually anyone who could modulate the pitch in their voice – would cause the appropriate digit lamp to light. (According to some accounts, the crowd of visitors typically reacted as if this were a high-wire trapeze act!)

These early endeavours have led to similarly constrained speech recognition applications that include voice dialling (e.g. *Call home*), call routing (e.g. *Connect me to the complaint department, please*), automated appliance control and content-based spoken audio search (e.g. *find a podcast containing the words '. . .'*), simple data entry (e.g. entering a credit card number), preparation of structured documents (e.g. a radiology report), speech-to-text processing (e.g. having your e-mails read out to you), and in aircraft cockpits (usually termed Direct Voice Input). Because we are accustomed to using speech communication to get things done, NLP has evolved principally around specific task and business applications.

Concept 5.1   **What is natural language processing?**

Natural Language Processing (NLP) is both a modern computational technology and a method of investigating and evaluating claims about human language itself. Some prefer the term Computational Linguistics in order to capture this latter function, but NLP is a term that links back into the history of Artificial Intelligence (AI), the general study of cognitive function by computational processes. NLP is the use of computers to process written and spoken language for some practical, useful, purpose: to translate languages, to get information from the web on text data banks so as to answer questions, to carry on conversations with machines about practical topics, getting a computer to decide if one screenplay has been rewritten from another or not. NLP is not simply applications but the core technical methods and theories that underlie these tasks.

Beyond this task orientation, speech communication has become the preferred mode of interaction in virtually every domain. Throughout human history, speech communication has been the dominant mode of social bonding and information exchange, because of the capabilities of speech for nuanced timing of interaction, layered meanings of content, and shadings of speaker intentions. Given these advantages of speech, which cannot be replicated in written form, our preference for spoken language communication as the primary medium of communication has persisted through multiple waves of technological development, for human-human interaction via computers and for human–machine interaction. An early development in this domain was Weizenbaum's (1966) 'simulator', which attempted to simulate basic human interaction: question and answer exchanges. This was achieved through a rudimentary form of 'artificial intelligence'. In this case, it was achieved through simple transformations of grammar, and insertion of standard sets of conversational gambits, as in the following interaction:

> Hello, my name is Eliza.

* Hello, Eliza. My name is Michael.

> Names don't interest me.

* Well, I'm here to talk about more than just my name.

> How long have you been here to talk about more than just your name?

* I just got here, but I've been putting it off a long time.

> What does that suggest to you?

* That maybe I'm a bit of a procrastinator. I should have contacted you earlier.

> Do you enjoy being a bit of a procrastinator? You should have contacted me earlier?

* No, I don't enjoy it.

> Why don't you enjoy it?

(Composed on an ELIZA simulation web site,
http://psych.fullerton.edu/mbirnbaum/)

Weizenbaum named this software ELIZA, after the George Bernard Shaw character who learned to emulate members of 'educated' society. The ELIZA software parodies a school of psychotherapy that echoes back the patient's own statements and queries the underlying motivation for making such statements.

This type of simulated interaction led to further developments in the human–computer interactive domain, including a range of **chatterbots** that became available in the 1990s. A **chatbot** – or **Artificial Conversational Entity (ACE)** – is a type of conversation agent, a computer program designed to simulate an intelligent conversation with one or more human users via auditory or textual methods. Most chatbots are still text-based, however, requiring the user to enter written text in order to interact.

Although advances are being made constantly, machine communication has been somewhat resistant to incorporating speech-based communication for two major reasons: (1) spoken language is considerably more complex than written language and (2) competent users of a language display an inordinate capacity for tolerating individual variation among users. To compensate for the complexity of spoken interaction, most human–machine communication, as well as human-human communication via computers utilises a **Graphical User Interface** (**GUI**), based on graphically represented language, interface objects (such as windows, icons, menus, pointers, files) and functions (key strokes, clicks, and other physical movements) to assist communication and to perform modifications to messages. Most computer operating systems and applications also depend on visual encoding of intentions, via a user's keyboard strokes and mouse clicks, and require a visual display monitor for feedback on communication effectiveness.

The goal of NLP since its inception has been to design and build a computer system that will analyse, understand, and generate natural human languages – in both spoken and written channels. This goal is clearly being reached, through specifically focused applications that 'understand' – within their defined domains – and do 'generate' natural language, again within their specified scope of operation. The remaining sections of this chapter will outline the ways in which linguistic processing, semantic processing, and pragmatic processing contribute to these goals.

5.2   Linguistic processing

NLP applications that utilise spoken language for their input are much more problematic than those that use written language. NLP applications using spoken language as input present one initial challenge: speech recognition. Once the input speech is recognised, it can be processed in the same way that written language is processed.

The first stage of speech recognition for NLP is phonological analysis of the input, or **Automated Speech Recognition** (**ASR**). ASR has been one of the greatest challenges in NLP because of a few persistent, inconvenient facts about spoken language:

- The large size of vocabulary that needs to be recognised.
- How fluent and connected the conversational input is, which prevents accurate recognition.
- The reliability of the instrument used for recording, which introduces 'noise' surrounding the speech signal.
- Accent and dialect characteristics, which introduce variations.

These challenges are not insurmountable, in large part because speech communication is redundant, as we have seen in earlier chapters. As with human-to-human speech processing, what is missed or misinterpreted in one channel or in one level of processing can be compensated for in other channels and levels.

Concept 5.2   **Speech recognition and speaker recognition**

There is a difference between *speaker recognition* (recognising who is speaking) and *speech recognition* (recognising what is being said). These two terms are frequently confused, as is *voice recognition*. Voice recognition is a combination of the two where it uses learned aspects of a speakers voice to determine what is being said. A voice recognition system cannot recognise speech from random speakers very accurately, but it can reach high accuracy for individual voices it has been trained with – usually by having the speaker read a 2,000 word set of texts that cover a range of sound clusters and intonation patterns.

When a computer receives speech input, its primary goal is to convert the speech signal into **spectral information** (mapping of **duration, loudness, pitch**) that it can deal with electronically. Speech recognition by computers seeks to emulate the processing outcomes that the human auditory system, using a more complex neurological architecture, is able to produce: recognition of most (if not all) incoming words, assigned lexical meaning for most (if not all) words recognised, a correct (or nearly correct) sequencing of the words, with precise (or at least acceptable) syntactic relationships calculated.

In essence, **Human Speech Recognition** by computers (HSR) or automated speech recognition (ASR), starts with the goal of human processing – comprehension of messages – and builds backwards to identify what parts of the signal contribute to that goal. As we have outlined in Chapter 2, our human auditory system performs a neurologically based analysis of speech using both top-down and bottom-up clues. HSR also uses bi-directional information, starting with an electronic spectrum analysis of incoming acoustic signals. (Figure 5.1.)

An automatic speech recognition device uses a microphone that converts acoustic pulses into electronic signals. Advances in microphones, using pulse density modulation now employed in hearing aids, have improved accuracy of capture, which in turn improves recognition (Schaub, 2009). The captured electronic signals are converted to a set of digital coefficients from which spectral information (pitch, loudness, duration) can be obtained. The key operation involved is cutting the incoming signal into a series of **acoustic snapshots**, each about a tenth of a second in length. The coefficients for the spectral information in a sequence of snapshots, or a **frame**, are analysed continuously to determine which sequence of phonemes in the programmed language is most likely to have generated them (Jiang *et al.*, 2006).

A frame does not necessarily correspond to specific words in an utterance. An additional probability calculation must be performed in order to derive the best possible match of frames to words. (This is essentially the

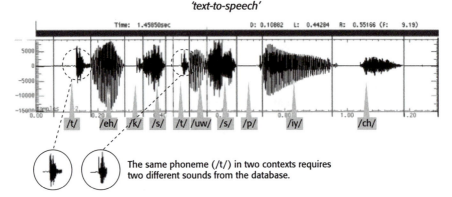

Figure 5.1   *The spectral signal used in speech recognition.* Speech recognition begins with a spectral signal. This is a simplified representation of the speech signal for the phrase 'text to speech'. The signal will be cut into very short 'acoustic snapshots' that will be stored as digital coefficients

feature detection model of speech perception described in Chapter 2, in which whole strings of input must be processed before likely candidates for words can be reliably recognised.) This calculation is never problem-free because the frame sequence for any spoken word can vary so widely, given the broad range of variation in spoken language from a single speaker and across multiple speakers. In addition to extraneous variables such as background noise and microphone sensitivity differences, there are phonological factors that contribute to this variability. As alluded to in Chapter 3, these variability factors include:

- different rates of speaking;
- different sounds preceding or following a particular word of interest (co-articulatory effects);
- different pronunciations, due to regional NS accents or NNS accents;
- different speakers: different vocal tract configurations lead to systematic spectrum differences;
- different styles of incomplete utterance, in which sounds or whole words are truncated or omitted.

The initial goal of an ASR device is to determine the words that were spoken. In order to determine words an ASR program must have both a database of possible candidate words and a means of matching the incoming signals to those words. The contents of the database and how it is constructed or programmed (called the **training of the database**) as well as the techniques used to find the best match are what distinguish one type of processor from another. All of the words in the HSR vocabulary are represented as phonemic patterns in the computer's database, against which input comparisons are made (Barker *et al.*, 2010).

Three basic methods are employed for pattern matching: **template matching**, statistical calculations and **neural nets**. Template-matching systems match patterns directly on sequences of spectrum frame. Systems that use words as units for recognition will have stored templates of each word in the system's vocabulary. The template contains a sequence of frames corresponding to a typical utterance of each word. When a sequence of speech is uttered, frame patterns are matched to measure the least difference or distance between the input and plausible words and sequences of words. As with human speech recognition, a best match can always be found, although this match may not necessarily be what the speaker uttered.

Statistical recognisers employ a technique known as **Hidden Markov Models** (HMMs), named after the Russian mathematician A. A. Markov. HMMs use statistical probabilities that represent the grammatical, lexical, and phonological aspects of speech as snapshots or frames (Aist *et al.*, 2005, 2006). The basic assumption underlying the HMM technique is that a temporal sequence of frames can always be described by probabilities of occurring, by comparing the observed frame sequence (with the large number of frame sequences in a computer data base. In particular, the probability of a single sound snapshot (called a 'state') transitioning to any other snapshot can be estimated, given a large database of words and phrases in the language and a large calculating capacity. The terminology of the hidden Markov model arises from the fact that the frame sequence for a specific word is not directly observable in the input data, and is therefore 'hidden'. HMMs are generally more efficient than template processors because they can decode full phrases rather than decode word by word. (See Figure 5.2 for an example.)

Neural Net Models (NNs) rely on simultaneous processing at multiple layers: phonetic, lexical and syntactic. Using information in one layer to help clarify partial information at any other layer, they can quickly rule out implausible candidates.

All three models improve their accuracy and efficiency by limiting the number of words to be considered at a given time. The goal is to gain efficiency by imposing constraints using an underlying model of how language is encoded. If a language model can specify vocabulary collocation rules (or probabilities) and grammar rules, the speech recogniser can more accurately determine what words are acceptable in specific strings of speech (Chan *et al.*, 2010).

Just as humans must deal with **mishearings** and missed signals, all speech recognition by computer must deal with the problem of error. Words with higher error rates include those with extreme prosodic characteristics (very loud/soft or very high/low pitch), those occurring turn-initially or as discourse markers, and *doubly confusable pairs*: acoustically similar words

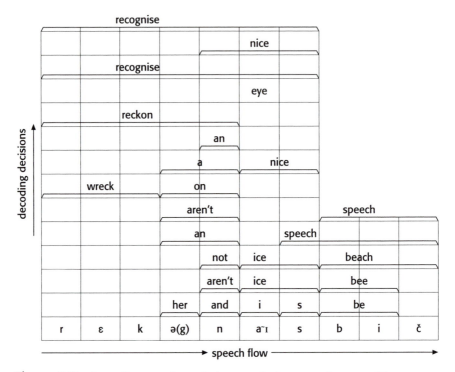

Figure 5.2 *Decoding words and phrases during speech recognition.*
Speech recognition involves activating multiple candidates for words
and phrases as the signal is being parsed. Here the incoming signal is
'recognising speech'. Multiple candidate words and phrases are activated
until the best candidate is decided

(e.g. breeder/bleeder/believer) or acoustically identical words (homonyms
like band/banned) that also have similar probabilities of occurring in the
data base. Words preceding disfluent interruption points (words before
fragments) also have higher error rates. In most domains, errors will not
disrupt continuous decoding. As with humans in most domains, '**good
enough recognition**' is considered to be less than 5–10 per cent error rate
in word recognition, and in some domains it can be even higher without
disruption of adequate comprehension. As with human listening, subsequent semantic processing can usually help the computer compensate
for ambiguities and recognition errors (Palmer *et al.*, 2010).

5.2.1 Syntactic processing

As we discussed in Chapter 2, we use grammatical knowledge to parse
incoming speech at two levels. The first level is a rough categorisation of

incoming speech into grammatical units within the heard utterance. The second level computes grammar relationship across utterances as they accumulate in short term memory. In NLP, there is a similar multi-stage process by which the computer analyses incoming text by checking for correct syntax, and then building a data structure – some kind of representation of the syntax in a hierarchy.

For example, if the input string is identified as 'I met the guy you were talking to yesterday,' the parser must represent two levels of input: an **embedded level** (= you were talking to a guy yesterday) and a **superordinate level** (= I met the guy). The first stage of syntactic processing will parse the sentence into constituents in a levelled hierarchy:

[level 1] meet (verb past tense = met, agent = I, object = **guy**)

|

[level 2] talk (verb past cont. = talked, agent = you, (object = **guy**), time modality = yesterday)

A **parse**, denoted in computer programming language as 'pi' (π), denotes a hierarchy of syntactic constituents, identified by a single **head word** with branches of **tags** related to it (Pauls and Klein, 2009). In our short example, the head words are 'meet' and 'talk', each with associated tags of Agent, Object, Modality.

The first stage of syntactic processing consists of **Probabilistic Context-Free Grammar** (PCFG) which is the bible of abstract syntax rules that is programmed into the computer. The PCFD is reinforced by a large database of acceptable utterances that it uses to estimate probabilities for needing to employ various syntactic rules (Higuera, 2010). In a sense, the parser 'learns' rules by extracting well formed examples from its **training data.** Modern parsers also take advantage of **lexicalised conditioning** to learn frequently occurring collocations. (This conditioning aids in rapid recognition of incoming strings, just as knowledge of lexical phrases aids humans in understanding speech.) For example, the parser will learn that the verb 'meet' commonly occurs with an object as a person (V + animate object + time) (e.g. *I met my future wife yesterday*) and less commonly with an object as abstract noun (e.g. *I met some difficulties along the way*).

The second stage of parsing is a text-level analysis that takes the input (π) and generates a cohesion map. A cohesion map for any chunk of input consists of a list of lexical entities (lexical items that have explicit relationships with other items in the text) and the anaphoric connections between them (Mitkov *et al.*, 2007). A composed example appears in Figure 5.3.

Calculating **cohesion** among text items is necessary in order to arrive at **coherence**: a more abstract, higher-level meaning in the input (Barzilay and Lapata, 2008). Coherence in NLP is defined as the congruent interaction between **linguistic representations** and **knowledge representations**, in which most if not all detected entities are interlinked. As with

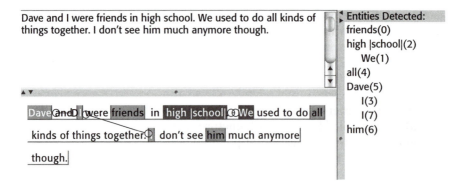

Figure 5.3 *A sample text analysis from an input.* As the text is parsed, the application creates a map of 'entities' and their syntactic and semantic interrelationships

human processing, coherence is considered a higher level goal of language comprehension than cohesion, which is simply the computation of intra-textual relationships of linguistic representations. However, in NLP, particularly with its focused, limited applications such as rough translations or calculation of readability indexes, cohesion is often all that is needed.

Different measures are weighted – given more or less value – in terms of determining cohesion. Some of these calculations can be used to determine objective levels of difficulty in a text, and are used in **readability indexes** and **listenability indexes**. For example, with readability and listenability indexes, such as the **Flesch–Kincaid**, **Strathcylde**, or **REAP** measures, all that is needed to compute the index is a random content extraction and automated counts and ratios such as: words per sentence, adjacency of nouns and antecedents, content word overlap, causal and temporal cohesion markers, density of conditionals, logical connectives, and relative frequency of content words in the database corpus (Gottron and Martin, 2008).

An early example of a syntactic parser was **HARPY** (Lowerre, 2005) a speech recogniser with the task of transcribing normally produced speech within limited lexical domains (initially with just 1,000 word vocabularies). The HARPY connected speech recognition system was the result of an attempt to understand the relative importance of various recognition choices. Knowledge is represented in HARPY as procedures as a Markov network, which consists of a flexible set of transition probabilities between units of input. Unlike earlier speech recognisers (like **HEARSAY** and **DRAGON**), HARPY searches only a few 'best' syntactic (and acoustic) paths (or **sub-nets**) in parallel to determine the optimal path, and uses increased segmentation to effectively reduce the utterance length, thereby reducing the number of sequential probability updates that must be done.

Several new **heuristics** have been added to the HARPY system to improve its performance and speed: detection of common sub-nets and collapsing them to reduce overall network size and complexity. This type of processing eliminates the need for doing an acoustic match for all phonemic types at every time sample. It also removes the need for learning the lexical representations and additional phonemic templates from training data. Inter-word phenomena (like **co-articulation** and **elided sounds**) are handled by the use of juncture rules which eliminates the need for time consuming application of phonological rules during the recognition phase.

5.3   Semantic processing

While the role of linguistic processing is to recognise as tangibly as possible what was said, the main goal of semantic processing is more abstract. The goal of semantic processing is converting incoming speech to idea units that will serve as the basis for a decision, an action, or a response (Song *et al.*, 2010). Semantic processing involves a formal, explicit representation of a set of concepts and their interrelationships, which is called an ontology (see Figure 5.4). Ontologies allow the application to use hierarchical reasoning to conduct searches and respond to the user in a 'reasonable' way.

An example of semantic processing is an NLP application for answering questions in a specific domain, such as TREC (Ittycheriah and Roukos, 2006; Song *et al.*, 2010). A Q–A system must proceed through the following steps of processing:

- *Question analysis*. A question in natural language is analysed into forms used by subsequent parts of the system.

- *Document collection pre-processing*. The collection is processed into a form which will allow question answering in real time.

- *Document selection*. A subset of files that are likely to contain the answers, is selected from the data base. The sub-set is typically several orders of magnitude smaller than the entire collection.

- *Document analysis*. A detailed analysis of the candidate files may be needed if the pre-processing was superficial. Clarification question may be narrow search.

- *Answer extraction*. Answers are extracted from the files and ranked according to the probability of being appropriate.

- *Response generation*. The system returns a response, possibly in a dialogue context.

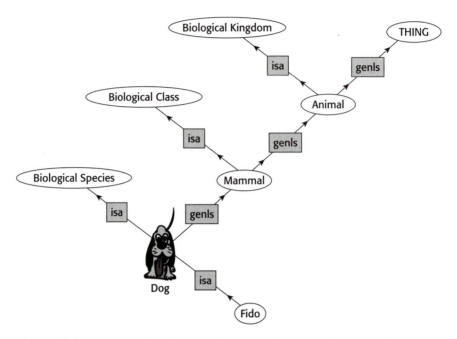

Figure 5.4 *An example of an ontology used in semantic processing.*
NLP employs ontologies, or hierarchies of knowledge, to aid in 'semantic reasoning'. Entities in a text have relationships to other entities, such as equivalence (isa) or generalisation (genls)

Early question-answering systems, such as Genial Understanding System (GUS; Bobrow *et al.*, 1977) were based on the computer asking the questions. Here is a sample interaction:

> *GUS.* Hello, my name is GUS. I can help you plan your trip. Where would you like to go?
>
> *Customer.* I'd like to go to Honolulu on May 28th.
>
> *GUS.* Honolulu. When would you like to go? [Note that only one part of response was recognised per turn.]
>
> *Customer.* May 28th.
>
> *GUS.* When would you like to leave?
>
> *Customer.* It doesn't matter, but morning would be preferable.
>
> *GUS.* There is a PSA flight that departs Los Angeles at 9:15 a.m. Is that flight suitable?
>
> *Customer.* When is the next flight?
>
> *GUS.* There is a United flight at 11:30 a.m.
>
> *Customer.* I'll take the earlier one.
>
> *GUS.* I will book you on PSA flight 122. It departs from Los Angeles on May 28th at 9:15 a.m. Is that acceptable?

GUS succeeded at semantically processing this relatively simple request by using **semantic role labelling** (destination, time) and **relationships between entities** (city names, directional relationships, temporal relationships). GUS was also able, again in a limited domain, to understand **context-sensitive paraphrases** of the responses to its questions.

A more complex level of semantic processing involves **Information Extraction (IE)** in more open discourse domains. Information extraction is a subfield of semantic processing in NLP that is concerned with identifying predefined types of information from text. For example, an information extraction system designed for a police department crime unit domain might extract the names of crimes, perpetrators, victims, physical targets, weapons, dates, and locations of attempted crimes. Or an information extraction system designed for a business domain might extract the names of companies, products, facilities, and financial figures associated with business activities.

Concept 5.3   **Ontologies and reasoning in NLP**

In NLP an **ontology** is a formal representation of the knowledge by a set of concepts within a domain, such as cooking or veterinary medicine or aeronautical engineering, and the relationships between those concepts. An ontology is used to identify entities within the domain and to 'reason' about the entities within that domain.

An ontology can be defined as an 'explicit specification of a shared relationship'. An ontology is important in any NLP application because it provides a shared vocabulary with human users.

Once a domain has been identified, information can be extracted using activating conditions and trigger words, called **extraction patterns**. For example, in a police department NLP application, 911 calls may be recorded and coded by type of call, using **triggers** (see Table 5.1). This type of semantic processing was launched with the development of Nijssen's Information Analysis Method **(NIAM)**, which utilises **conceptual schemata**. The earliest versions, such as those developed at Yale University by Roger Schank's artificial intelligence research group (Schank, 1980), focused on story comprehension. Each application was dedicated to a particular **Universe of Discourse (UoD)**, such as fairy tales, international fables, or detective stories. In a UoD the key design factor is creating a relational database from large numbers of input texts that contain exemplars of the genre. From these exemplars, the program can generate Memory Organising Packets (**MOPs**) that contain likely variations for each concept in the story and **scripts**, which contain likely routines and sequences of events.

Table 5.1   A sample extraction pattern

Name: %MURDERED%

Event type: MURDER.

Trigger word: MURDERED, KILLED, SHOT, STABBED, EXECUTED, ASSASSINATED, BUMPED OFF

Activating conditions: Passive verb, past tense

Semantic slots:

VICTIM subject (*human*)

PERPETRATOR

<prep-phrase, by>

(*human*)
INSTRUMENT

<prep-phrase, with (*weapon*)>
TIME <prep-phrase, at (*time*)>
LOCATION <prep-phrase, on, near, at (*place*)>

Computer programs can demonstrate their understanding of a story through paraphrase and question answering. For example, after 'hearing' the story 'Little Red Riding Hood', Plan Applier Module, PAM (Wilenski, 1981) or MARGIE (Schank, 1982), could readily answer these questions:

- Who is the main character in the story?
- Why did the girl visit her grandmother?
- What happened after the wolf said . . . ?
- When did the wolf say . . . ?
- What is the outcome of the story?
- What is the point of the story?

Similarly, PAM, MARGIE, and other story applications could also generate these questions to test whether you have understood the story as completely as it has! Applications in which either the computer or the user can control the questioning is called a **mixed initiative system**. These systems are more attractive than a **single initiative system** in that they more closely resemble real-world communication, and will be considered more relevant to the user.

Schank claimed that a viable story comprehension application, such as MARGIE, should be able to demonstrate multiple levels of understanding of the story which entail logical inferencing: event characterisation, event connection, contextual understanding, global-contextual understanding.

Essentially, during semantic processing of a story, or of any other UoD, the NLP application will be activating **concept maps**. A concept map is a kind of structural diagram that contains a schema for the type of discourse, and looks to fill in slots in the schema with each key word and each proposition that it identifies. (This parallels human use of default values in schemata in making inferences when listening or reading.)

Concepts are connected in a hierarchical structure. The relationship between concepts can be articulated by way of **semantic operators** such as 'gives rise to', 'results in', 'is required by,' or 'contributes to'. Because a complete semantic processing involves filling in all of the slots in the hierarchical structure, the application will know what it does not know, and can ask specific questions to be sure it 'understands' the discourse completely.

5.4   Pragmatic processing

The goal of pragmatic processing in NLP is to derive knowledge from external commonsense information, integrate that knowledge with knowledge gained from semantic processing, and come up with a suitable response. One widely respected roadmap document for NLP research (Hirschman and Gaizauskas, 2001) has identified five pragmatic standards that users may expect from an NLP system:

- *Timeliness.* The system should be able to respond to the input or user in real time, even when accessed by thousands of users, and the data sources should be kept up to date.
- *Accuracy.* Imprecise, incorrect responses are worse than no answers. The system should also discover and resolve contradictions in the data sources.
- *Usability.* The knowledge in the system should be tailored to the needs of the user.
- *Completeness.* Responses that come from multiple databases should be fused coherently.
- *Relevance.* The answer should be relevant within a specific context. The evaluation of the system must be user-centred.

An example of this would be in a Q–A system, in which the user asks questions about world history. In order to meet the criteria above, the NLP application should aim to identify the user's question accurately, and then provide a response that is (1) given in a timely manner that is consistent with the user's communicative rhythm, (2) accurate in providing what the user has asked, (3) usable at the user's level of knowledge and need to know, (4) complete, and if using multiple sources of information, prioritised and coherent, and (5) relevant and contextualised for the user. Burger *et al.* (2002) has identified four levels of users, based on the patterns of questions asked by the particular user. 'Casual questioners' are seeking surface information, and information sources used for the responses need not be 'deep' – that is, consulting and comparing multiple data files. For the more discerning questioner, the 'professional information analyst', more sources need to be compiled and synthesised in order to satisfy the user's criteria. (Table 5.2 illustrates levels of questioning.)

Because user relevance is a primary goal of NLP, pragmatic processing involves interpreting the input in terms of its social or action-oriented value – knowing how to respond to the user. **Response processing**, which is considered part of pragmatic processing, is based on a correct calculation by the SLS of **intention** in discourse processing. Moviegoers will recall the famous SLS response in Kubrick's film *2001: A Space Odyssey*:

Dave Bowman. Open the pod bay doors, HAL.

HAL. I'm sorry, Dave, I'm afraid I can't do that.

In this interaction the SLS (HAL) understands Dave's intention to 'kill' HAL and invokes its overriding 'training base' intention to complete the mission successfully (even if without Dave).

Response processing by an SLS always selects the most appropriate response from the trained database that matches intention. It then generates an output, either through speech or writing, or other symbolic system, and anticipates a next, likely discourse move from the human. All SLSs are domain-specific, that is, operate on a trained data base in a relatively small and fixed domain, such as travel planning, or answering general knowledge questions, or perhaps monitoring the goals of a space mission.

For instance, if an SLS is set up to help museum visitors, it may be trained to anticipate questions such as *Where is the dinosaur exhibit?* and *What is the most popular exhibit in the museum?* It would provide pre-set responses once the input had been recognised, pragmatically, as a 'request for (location) of (specific item)'. Effective semantic analysis assigns a proposition to an appropriate content schema, in which vacant slots in the schema – those not provided in the input – can be filled by the SLS. An appropriate response effectively predicts what information the user requires and provides it in a usable form.

Summary: automatic processing and human language processing

Although there have been great gains in NLP over the past few decades, some persistent problems remain, particularly relating to the user of SLSs:

Table 5.2   Illustration of levels of questioning and response processing

LEVEL	QUESTION	TAGS USED FOR SEARCH	SOURCE FILES FOR RESPONSE	RESPONSE GIVEN TO USER
		Level 1		
Casual questioner	When was Queen Victoria born?	When born (person)?	*Text 1.* Queen Victoria (1819–1901) ruled Britain with an iron fist.... *Text 2.* British monarchs: Victoria, (1837–1901); Edward (1901–10);	1828
		Level 2		
Template questioner	How many casualties were reported last week in Fredonia?	How many (category of person), (date), (location)?	*Text 1.* Last Monday two people were killed on the streets of Beautiville, Fredonia, after a bomb exploded *Text 2.* The terrorists murdered a family with a small child in Fredonia last Friday, near its border with Evilonia. The father just returned home the day before	Five people
		Level 3		
Cub reporter	How many US households have a computer?	How many, (group) have (own) (item)?	*Text 1.* Two families in three are connected to the internet in the US *Text 2.* Last year IRS received 150 million individual return forms	90 million
		Level 4		
Professional information analyst	Why were there hacker attacks on the computers at University of California, Santa Barbara?	Why, (existence), (category of person), (action), (location)?	*Text 1.* US colleges have powerful computing facilities *Text 2.* Computer hackers need speedy processors to break security passwords	To use their computers for password cracking

Sources. Based on Burger *et al.* (2002) and Gabay *et al.* (2010).

- *User logic problem*. How to design dialogue between computer interface and user to approximate the user's logic. As we saw in Chapter 3, human logic is often 'creatively flawed' and memory imperfect. As a result, the SLS may need to think more like a human in order to communicate effectively.
- *Ambiguity problem*. How to arrive at solutions to comprehension problems. Should the SLS seek to clarify ambiguities or simply proceed with 'best guess'?
- *Recovery problem*. How to manage dialogues with the user and recover from breakdowns; how to diagnose ambiguities and potential understanding problems before they 'snowball' (Fernandez *et al.*, 2004).
- *Sufficiency problem*. How to extract the needed information from the user's utterances.
- *Variability problem*. Because the same target speech sounds are encoded differently by speakers of the same language (speaker and dialect variations) how can the 'same' sound be recognised?
- *White space problem*. How to handle the uncertainty about what the units of processing are, as there is no 'white space' between words in speech.
- *Reference problem*. How to understand real-world references that the speaker introduces which may be initially unfamiliar (Stoness *et al.*, 2005).
- *Time problem*. How to solve ambiguity problems, integrate relevant information quickly and still keep up with the input, or handle overlapping tasks. ('Real Time' Factors, RTFs, are often used as a measurement of efficacy for speech recognition systems; the lower the RTF the more efficient (Kokubo *et al.*, 2006).

Chapter 6

Listening in language acquisition

As we have demonstrated in the preceding chapters, listening is an integrated ability that requires a number of overlapping psycholinguistic abilities. The main abilities can be grouped as linguistic processing, semantic processing and pragmatic processing. We often think of **linguistic processing** (sound perception, word recognition, syntactic parsing) as the fundamental skill in listening, and the one that must be acquired first, as a foundation for further development. Likewise, it is logical to think that once a person's linguistic processing ability is developed to a high degree that only then can **semantic processing** (linking of words to concepts and access of schemata in memory) develop fully. However, it is the need for more competent **pragmatic processing** – the need to express oneself and to connect with others in an array of social environments – that seems to drive the acquisition of both linguistic and semantic processing.

This chapter undertakes the broad task of discussing the role of listening in both first language (L1) and second language (L2) development. Because of its extensive nature, this chapter will provide brief outlines of topics and issues that will be treated more fully in the subsequent sections of the book dealing with teaching listening (Section II) and researching listening (Section III).

This chapter will address how listening is acquired, first in one's L1 and then in an L2:

- development of linguistic processing;
- development of semantic processing;
- development of pragmatic processing.

6.1 Listening in L1 acquisition: development of linguistic processing

Under normal circumstances, and given a healthy neurological system, we all manage to acquire our first language (L1) successfully. In nearly all cases, our L1 is acquired primarily in an oral mode, although multiple sensory and experiential systems are involved. We acquire the ability to use oral language through a lengthy immersive process which involves an abundance of listening. Deaf children, who do not have functional hearing, also engage in the same essential acquisitional processes, relying more on visual input and visual coding of oral input.

Because L1 acquirers always begin the process as infants, the L1 immersion process involves simultaneously the acquisition of multiple cognitive and social skills through interaction with other L1 speakers. There is an essential and seamless connection between learning to observe, to listen, to think, to interact and acquiring our L1. We acquire listening ability in our L1 as part of this larger process, in a seemingly effortless way, and, regardless of what our first language is, we manage to complete this process in about the same amount of time. Interactive language abilities emerge within the first year of one's life, and a full repertoire of communicative abilities that identify a person as a native speaker is often displayed within just three years (Santrock, 2008).

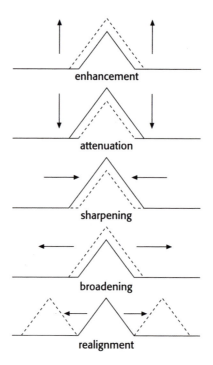

Figure 6.1 *Changes in perception during the first year of life.* When learning a first language, the child uses several kinds of perceptual adjustments to tune into the sounds of the language. By the end of one year, through regular exposure to spoken language, a child will know which sounds belong to the native language

Though all psycholinguistic systems (phonological, lexical, syntactic, semantic, pragmatic) are developing in parallel, we often think of sound perception occurring first because it has the most definable physical correlates. Developmental studies of speech perception across languages demonstrate that all infants begin with a **language-general capacity** that provides a means for discriminating *thousands* of potential **phonetic contrasts** in any of the world's languages. Over time, based on the input received from significant caretakers in the child's world, each child sifts the set of contrasts to the ones most relevant to what is to become his or her native language or languages. This notion is consistent with other accounts about general neurological development, in which the child employs **learning by selection**. It is claimed that the nervous system of an infant starts with an **overexuberance of connections** that are pared down in the course of development to **templates** that are tuned to the **phonotactic system** of the language being acquired (Vihman and Croft, 2008).

L1 studies have shown that over the first year of life, learning by selection of available environmental sounds results in **directional changes in perception** (Kuhl *et al.*, 2008; Kuhl, 2000). The child's experience (exposure and selective attention) is known to affect the **magnetic tuning** of neural transmissions in the cortex: through enhancement, attenuation, sharpening, broadening and realignment of sound prototypes.

During their first year of life, infants develop the perceptual ability to discriminate various kinds of differences in the utterances they hear around them. This ability provides them with a way of distinguishing one utterance from another and one speaker from another, and serves as a precursor to developing the ability to listen to connected language in context.

Quote 6.1   Moore on innate learning processes

Leslie Moore (2004) notes: Infants are innately equipped to process tone, stress vowel length, etc. of *any* of the world's languages and they become attuned to phonemic contrasts in their linguistic environment during the first year.... Once established, these processes are used to discover regularities in speech where infants by nine months, show a 'preference' for listening to words rather than non-words.... Infants show a 'preference' for listening to phoneme structures conforming to their own language ... implying language regularities are used to hypothesise word boundaries in speech streams. Furthermore, infants use the rhythm type to decide which segmentation unit to use for further speech analysis.

Words are very seldom isolated from one another in fluent speech, and even **Child-Directed Speech** (CDS) is generally in phrasal forms. Consequently, part of what the child must acquire has to do with learning how word boundaries are marked in the language. Learning what features mark word boundaries in utterances from a particular language seems to involve discovering how the sounds can be ordered, phonetically and prosodically, within words in the language. This exposure and gradual discrimination of allowable features is known as gaining **phonotactic knowledge** of the language.

Words from other languages will frequently differ with respect to the properties of the child's first language, and the infant must acquire a sense of what is and is not allowable in the native language. Hence, one of the things that is essential for infants to learn is what sound properties are characteristic of utterances they hear in their native language. Over the course of the first several months of being surrounded by sound, this ability seems to emerge naturally.

By the end of the first year, sensitivity will decline for many distinctions that are not frequently found in the native language input. At the same time, infants seem to be absorbing information about regularly occurring features of the native language sound patterns. In a cumulative fashion, sensitivity is thus developing to precisely those features that are helpful in segmenting words from the input. This is an important transition in listening development. This means that infants' skills at word segmentation are developing along with their knowledge of the way sound patterns are structured in their native language. Speech segmentation and word recognition are the essential properties of perception.

Table 6.1 Development of listening abilities in the first year

MONTHS	LISTENING ABILITY
1	Responds to the sound of human voices
2	Distinguishes between different sounds
3	Turns head in response to direct voices
4	Imitates heard tones
5	Discriminates between 'negative' and 'positive' attitudes in human voices
6	Imitates volume, pitch and speech rate of heard voices
7	Attends to vocalisations of adults around her
8	Recognises some frequently repeated words
9	Begins to imitate complex sounds
10	Imitates syllables (combined phonemes) of adult speech
11	Imitates inflections and rhythms
12	Recognises familiar words, such as own name

Source. Based on Owens, 2007.

In summary, there are two primary features of the early development of learning to listen:

- Infants develop **categorical perception**, the capacity to discriminate speech sound contrasts in their native language in a number of different phonetic dimensions, in addition to **continuous perception**, the ability to hear continuous speech as combinations of sound sequences (See Table 6.1.)

- Infants develop **perceptual constancy**, the ability to tolerate the kind of acoustic variability that accompanies changes in rates of speech or differences in speakers' voices. This ability to generalise across variable input is exactly what is required to relate sound differences to changes in meaning.

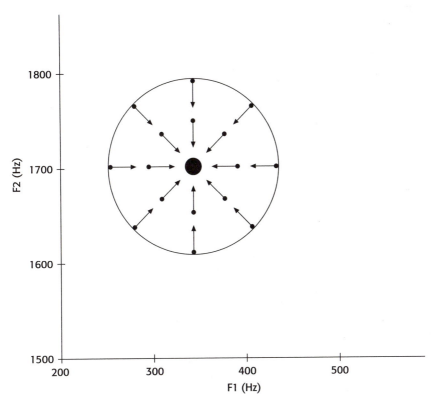

Figure 6.2 *Perceptual magnet effect.* The child learns to recognise sound variations according to a prototype for each phoneme in the language. This is called the 'perceptual magnet effect'. This illustration shows the prototype for the sound /i/ (F1 = 350 Hz; F2 = 1,700 Hz). Sounds within a small physical variation of the target will be recognised as belonging to that phoneme

Concept 6.1   **Methodology used in studies of infant speech perception**

When working with infants and very young children, researchers have to devise ways for the children to participate in experiments. Because young children cannot yet verbalise their responses, non-verbal responses have to be utilised. Here are the two main procedures that have been used.

High Amplitude Sucking Procedure (HAS)

The HAS technique is used with very young babies and takes advantage of the fact that infants like to hear new sounds and will readily suck on a soft object. In this procedure, infants are given a pacifier that is connected to a pressure transducer, which measures the sucking rate of the infant. Although this procedure seems absurd at first glance, the HAS procedure has been a highly productive tool in speech research with infants. Because infants often show increased interest in novel stimuli, it has been found that they will increase their rate of sucking on a pacifier in response to new stimuli. In order to test whether an infant can discriminate between two sounds, the researcher might present a tape of a sound sequence /a/ /a/ /a/ /ae/ /a/. If there is an increase in the HAS response over a number of trials, the researcher may conclude that the child perceives a difference in the sounds. (For example, see Rochat and Striano, 1999; Werker and Tees, 2002.)

Head Turn Preference Procedure (HTPP)

For babies older than four months, the HTTP is used. This technique cannot be used with younger babies because it requires sufficient muscular control over the head and neck. Like HAS, this technique takes advantage of the baby's interest in hearing as well as the fact that a child naturally looks in the direction of a novel stimulus or in the direction of a desired object. The HTTP technique, known in audiology research as Visual Reinforcement Audiometry (VRA), is based on principles of operant conditioning (it was initially called Operant Head Turn Procedure to reflect this orientation) in which the child seeks a reinforcement, like being able to see a toy, when he or she exhibits a specific action. In the protypical experimental situation, an infant is seated on a caregiver's lap facing the experimenter across a table in the testing room. To the side of the infant is a loudspeaker, in front of the loudspeaker is a dark Plexiglas box, and concealed inside the box is a mechanical toy (such as a monkey banging cymbals) that is used as a visual reinforcer. During the experiment, whenever the infant detects a change in the auditory stimulus, he or she is supposed to turn his or her head toward the box, which of course is also the direction of the loudspeaker. An observer, outside the room looking through a one-way mirror, presses a button linked to a computer timing the presentation of the auditory stimuli whenever the infant makes a head turn toward the box. The correlations between head turns and presentation of auditory stimuli is later calculated. Because this procedure can be used successfully with infants between six and twelve months old, it has been used to study the development of speech-perception capacities in young children. (See Jayarajan *et al.*, 2005; Benasich and Talal, 2002, for examples of this procedure.)

6.1.1 Lexical acquisition

In L1 development, acquisition of lexicon is an ongoing process. At any point, a child will be in various stages of acquisition for different words and concepts. For Aitchison (2003) **labelling** is the first of three related tasks a child has to perform during the acquisition for any new word. 'Children have to discover that sequences of sound can be used as names for things.' This challenge of **symbolisation** is often simply depicted as a process in which parents point at an object and say the name of it so that the child can understand the connection between sound, object and meaning. Of course, acquisition of the ability to actually label a word is not that simple from the child's perspective. Usually, many early words are simply ritual accompaniments to a whole situation and therefore, a child's babbling is unlikely to be a sign of meaning acquisition but rather of spontaneous sound productions.

The labelling task can be accelerated by use of the two strategies: **generalisation** and **differentiation**. Generalisation refers to the child labelling numerous things and situations with the same words. Only after encountering these things in different contexts does the child start to differentiate each word from a whole event and start to use it as a label for a specific object or event. Somewhere between the ages of one and two children reach an amplified labelling stage and various researchers have remarked on a vocabulary spurt around this time. This may be due to the child's cognitive discovery that things have names, leading to a passion for attaching labels (Tomasello, 2003).

The second task of meaning acquisition is the **packaging task**. The crucial question is how a child manages to apply a label to a wider range of objects of the same type but simultaneously to restrict the label when appropriate. Aitchison answers this question with the concepts of **underextension** and **overextension**. Underextension means that the child oversimplifies concepts and fails to apply them to more than only one prototypical object. Aichison (2003: 192) says: 'A period of underextension for a word . . . is quite normal, and the gradual enlarging of meaning to include an increasingly wide range does not seem particularly puzzling.' In contrast, while overextensions are less common than underextensions, they are more noticeable to caretakers. In these cases the child applies labels to too wide a range of concepts. The primary reason for such packaging mistakes is **gap filling**: the child does not yet know the right term for an object and then uses another label for it.

In order to acquire fuller meanings of words the child has to achieve the third task which is the **network-building task**. The challenge for the child is that relations between words and concepts have to be worked out explicitly. This connecting task takes place slowly and proceeds initially through collocational links, for example, when the child links *table* with *eat* in one network. Later the child co-ordinates words with other contexts and gradually builds broader networks. Other important aspects of this network-building task are the connection of sounds and their meanings to visual concepts, grammatical information and orthography to develop a more advanced level of lexical competence, which leads to the development of vocabulary in the context of literacy (Lieven and Tomasello, 2008).

6.2   Listening in L1 acquisition: development of semantic processing

As a child learns a first language, a number of cognitive developments are taking place simultaneously. These cognitive changes serve as an experimental playground for the child to try out new language and also as a motivator to help the child seek new language that fits new concepts that the child is experiencing for the first time. Because of this harmonious fit between growth and motivation, first language development and cognitive development cannot be separated. Vocabulary and syntax develop to meet the child's burgeoning needs for comprehension and self-expression, as well as a need for social exploration and integration.

The concept of **cognitive structure** is central to understanding how these vectors of development coincide in the child. Cognitive structures are patterns of physical or mental action that underlie specific acts of development of intelligence.

According to Piaget, in his seminal research on the development of language and intelligence, these patterns seem to correspond to definable stages of child development. According to Piaget and followers of his theory of mind development, there are four primary cognitive structures that are triggered during four development stages: (1) sensorimotor operations; (2) preoperations; (3) concrete operations; and (4) **formal operations** (Piaget, 1951, 2007; Flavell, 1999). Although there have been challenges to Piaget's fixed concept of stages (Brainerd, 1978; Kesserling and Muller, 2010), the notion of benchmarks or transitional stages in development can inform our monitoring of the acquisition process.

In the **sensorimotor stage** (birth to two years), intelligence takes the form of motor actions. Intelligence in the **preoperation period** (three to seven years) is intuitive in nature. The cognitive structure during the concrete **operational stage** (eight to eleven years) is logical but depends upon concrete referents. In the final stage of formal operations (twelve to fifteen years), thinking involves abstractions.

Cognitive structures invariably change as the child grows older, and this modification can be amplified through experience and education. Piaget calls these experiences the processes of adaptation: assimilation and accommodation. **Assimilation** involves the interpretation of events in terms of existing cognitive structure, whereas **accommodation** refers to changing the cognitive structure to make sense of the environment. Cognitive and linguistic development consists of a continual effort to adapt to the environment in terms of assimilation and accommodation. The child's use of language – both receptively and productively – is a reflection of his or her efforts to adapt to the environment. In this sense, Piaget's theory shares a similar perspective to constructivist theories of learning, such as Vygotsky's 'mind in society' theory (see Vygotsky, 1978; van der Veer, 2007) that posit a **proximal zone** in which the learner is actively experimenting with structures not yet mastered. While the Piagetian and Vygotskian perspectives differ in relation to the notion of stages and the role of social environment, in both views, guidance by a caretaker is seen as facilitating, and occasionally accelerating, the child's cognitive and linguistic development.

While the stages or sequences of cognitive development are associated with characteristic age spans, they vary for every child. Furthermore, each stage has many detailed structural forms that individual children will come to master in different ways. For example, according to Piaget, the concrete operational period has more than 40 distinct structures covering classification and relations, spatial relationships, time, movement, chance, number, conservation and measurement. It would be ludicrous to assume that all children would acquire mastery of these cognitive structures in the same sequence or in the same way.

Caretakers and teachers can facilitate the cognitive and linguistic development of the child, by providing environments, stimulation and listening opportunities that will fully engage the child in concepts that the child is beginning to explore (Saxton, 2009). For example, with children up to seven years in age, the teacher's primary role may simply be to provide a rich and stimulating environment with ample objects to play with, and ample discourse – and active listening experiences – about the objects and actions that are employed. On the other hand, with children above the age of seven, learning activities can include more tangible problems of classification, ordering, and location using concrete objects and tasks (Mercer, 2000).

Another critical aspect of the child's cognitive and linguistic development is social. It is now well established that social interaction plays a fundamental role in the development of cognition and language.

> **Quote 6.2** Vygotsky on social development
>
> Every function in the child's cultural development appears twice: first, on the social level, and later, on the individual level; first, between people (inter-psychological) and then inside the child (intra-psychological). This applies equally to voluntary attention, to logical memory, and to the formation of concepts. All the higher functions originate as actual relationships between individuals.
>
> (1978: 57)

A critical aspect of Vygotsky's theory is the idea that the potential for cognitive development is limited to a certain temporal span which he calls the **Zone of Proximal Development (ZPD)** (Tudge and Rogoff, 1999; Lantolf, 2006). Furthermore, full development during the ZPD depends upon intensive social and oral interaction. The range of skill that can be developed with adult guidance and peer collaboration far exceeds what can be attained through individual discovery alone. Vygotsky's theory places consciousness as the end product of social development. For example, in the learning of language, our first utterances with peers or adults are for the purpose of communication, but once mastered they allow for **inner speech**, which is essential for the development of mental concepts and cognitive awareness (Van der Veer, 2007).

While the child is continuously restructuring cognitive connections, he or she is also working on restructuring internal modelling of the grammar of the L1. Restructuring is achieved through active processes of using intake to formulate the underlying grammar rules of the language. Formulating a grammatical system can be achieved only through the processes of **extraction** (finding recurring temporal units in speech that are bound by silence, and hence are likely to be important units of communication) and **segmentation** (breaking off pieces of extracted units to make internal comparisons). Throughout the first few years of listening to ongoing elaborated examples of speech being used appropriately and contextually, the child gradually restructures his or her understanding of the rules of language toward an adult standard, though speech performance is constrained by developmental factors (Iverson and Goldin-Meadow, 2005).

An additional area that is related to the child's cognitive development in L1 is the **mutuality of development** between caretaker and child and between child and other children. Recent ethnographic studies of children in their everyday interactions have challenged simplistic socialisation accounts of child development that focus only on the unidirectional influence of adults and caretakers on children. These recent studies are helping linguists and educators see the ways that children can propel their own development. From an early age, children often take initiative by asking questions, observing, or choosing to take part in ongoing activities (Rogoff, 2003). Children also contribute creatively to ongoing activities within their families and peers by introducing or modifying routines and ways of playing (Goodwin, 1997; Corsaro, 1985), creating new vocabulary and forms of talk (Eckert, 1998), and utilising the tools of their culture (particularly technological tools) in ways unimagined by their caretakers. In turn, parents and other caretakers nurture development not only by providing personalised explanations, but through the manner in which they structure time, introduce topics, toys or other materials, and allow children opportunities to participate in ongoing activities (Ash, 2003; Rogoff, 2003; Sawyer, 2006).

The complex intertwining of contributions of both the child and his or her caretakers to cognitive development is exemplified in studies of preschoolers' scientific knowledge. Crowley and Jacobs (2002) introduced the idea of **islands of expertise** to reflect the fact that young children often develop considerable knowledge about topics of interest well before they begin going to school. In my own case, my son became increasingly interested in building structures after receiving a set of Lego blocks. Repeated, concentrated playing with the blocks, supported by his curiosity toward buildings he saw around him allowed him to build up a great deal of specialised vocabulary and schemata for building. This shared knowledge in turn allowed the family to have rich conversations that included explanations, elaborations, and analogies to related domains.

Peers and siblings are also active learning partners and share knowledge about cultural tools, toys, and practices. For example, children share songs and stories and games and use them to signify and build friendships (Joiner, 1996), and they share knowledge of how to create and learn with new technologies (Barron, 2004; Chandler-Olcott and Mahar, 2003). With age children expand their social networks and peers become more important and influential within the child's social and linguistic development (Hartup, 1996).

6.3 Listening in L1 acquisition: development of pragmatic processing

While the child spends his or her first year of linguistic development learning to process the L1, the child is also being assimilated into a social unit, usually with familiar adult caretakers, and gradually with a wider circle of friends and acquaintances. Children's innate language ability, coupled with a natural curiosity about the world of ideas and feelings and experiences around their desire to integrate into the family unit provide the motivation and the means for acquisition of language. While the child can be seen as the motivator for this acquisition process, the role of caretaker is critical in providing challenges, support and congruent feedback for the child as she develops. Further, these interactions provide a useful record of the kind of linguistic development the child is undertaking, along with all of the concomitant cognitive, moral, social, emotional, and identity development that the child is going through (Johnson-Pynn *et al.*, 2003; Stern, 1999).

In nearly all cultures adults and other caretakers commonly use special speech styles when talking with young children, styles that feature repetitive patterns and frames, manipulate intonation, increase voice onset timing, reduce utterance length, coin special words and utilise special lexical selection (Mintz, 2003). In terms of language development, it has been established that this form of **Child-Directed Speech** (**CDS**) facilitates children's **noticing** and subsequently more effective learning of the phonology, syntax, lexis and discourse patterns of the native language. In addition, the personalised form and style of CDS assists the child in developing, identifying, controlling, and expressing and gaining feedback about her 'temporal contour of feelings' as she experiences her life of increasing complexity and intensity (Stern, 1999).

Empirical study of CDS from a linguistic perspective dates back to the 1960s and has been summarised in recent years. Cameron-Faulkner *et al.* (2003) and Saxton (2009) provide an overview of L1 acquisition studies, listing the range of ways in CDS facilitates language acquisition. These include:

- managing attention;
- promoting positive affect toward interacting with others;
- improving intelligibility of language directed to children;
- facilitating segmentation of input;
- providing feedback on comprehension;
- providing correct models for imitation;
- reducing processing load;
- encouraging conversational participation;
- providing repetitions for learning social routines.

There is not a complete consensus among child language specialists, however, about exactly how all of these potential facilitating factors in language acquisition actually do facilitate acquisition. A couple of points seem to be agreed. One is that CDS is typically **semantically contingent**, that is, caretaker talk with the child tends to be about objects and events to which the child is already paying attention. Thus, it may be that semantic contingency and the establishment of a mutuality with the caretaker (Thibault, 2006), rather than the linguistic features of CDS itself, is what is consistently triggering language acquisition. Studies of caretaker–child interaction from other cultures (e.g. Burman, 2007; Ochs and Schieffelin, 2009) have shown that while the process of acquiring a language is deeply affected by the language learner's desire to become a competent member of a society, CDS *per se* is not a universal practice. What is universal is that children are always in the presence of multimodal **contextual language routines**, such as eating, getting dressed, playing with toys, taking a bath, going to bed. In these situations, salient features of the context as well as habituated routines help the child understand the role of language in the routines and the amplificatory meaning of the language used.

Another common observation is that in CDS explicit formal correction of the child's productions is highly unusual, though contextualised **recasts** are quite common. These recasts – restating and emphasising a more correct or appropriate formulation – provide opportunities for the child to notice gaps between her own speech and comprehension processes and those of her adult interlocutor.

Child-directed speech is principally constructed to help the child understand linguistic or social concepts more easily and to learn how to participate in social events. At a linguistic level, CDS also provides both positive and negative evidence to help the child develop productive and receptive language skills, though the adult language that is used is most often unsimplified lexically or syntactically, and is thus well beyond the child's productive abilities (Ochs and Schieffelin, 2009).

In Table 6.2, Jacqueline (J), aged two, interacts with her mother (M). M attempts to understand J's meaning, to help J clarify her understanding of the situation, to help J formulate the language needed to express that understanding, and to offer opportunities to be understood. In this setting, Jacquelyn has just noticed a pair of her socks in a pile of laundry that Mother is doing and recalls that she received the socks from her Aunt Linda. She is now trying to share this interesting discovery with her mother.

Although the style of child-directed speech varies from culture to culture, it appears that children in all language backgrounds are constantly present in group settings and are surrounded by contextual talk routines to which they can and do pay attention. Both exposure to and attention to a wide range of live contextual talk routines appear to be necessary conditions for language acquisition to occur. At early stages of development, language acquisition is primarily learning to understand, which means having the opportunities to work out the meaning of language in context, to make sense of their social environment.

Table 6.2 **Child-directed speech**

1	Jackie	**Linda** bought you **socks, Mum.**
2	Mother	(f) **Yes**, Linda bought you (f) **socks.**
3		They're (f) **dirty.** They've got to be (f) **washed.**
4	Jackie	Linda bought you – me got . . . (r) washed.
5	Mother	(f, r) **Pardon?**
6	Jackie	(f) **Linda** wa – (r, f) **wash** them.
7	Mother	(f) **No.** (f) **Mummy's** going to wash them.
8	Jackie	(f) **Linda** wash them.
9	Mother	(f) **No.** Linda's (f) **not** going to wash them.
10	Jackie	(f) **Linda's** not going to (r) **wash** them.
11	Mother	(f) **No.** (f) **Mummy** wash them.

Note. We can see how the mother employs features of CDS to encourage participation and improve intelligibility.
Source. Wells (2009: 61).

Quote 6.3 **Elena Lieven on the role of environment**

. . . the study of child language development cross-culturally supports the idea that children will only learn to talk in an environment of which they can make some sense and which has a structure of which the child is a part . . . there are systematic ways in which the structure in which the child is growing up gives the child access to ways of working out the language . . .

Lieven (2005)

6.4 Listening in L2 acquisition: development of linguistic processing

As anyone who has worked on acquiring an L2 knows, the acquisition of an L2 is clearly different from the acquisition of an L1. Second language learners, particularly adult second language learners, rarely if ever achieve the same native competence that children do learning their L1. This disparity between L1 and L2 acquisition is evident in all psycholinguistic systems (phonological, syntactic, lexical, semantic, pragmatic), but the disparity is often most apparent with respect to acquisition of an L2 phonological system.

While children consistently achieve native competence across a full range of subtle and complex phonological properties of their L1 – that is, they master the phonotactic system of their language – L2 learners often have extraordinary difficulty first perceiving and subsequently mastering the pronunciation and intonation patterns of their L2 (Hayes, 2004).

Kuhl and colleagues explored potential mechanisms underlying critical periods in early language development (Kuhl *et al.*, 2008). The idea behind the studies relies on the concept of **neural commitment** to language patterns. Recent neuropsychological and brain imaging work suggests that language acquisition involves the development of neural networks that focus on code-specific properties of the speech signals heard in early infancy, resulting in neural tissue that is dedicated to the analysis of these learned patterns. This means that early neural commitment to learned patterns can also constrain future learning. Neural networks dedicated to native-language patterns do not detect non-native patterns, and may actually interfere with their analysis (Iverson *et al.*, 2003; Kuhl, 2004; Zhang *et al.*, 2005).

In terms of auditory processing for L2 listeners, the fundamental goal of phonological processing is word recognition. Lexical processing in the L2 is the means by which the L2 user comes to use conceptual knowledge needed for understanding. The area of bilingual speech processing is particularly important as it relates to **cognitive transfer** from the L1 to the L2. Several factors are attended to in speech perception: phonetic quality, prosodic patterns, pausing, pacing and speed of the input. All of these factors influence comprehensibility. While it is generally accepted that there is a common store (or **single coding**) of semantic, real-world information in memory that is used in both L1 and L2 speech comprehension, there seems to be a separate store information (or **dual coding**) of phonological for speech (Finardi, 2007). The semantic knowledge that is required for language understanding (the background knowledge related to real-world people, places and actions) is accessed through **phonological tagging** of the language that is heard, and facility with the phonological code of the L2 will be the basis for keeping up with the speed of the spoken language (Magiste, 1985; Sanchez-Casas and Garcia-Albea, 2005).

Use of the phonological code of an L2 has been widely studied in the context of word recognition experiments (often called *word spotting* in psycholinguistic literature). The essence of phonological competence in an L2 is the appropriate use of **lexical segmentation strategies**. Each language has its own preferred strategies for listening, which are readily acquired by the L1 child but often only partially acquired by the L2 learner. In English, for example, L2 listeners must come to use a **metrical segmentation strategy** that allows them to assume that 'every strong syllable is the onset of a new content word' (See Table 6.3). Because English is a **trochaically**

timed language, stress peaks are important indicators of processing segments (Cutler and Butterfield, 1992; Sajavaara, 1986). The similarity of metrical segmentation strategies between one's L1 and L2 (e.g. Dutch and English) will tend to lead to positive transfer, making aural perception in the L2 easier.

Lexical segmentation is the processes of recognising words in the stream of speech. Because there are few reliable markers in the speech code for word boundaries, even a fluent listener may require one or two seconds to recognise words in the speech stream.

Studies of error analysis focus directly on phonological coding and reveal the kind of word recognition difficulties that L2 listeners face (Cutler, 2005; Kim, 1995; Field, 2008). In order to decode incoming speech, the L2 listener has to deal with what she may perceive as degraded phonetic quality due to assimilation, prosodic patterns disguising unstressed words and varying speed of the input. All of these factors influence comprehensibility of speech in real time, even though the listener may know all of the words being used.

Speech perception and word recognition are considered the **bottom-up processes** in listening: They provide the tangible data for comprehension. If the listener does not recognise enough of these bottom-up cues in order to process the speech in real time, he or she will need to rely more on **top-down processes**: semantic expectations and generalisations.

6.4.1   Syntactic development

L1 listeners acquire an ability to process increasing complexity syntax at the same time as they are gaining cognitive and social maturity. L2 listeners, if they have already acquired an L1, will not have this concurrent acquisitional process, and will therefore forfeit this apparent motivational advantage (Wode, 1992:58 ff). Indeed, L2 listeners, because they may already be cognitively advanced, are likely to experience the need to process syntax as a detriment to understanding messages. By aiming to understand messages through focusing primarily on lexis, which is called the **lexis-first comprehension principle** (see Ortega, 2007), L2 learners may learn to

Table 6.3   **Use of metrical segmentation to identify word beginnings**

i	TOLD him	GO	FIND	PLACE
	to	and	a	
	w1	w2	w3	w4

suppress syntax processing, and fail to use syntactic cues that would help them become better listeners.

According to VanPatten (1996; 2005), much of the syntactic aspect of input never becomes intake for L2 listeners. This can of course have a deleterious or slowing effect on the learner's acquisition of the L2. When input does become intake, the learner restructures his or her internal knowledge of the language, and this change becomes a permanent, or **fossilised** to use the term coined by Corder (1967), development in language growth.

Transfer is pervasive in the arena of syntax development. There are now over a dozen competition model studies that have demonstrated the transfer of a **syntactic accent** in sentence interpretation, a tendency to maintain L1 syntactic settings in both reception and production (e.g. MacWhinney, 2001; Liu, Bates and Li, 1992). These studies have shown that the learning of oral sentence processing cues in an L2 is a gradual process. The process begins with L2 cue weight settings that are close – only minimally different – from the L1. Over time, these settings change in the direction of the native speaker's setting for the L2.

In order to make a cognitive shift that allows for L2 based processing without bilingual processing through the L1, the learner must address the issue of cognitive capacity for processing information. Until a learner's cognitive capacity increases, acquisition is bound to remain stagnant. Though the learner may come to understand more of the L2 through strategic compensations (e.g. inferring meanings from situational cues), her ability to process information from linguistic cues in real time remains more or less the same.

A common point of agreement among L2 processing models (the **information processing model, input processing model**, **competition model, multidimensional model**) is that in order to increase cognitive capacity for processing, the learner must begin to **detect** new forms in the L2 spoken input. Detection (i.e. discovering a new phonological or syntactic form in the input, in real time, form without being told) is the key cognitive process that makes the piece of information in the input available for further processing. In order to detect a particular form (e.g. subject–verb agreement), the learner must attend to form generally. A key problem in L2 listening occurs because a struggling learner is typically unable to attend to both content (lexical items) and grammatical form of a message (VanPatten, 2005). When a learner attends to the form of the message, this attention to form competes for the processing capacity in short-term memory that is available to attend to content. As is well known, L2 listeners can attend to only so much linguistic information at a time, and under normal processing constraints, detecting any new linguistic information is unlikely.

6.4.2   Lexical development

Just as the child learning her L1 proceeds through predictable stages of lexical acquisition, the L2 learner also must engage in gradual acquisition of the lexis of the new language. These processes involve mapping concepts on to words, generalising and eventually discriminating between lexical items. Listening and reading are the only avenues for lexical acquisition; therefore, the more an L2 learner listens to and read input that is comprehensible, yet contains *some* new and challenging items (the **i + 1** concept, which is discussed in Section II), the more lexical acquisition will take place.

Mapping is regarded as the initial phase of lexical acquisition in which grammatical, contextual and communicative information from the linguistic and non-linguistic context are being processed (Nation, 2006). This processing initiates a developing map of referent and meaning in the mental lexicon. Successful language learners are able to access these mental representations when necessary in order to further develop, revise or differentiate their maps. According to connectionist principles of acquisition, frequency of input is an important factor of the quality and speed of fast-mapping (Ellis, 2006). In this type of model, exposure to new words in contexts of reading, listening, and interaction are the means of acquisition of lexis in an L2, which parallels acquisition of L1 lexis.

Of course, there is a major difference between L1 and L2 lexical acquisition through mapping. When language learners acquire their L1, **mutual exclusivity strategies** are often used, in which the L1 acquirer differentiates new words while learning new concepts, with numerous lexical maps being updated by the child every day (Bialystok, 2007). As soon as a language learner starts to learn an L2, the learner has to accept that there are counterparts for already known words and concepts of their L1 in the L2: There is no new discovery process. This principle may decrease the L2 learner's motivation to discover new words in the L2.

One significant difference in the acquisition of lexis in L1 and L2 is the possibility of **lexical transfer** between two related languages. The two basic kinds of transfer are cognate transfer and loan transfer. Both of these, when used successfully, can vastly increase an L2 users receptive and productive vocabulary. Cognate transfer refers to an underlying semantic and phonological similarity between words in the L1 and L2:

Cognates are words that have a common etymological origin. A common example of a cognate in Indo-European languages is the words *night* (English), *nuit* (French), *Nacht* (German), *nacht* (Dutch), *natt* (Swedish, Norwegian), *nat* (Danish), ночь, *noch* (Russian), *nox* (Latin), *nakt-* (Sanskrit), *noche* (Spanish), *noite* (Portuguese and Galician), *notte* (Italian). All are derived from the Proto-Indo-European (PIE) *nókts, 'night'. Learners of an L2, when they become aware of cognates, can generally learn the L2 target word faster, often immediately, without needing to go through the mapping processes involved in semantic acquisition of words. (But see Table 6.4 for exceptions to the rule.)

Another form of transfer is the use of loan words that have come into the learners L1 from the L2 that the learner is acquiring. This section is highly relevant and explanatory Loan words are usually borrowed whole from another source language, and involve a process of **transliteration** and **transvocalisation** into the L2. A notable case of loan transfer is the rampant borrowing of foreign words into Japanese (a phenomenon called *gairaigo*), which has an estimated 3,000 loan words from English, with a smaller number from French, German, Dutch and Portuguese (Daulton, 2008). The L2 learner can take advantage of the loan words in his or her L1 when learning the L2, but must be aware of the transformation process that occurs during the loan process.

Loan words will undergo the following processes of transformation:

- *Transliteration:* adapting the word to the writing system of the new language (in gairaigo all borrowed words are written in katakana, one of the three writing systems integrated into Japanese).

Table 6.4 Examples of false cognates in Spanish and English

SPANISH WORD	FALSE COGNATE (INACCURATELY USED TO MEAN)	ACTUAL MEANING	CORRECT TRANSLATION
actualmente	actually	at present	actually – *la verdad es que*
asisistir	assist	to attend	assist/help – *ayudar*
carpeta	carpet	folder	carpet – *alfombra*
chocar	choke	to crash	choke – *ahogar/sofocar*
embarazada	embarrassed	pregnant	embarrassed – *avergonzado*
éxito	exit	success	exit – *salida*
largo	large	long	large – *grande*
parientes	parents	relatives	parents – *padres*
realizar	realise	to actualise	realise – *darse cuenta*
recordar	record	remember	record – *grabar*
sensible	sensible	sensitive	sensible – *razonable, sensato*
soportar	support	put up with	support – *mantener*
últimamente	ultimately	lately	ultimately – *al final*
vaso	vase	drinking glass	vase – *jarrón*

Source. Examples from Golan and Acenas (2004).

- *Phonological transformation:* typically around the world, loanwords are initially marked as foreign by retaining close to their original pronunciations and spellings (by contrast, loanwords into Japanese are phonologically transformed and almost always transliterated; for example English becomes *ingurishu*).
- *Shortening* (sometimes called clipping or truncation): typically the most semantically important phonemes will be preserved; shortening facilitates integration into the language example.
- *Hybridisation and coinage* (e.g. *dai-hitto* = big (*dai* in Japanese) + hit (from English); *sukin-shippu* (skin + ship, denoting close physical relationship).
- *Grammatical transformation:* usually only one form of the borrowed word is used (e.g. *sabisu* (service) becomes fixed expression used as a noun phrase, *sabisu-suru* (give it away for free).

6.5   Listening in L2 acquisition: development of semantic processing

Semantic processing can be a problematic aspect of L2 listening, and L2 acquisition in general, because L2 learners may not be conscious of the schemata they are using in comprehension, and may not realise that some of their default reasoning and inference processes that they use in their L1 are not effective in their L2. These processes can be changed consciously, through normal deductive means of acquiring a new skill, but the L2 learner must first become aware of any schemata or reasoning processes that may need to be altered.

Just as we noted that there are broad individual differences in inferencing and reasoning processes, there are also broad (and sometimes broader) cultural differences that can be observed in these processes. Shaules (2009) refers to a classic categorisation experiment in which subjects look at three pictures: a cow, a chicken, and some grass. They are asked if a cow belongs more naturally to a category with a chicken or with grass.

In these experiments, it turns out that Westerners (people from Europe and North America) more often associate the cow with the chicken (based on them sharing a category: animals) while Easterners (people from Eastern Asia) relatively more often associate the cow with the grass (based on them sharing a relationship: Cows eat grass). This is one of many experiments that have indicated how ingrained culture differences in cognition may be, and how pervasively these differences may affect comprehension.

Results like these may indicate differences in the type of thinking that the listener uses during comprehension of a metaphor, an axiom, or a story. These differences originate in cultural institutions of family, school, religion, literature, and are also keyed to the patterns of one's language that are used in the reasoning process. In the case of English, origins in reasoning can be traced to ancient Greece, where there was an overt value placed on the detachment of subject–object thinking. According to Shaules (2008), the Socratic Greeks assumed that pure thought or reasoning could bring us towards absolute truths and help us identify essential qualities in the world around us. He speculates that this style of thinking led Western thought towards a dualism of subjects and objects, body and spirit, mind and matter, good and evil. In parallel, the ancient Chinese philosophers were as influential as the Greeks in influencing eastern Asian cognition. By contrast, they assumed that it was futile to try to identify essential qualities using thought alone, and by analysing objects into separate entities. This conclusion may have been based on observation or patterns in nature. Thus, where Westerners saw subjects and objects, East Asians have been influenced by context and relationships.

However cultural differences in thinking may arise, it seems apparent that cultural styles of thinking influence the **cognitive anchors** and **schemata** we use when we understand and interpret texts (See Chapter 3 for discussion of schemata.) When L2 learners are confronted with a topic regarding another culture about which they have no anchoring ideas, the potential for misunderstanding is heightened. One of the most obvious reasons why a particular content schema may fail to exist for the learner is that the schema is culturally specific and is not part of a particular learner's cultural background (Alpetkin, 2006; Martinez, 2009).

One difference that sometimes emerges in cultural interpretations of texts concerns detection of conflicts and contradictions between speakers or within speakers. In East Asian cultures, and particularly in Japanese, it is not uncommon for a listener to say *I understand* when he or she clearly does not understand the propositional content of what is being said, or even when he or she may understand and radically disagree with the actual proposition. For me, a key breakthrough in learning to listen and interact in Japanese was realising that I could use *wakarimashita* (*I understand* or, more literally, *I have understood*) fervently and often, to mean 'I understand your feeling' (*wakarimashita so yuu kimochi*) or 'I understand why you're saying that' or 'I see how that came about' (*doushite sounatta noka wakari-mashita*) and *not* to mean 'I get what you're saying' or 'I agree with you', which would be my typical meaning for 'I understand' in my native lan-guage. I found that learning to live with this apparent contradiction made learning and participation much easier.

This type of schematic difference in the meaning of *understand* has clear implications for learning to listen (or achieving understanding) in an L2. L2 learners must often deal with semantic contradictions as they listen in their L2. It has been claimed that many Asian learners, for example, take a dialectical or compromise tack to understanding problems by retaining basic elements of opposing perspectives, and thereby seeking a 'middle way'. On the other hand, it is claimed that European and North American learners, deriving from a tradition of Aristotelian logic, prefer a stronger differentiation model – one that polarises contradictory perspectives in an effort to determine which position is correct (Hamamura *et al.*, 2008; Peng and Nisbett 1999). Learning to listen in an L2 requires initially some awareness of cultural and individual differences in use of schemata, and an ability to adjust or expand interpretations and interpretive possibilities when necessary.

6.6 Listening in L2 acquisition: development of pragmatic processing

The acquisition of pragmatic competence in an L2 is widely recognised as one of the most challenging – and one of the most fascinating – aspects of language acquisition, particularly in an EFL context. Pragmatic competence involves listening and spoken interaction in many ways:

- knowledge of rules for taking speaking turns, including silences;
- when to talk, how much to say, pacing and pausing in and between speaking turns;
- when and how to give 'listenership cues';
- how to interpret intonational emphasis;
- how to interpret a range of idioms and formulaic expressions;
- how to interpret styles of cohesion and linking devices in discourse;
- how to interpret communication styles, including non-verbal communication;
- how to interpret types of indirectness, including apparent deception.

Research in cross-cultural pragmatics has been vital to our understanding of the dynamics of L2 listening. It has been shown that, in general, cultures differ in their use of key conversation features that a learner may initially – and often erroneously – as the same criteria as in his or her L1 culture: when to talk, how much to say, how loud to talk, what gestures to use, backchannelling cues for the speaker, intonational emphasis, and so on. Research in cross-cultural pragmatics (e.g. Bardovi-Harlig, 2006; Rose and Kasper, 2001) has documented examples of formulaic differences in accepted communication in various cultures. One key dimension is in the enactment of **politeness** and **directness–indirectness**, which is observable across a number speech acts, notably apologies, requests, and promises, and in a range of social contexts. Knowledge of the cultural norms in pragmatics, particularly identification of acceptable formulas and recognition of situation cues for levels of politeness, is critical to listening success.

Most analyses of intercultural communication have been based on a model of mismatch ('crosstalk') which derives from the cultural anthropological tradition (Gumperz, 1990). According to the mismatch view, conversations between speakers of different cultural backgrounds often become problematic because of contrasting discourse styles and a **mismatched interpretation** of **participant** and **activity frames**. If misunderstandings multiply due to mismatches of discourse styles, the speakers become entangled in a dangerous spiral of miscommunication that tends to reinforce the negative stereotype that people from the 'other' culture are unco-operative or rude or 'strange' (Auer and Kern, 2001). And, of course, an unpleasant by-product of this cycle is that miscommunication then serves to 'reify' cultural differences (Sarangi and Roberts, 2001).

An alternate point of view is that *inter*cultural interaction follows the same **inter-subjective rules** as *intra*cultural interaction, with speakers and listeners seeking to find balanced, reciprocal participation. Discourse with participants from differing cultural backgrounds, particularly if one is a Native Speaker (NS) and one is a Non-Native Speaker (NNS), is often mediated by the NS distorting – either amplifying or reducing – the responses from the NNS (Shea, 1995). This is often realised by the NS *not* incorporating the NNS's perspective into the conversation, due either to limited recognition of the information provided by the NNS or to a desire to avoid joint orientation to the conversation at hand. In conversations of this kind, the NNS is reduced to a 'passive listener' who simply affirms the talk of a 'superior', more 'knowledgeable' native speaker, with little opportunity to voice his or her own ideas and opinions.

Being reduced to a passive listener is one of the key problems that the NNS faces in interaction. The dissatisfaction that the NNS experiences in a passive listening role is often triggered initially by language understanding problems. However, understanding difficulties in conversation arise not only at the levels of phonological processing, grammatical parsing, and word recognition, but also, as has been discussed in Chapter 3, from informational packaging and conceptual difficulty of the content. Other understanding problems that have been identified include understanding problems triggered by elliptical utterances (in which an item is omitted because it is assumed to be understood) and difficulty in assessing the point (or speaker's intent) of an utterance (Hinds, 1985). These problems can be cumulative in any interaction, leading to misunderstandings and breakdowns in communication, particularly if the NS partner does not recognise ways to co-operatively repair problems as they arise.

Bremer *et al.* (1996) have documented many of the social procedures that L2 listeners must come to use as they become more successful listeners and participants in conversations, including identification of **topic shifts**, providing backchannelling or **listenership cues,** participating in conversational routines (providing obligatory responses), shifting to topic initiator role, and initiating queries and repair of communication problems. A clear conclusion of much research on L2 listening in conversation is that the listener needs to do a great deal of **interactional work**, including using clarification strategies, in addition to linguistic processing, in order to become a successful participant in TL conversation. The research also indicates how NSs play a very significant role in enhancing (or impeding) comprehension by the ways in which they (NSs) respond to NNS input.

Bremer *et al.* note that acquisition of pragmatic competence is critically tied to motivation and successful learning of the L2. It is important that L2 learners have early and continuing positive experiences interacting with speakers of the L2 – experiences in which they feel their full identity is being honoured and in which they are interacting with the TL speakers on a equal basis. Successful pragmatic experiences lead to an upward spiral, leading to greater engagement and more feedback, whereas unsuccessful experiences feed a negative cycle of less engagement, less feedback, and less ultimate attainment in L2 acquisition.

Summary: comparison of L1 and L2 language acquisition

In this chapter we have explored the complex issue of language acquisition and the role that listening plays in it. We compared three fundamental aspects of language development in L1 and L2 acquisition: development of linguistic processing, including lexical acquisition; development of semantic processing, and development of pragmatic processing.

There are many similarities between L1 and L2 acquisition. Both L1 and L2 acquirers are acquiring the same underlying phonology, syntax, lexis, and pragmatics. The 'what' of language acquisition is the same for both L1 and L2 learners, so descriptions of the language system, and what must be acquired, are valid for both groups of learners.

There are of course some fundamental differences between L1 and L2 acquisition, as we have outlined in this chapter. Two principal differences are related to neurolinguistic changes that occur after a first language is acquired, and subsequent changes in motivation to learn a new language after a native language has begun to be acquired. Neurological changes which help lock in our L1, particularly the phonology and syntax, can never be reversed, but L2 acquirers can work within the neurological constraints to acquire a new language to near-native proficiency. Motivational issues similarly need to be addressed: It is not possible to gain proficiency in an L2 without strong, sustained motivation to acquire it, including development of learning strategies for overcoming obstacles and possible resistances from the TL community (Dornyei and Ushioda, 2009).

A third difference between L1 and L2 acquisition, particularly acquisition of listening ability, concerns access to input and interaction. L1 input and interaction, the only means of gaining listening ability, are generally in abundant supply for the child learning an L1, while for the L2 learner useful sources of input and interaction may be lacking.

A final difference should be mentioned. While L2 acquisition is decidedly more problematic than L1 acquisition, L2 acquisition has some markedly positive aspects. L2 acquisition, regardless of the level of attainment, can offer a personal, social, cultural, and professional enrichment that is inaccessible to someone who has only acquired one language.

II Teaching listening

Section Introduction:
The role of instruction
in listening

This section explores approaches and methods for teaching listening. Section I defined listening in terms of neurological, linguistic, semantic, and pragmatic processing. The teaching of listening encompasses a conscious attempt to develop all of these processes.

Chapter 7 provides an overview of approaches for teaching listening. It first outlines a way of identifying teaching and learning contexts in order to identify the relative importance of listening and type of listening within each context. The chapter then reviews six research initiatives that have influenced the ways in which listening can be taught most effectively. The chapter ends with a synthesis of key principles to include in an instructional design, in any context.

Chapter 8 discusses the central role of input and interaction in the teaching of listening. It deals with the central concepts of input relevance, difficulty, and authenticity and describes the processes that learners use to make input comprehensible and useful for language acquisition purposes.

Chapter 9 is the focal chapter of the section in that it integrates ideas on research into recommended designs for instruction. It examines six overlapping types of listening instruction: intensive listening, selective listening, interactive listening, extensive listening, responsive listening, and autonomous listening.

Chapter 10 deals with issues involved in assessing listening. It describes a way of defining the contexts for assessment and ways of defining listening constructs for assessment. The chapter revolves around a model of assessment and provides examples of assessment formats.

Chapter 7

Approaches to teaching listening

Early views of teaching listening considered listening to be a passive skill that would develop naturally with speaking and reading. To some extent, this is true since there are underlying competences for all language skills. However, listening is now receiving fresh attention as an active skill that can be taught directly. In the last part of the twentieth century, a number of teaching methodologies developed that included a key role for listening, among them: the Audio-Lingual Method (ALM), with its focus on presentation of models; Communicative Language Teaching (CLT), with its focus on authentic conversation; Content-Based Instruction (CBI), with its focus on rich input; the Natural Approach, with its focus on immersion in comprehensible input (and its proposed avoidance of speaking).

The development and adoption of methods gave way to a post-methods view of teaching that draws upon principles of language acquisition (Kumaravadivelu, 2006). Currently, there are several viable, complementary theories of language development and instruction that articulate a clear role for listening, and a positive role for explicit instruction of listening as a skill (Norris and Ortega, 2000). This chapter reviews a number of approaches to teaching listening with the intent of focusing on key areas that need to be included in any successful pedagogy.

7.1 Contexts for teaching listening

Language learning is essentially an abstract psycholinguistic process, but one that *always* takes place in concrete social contexts. The contexts, rather than the listening process, provide learners with definable goals, standards, and expectations. As such, before we discuss or recommend teaching and learning methodologies, it is important to define what this social context is for a particular learner or group of learners. This, by itself, will aid in selecting types of input and activities that will helps learners improve their listening. To be realistic, it is important to also consider the goals and expectations of other principal participants in that context who influence the learners: teachers, administrators, learners' families, and learners' peers and colleagues (Candlin and Mercer, 2001).

There are several specific criteria that we can consider in defining the social context and learning background:

- *Contact.* What is the origin and type of the contact with the second language? In other words, when does the learner come into contact with the L2, and how often and how intense is this contact with the L2?
- *Identity.* How does the learner identify himself or herself as a user of a second language? In other words, to what extent does the learner see himself or herself as **bilingual**?
- *Competence.* What is the **target competence** that the learners are expected to attain in the second language?
- *Function.* For what communicative functions will the second language be used?
- *Goal.* What is the ultimate or eventual goal of the learner in acquiring a second language?

Answers to these questions – even if the range of answers is relatively broad – are helpful in initiating an approach to listening instruction. Table 7.1 shows a range of possible answers to these questions. Identification of learners within this type of framework is useful in estimating **intensity** (how intense L2 instruction should be in relation to other aspects of the learners' educational and social lives), value of **oracy** (the relative role of the spoken language in L2 instruction, including listening), and **authenticity** (the relative role of the source of L2, which may include local and international sources).

This matrix provides five variables (**contact, identity, competence, function, goals**) and four descriptors of each variable. Placing a learner group in the matrix helps define instructional goals, and can be applied for purposes of assessment (based on Skutnabb-Kangas, 2008; Willis, 2009; Cummins, 2009). (See Chapter 10 for a treatment of assessment.)

Another key consideration, one that parallels the identity of the learner, is the description of the educational setting. Educational settings vary widely in terms on how the L2 is treated – as a subject matter, as a professional or social tool, or as a medium for communication in the learner's community. Educational setting also concerns the perceived status of the L1 and the L2, as the desirability and acceptability of gaining competence in and using the L2. By understanding the variables in the educational setting, the language teacher or planner can better choose an approach for teaching listening that is most likely to be effective.

The stated or observed norms of the educational setting will interact with the instructional goals as well, and provide a useful starting point for decisions about maintenance of or change to these norms and expectations.

Table 7.1 Criteria for identifying social context for language learning

CRITERION FOR DEFINING L2 INSTRUCTION	A (STRONGEST) THE LEARNER . . .	B THE LEARNER . . .	C THE LEARNER . . .	D (WEAKEST) THE LEARNER . . .
1 *Contact* with the L2	has learned two languages in the family from native speakers from infancy	has used two languages in parallel as means of communication from infancy, with one language clearly dominant	has made contact with a second language at school	has made contact with a second language later in life in social contexts only
2 *Identification* of the learner	identifies himself/herself as bilingual/with two languages/or two cultures (or parts of them)	is identified by others as bilingual/as a fluent user of two languages	identifies himself/herself, or is identified by others as an advanced learner of a second language	identifies himself/herself and is identified by others as a recent learner of a second language
3 *Competence* of the learner	has complete or equal mastery of two languages	has nearly native-like control of two languages, at least in some domains	can produce complete meaningful utterances in the other language or has at least some knowledge and control of the other language	has come in limited contact with another language, not enough to establish any control
4 *Function* of the L2	uses or can use two languages in most situations	uses or can use two languages in a variety of situations	uses or can use the other language in at least one significant social domain, with a small range of functions	uses a second language in limited situations, across limited functions
5 *Goals* for attainment	wishes to use two languages in most situations, wishes to comply with the demands of the community	wishes to use the second language in at least one social context, in a sustained way	wishes to use the second language in at least one social or academic context, for only a limited time	wishes to maintain minimal, limited contact with the L2 community

Table 7.2 Types of educational setting

LANGUAGE USE	TYPE OF EDUCATIONAL SETTING	DESCRIPTION	EXAMPLE
L2 focus	Subject matter	The language of the school curriculum is the learners' L1; the L2 is taught as a subject for academic mastery	English taught as a foreign language in Japan
	Submersion	Linguistic minority students with a low-status L1 are taught the school curriculum through the medium of a high status L2	English as a medium of instruction in anglophone Africa
	Segregation	Linguistic minority children with a low-status L1 are taught the school curriculum through the medium of their L1. The L2 may be taught as a subject	Mother tongue medium schools for the children of Turkish migrant workers in Germany
Dominance of L1 use	Transitional	Linguistic minority children with a low status L1 are instructed through the medium of the L1 until they have acquired sufficient competence in the L2 for that to become the medium	Use of students' L1 in early primary school in anglophone Africa, e.g. use of Hausa in Nigeria. L2 English takes over in late primary and secondary
Balanced use of L1 and L2	Mother tongue maintenance	Linguistic minority children with a lower status L1 receive instruction in their L1 with a view to maintaining and developing skills in that language	The programme in Italian for children of Italian-speaking parents in Bedford, UK (Tosi, 1984)
	Immersion	Linguistic minority children with a high status language are instructed through the medium of a foreign/minority language in classes consisting entirely of L2 learners	French immersion programmes in Canada
	Dual language	A mixed group of linguistic minority and majority students are taught through the medium of the learners' L1 and L2, with the dominant language taught as a subject	Two-way Spanish–English programmes in the US
	Alternate days	A mixed group of linguistic minority and majority students are taught using their L1 and L2 on alternate days	The alternate-day programme in English and Spanish in Calistoga, California
	Plural multilingual	Students with different L1s are taught the school curriculum through the medium of their L1 with an L2 taught as a foreign language in grade 1. This increasingly becomes the medium of instruction in later years when other L2s are also offered as foreign languages	The ten European Union schools in six countries

Sources. Based on Pavlenko and Norton (2007), Miller (2004) and Ellis (2006).

Understanding norms and expectations can be particularly helpful to a new teacher in an unfamiliar context. (I know in my own teaching experience, in West African high schools, in South East Asian refugee camps, and in Japanese universities, that clarifying the social context and expectations of the educational setting, over time, aided me in teaching and assessing progress more effectively and in collaborating more congruously with my local colleagues.)

7.2   SLA research and language pedagogy

A number of academic fields and traditions exert an influence on the way that languages are taught. It is now widely recognised that Second Language Acquisition (SLA) research has emerged as a valid scholarly field in its own right, and one that is exerting considerable impact on the world of language teaching.

Ellis (2009) notes seven positions that have been taken toward SLA research over the past decades:

- SLA has no influence. SLA does not have enough certainty to exert an influence on to language education.
- SLA should constitute the basis of teacher education, but should not support teacher training or teaching practice.
- SLA should show how languages are learned and taught, and also determine language teaching methodology.
- SLA can participate in design and construction of tasks that teachers can test out and adapt for particular learning environments.
- SLA should define research issues that need to be addressed in language education.
- SLA should be at the service of language pedagogy: SLA should address only those issues of concern to language pedagogy delivery systems.
- SLA should have a reciprocal relationship with language pedagogy: SLA should inform language pedagogy, and at the same time language pedagogy should inform SLA.

The view taken in this chapter is a combination of a few of these perspectives: SLA can show how languages are learned, and can offer insights into the formulation of principles that language teachers can use in their pedagogy. From this perspective, several strands of SLA research will be reviewed here, in order to formulate principles that can be incorporated into the teaching of listening.

This section outlines six key influences that are derived directly from second language acquisition research: the affective filter hypothesis, the input hypothesis, the interaction hypothesis, the processability hypothesis, the metacognition hypothesis, and the sociocultural hypothesis.

7.2.1   Affective filter hypothesis

The **affective filter** was first proposed by Dulay and Burt (1977) to account for how affective variables – motivation, attitude, etc. – influence the process of L2 learning. (They initially used the term 'affective delimitors'.) In subsequent work by Krashen (1982, 1985) the concept was given more extensive treatment.

The filter is proposed to be a part of the internal processing system that subconsciously screens incoming language based on affect: the learner's motives, needs, attitudes and emotional states. According to the hypothesis, those aspects of the learning experience (including the input itself) that are congruent with the learner's motives, needs, attitudes, and emotions tend to lower this filter, and allow increased learning to take place. Those aspects of the learning experience that are incongruent tend to raise the filter and inhibit learning.

Applicable principles for teaching

- Listening experiences that help students lessen their anxiety about listening will generally be beneficial. Using student-centred and collaborative learning formats, such as pair and group work, and employing task types, such as collaborations, friendly competitions and listening games, and technology tools that learners enjoy, may help learner relax, become more engaged, and make greater progress in listening (Finch, 2001; Sindrey, 2002; Du, 2009).
- By taking into account learners' motives and their attitudes about listening, the instructor can better select input or point learners to the best resources and opportunities for input. Choosing listening content that appeals to the students – current dramas and television programmes, music, comedy, or relevant political discussions – can help students lower their affective filters toward listening, and get more out of the learning experience (Gay, 2000).
- Because learners differ in many aspects, effective instruction needs to take into account differences in learners. This includes individual opportunities to select input of interest, and experimentation with learning styles and task types that may best trigger involvement and acquisition for each learner (Breen, 2001).

7.2.2   Input hypothesis: selecting accessible input for acquisition

Krashen's (1982) **input hypothesis**, which was part of his overall monitor model of L2 learning, has had a sustained effect on teaching approaches to listening. The input hypothesis was developed as a corollary to what Krashen referred to as the **natural order hypothesis**. Krashen suggested that *if* there is a natural order of acquisition for all language learners, there must be a consistent way to map and guide progress for all learners. The input hypothesis suggested this underlying consistency: second languages are acquired 'by understanding messages or by receiving **comprehensible input**' (Krashen, 1985).

By receiving input that is progressively more complex, the learner naturally acquires listening ability.

This hypothesis has two main corollaries:

- Speaking is the result of acquisition and not its cause. Speech cannot be taught directly, but rather emerges on its own as a result of building overall competence via comprehensible input.

- If input is understood, and there is enough of it, the necessary grammar the learner needs to learn is automatically provided. The language teacher does not need to teach the structures (syntactic or lexical) along a continuum of learnability or difficulty – a natural order will be provided in just the right quantities and automatically reviewed if the student receives a sufficient amount of comprehensible input.

Applicable principles for teaching

- Instruction should aim only to provide comprehensible input, that is, input at an **i + 1 level**, slightly above the learner's current level of competence in terms of vocabulary, syntax, discourse features, length and complexity. Planning large amounts of appropriate input that is scaled to the right length and graded according to overall receptive difficulty will help build up learners' capacity for managing L2 input, and stimulate learner's **built-in syllabus** (Corder, 1967; Ellis, 2006).

- Comprehensible input may be aural or written, or both. Context should be enhanced to ease processing; input with visual and other sensory support will tend to be more comprehensible. Using multimedia involving visuals and audio, and with multiple modes of presentation (e.g. video with subtitles), will increase context, reduce cognitive load, and improve comprehension (Clark *et al.*, 2006; Jones and Plass, 2002). Instruction should also include extensive listening to assure ample amounts of input (Rendaya and Farrell, 2010).

- While the successful development of a listening ability – and successful language acquisition – requires extensive L2 input, successful learning also requires opportunities for output (Swain, 2000). Speaking ability will tend to emerge naturally as a result of extensive work with authentic listening input. (See Chapter 8 for a discussion of authenticity.)

Particularly in EFL contexts that may have a paucity of authentic input, teachers should aim to provide rich listening input that contains useful models of culture, interaction styles, and colloquial pronunciation and vocabulary, so that students' emergent speaking can be modelled on this input (Zhang, 2009).

7.2.3   Interaction hypothesis: using interaction to make input accessible

Input alone is generally not sufficient to sustain acquisition because meaning has a social dimension. Participation in verbal interactions following a listening experience offers a learner the opportunity to engage in creating social meaning, specifically by following up on words and discourse structures that may be unfamiliar. By itself, social interaction has long been considered of great value for language learning, though the reasons given for its value vary. According to the interaction hypothesis, interaction contributes directly to language acquisition in three ways: (1) through allowing the learner to provide himself or herself with comprehensible input through interaction adjustments (e.g. requests for clarification which elicit repetitions and paraphrases); (2) by providing negative feedback that allows the learner to see where he or she may be producing errors (e.g. through recasts or reformulations by the conversation partner); and (3) by presenting opportunities for '**pushed output**', in effect forcing the learner to try out new words and structures to get his or her ideas across in a social context (Gass and Mackey, 2006).

In particular, the kind of negotiation of meaning that routinely takes place during interactions (both NNS–NNS and NNS–NS interactions) is a primary means of listening development as well as language acquisition. The most effective source of comprehensible input is often conversational exchanges following lack of comprehension because the learner must use active clarification strategies to **negotiate meaning**. Negotiation between learners and interlocutors takes place during the course of their interaction when either one signals with questions or comments that the other's preceding message has not been successfully understood. The other then responds by repeating or modifying the original message.

Applicable principles for teaching

- Listening instruction should allow learners to figure out meanings for themselves and not depend on deductive presentation by the instructor. Listening instruction should promote the use of clarification checks, comprehension checks, and collaborative strategies for approaching meaning (Nation, 2007; Mackey and Abdul, 2005).

- Listening instruction should include a wide range of oral interaction tasks that present a need and opportunity for **negotiation of meaning** and **pushed output**, such as **information gap** and **opinion gap tasks** and **role plays**, as well as opportunities for learning how to incorporate feedback from learning tasks (Lynch, 2009; Maleki, 2007).

7.2.4 Processability hypothesis: tuning input to trigger acquisition

There are two similar pedagogic approaches to help L2 learners develop their syntactic processing of oral language. The first, **enriched input**, provides learners with oral texts that have been deliberately 'flooded' with exemplars of the target syntactic structure in the context of a meaning-focused task. This approach caters to incidental learning of the target grammar structure through **focus on form** (see Long, 2009, for a review). The second is through **processing instruction**, in which pedagogic tasks are designed based on predictions about features of grammar that interfere with acquisition. Learners attend to listening tasks that require them to engage in intentional learning by consciously noticing how a target grammar feature (e.g. passive voice) is used in the spoken input, even though the feature is not explicitly emphasised or 'flooded' in the input (VanPatten, 1996, 2005).

Ellis (2010) reviews a number of studies using these two approaches. Concerning the enriched input approach, Ellis concludes that enriched input can help L2 learners acquire new grammatical features and help learners use partially learned features more accurately. Ellis contends that this form of grammar instruction is at least as effective as explicit instruction in grammar. Clear positive effects, however, seem to be evident only when the treatment is prolonged. Concerning input-processing instruction, Ellis concludes that processing instruction in conjunction with explicit grammar instruction leads to the most consistent gains in the ability of learners to comprehend target structures being taught. Further, Ellis concludes that effects of processing instruction on both comprehension and accuracy in production are more durable than explicit instruction alone.

While access to suitable input is crucial in language acquisition, successful acquisition depends not so much on what transpires in the ambient linguistic environment, but rather on what transpires in the *mind of the learner*. There is no isomorphic relationship between input and accessibility, because access to input may be triggered by both external factors (characteristics of the context and input) and internal factors (readiness of the learner). As Carroll (2006) notes, a learner can, on a given occasion, attend to some stimulus in the speech environment, process it, and permanently acquire some bit of knowledge about the L2. On a different occasion, however, the same learner may not attend to the same physical stimulus, may not process the same linguistic input, and may not learn or retain anything about the language. In the final analysis, **intake** is determined by the listener, not features of the text.

Because acquisition of the grammatical system of a second language tends to follow a stage-like pattern corresponding to the complexity of the language, certain linguistic forms in oral input are salient or *noticeable* to learners *only* after they have acquired other features. Before certain syntactic forms and certain lexical items are noticeable, these features may be heard by the L2 listener simply as a blur of sound surrounded by other more comprehensible parts of discourse that they are able to pick out.

Within the processability hypothesis, there are specific principles by which learners come to notice new features from the blur of input. It has been proposed that successful listeners consciously use **operating principles** that were outlined by Slobin (2004). Operating principles are cognitive strategies that underlie our innate ability to acquire language – presumably in both an L1 and an L2. By using operating principles, the learner can strategically link incoming sound with linguistic rules, and readily discover the way the grammatical system of the spoken language works. Slobin's operating principles are as follows:

- Pay attention to the ends of words. They often signal relational meanings.
- Be aware that there are linguistic elements which encode relations between words.
- Avoid thinking about exceptions; try to find a consistent rule.
- Attend to underlying semantic relations; they should be marked overtly and clearly.
- Assume coherence; the use of grammatical markers should make semantic sense.

Applicable principles for teaching

- Because different features of the grammatical, lexical, and discourse systems of the L2 are available to learners at different times, depending on their readiness, listening instruction should select oral input that contains the necessary features for acquisition and create activities that promote noticing of those features. This is what Richards (2005) called **listening for acquisition**, different from **listening for comprehension**.
- Learners must use operating principles to notice formal features of the spoken language in order to make progress in listening. Teachers can incorporate intensive listening techniques, such as Lynch's (2001a) proposed **proof listening**, to enable learners to go over transcripts of natural oral texts systematically, successively identifying particular features that they may otherwise not notice. Teachers can also incorporate input enhancements and design interventions that help learners notice new features (Cárdenas-Claros and Gruba, 2009).

- Attending to structural form while listening for meaning requires a gradual increase in processing capacity. Since it is necessary only in speaking or writing to focus explicitly on form, it is helpful to link listening with **'pushed output' tasks** that force learners to articulate in speech or writing exactly what they have heard. Reconstruction of oral input, especially when done as part of a collaborative task, can assist learners in developing more focused attention as they listen.

7.2.5   Metacognition hypothesis: using explicit strategies to activate listening capacity

The employment of listening strategies is part of a cognitive approach to learning that emphasises metacognition – thinking about the ways one processes language. Metacognitive processing is a form critical thinking, in which we seek to overcome – or at least counterbalance – our instinctive reactive thinking.

A good deal of listening research since the 1990s focused on strategies, ways that learners think about, plan, and adjust their own listening processes. The underlying hypothesis in this line of research is that better listeners and listeners who tend to make the most sustained progress are those who are able to learn and implement effective strategies (e.g. Rost and Ross, 1991; Vandergrift, 1999).

Instruction in critical thinking can assist listeners with monitoring their own comprehension, clarification requests, and responses. Specifically, they can begin to evaluate input texts as clear versus unclear, relevant versus irrelevant, logical versus illogical, fair versus one-sided, etc. This type of comprehension instruction goes beyond simple comprehension of information into situation comprehension and strategic training in approach comprehension problems (Duffy *et al.*, 2010).

Learning strategies is a term now used to refer to any attitudinal plans or behavioural devices that students use to acquire knowledge or skills. In particular, the notion of learning strategies is used to focus on those plans that aim to increase transfer of learning from a controlled, pedagogic experience to a more generalised realm. Learning strategies can range from techniques for improved memory of vocabulary to approaches for sustaining conversations with native speakers. Learning strategies have been studied extensively, both in general education and in language education, though precise definitions of what constitutes a strategy and claims about the effectiveness of strategy instruction are seldom agreed upon (Grenfell and Macaro, 2007; Oxford, 2010).

Historically, and across a variety of disciplines, the purpose in advocating learning strategies has been from a behaviourist perspective. The goal of introducing strategies is to make instructional goals clearer and learning ultimately easier, effectively allowing learners to reach learning objectives with less time on task, less practice, and less effort. Instructional models that attempt to increase the efficiency of learning transfer by supplying supportive information and procedural tips are often called **mathemagenic models** (Spector *et al.*, 2008).

Second language learning strategies are generally divided into two basic classes: those types of plans and decisions adopted to benefit *long-term learning* (e.g. joining a conversation club, listening to a news podcast every evening, making, reviewing vocabulary cards every day) which are often recursive and those adopted for using the language in a *current* contact situation (e.g. noting down key words, formulating clarification questions to ask the speaker, reading a related article in the L1 before listening to a news report in the L2) which are often time-sensitive.

The latter category, **strategies for current use**, include four sub-sets: retrieval strategies, rehearsal strategies, covert strategies (to exert control), and communication strategies (to convey or receive a message) (Chamot, 2005). Language learning strategies and language use strategies can be further differentiated according to whether they are primarily **cognitive, metacognitive, affective,** or **social**.

The cross-section described here already creates sixteen sub-categories of language use strategies, and it is easy to see ways to multiply the sub-categories further, for instance, by language modality (listening versus reading). The penchant of researchers for creating strategy lists has obviously become unwieldy and as the lists expand, they become of marginal use. It is important for teaching purposes to find ways to reduce strategy lists to the essential ones that promote learning in a specific context.

As most learning strategy specialists advise, the goal of incorporating strategy instruction into language teaching is *not* to have students employ (I have even heard the term *accomplish*) as many strategies as possible. Rather, the goal is to focus learners' attention on cognitive plans that they can personally employ to overcome obstacles in language use, and to develop realistic, efficient plans for long-term language learning.

Applicable principles for teaching

- Integration of learning strategies helps students listen more efficiently, and become more autonomous learners who can acquire language on their own. The introduction of listening strategies needs to be done explicitly, with opportunities for students to identify and explore various strategies and evaluate their effectiveness throughout a language course (Vandergrift *et al.*, 2006).

- Use of explicit listening strategies can enable students to handle tasks that may be more difficult than their current processing might allow. This stretching of capacity can be instructive to learners, and may motivate them to listen to more challenging authentic input, and find ways to comprehend more than they thought possible (Mendelsohn, 2006; Graham *et al.*, 2007)

- Listening strategies that are associated with successful learning can be demonstrated and modeled for less successful learners. Over time, less successful learners can consciously adopt these strategies, and due to the change in learning style, make significant gains in their listening comprehension skills and intrinsic motivation toward listening (Rost, 2006).

7.2.6   Sociocultural hypothesis: seeking appropriate contact to promote development

Sociocultural Theories (SCT) of language acquisition posit that language learning is a complex activity, a socially situated phenonemon that goes beyond paradigms of psycholinguistics (Lantolf, 2000). Within SCT, the goals and motives of the learner are of paramount importance, as are the learners' perception of themselves within their social environment.

One implication of SCT is that second language acquisition is seen as part of **acculturation**. The degree to which a learner is motivated to acculturate with the target language group will determine the success which he or she acquires the second language. As Pit Corder famously claimed, 'Given motivation, it is inevitable that a human being will learn a second language if he is exposed to the language data' (Corder, 1974, in Mishan, 2004). To the extent that this view is correct, the role of teaching concerns developing and fuelling motivation.

Motivation for a long-term process like L2 learning, however, is not quite like a light switch that the learner can flick on and off at will. Language learning motivation is developed through positive experiences with acculturation. As such, in SCT language acquisition is determined largely by the degree of **social and psychological distance** – the gap between the learner and the target language culture. Social distance pertains to the member of a social group that has contact with another social group whose members speak a different language. Psychological distance is the result of various affective factors that concern the learner as an individual, including culture shock, stress, motivation to be part of the culture and personal ego (Block and Parris, 2008; Lantolf and Thorne, 2006).

Applicable principles for teaching

- Learners who have positive (minimal) distance, socially and psychologically, from the target language will learn more efficiently and more enjoyably. Instruction must seek to gauge the appropriate input and design based on the social distance of the learners.

- Learners who experience positive social and psychological distance will more readily gravitate toward target language standards in their language learning efforts.

Summary: a balanced approach for teaching listening

This chapter has outlined some of the key considerations for selecting an approach to teaching listening. The chapter began by proposing an analysis of contextual, cultural, and educational factors before selecting or developing a method for teaching. Key factors in this analysis are identity and personal goals of the learners and cultural factors that impact the educational setting. A central factor, of course, is the relative emphasis on oracy and listening.

Following this essential overview, we examined six theoretical positions within SLA research that include a central role for listening: the *affective filter* hypothesis, the *input* hypothesis, the *interaction* hypothesis, the *processability* hypothesis, the *metacognition* hypothesis, and the *sociocultural* hypothesis. For each of these hypotheses about language learning, we derived principles that the teacher can aim to apply in his or her teaching context.

A balanced method teaching listening will include key elements from the approaches outlined in this chapter:

- Provide a lot of accessible input for learners, in a variety of audio, video and interactive media. Use text support to enhance the input and promote comprehension.
- The key is for learners to want to listen to the L2.
- Embed listening input in tasks that involve negotiation of meaning: the learner has to seek clarification and collaborate with others to enhance what they have understood. Add 'pushed output' to tasks so that learners have to reconstruct and incorporate what they have understood in speaking or in writing.
- Create opportunities for learners to notice new language (vocabulary, phonology, grammatical structures, discourse structures) and new cultural elements (gestures, interaction styles, allusions to cultural information) as part of their listening experience.
- Incorporate strategy training into listening instruction, in order to allow learners to monitor their own progress and make decisions on how to listen more constructively.
- Incorporate ways of personalising the listening experience to maximise long-term motivation and commitment to learning.

The following two chapters will examine specific ways of selecting appropriate input and planning instructional design to activate these concepts.

Chapter 8

Input and interaction

The previous chapter outlined principles for listening instruction based on research in language acquisition. The six areas of research that were reviewed all posited a crucial role for input and interaction. This chapter will examine the role of input and interaction in more detail.

As children we learn to listen in our L1 by paying attention to input around us and intentionally interacting with people in our immediate environment. Learning to listen in an L2 is different in many ways from learning to listen in an L1, but the essential role of input and interaction is similar. Therefore, the selection and use of input and the planning and guiding of appropriate interaction are central aspects of teaching listening.

This chapter will:

- define the concept of relevance in input and argue that relevance has a central role in the teaching of listening;

- outline the concept of authenticity in input and argue for a moderated view of authenticity;

- examine the notion of input genres and exemplify the use of different genres in teaching listening;

- define the notion of difficulty of input in terms of cognitive load and suggest using this measure for grading listening material;

- examine the practice of simplification, and present an argument for elaborated simplification in teaching listening;

- introduce the role of interaction in teaching listening and examine the variables that make such interaction most effective.

8.1   Relevance

We learn to listen primarily through attention to input and by engaging in intentional interaction. We can make gains in our listening capacity in more indirect ways also, including increasing our vocabulary, sharpening our reasoning skills, and expanding our content and cultural schemata to prepare us for new listening experiences. But it is through listening to **relevant input** and taking part in meaningful interaction that the actual gains are made.

The concept of **relevance** is gaining importance in educational and communication contexts. According to Sperber and Wilson (1995), human cognition has a single goal: we pay attention *only* to information which seems relevant to us. If our entire cognition – our power of attention, perception and interpretation – is co-ordinated most naturally and most readily around the notion of relevance, it makes sense to place this aspect of listening as the top priority in teaching. Engaging learners with relevant material – the 'right stuff' (a term originated in this context by Beebe, 1988) for triggering true motivation for learning – is essential for progress in language learning.

Relevant material for listening can be obtained through discovery of naturally occurring local input sources – that is, those sources already part of the learner's linguistic environment, whether they are, for example, L1 sources in an ESL or EFL environment, or ELF (English as a Lingua Franca) resources in an environment without native speakers of English. At the same time, materials can be obtained through selection or adaptation of distant sources – that is, those sources not currently familiar to or readily available to the learner. A pedagogic study conducted by Day *et al.* (2009), is an example of selecting material for maximum relevance. They surveyed a target population of university students to identify the types of topics that students found most interesting and most useful for their English study. Given a list of topics and subtopics, students ranked the choices in terms of interest or relevance to them as discussion topics. Materials for listening were then found and developed for each of the topics selected as relevant by a majority of students. While no approach to topic selection will ever guarantee initial relevance for all students, the approach used in this materials design study used the aim of relevance as its guiding principle. Moreover, through instructional design that includes personalisation options, even marginally relevant material can become relevant through exploration and interaction.

Teaching principle: aim for maximum relevance

Learning materials (topics, inputs, tasks) are relevant if they relate to learner goals and interests, and involve self-selection and evaluation.

8.2   Genres

Learning to listen involves exposure to a range of genres of language use. The notion of genres in linguistics refers to culture-specific ways in which communication is organised. This includes communicative function and identification of communicative situation in which certain text types are employed, as well as formal characteristics of texts and textual organisation. (Charaudeau and Maingueneau, 2002).

For example, we can think of literary and film genres such as: action, adventure, comedy, crime, documentary, and so on. When we watch a film or hear or read a story, we utilise our expectations about these genres to guide our interest, expectations, and our comprehension. We also utilise our knowledge of genres when we recall those stories and experiences of first watching or hearing them, and we utilise metaphors for communication based on these genres. Experience with these genres constitutes a large part of our schematic knowledge. (See Chapter 3 for further discussion.)

Just as we utilise genres in our own cultural experience to generate and guide further comprehension, we can see that within different cultures, the types of texts that fit in each group will differ. Familiarity with genres, and particularly with current or popular exemplars of those genres contributes indirectly to listening ability, through activation of these cultural schemata.

The following subsections provide illustrative overviews of the listening processes for two main genres, narratives and descriptions.

Ideas from practitioners

Selecting suitable listening texts

A combination of factors needs to be considered in selecting suitable listening texts for learners. Though it is not possible to satisfy all criteria with every selection – and it is important to expose learners to a range of listening text types – understanding the importance of the most common factors assists instructors grasp the subjective difficulty of a listening text:

- *Interest factor*. Is the text intrinsically interesting? Do the listeners have a stake in understanding it?
- *Entertainment factor*. Is the text engaging? Funny? Dramatic? Are there any special features or effects that make it enjoyable to listen to?
- *Cultural accessibility*. Does the text require a great deal of cultural knowledge to interpret?
- *Speaker roles and intentions*. Are the roles of the speakers recognisable? Are the intentions of the speakers clear or readily recoverable?

JJ Wilson, teacher trainer, New Mexico, US

8.2.1   Narrative

The narrative is the most universal rhetorical form across the cultures of the world. Narratives follow a time, event, and change sequence that is understood and embellished by people in every culture. Because of their universal appeal, narratives are an unparalleled teaching device for cultural values and facts as well as for discussion of relationships and morals.

Narratives will vary in complexity, but they always involve some element of time orientation, place orientation, character identification, events, complications, goals and meaning

- *Time orientation.* When are the actions happening? What is the historical setting? In what order, what events are left out?
  Listening expectation. Listeners typically assume **paratactic organisation**, forward sequencing, unless time markers indicate backtracking or jumping forward in time.

- *Place orientation.* Where is the action happening? What aspects of the setting are significant for the narrative?
  Listening expectation. Listeners typically assume **prototypical settings** – that is, prototypes, or typical cases, based on their personal experience – unless specific descriptions contradict them.

Table 8.1   **Genre and listening purpose**

	TYPE	INFORMATION ORGANISATION	PURPOSE OF LISTENING	SPEAKER FOCUS
1	Narrative	Temporal sequence	To find out what happened, who was involved, personal responses to events	Events, actions, causes, reasons, enablements, purposes, time, proximity
2	Descriptive	Spatial/sensory sequence and coherence	To experience what something looked or sounded or felt like	Objects, situations, states, attributes
3	Comparison/ contrast	Point-by-point organisation, leading to single conclusion	To discover how two things are alike and unalike	Instances, specifications, equivalences
4	Causal/ evaluation	Syllogistic/logical explication	To understand the causes and effects of certain actions	Value, significance, reason
5	Problem/ solution	Problem/ proposal/effect of proposed action	To generate hypotheses on the effects of proposed solutions	Cognition, volition

- *Character identification.* Who is in the story? Who are the main characters? Who are minor characters? Who are peripheral characters? What are the key relationships?
  Listening expectation. Listeners typically assume one or two main characters, a range of minor characters, with the relationships to the main characters driving the story.

- *Events/problem/complication/goal.* What about the setting is especially problematic? What factors complicate the story? How will the story be resolved?
  Listening expectation. Listeners typically assume there is a complication in the story that will be resolved, probably in some dramatic fashion.

- *Meaning of the story.* Most stories are told with some encompassing point, often with a moral lesson or a principle that confirms some aspect of the relationship between the speaker and listener. What is the special meaning of this story?
  Listening expectation. Listeners will assume that the story has some unique meaning, though one that conforms with accepted principles (such as 'good over evil').

Although the underlying semantic structure of narratives have a great deal in common, the surface features of narratives will obviously vary widely. In order to teach listening to narratives, the teacher also needs to help learners identify **transitional elements** that help them follow the story as well as absorb content themes in the story (cf. Pavlenko, 2006).

8.2.2   Descriptive

Like narratives, descriptive texts – descriptions of people, places, and events – are universal. However, unlike narratives, there are many more variations in organisation, and cultural differences in how descriptions are likely to unfold.

Oral descriptions of people, places, and things tend *not* to follow a fixed pattern, but often exhibit – *somewhere* in the text – characteristics of prototypical descriptions: features that are specific or peculiar or otherwise memorable, features that evoke a feeling or strong impression in the speaker, features that lead to a story or anecdote about the object or place or person being described, features that provide a link to other topics shared by the speaker and listener.

- Objects: appearance, parts, functions.
- Places: spatial/geographical arrangement (left to right, front to back, etc.).

Linde and Labov (1975) studied apartment descriptions and found that many speakers gave their listeners a spatially oriented walking tour of sorts, pointing out their own likes and dislikes in terms of layout and furnishings as they proceeded. They also found that much of the description of an apartment – or other place assumed to be familiar to the listener – is considered given, and is not described. Only those aspects of the description that differ from the norm, and are therefore 'new' are included in the description. (See Chapter 2 for discussion of 'given' versus 'new' information.)

Part of our sociolinguistic competence is knowledge of different genres and the structures to expect within each genre. When we listen to certain genres, we expect characteristic syntactic, lexical, and discourse patterns. For example, in descriptions, we tend to find copula sentences (*it's unbelievably warm, it's basically blue*), relative clauses (*it's a narrow room that leads to the outside porch*), presentatives (*there's a big oak door, you'll notice two small windows in the back wall*), as well as descriptive adjectives of size, shape, colour and number.

8.3   Authenticity

Situated language is the basis of natural, real-time language use, and comprehension of this situated, **authentic language** is the target of virtually all language learners.

This issue of **authenticity** is one of the most controversial issues in the teaching of listening, one that engenders heated discussion among teachers and linguists. *Genuineness, realness, truthfulness, validity, reliability, undisputed credibility*, and *legitimacy* are just some of the concepts involved when we talk about authenticity. At one end of the spectrum are those who define authenticity as any language that *has been used* by native speakers for any real purpose, that is, a purpose that was real for the users *at the time* the language was used by them. While this approach has value in terms of targeting *real context* and *real language* as central to language instruction, it perhaps devalues the role of the addressee in *making* the language authentic. In other words authenticity is relative; what's relative to one listener may not be relative to another (cf. Widdowson, 2007).

As is now well established in pragmatics, the closer a participant is to the 'control centre' of an interaction, the more immediate the purpose for the interaction, and therefore the more authentic and meaningful the discourse.

If we accept the notion of discourse control as leading to authenticity, then for purposes of language education, those inputs and encounters that involve the students' own purposes for listening can best be considered authentic. In this sense, any source of input and interaction that satisfies the learner's search for knowledge and allows the learner the ability to control that search is authentic.

Table 8.2 Facets of authenticity

- Authenticity of language
- Authenticity of text used as input data for learners
- Authenticity of the learner's own interpretation of such texts
- Authenticity of task
- Authenticity of the tasks conductive to language learning
- Authenticity of situation
- Authenticity of the actual social situation of the language classroom

Sources. Based on Taylor (1994) and Breen (1985).

What many teachers are referring to when they seek authentic input is the characteristic of *genuineness*. **Genuineness** refers to features of colloquial style of spontaneous planning that are characteristic of everyday spoken discourse:

- Natural speed, speaking in short bursts, irregular timing.
- Natural phonological phenomenon, natural pauses and intonation, use of reduction, assimilation, elision.
- High-frequency vocabulary, as a function of short-term memory limitations during spoken discourse planning.
- Colloquialism, such as short formulaic utterances, current slang, that show sensitivity to the audience.
- Hesitations, false starts, self-corrections, as indicators of the speaker's real-time cognitive processes.
- Orientation of the speech toward a 'live' listener, including natural pauses for the listener to provide backchannelling (e.g. nodding, *uh-huh*) or responses (e.g. *Yes, I think so.*).

The reasons for preferring genuine input are obvious. If the target of the learners is to be able to understand genuine spoken language, as actually used by native speakers, then the targets need to be introduced into instruction.

Another issue relating to authenticity is the medium of the input itself and the quality of that medium. If at one end of the spectrum are those who argue for authenticity input at all times, then at the other end are those who believe that authentic input is too difficult for the students to handle or unrealistic for the instructor to provide. A mediating factor in the use of authentic listening material has been task design (Nunan, 2004). By designing tasks which preview key vocabulary and discourse structures in the input, by chunking the input into manageable segments and providing selective focus on its particular elements, teachers can make use of authentic material in ways that are motivating and useful to learners at all levels.

Ideas from practitioners

How important is authenticity in L2 listening?

I know from my experience with L1 teaching that developing reading skills early turns out to be one of the strongest predictor of student success in school. My sense of teaching L2, something I came to later in my career, is that something quite similar is going on. Those who can develop listening skills early on in their language learning career – or who seem to have an aptitude for listening – have the best chance for success, and ultimately for higher level of attainment in the L2. So I emphasise listening, especially out of class listening, for all of my students.

I don't need to amplify the idea of 'authenticity'. For me, and for my students, anything that is in the target language that they want to listen to is authentic. This includes songs, YouTube videos, interviews, TV shows, films, you name it. If they like it, I generally go with it.

Katherine Rose, Paraiso, Costa Rica

Teaching principle: focus on authenticity and genuineness

- Language input should aim for user authenticity, first, by aiming to be appropriate to the current needs of the learners, and second, by reflecting real use of language in the real world.
- Language input should aim to be genuine, i.e. involving features of naturally occurring language with and between native speakers: speed, rhythm, intonation, pausing, idea density, etc.

Ideas from practitioners

Adjusting learner roles to activate learning

It seems clear that the methodology of teaching listening needs to change in a number of ways, in order to provide students with some opportunity to play an active role in their learning of the listening skill, and to engage with listening materials that interest and motivate them. Many of the problems associated with the traditional model of teaching listening can be lessened if teachers can find ways of allowing students to:

- choose what they listen to;
- make their own listening texts;
- control the equipment (being in charge of replaying difficult parts of the listening text, for example);
- give the instructions;
- design their own listening tasks;
- reflect on their problems in listening.

Goodith White, teacher trainer, London, UK

8.4 Vocabulary

Vocabulary acquisition is an important goal of listening instruction, as there is a robust relationship between effective listening and vocabulary accessibility. In principle, listening is facilitated by the size of an individual's mental lexicon and the listeners' facility in spoken word recognition. The activation of background knowledge (**content schemata** and **cultural schemata**) that is needed for comprehension of speech is linked to and launched by word recognition. Speed and breadth in word recognition have been shown to be a consistent predictor of L2 listening ability. (Segalowitz *et al.*, 1998; Laufer and Hulstijn, 2001).

Corpus studies show that a recognition vocabulary of 3,000 word families is necessary for comprehension of everyday (non-specialist) conversations, if we assume that a listener needs to be familiar with – and able to recognise – about 90–95 per cent of content words and lexical phrases to understand a conversation satisfactorily (Waring and Nation, 2004; Read, 2000; Schmitt, 2007). There is evidence that occurrences of **out-of-vocabulary words** in a spoken text (i.e. words outside of one's vocabulary knowledge, either nonsense words or unacquired words) create attentional problems that interfere with comprehension of both the immediate and subsequent utterances (Rost, 2005; Nation *et al.*, 2007; Graves, 2009).

Recognition vocabulary is not a simple concept because word knowledge involves a number of aspects and continuously expands. Word knowledge includes, on a surface (**syntagmatic**) level, recognition of the word's spoken form (including its allophonic variations), its written form, and grammatical functions, and on a deeper (**paradigmatic**) level, its collocations, relative frequency in the language, constraints on use, denotations and connotations (Bieliller, 2009; Schmitt, 2001; Kaivanpanah and Alavi, 2008). There is evidence that a listener's depth of knowledge of words influences the speed of spoken word recognition, by way of **priming effects**. Where **neighbourhood density** is greater, that is, when semantic connections in the mental lexicon are more dense, word recognition becomes easier. This means that the depth of individual word knowledge determines a given word's degree of integration into the mental lexicon, and therefore the facility with which it is accessed in real time (Luce and Pisoni, 1998).

How one activates vocabulary knowledge while listening has not been widely studied in L2 contexts. Based on L1 research, it is assumed that activation is more readily achieved for high frequency (i.e. frequently used) words than for low frequency words. It is also assumed that vocabulary knowledge interacts with other competencies in the process of listening, such as syntactic processing and discourse processing. In L2 contexts, the four major views on the role of vocabulary in language comprehension are:

- The *instrumentalist* view, which sees vocabulary knowledge as being a major prerequisite and causative factor in comprehension.

- The *aptitude* view, which sees vocabulary knowledge as one of many outcomes of having strong general 'intelligence' or 'feel' for a language.

- The *knowledge* view, which sees vocabulary as an indicator of strong world knowledge. This world knowledge enables listening comprehension.

- The *access* view, which sees vocabulary as having a causal relationship with comprehension provided that the vocabulary can be easily accessed. Access can be improved through practice. This access can involve several factors including fluency of lexical access, speed of coping with affixed forms, and speed of word recognition.

                    (Adapted from Nation, 2008, and Tseng and Schmitt, 2008)

Because word recognition and vocabulary knowledge play such an important role in L2 listening and second language acquisition, most approaches to teaching L2 listening involve explicit efforts for vocabulary development. Five types of instructional methods are commonly used:

- Priming of lexical knowledge through pre-teaching of vocabulary items known to be unfamiliar to L2 learners (Ellis and Heimbach, 1997; VanPatten, 1990).

- Concurrent lexical support while listening, either through captioning of videos (Baltova, 1999) or overt signalling and paraphrasing of unfamiliar lexical items in face-to-face delivery (Chaudron, 1988).

- Prior simplification of vocabulary in oral texts, including restatements and paraphrases to promote vocabulary learning (Chaudron, 1988).

- Emphasis on negotiation of meaning of unknown lexical items during conversational interactions, to promote awareness of lexical gaps in input processing, and on increasing use of contextual strategies for inferring meanings of unknown words (Chaudron, 1988; Pica *et al.*, 1987).

- Group reconstruction activities following listening (sometimes called *dictogloss*) to promote awareness of unfamiliar lexical items and to deepen and extend partial vocabulary knowledge (Wajnryb, 1990).

All five methods have demonstrated gains in vocabulary knowledge, as measured through pre- and post-test comparison in comparison to control groups, though part of this gain must be attributed to the additional time of lexical processing provided in each method.

Table 8.3   **Percentage of coverage by word type in English**

LEXICON TYPE	NO. OF WORDS	TEXT COVERAGE (%)
High-frequency words	2,000	87
Academic vocabulary	800	8
Technical vocabulary	2,000	3
Low-frequency words	123,200	2

Sources. Nation and Newton (2009) and Schmitt (2008)

8.5   Difficulty

The discourse framework of a text (often called **formal schema**) contributes to the ease or difficulty of understanding it. For example, understanding an argument that introduces contrastive reasons is, in principle, more difficult to understand than a story that proceeds through an orderly sequence of events because it requires deeper cognitive processing. Similarly, the surface language of the text itself contributes to its difficulty. For example, a text with an abundance of complex and embedded sentences is predictably more difficult to understand than a text with only short, simple sentences. However, it is important to note that these are only predictive aspects of difficulty. Brown (1995) has argued that the central, governing feature in difficulty of a text is not the language itself, but the complexity of the content – its intrinsic **cognitive difficulty**.

Brown defines cognitive difficulty as the factors that make the four central listening processes (*identifying* information, *searching* memory for information you already have, *filing* or storing information for later cross-referencing, and *using* information in some way) easier or more difficult to perform. Having conducted a long series of interactive listening experiments (Brown, 1995), Brown proposed six principles of **cognitive load** that affect listeners:

- *Cognitive load, principle 1.* It is easier to understand any text (narrative, description, instruction, or argument) that involves FEWER rather than MORE individuals and objects.
- *Cognitive load, principle 2.* It is easier to understand any text (particularly narrative texts) involving individuals or objects which are clearly DISTINCT from one another.
- *Cognitive load, principle 3.* It is easier to understand texts (particularly description or instruction texts) involving simple spatial relationships.

- *Cognitive load, principle 4.* It is easier to understand texts where the order of telling matches the order of events.

- *Cognitive load, principle 5.* It is easier to understand a text if relatively few familiar inferences are necessary to relate each sentence to the preceding text.

- *Cognitive load, principle 6.* It is easier to understand a text if the information in the text is clear (not ambiguous), self-consistent and fits in readily with information you already have.

The implications for teaching and testing are that if we wish to grade the texts and tasks that listeners will encounter, we need to take into account the cognitive load of the texts and tasks we are presenting. If we wish to simplify a text (e.g. by shortening it) or a task (e.g. by providing initial vocabulary or other information), we need to first consider the factors of cognition – the listening processes – that make a listening activity difficult.

Ideas from practitioners

Ways to adjust difficulty

Some texts are inherently difficult for learners. Rather than adjust the text difficulty, I prefer to adjust the *task* difficulty. Here are some 'tricks' that will help learners deal with difficult texts.

- Do a 'pre-listening warm-up' activity to remind them of the content and vocabulary they will need (schema activation).
- Have learners do a task in pairs as they listen. That way, they can share what they did understand instead of worrying about what they missed.
- Do a *micro-task* before the main task.
  - Brainstorm words likely to be in the listening text. When your learners listen, have them raise their hands when they hear one of the words. This shows recognition and is a cue for other learners.
  - Give a list of events or items that will be mentioned in the listening text. Then have students listen and identify the sequence.
  - As students listen, pause the recording to give them time to think and process what they hear.
  - If the listening is a close activity where students listen and write missing words in a reading passage, have the learners read the passage first. They may want to guess at the words or types of words they expect to hear.
- Give students a copy of the script and have them read it. Then ask them to put the script away and listen to the text.
  - After they listen, give them a copy of the script. They listen and underline a key feature (e.g., the information that contained the answers, a certain grammatical form, etc.).

- Have students choose their own style of review. After doing a task and checking it, play it again. Invite the students to choose their own level for review:
  - Those who found it very difficult follow your prompts. As you play the recording, point to the answers on the board or an OHP as they are mentioned.
  - Those who found it of average difficulty look at their books. They try to hear the answers and touch them as they do so.
  - Those who found it easy close their eyes. As they listen, they 'watch the movie in their minds'.

Marc Helgesen, author, Sendai, Japan

8.6   Simplification

Simplification of input is a form of **social accommodation**, a term first used in social psychology (Giles and Smith, 1979) to refer to mutual movements of interlocutors toward the language and behaviour standards of the other. Simplification of input is one common method of making discourse accessible to L2 users and rendering difficult texts more accessible for language-learning purposes.

Simplification of input can be achieved in two basic ways:

- *Restrictive simplification* operates on the principle of using and highlighting familiar linguistic items and frames:
  - *Lexical:* using a simpler term (or higher-frequency term) for a more complicated one (or lower-frequency one), less slang, fewer idioms.
  - *Syntactic:* using simpler syntax, shorter utterances, topic-fronted utterances (e.g. *The man at the reception desk, I gave the package to him*), less pre-verb modification (*I only want coffee* versus *I want only coffee*) to make utterance easier to process and study.
  - *Phonological:* overtly marking word and phrase boundaries by slowing down or exaggerating speech patterns.
  - *Discoursal (for conversation):* using prototypical question–answer patterns (yes/no questions), non-inverted questions (*You can sing?*), either–or questions (*Where do you live? Do you live in the city?*) or other familiar patterns (e.g. tag questions: *You're from Osaka, aren't you?*).
  - *Discoursal (for monologues):* using prototypical rhetorical patterns such as direct temporal sequencing, avoidance of tangential information.
- *Elaborative simplification* operates on the principle of enriching the input rather than cutting out presumably difficult parts (Granena, 2008; Long, 2009):

○ *Phonological:* using higher pitch and more pitch variation to promote attention.
○ *Lexical:* providing rephrasing of key words and ideas, use of definitions, use of synonyms.
○ *Syntactic:* providing rephrasing of difficult syntactic constructions, to provide more time for processing of meaning.
○ *Syntactic:* using more subordinate clauses and embeddings to make utterance relationships more transparent (e.g. *I have relatives in the Cincinnati area. That's the place where I grew up*).
○ *Syntactic:* supplying optional syntax (*I think that he's here* versus *I think he's here*).
○ *Discoursal:* providing explicit frame shifts (*well, now, so, okay, The next thing I want to mention is, One of the main issues is . . .*) to assist in identifying of idea boundaries and relationships. (Temporal relationships: *and, after that*; causality: *so, then, because*; contrast: *but, on the other hand*; emphasis: *actually, in fact*).
○ *Discoursal:* providing direct repetition of words, phrases, whole utterances.
○ *Discoursal:* providing narrative examples of key ideas.

Simplification often has the immediate beneficial effect of helping learners understand the ideas in what otherwise might be an inaccessible text, and thus reducing frustration and increasing motivation. But because simplification of the input itself necessarily alters the original text and may reduce the learner's satisfaction of having a genuine listening experience, it is important for teachers to use simplification judiciously.

Teaching principle: increase shared knowledge rather than simplify texts

Simplification of input is effective for language learning only if it helps the listener become more active as a listener, that is, more able to activate background knowledge and make inferences, and more willing and able to respond to what he or she hears. Speakers generally do not consciously script features of simplified language into their speech. Rather, they tend to 'pitch' their discourse at their intended audience, taking into account their own perceived importance of the topics and subtopics as well as the interests and expectations of their audience and the amount of background information available to them.

Other means of achieving greater comprehension without altering a text are often preferable and typically much easier to administer. They include:

• *Direct repetition:* repeating the text by replaying the audio or video extract or repeating the text orally.

- *Simplification of the context:* preparing for key concepts in advance is the chief means of simplifying the context for the listener. Presenting or eliciting vocabulary and ideas that will be part of the text generally helps adjust the listener's cognitive context. As Lynch (1996: 26) says, 'The more we know, the less we need to rely on language to understand the message.'
- *Chunking the input:* presenting the input in short chunks (e.g. one- to three-minute segments), followed by opportunities for clarification before continuing.

8.7   Restructuring

Restructuring is an interactive technique for simplifying or elaborating in face-to-face discourse, depending on the needs of the listener in the moment.

Based on a survey of successful restructuring moves in NS–NNS discourse across a number of languages, Bremer *et al.* (1996) offers a helpful summary of the range and types of discourse structuring that will help prevent understanding problems and promote repair of problems when they occur (see Table 8.4).

8.8   Interaction

Access to input alone is rarely sufficient to assure successful and sustained acquisition of listening ability in an L2. Some type of sustained, meaningful interaction is required if the L2 learner is to deepen and expand comprehension, and develop an ability to respond to what he or she hears.

While virtually all children learn to listen in their first language as part of their language acquisition process, even when their environment is only minimally supportive of their efforts, the case for second-language learning is not nearly as optimistic. Indeed, as noted by Bley-Vroman (1990) the typical case is that the L2 learner achieves an incomplete grammatical, lexical, and pragmatic mastery of the L2.

It is now axiomatic that for a person to learn a second language to any high functioning degree, three major conditions are required: (1) a learner who experiences the need to learn the second language and is motivated to do so; (2) a speaker or speakers of the target language who know it well enough to provide the learner with access to the spoken language and the empathic support (such as simplification, selective repetition and targeted feedback) needed for learning the target language; and (3) a social setting

Table 8.4   **Range and types of discourse structuring to promote active listening**

ENCOURAGING PARTICIPATION	RAISING EXPECTABILITY	RAISING TRANSPARENCY RAISING ACCESSIBILITY	RAISING EXPLICITNESS
Open-topic management	*Discourse:* metadiscursive comments on: activity type, topics, shared knowledge	*Perceptual:* short utterances, salience of elements (articulation, volume), segmentation (pauses, rate of delivery, chunking, avoid false starts)	Full forms instead of ellipsis, pro-forma reduced forms, lexicalisation of important information
Slow down rhythm for turns	*Topics:* announce by paralinguistic markers, announce content explicitly	*Lexical meaning:* high-frequency vocabulary, recourse to L1 code switching	*Metadiscursive:* comments on discourse function of utterance, discourse structuring, discourse context
Acknowledge language problems	*Locally:* left topic dislocation	*Conceptual meaning:* linking complex topics to 'here and now' absolute instead of relational reference to time	Possibility of re-runs by modified repetition
Giving room: offer turns, open questions, allow for pauses, help other with formulations			

Sources. Based on Bremer *et al.* (1996) and Roberts *et al.* (2005).

that brings the learner in frequent enough and sustained enough contact with target language speakers to make permanent language acquisition possible. Predictably, most cases of experienced difficulty or failure by a learner, either a child or an adult, to acquire a second language to the desired level are generally due to a lack in one or more of these factors (Wong-Fillmore, 1991).

Listening plays a vital role in the relative success or failure of the L2 learner. Listening is required in two of these conditions (access to a learnable version of the spoken language, sustained contact), and is therefore an essential means of language development.

Ideas from practitioners

Using specific models to promote listener interaction

I often have found that just exhorting students to be more interactive doesn't really help a lot of them. I now present just four or five concrete examples of how they can become more interactive:

- *Extenders*. Signals you are trying to understand and are emotionally involved. (*Uh-huh. Right, I see. Oh, oh really? Wow, great. Oh, that's too bad.*)
- *Repeating*. Repeating word or sentence or question to show understanding. (*Colorado? You went there for your holiday?*)
- *Extra question*. Direct question to prompt the speaker to continue or to reveal more. (*What's it like there? What was the most surprising thing for you?*)
- *Comment*. Short comment on what the speaker has said, showing something about you. (*That sounds like fun. I'd like to try that some time.*)

Because my students tend to be competitive about learning anything in school, if I can quantify communication for them in some way it seems to help them make progress.

Todd Beuckens, teacher, Bangkok, Thailand

In Second Language Acquisition (SLA) research, listening opportunities are often considered to be part of the **linguistic environment** – the stage for second-language acquisition (Gass and Selinker, 2008). This environment, that is, the speakers of the target language and their speech to the L2 learners, provides linguistic input in the form of listening and interaction opportunities embedded in informal social encounters as well as in more formal pedagogic situations. The learner, in order to acquire the language, must come to understand the input in terms of its cognitive and social meanings *and* pay attention to structural form within the input. As in L1 acquisition, motivation and access to developmental opportunities are required. Access is made possible in part through accommodations made by L2 speakers to render their language more comprehensible *and* in part through strategies the learner employs to create meaning from limited (yet ever-expanding) linguistic resources.

In order to listen in the L2, for purposes of message comprehension and for language acquisition, the listener must gain access to the spoken-language code. Research on speech to children learning their L1 prompted SLA researchers in the mid-1970s to enquire how much 'code modification' was typically being offered to L2 learners in order to increase their access to the L2. It is often assumed that **modified input** or **accentuated input** in SLA is of even greater potential importance, given that many learners are adults (without caretakers) and their opportunities for access to input in the L2 may be limited.

Because the language presented to second-language learners is often in the form of a modified input similar to child-directed speech, SLA researchers in the 1980s began to document the kind of linguistic adjustments that were evident in this newly named 'foreigner talk'. Linguistic adjustments have been noted in several areas (Rost, 2005).

- *Phonology:* slower rate of delivery, more use of stress and pauses, more careful articulation, wider pitch range, more use of full forms/avoidance of contractions.
- *Morphology:* deliberately well formed utterances, shorter utterances, less complex constructions, more retention of optional constituents/less ellipsis, more questions.
- *Semantics:* more redundancy of information, higher frequency of content words, fewer idiomatic expressions, more concrete references.

An important research and pedagogic issue arising from SLA studies of this nature is the degree to which modified input and **compensatory strategies** for dealing with difficult input actually facilitate L2 learners' acquisition of the language. Vandergrift (2007), for example, has recommended that, for purposes of pedagogy, it is preferable to modify the input in the direction of elaboration (providing rephrasing, examples, confirmation checks) rather than syntactic simplification (slower rate of delivery, etc.), as this is more congruent with native speaker to native speaker (NS–NS) norms.

8.9   Strategies

Interaction can take many forms and serve many purposes, but it is the kind of interaction linked to input processing that is of most interest in the development of listening ability. In L1–L2 interactions, both speakers and listeners enact **strategies** that they assume will make the interaction smoother and the content more comprehensible. L1 speakers often make **conversational adjustments** for content (narrower range of topics, more predictable topics nominated, more here-and-now orientation, shorter treatment of topics) and also for interaction structures (more acceptance of unintentional **topic shifts**, more **confirmation checks**, more clarification requests, more question-and-answer strings). These conversational adjustments are most often made by the NS or more fluent of the two interlocutors in L2–L2 interactions, but the L2 participant can also employ these same moves as **listening strategies** in order to make the input more accessible and learning from the interaction more durable (Mondada and Doehler, 2005; Gass and Mackey, 2006; Pica, 2005).

Comprehension and clarification checks are the most overt form of L2 listener interaction strategies leading to listening development, and to language acquisition, but there are other important strategy types as well. Listener displays of uptake, backchanneling, and follow-up acts can be seen as part of 'pushed output', leading to listening development and acquisition as well.

Listener response is often considered part of the listening process, as it is interwoven with interpretation and adoption of a pragmatic perspective. Listener response generally involves display of uptake, backchannelling, and follow-up acts.

When a speaker initiates topics in conversation, the listener has the choice of uptaking any initiating move or ignoring it. Typically, the speaker intends the listener to uptake the topic in a specific way, incorporating both verbal and non-verbal means that constitute a normal, or **preferred response**. For example, an invitation leads to a preferred response of an acceptance or a polite refusal. A listener response that expresses inability or reluctance to provide completion, or otherwise comply with the speaker's initiating move forms a challenge. A dispreferred response confronts the presupposition that the addressee has the information or resource the speaker needs and is willing to provide it, or it challenges the speakers right to make the initiating move, as in the following example:

> *Speaker 1.* Would you like to come to Kaoru's wedding?
> *Speaker 2.* What for?

Challenges are by nature face-threatening – they upset the participation frame by demoting the speaker's power. Of course, some challenges are less face-threatening than others. Specifically, challenging the presupposition that one is *able* to provide the information is less face-threatening than challenging the presupposition that one is *willing* to provide it. This is why in most cultures it is more 'polite' to declare ignorance than refuse to comply with a request or an initiating move (Tsui, 1994).

Another type of listener interaction token is **backchannelling**. Backchannelling responses are short messages – verbal, semi-verbal and non-verbal – that the listener sends back during the partner's speaking turn or immediately following the speaking turn. These messages may include brief verbal utterances (*yeah*, *right*), rhythmic **semi-verbal utterances** (*uh-huh*, *hmm*), laughs or chuckles, and postural movements, such as nods and raising of the eyebrows. Backchannelling, differing from culture to culture and within subcultures, is important in conversation for showing a number of listener states: reception of messages, readiness for subsequent messages, agreement on turn taking, and empathy with the speaker's state, or change in emotional state, or communicative intentions. Backchannelling occurs more or less constantly during conversations in all languages and settings, though in some languages and in some settings, it seems more prevalent. Miyata and Nishisawa (2007) note that in Japanese, a language noted for its high level of overt backchannelling, a listener is expected to provide backchannelling on average every two and a half seconds, technically once for every pause unit in the utterance. Because of its rhythmic elements, Maynard (2002, 2005) terms the interplay between speaker and listener as the **interactional dance**. Naturally, when backchannelling is withheld or disrupted, the dance stops: The interaction becomes perceptibly disrupted.

A. She was really upset when Helen suggested that they might move her to the other facility.

B. Um-hm.

A. Even though Helen only mentioned it once in maybe the past two months. It wasn't like she was insisting on it or anything. (*Pause.*) Are you listening to me?

B. Yeah, yeah. You were saying that Helen is getting on her nerves, right?

A third category of listener interaction in discourse is the follow-up act. Follow-up acts are responses to a discourse exchange, and can be provided by either the listener or the speaker from the previous exchange.

Speaker 1. [Elicit.] I'll see you tomorrow.

Speaker 2. [Response.] Okay, see you. [Follow-up act.] Could we meet at the Shinjuku Starbucks around nine?

Follow-up acts can be endorsements (positive evaluations), concessions (negative evaluations), or acknowledgements (neutral evaluations). A follow-up act may include a move to reframe the interaction by adjusting the participation frame or by redirecting the topic

Speaker 1. I'll see you tomorrow.

Speaker 2. Wait, don't leave yet. I need to tell you something.

Because learning to listening in face-to-face interactions is such a critical part of language learning, and by some counts is the most face-threatening aspect of L2 learning, L2 pedagogical approaches now incorporate direct instruction on interaction. L2 pedagogy dealing with interpretation in face-to-face encounters has generally integrated three approaches: (1) exploring options for listener roles and using interactive procedures for enhancing listening effectiveness (2) two-way (collaborative) tasks and (3) **meta-pragmatic** treatment of speech acts and listener behavior in interactions (Kasper, 2006).

Enhancing interaction and output options for NNSs in conversation has become an important tool for language training. Using longitudinal studies of NNSs acquiring host languages in non-tutored environments in European settings involving multiple L2s, Bremer *et al.* (1996) have documented many of the social procedures that L2 listeners must come to use more comfortably and confidently as they become successful listeners and participants in everyday conversations. These procedures include the forms of interaction we have discussed here (identifying topic shifts, providing backchannelling, participating in conversational routines, providing obligatory responses) and, most significantly in this study, the listener shifting to topic initiator role, and the listener initiating queries and repair of communication problems.

Metapragmatic approaches are now being employed in listening pedagogy in order to assist learners to become aware of their active role in interactions. Some metapragmatic approaches draw support from the **sociocultural theory of mind** (Vygotsky, 1978) to claim that development of metacognition of L2 largely takes place in **dialogic interaction** (Cross, 2009b). It is felt dialogic interaction initiated by listeners allows them to employ collaborative strategies to construct understanding, gain insights into the nature of their dialogue and its impact on their own learning.

Summary: quantity and quality in input and interaction

This chapter has dealt with the interrelated topics of input and interaction. Development of listening ability is directly related to the quantity and quality of input a learner seeks. We all know that simply being surrounded by input will not ensure listening ability development. The input must somehow be made accessible to the learner and the learner must somehow make a cognitive commitment toward understanding the input if language development is to take place.

The chapter explored some of the techniques by which input itself can be made more accessible, through controlling the external factors that increase the cognitive load for the listener. In face-to-face interaction, these kinds of cognitive load reductions, or simplifications, occur as part of a normal accommodation process. In distant contact situations, such as online listening, in which the listener does not have any means of simplifying the input, other strategies must be used to make the language and content more understandable.

Language learners often wonder *how much input* and *how much interaction* is needed for language acquisition. All SLA researchers avoid giving a direct answer to this question, but a simple answer must be that thousands of hours of *active* input processing is required to attain a high level of proficiency in a language, and a similarly large number of active, engaged hours with oral input is necessary to gain a high level of listening proficiency. However, quantity of input and interaction is not the main issue in language acquisition or listening development. What is essential for development is a process of engaging with input and interlocutors, attempting to understand new – and relevant – texts and striving to connect more deeply and for more sustained periods of time with TL speakers. This seeking action, along with the development of appropriate strategies, is what triggers acquisition.

Chapter 9

Instructional design

There are several keys to effective instruction, but perhaps the most important key is instructional design: the selection and adaptive design of input, tasks, interactive and collaborative elements, feedback, sequences, and evaluation that guide learning.

This chapter aims to provide details of instructional design to implement the principles and materials discussed in Chapters 7 and 8. Although many of the forms of instructional design in this chapter include an element of assessment, the following chapter, Chapter 10, outlines principles and forms of assessment of listening in more detail.

This chapter provides an overview of six types of listening practice, with task types and activities for each. The six types of listening discussed are:

- Intensive listening.
- Selective listening.
- Interactive listening.
- Extensive listening.
- Responsive listening.
- Autonomous listening.

In lieu of providing published examples of these types of listening, the chapter offers generative frameworks and specific ideas of practitioners to stimulate the reader in selection and design of suitable learning tasks and materials.

9.1   Designing instruction to include a range of listening types

In the 1980s, at about the time that Tom Wolfe's novel *The Right Stuff* was made into a Hollywood film, an influential SLA book hit the market. Wolfe's story is about air force test pilots who live by an unspoken set of standards and assumptions summed up as having 'the right stuff.' In her (SLA) book, sociolinguist Leslie Beebe writes about the role of input in language acquisition, and states that the key to successful language acquisition is for the learner to find 'the right stuff'.

Carrying this metaphor a bit further: while finding the right input may be key to language acquisition, ultimately it is *how* learners interact with that input that allows them to 'fly'. We can categorise ways of interacting with input, and how those ways allow learners to understand and to glean more from the input. This chapter outlines six types of practice, highlighting the learning focus and activity focus of each type (see Table 9.1).

Table 9.1   **Types of listening practice**

LISTENING TYPE	LEARNING FOCUS	ACTIVITY FOCUS
Intensive	Focus on phonology, syntax, lexis	Learner pays close attention to what is actually said. Teacher feedback on accuracy
Selective	Focus on main ideas, pre-set tasks	Learner attempts to extract key information and construct or utilise information in a meaningful way. Teacher intervention during task and feedback on task completion
Interactive	Focus on becoming active as a listener; attempt to clarify meaning or form	Learner interacts verbally with others, in collaborative tasks, to discover information or negotiate solutions. Teacher feedback on form and outcome of interaction
Extensive	Focus on listening continuously, managing large amounts of listening input	Learner listens to longer extracts and performs meaning oriented tasks. Teacher direct instruction on comprehension strategies; global feedback from teacher
Responsive	Focus on learner response to input	Learner seeks opportunities to respond and convey her own opinions and ideas. Teacher 'pushes output' from learner
Autonomous	Focus on learner management of progress, navigation of 'Help' options	Learner selects own extracts and tasks, monitors own progress; decides on own patterns of interaction with others. Global feedback from teacher on learning path

A balanced approach to listening instruction would aim to include all six types, with an instructional priority on those types that offer the most engagement and are consistent with learning and assessment goals.

9.2   Intensive listening

Intensive listening refers to listening closely – for precise sounds, words, phrases, grammatical units and pragmatic units. Although it does not seem that listening intensively is called for in most everyday situations, accurate perception is involved in higher level comprehension and listening. The ability *to* listen intensively *when required* – as in listening for specific details or to spot a particular word – is an essential component of listening proficiency.

Concept 9.1   **Intensive listening**

Intensive listening refers to listening to a text closely, with the intention to decode the input for purposes of analysis.

In addition to its value in increasing listening proficiency, intensive listening offers an avenue to **language-focused learning**, which is an essential aspect of permanent language acquisition (Nation and Newton, 2009). As such, it is beneficial to include intensive listening in instruction, if only as a small part of each learning session. Types of intensive listening practice include: dictation, elicited repetition, shadowing (for a review of shadowing types and techniques, see Murphey, 2000), word spotting, error spotting, grammar processing, and mediation (translation or simultaneous interpretation).

Ideas from practitioners

Using timely texts for dictation

Most teachers come across bits of text which interest them and would be of interest to their students – newspaper articles, magazines, bits of books, even bits of textbooks. Often such texts have a topicality or curiosity that will attract students in spite of potential linguistic difficulties. The teacher who has a range of dictation strategies at her disposal will be able to exploit these texts as they arise, employing techniques that will increase or decrease the difficulty of the text to match the needs and abilities of the group. And students will respond to the effort and opportunism of their teacher – perhaps adding their own finds to the collection.

Mario Rinvolucri, teacher trainer, Canterbury, UK

The prototypical intensive listening activity is **pure dictation**, the transcription of the exact words that a speaker utters. Dictation, with its many practiced variations such as **dicto-comp** and pair info-gap dictations, is a focused instructional tool because it involves processing phonology, vocabulary, grammar and draws on the ability to make specific inferences from context.

Because pure dictation of extended passages can be tedious and time-consuming, many teachers have developed variations. These variations provide more efficient use of time, more interaction, and clearer focus on specific language items. (See Nation and Newton, 2009, Wilson, 2008, and Davis and Rinvolucri, 1988, for examples.) Some popular variations follow:

- *Fast-speed dictation*. The teacher reads a passage at natural speed, with assimilations, etc. The students can ask for multiple repetitions of any part of the passage, but the teacher will not slow down her articulation of the phrase being repeated. This activity focuses students' attention on features of fast speech.

- *Pause and paraphrase*. The teacher reads a passage and pauses periodically for the students to write paraphrases, not the exact words used. (Indeed, students may be instructed not to use the exact words they heard.) This activity focuses students on vocabulary flexibility, saying things in different ways, and in focusing on meaning as they listen.

- *Listening close*. The teacher provides a partially completed passage that the listeners fill in as they listen or after they listen. This activity allows focus on particular language features, e.g. verbs or noun phrases.

- *Error identification*. The teacher provides a fully transcribed passage, but with several errors. The students listen and identify (and correct) the errors. This activity focuses attention on detail: the errors may be grammatical or semantic.

- *Jigsaw dictation*. Students work in pairs. Each person in the pair has part of the full dictation. The students read their parts to the other in order to complete the passage. This activity encourages negotiation of meaning.

- *Group dictation*. Learners hear an extended passage, perhaps two minutes long, usually a monologue. It can be a relatively complex exposition or a narrative. The passage deliberately contains challenging vocabulary and structures, and considerably more information than can be recalled by a single listener after listening just once. A key element of this activity is that the learners do not take notes, but rather rely on short-term memory building. Following the hearing of the passage, which may be read more than once, the learners are asked to collaborate to reconstruct the passage as completely and as accurately as they can (see Nation and Newton, 2009; Kowal and Swain, 1997; Wajnryb, 1990).

- *Communicative dictation*. There are several variations of this type of dictation, all focusing on student-to-student exchanges. In a **jigsaw**

listening variation, students hear different parts or versions of a text. They then pair up to share their information. Or students add an opinion to each sentence they hear (*I think that . . .* or *I don't think that . . .*) and then compare.

- *Listening games.* There are a variety of listening games, particularly designed for younger learners, that involve partial dictation, writing down key words, 'word spotting' (e.g. 'I spy', 'Simon says', 'Mother, may I?'), passing along messages verbatim, etc.). (See Gurian, 2008 for more examples.)

Ideas from practitioners

Using input processing techniques to teach grammar

It is more effective in the long term to teach grammar through input processing rather than through deductive presentations. We can do this by helping learners to attend to particular grammatical features, training the skills of noticing. This contrasts with traditional approaches which aim to teach grammar through production practice of one kind or another. In input processing tasks, we make use of oral texts on the grounds that learners need training in being able to notice grammatical features when they are listening. This is very difficult for learners, particularly if the features are redundant (i.e. are not essential for understanding the meaning). In doing this, we are using a **grammar discovery approach**. Learners are shown how to analyse the data in order to arrive at an understanding of how a grammatical feature works. This means that we are providing practice in monitoring – the learners are asked to use their explicit knowledge to identify and correct errors of the kind that they typically make.

Rod Ellis, author, Auckland, New Zealand

9.3 Selective listening

Selective listening tasks may be the most salient form of listening instruction in use today. Joan Morley, a pioneer in this area, offered perhaps the first comprehensive set of materials for selective listening in her work *Improving Aural Comprehension* (1972). As Morley stated at the time, 'The only way to improve aural comprehension is to spend many hours practicing listening . . . However, a directed program of purposeful listening can shorten the time.' Morley considered the two tenets of improving aural comprehension (what she then called 'listening with understanding') to be concentrated, disciplined listening, and immediate task completion to provide 'an urgency for remembering'.

Ideas from practitioners

Using internet sources for selective listening

My students are naturally interested in local and world news and global trends, so I use news clips from the internet, like afrikainfo.com or e-tv from South Africa. The students see this addition to class as a kind of bonus, because they know it's authentic, so they really pay attention. (I wish they'd pay such rapt attention to me when I talk!) I've found it's best when I use clips two minutes or so in length, and prepare some kind of quiz or fill-in-the-blanks exercise. I've also created subtitles for some of the pieces I use. Of course, it's time-consuming to prepare, but the pay-off is definitely worth the effort.

Eric Tevoedjre, teacher, Cotonou, Benin

Morley viewed selective listening as a prerequisite for the more complex and more extended listening that learners in an academic course would need to undertake. Morley believed that using carefully planned and graded listening lessons would help students learn to listen and get facts so they become ready to listen and get ideas. Lesson content included:

- Numbers and numerical relationships.
- Letters, sounds, abbreviations, spelling.
- Directions and spatial relations.
- Time and temporal sequences.
- Dates and chronological order.
- Measurements and amounts.
- Proportion, comparison, and contrast.
- Getting the facts (factual readings).

Concept 9.2 **Selective listening**

In language teaching, selective listening refers to listening with a planned purpose in mind, often to gather specific information to perform a task. In its vernacular use, selective listening is used to refer to 'attending to only what you want to hear' and 'tuning out everything else'.

For extended texts, longer than the one-minute extracts, a useful form of selective listening is note-taking. Note-taking is widely viewed as an important macro-skill in the lecture–listening comprehension process, a skill that often interacts with reading (when note-taking is integrated with reading material accompanying the lecture), writing (the actual writing of the notes or subsequent writing based on the notes) and speaking (posing questions, or oral reconstruction of the notes or discussion based on the notes).

Ideas from practitioners

Learning to take notes

Students' ability to take clear, comprehensible notes for study and test preparation has to be seen as a key element in their academic success. Even though there is no consistent correlation between specific types of notes or quantity of notes and comprehension scores, as a teacher I have consistently seen a positive effect of note-taking instruction on student participation and an increase in student responsibility in trying to understand. I have seen advantages of providing illustrative strategies via interventions *while* students are actively engaged in listening to academic lectures – not before or after. Interventions – short instructional episodes during a language processing experience – provide a way for students to focus their attention and learn specific note-taking strategies that promote comprehension. I also think that the note-taking interventions improve long-term memory during and after listening.

Jeanette Clement, author, Pittsburgh, US

Note-taking is a commonly used selective listening task, and one with a high degree of **face validity** (i.e. it is recognised as having practical value in the real world) and **psychological validity** (i.e. it is recognised by learners as reflecting their listening ability). For purposes of developing students' selective listening ability, instructors may cater their requirements in note-taking, such as writing down certain words or phrases, copying material on board in appropriate places in their notes, listing topics, or labelling parts of their notes. Examples of different note-taking systems that are widely taught are provided in Table 9.2. As noted by several researchers, however, it is not the note-taking itself that fosters increased listening ability but the preparation for note-taking, and the follow-up reconstruction and review activities based on the learner's own notes (cf. Clement, 2007; Flowerdew and Miller, 2010).

An important aspect of selective listening is the **pre-listening** portion of the instruction. Pre-listening is a stage of instruction designed to prepare students for listening. This phase may consist of a short activity to preview upcoming vocabulary or concepts or discourse frameworks that will help students engage with the listening extract.

Prior to listening, the class can discuss pictures, photos or cartoons that may pique interest in the listening topic and provoke some predictions about the extracts. The teacher can also elicit what students already know about the topic or add a personal experience to pique interest. Or, to

Table 9.2 Note-taking functions, goals, techniques

NOTE-TAKING FUNCTIONS	NOTE-TAKING METHODS	NOTE-TAKING TECHNIQUES
Retrieval	*Outlining:* showing macro–micro relationships	Indentation, spacing, charting, review (e.g. Cornell method)
Storage	*Linear:* showing sequencing of presentation	Key words, sequencing, abbreviations (key word method)
Application	*Matrix:* showing connectivity and relevance	Graphic imagery, connectives, personalisation (e.g. Mind Maps scheme)
Language learning	*Task:* completing explicit activity	Group collaboration, reconstruction, question answering (e.g. Contemporary Topics system)

promote interest in the topic, the teacher may provide a short list of provocative questions (such as *Do you agree or disagree with the following statements? . . .*) on the upcoming topic to help activate schemata and emotions related to the listening extract.

Any of these activities, alone or in combination, may serve to activate the background knowledge students will need to listen well. Effective pre-listening activities heighten the degree of relevance for listening, which fuels motivation.

Ideas from practitioners

Incorporating pre- and post-listening steps

It is unfair to plunge students straight into the listening text, even when testing rather than teaching listening comprehension, as this makes it extremely difficult for them to use the natural listening skills (which we all use in our native language) of matching what they hear with what they expect to hear and using their previous knowledge to make sense of it. So before listening, students should be 'tuned in' so that they know what to expect, both in general and for specific tasks.

Although listening *per se* takes place while students are actively processing texts, the pre-listening and post-listening stages of listening are vital. Pre-listening activities help students tune in to what they're going to hear. These are essential – otherwise, students are just listening 'cold', which can be very discouraging. Post-listening activities help students structure what they have heard and exercise their memories in the L2. So, like a lot of teachers, I usually think of listening practice as having three phases: pre-listening, while listening, and post-listening.

Mary Underwood, author, Surrey, UK

9.4 Interactive listening

Interactive listening refers to listening in a collaborative conversation. Collaborative conversation, in which learners interact with each other or with native speakers, is now well established as a vital means of language development and as a benchmark of listening performance. Its potential benefits seem to be both in 'forcing **comprehensible output**', that is, compelling the learner to formulate ideas in the target language, and in 'forcing negotiation', that is, leading the learner to come to understand language that is initially not understood. (See Chapter 8 for discussion of these concepts.)

Learners acquire new linguistic forms (syntactic structures, words and lexical phrases) as a product of attending to them in the communicative contexts that collaborative discourse provides. Because learners frequently experience difficulty in producing accurate forms, collaborative discourse provides an ideal opportunity to attend to and query target forms that are necessary to arrive at meaning (Long and Robinson, 1998).

Concept 9.3 **Interactive listening**

Interactive listening refers to a type of conversational interaction in which the listener takes a leading role in understanding, through providing feedback, asking questions and supporting the speaker.

In language teaching, selective listening refers to listening with a planned purpose in mind, often to gather specific information to perform a task. In classroom language learning situations, the primary opportunity for collaborative conversations is learner–learner interaction. In order for learners to benefit from this NNS–NNS interaction, it is important to incorporate necessary learning elements. First, there needs to be a **communicative task**, that is, a tangible outcome of the interaction, and therefore a problem that requires negotiation of linguistic form to achieve that outcome. Collaborative tasks usually require some negotiation and clarification of meaning in order to arrive at an outcome, although real-world communicative outcomes may be indirect and unstated. For pedagogic purposes, tasks often need to be contrived to some extent (i.e. they are structured as 'pedagogic tasks') in order to make problems explicit and outcomes expressed. Commonly used text–task combinations are information gaps for pair exchange or ambiguous stories for reconstruction (e.g. Cullen, 2008).

Ideas from practitioners

Learning social procedures

Effective listening involves social procedures that the person must use to become an equal partner in conversation – such as backchannelling, providing obligatory responses in conversation routines, and initiating repair when there is a communication problem. Although exposure and indirect feedback sometimes help, explicit instruction is often needed to formulate these strategies and provide learners feedback on their use. There are a few things teachers can do:

- Focus on the use of explicit responses to understanding problems (e.g. metalinguistic comments (such as *I'm not sure I understand this*) and the use of partial repetition to distinguish the elements that were not understood. (Speaker: 'It's the perfect antidote to depression...' Listener: 'Perfect *antido*...?')
- Encourage learners to formulate hypotheses, to develop high inferencing capacities, to stay active in the struggle for understanding.
- Raise awareness of issues of 'face' in conveying problems in understanding and in mitigating face threats to gatekeepers.
- Encourage learners to take initiatives in topics as a way of reducing some frame and schema difficulties in understanding.

Katharina Bremer, sociolinguistics researcher, Heidelberg, Germany

In classroom settings, **two-way collaborative tasks** are widely used to promote interactive listening skills. Use of structured communicative tasks involving two-way communication promotes listener control of conversations, including regulating turn-taking, and seeking feedback through clarification, and confirmation checks (Lynch, 1996). According to Ellis (2002), the key characteristics of an effective two-way collaborative task are (1) a **primary focus on meaning** (rather than on language form) (2) the learner selecting from a menu of linguistic resources needed for task completion, and (3) a tangible outcome (which can be evaluated for its correctness or appropriateness). These features are seen as necessary in promoting learner **uptake** during the task, rather than mere completion of the task.

Here is an example of interactive listening involving two students of French as a foreign language performing a pedagogic task. Note that the comprehension problem is left unsolved.

Speaker 1. *Un passage étroit, à la métro?*
  A narrow passage, at the subway?

Speaker 2. *C'est 'dans' la chose.*
   It's 'in' the thing.

Speaker 1. *Dans la métro ou à la métro?*
   In the subway or at the subway?

Speaker 2. *Non, c'était quelque chose comme à l'endroit, ou à la métro.*
   No, it was something like at a place, or at the subway.

Speaker 1. *Je pensais que c'était, je marchais dans un passage étroit à la métro.*
   I thought it was, I was walking down a narrow passage at the subway.

Speaker 2. *Un passage à l'étroit dan le métro* . . . in the . . . in the subway . . .
   A narrow passage in the metro . . . in the . . . in the subway . . .

Speaker 1. *À la métro.* I just don't know.
   At the subway, I just don't know.

Speaker 2. *Mais c'est comme 'dans'.*
   But it's like 'in'.

Speaker 1. OK. Anyway, *on va continuer.*
   OK. Anyway, let's continue.

(From Watanabe and Swain, 2007)

Though there are inherent advantages to interactive listening, not all interaction or collaboration is guaranteed to lead to effective learning or to improved attitudes about listening. Teachers who have worked extensively with interactive listening have formulated schematic frameworks for evaluating the success, and for leading learners toward more successful and rewarding interactions. For example, Lynch (2001b) has developed a framework (Achieving Communicative Outcomes, ACO) that focuses on ways that learners come to achieve better outcomes in problem-solving negotiations, particularly in academic settings in which students work together to discuss complex issues (see Table 9.3).

In the following extract we can see how two learners engage in a negotiation:

Lian. I'm sorry I didn't catch + what you mean by 'the shock' + that's the first question + and the other one is I am not clear + who organises the transfer between companies + so + there are two questions here

Kazu. um + + for the first question + 'shock'?

Lian. yes I didn't catch what 'shock' means here

Kazu. 'shock'?

Lian. 'after the shock'

Kazu. it's the oil shock + in 1973

Lian. I don't + +

Kazu. sorry + I didn't mention it?

Teacher. perhaps I can + just ask you to explain the word 'shock' because there may be others in the room who don't understand it + + you've explained 'shock' by saying 'it's a shock' + can you explain it in any other words?

Table 9.3 Achieving communicative outcomes

1. *No problem*. A problem exists but is not identified by either the sender or the receiver.

2. *Non-negotiated solutions*
   a. *Unacknowledged problem.* A problem is identified by the receiver but not acknowledged by the sender.
   b. *Abandon responsibility.* A problem is identified by the receiver and acknowledged by the sender, but the sender does not take responsibility for solving the problem, either by saying they will skip it, leave it, never mind it or forget it, or by telling the receiver to choose any location or path.
   c. *Arbitrary solution.* A problem is identified by the receiver and acknowledged by the sender, who then makes an arbitrary decision about some defining feature of the location or path. The key element here is not accuracy but the arbitrariness of the decision, which does not attempt to take the receiver's world into account or to make the receiver's world match the sender's.

3. *Negotiated solutions*
   a. *Receiver's world solution.* A problem is identified and acknowledged by the sender, who then tries to find out what is in the receiver's world and uses that information to instruct the receiver, based on the receiver's perspective.
   b. *Sender's world solution.* A problem is identified and acknowledged by the sender, who then instructs the receiver to make the receiver's world match the sender's, ignoring whatever information the receiver provides which does not fit the sender's perspective.

Source. Based on Lynch (2001b).

> *Kazu.* in any other words? + the oil shock?
>
> *Teacher.* Lian doesn't know what the word 'shock' means
>
> *Nobu.* prices
>
> *Kazu.* ah yes + the oil prices increased at one + very alarming rate + so as a result + companies have to change their structure + in the 1970s + + + ok

Lynch uses this ACO framework, not only for assessment, but for teaching: learners come to see how they can take responsibility for achieving desirable outcomes in their classwork.

9.5   Extensive listening

Extensive listening refers to listening for an extended period of time, while focusing on meaning. Extensive listening can include **academic listening,** also known as **listening for academic purposes** and **sheltered language instruction**. It can also include extended periods of listening in the target language outside of classroom settings, paralleling what in reading instruction is referred to as 'reading for pleasure'.

Concept 9.4 Extensive listening

Extensive listening refers to listening for several minutes at a time, staying in the target language, usually with a long-term goal of appreciating and learning the content. Extensive listening includes academic listening, sheltered language instruction, and 'listening for pleasure'.

For extensive listening to be successful for an L2 learner, it is necessary for the learner to have access to listening input that can be understood reasonably well on the **first listening**. It is important to aim for high levels of learner satisfaction and comprehension, providing whatever preparation is needed (e.g. prior reading, pre-learning of key vocabulary) and providing additional support (e.g. graphics, subtitles, help menus) during the actual listening process (cf. Kanaoka, 2009; Clement *et al.*, 2009; Camiciottoli, 2007).

Incorporating these support elements into academic listening has been described under the nomenclature of '**sheltered instruction**', in which learners are literally protected from being overwhelmed by too much information to process effectively. One comprehensive system is the Sheltered Instruction Observation Protocol (SIOP). The SIOP guides teachers in several steps to support students in an extensive listening environment:

- Lesson preparation:
  - ○ Check that content objectives are clearly defined for students.
  - ○ Check that language objectives are clearly defined.
  - ○ Check that content concepts are appropriate for age, educational background.
  - ○ Provide supplementary materials to prepare students.
  - ○ Adapt content to level of student proficiency.
  - ○ Prepare meaningful activities that integrate lesson concepts with language practice.
- Building background:
  - ○ Link concepts to students' background and relevant experience.
  - ○ Review past learning to link to new concepts.
  - ○ Emphasise key vocabulary.
- Comprehensible input:
  - ○ Accommodate speaking style for English language learners.

- o Be sure to explain or demonstrate all academic tasks.
- o Use techniques to supplement language, graphics, demonstrations, gestures.
- Strategies:
  - o Promote student questioning strategies during the lesson.
  - o Use scaffolding techniques focusing on learning of content.
  - o Use two-way questioning during the lesson to check comprehension.
- Interaction:
  - o Provide abundant opportunities for interaction.
  - o Link oral language development to the lesson.
  - o Use multiple grouping configurations to assure collaboration.
  - o Be sure to employ ample wait time.
  - o Clarify key concepts repeatedly.
- Practice/Application:
  - o Be sure to have hands-on materials and/or manipulatives for students to practise using new content.
  - o Prepare follow up activities that allow students to apply new content and language skills.
- Lesson delivery:
  - o Check that content objectives are clearly supported by lesson delivery.
  - o Aim to have students engaged 90 per cent-plus of the period.
  - o Check that pacing of the lesson is appropriate to students' ability levels.

(Based on Echevarria *et al.*, 2008)

Whether extensive listening is done in an academic context or in an autonomous learning context (e.g. as homework or in a learning lab), this form of listening practice is useful for improving automaticity in oral language processing. As Brown *et al.* (2008) note, extensive listening is also valuable for building confidence and simply enjoying listening in the target language, and for experiencing 'knock-on effects' such as indirect pronunciation and intonation practice, and providing rich content for projects and presentations.

Extensive listening is generally considered appropriate for all students above a beginner level (Waring, 2010). Table 9.4 provides an outline of an Extensive Listening (EL) approach.

An important aspect of teaching extensive listening is the need to provide **comprehension strategy** instruction so that learners can avoid becoming overwhelmed by the quantity of input and so that they can get back on track when they are experiencing comprehension difficulties. Researchers in both reading and listening have derived a small number of principles to guide comprehension strategy instruction. (See Table 9.5.)

Table 9.4   Guidelines for an EL programme at intermediate and advanced levels

Intermediate. EL should be a significant part of language instruction	*Advanced*. EL should be a major aspect of language learning
• Listening to long graded texts (e.g. graded readers)	• Watching movies, television (with subtitles as necessary)
• Watching easy movies or easy television broadcasts with subtitles	• Radio programmes and podcasts
• Listening to easy songs	• Listening to songs
• Listening to simplified lectures	• Lots of natural conversation, including radio and television interviews, variety shows, dramas, new shows
• Repeated listenings are important	• Listening to authentic lectures
	• Lots of narrow listening (extracts or lectures on the same topic from different perspective)

Drawing on elements from all four of these approaches to comprehension strategy development, Block and Duffy (2008) recommend that teachers focus on the following comprehension strategies:

- *Predict*. Size up the text (story, lecture, etc.) in advance by looking for titles, pictures, captions; relating to prior readings, etc.
- *Monitor*. Activate and remind yourself of as many comprehension strategies as you can, make a plan for how to continue if you encounter difficulties; don't give up
- *Question*. Stop to re-listen and ask yourself questions about what you understand and what you don't understand
- *Image*. Construct images and mental pictures that help you visualise the story
- *Look back*. Go over sections that are unclear, keep thinking about the text after you stop listening
- *Infer*. Connect ideas based on what you already know; make good guesses
- *Find main ideas*. Pause to summarise what you understand so far, try to focus on the main elements of the lecture or story
- *Evaluate*. Formulate opinions about the story or lecture; evaluate your own emotional reactions to the text
- *Synthesise*. Consider all the facts, scene observations and parts of the dialogue that help you understand
- *Collaborate*. When possible, ask others who have heard or read the same text for their ideas, compare your understandings

Table 9.5   Principles of comprehension strategy instruction

METHOD FOR TEACHING COMPREHENSION STRATEGIES	DESCRIPTION	EXAMPLE
Experience–text–relationship method	Emphasises tying learners' own experiences with text cues to arrive at meaning (Au, 1979; Vandergrift, 1997)	(Accompanying the film *God Grew Tired of Us*, about Sudanese refugees) As you watch the story, think of similar events in your own life when you felt out of place. Note some key events or interactions in the story that bring up memories for you
K–W–L sequence ('What you Know', 'What you Want to know', 'What you Learned' from listening or reading)	Focuses listeners and readers on the process of learning from text (Ogle, 1986; Rubin, 1988)	(Accompanying audio clips of three job interviews for Apple Computer Company) Before you listen to the interview, think of three direct questions you would ask the interviewee. Think of one extra question that might surprise the interviewee
Reciprocal teaching approach	Prompts teacher and students to query each other around the four specific strategies: predicting, questioning, clarifying, summarising (Palinscar and Brown, 1984; Robbins *et al.*, 1999)	(Prior to watching a scene from *Mulholland Drive*) After you watch this scene, write down three questions to ask your classmates to make sure that they have understand the scene clearly
QAR method (Question–Answer Relationships):	Teaches learners to look for specific links concerning how the information is presented (Nix, 1983; Raphael and Wonnacott, 1985)	(Accompanying a scene in *Little Miss Sunshine*) In this scene Grandpa is trying to boost Olive's confidence. What does he say to show this?

9.6   Responsive listening

The notion of culturally influenced schemata are particularly important in L2 comprehension because L2 listeners continuously come in contact with assumptions and expectations that are in variance to their own. As we discussed in Chapter 3, comprehension problems arise not only when schemata are markedly different, but also when the listener is unaware of what these schematic differences might be. (For example, when I watch game shows in Japanese, an L2, I frequently encounter comic routines between a male host and female contestants that I would consider sexist in my own culture, but which are apparently considered acceptably playful and entertaining in the Japanese 'game show culture'. The time I spend figuring out what actually transpired in these 'sexist' encounters usually interferes with my comprehension of the actual content of the game.)

Concept 9.5   Responsive listening

Responsive listening refers to a type of listening practice in which the listener's response is the goal of the activity. The listener's response in this type of activity is 'affective' – expressing an opinion or point of view – rather than 'informational' – giving back facts based on what was heard.

L2 pedagogy has taken a significant interest in the notion of schemata and the activation of appropriate background knowledge for listening. Training methods typically incorporate pre-listening activities to raise awareness of cultural schemata that will be needed for comprehension, and follow-up discussion of cultural allusions, cultural preferences, etc. that were included in the listening text (Buck, 2001). Some methods stress the interrelatedness of gaining intercultural competence (awareness of cross-cultural factors in language learning and L2 use) and skill development (Sercu, 2004; Bremer *et al.*, 1996). Methods for teaching academic listening directly incorporate an awareness of cultural and content schemata in extended listening and recall (Flowerdew and Miller, 2010). These methods are consistent with general L1 educational methods for promoting use of schematic maps in developing critical thinking and understanding extended texts (e.g. Willingham, 2007).

One structured method of using ongoing listener response is a **paused task**. Listening task design using short inputs (typically one or two minutes long) and overt listener response have great benefits for listening training. There are known limitations to short-term memory that occur after about sixty to ninety seconds of listening – for listeners of all ages and backgrounds (cf. Florit *et al.*, 2010; Cowan, 2005). Because of these limitations, one minute may be an optimal 'training window' for new listening skills and strategies. When learners are listening beyond this time limit, it is often not clear what mental activities they are performing. Guided instruction and feedback becomes more difficult in extended listening activities.

One way to work within the limitations of short-term memory and still employ longer texts is to use paused tasks. Paused tasks require the

instructor to pause at specific points during the input phase of the activity
– either by pausing the audio or video or by stopping the narration if the
teacher is providing the input directly.

Ideas from practitioners

Using prediction tasks for responsive listening practice

Here is an activity I use often to encourage attentive listening, and to create
student-led interactions.

- *Purpose.* The purpose of this kind of task is to encourage students to make
  explicit predictions about what they will hear next.
- *Focus of the activity.* Students aim to comprehend enough of the story plot
  and characters to be able to predict.
- *Input.* A narrative with frequent pause points (I decide these in advance,
  based on the script), one pause after each fifteen seconds or so, at which
  points the students will be asked to make a prediction.
- *Procedure*
  - Read aloud or play a recording of the story
  - Stop at pre-set points (at least five per story) to have students say their
    predictions to each other for the upcoming parts (they also help each
    other understand things they may have missed)
  - Elicit some predictions at each pause point, then proceed with remain-
    ing part of the text (predictions are often in the form of opinions about
    a character).
- *Strategy focus.* Students make explicit predictions, without worrying if their
  prediction is exactly correct.
- *Outcome.* Statements of predictions for each pause point, interaction from
  all students.

Example (beginning level):

A folk tale

Once there was a very proud fox. One day, he was walking in the woods and
[(pause point) he stepped into a trap.] His tail was caught in the trap. He
pulled and pulled and [(pause point) he escaped], but his tail was left in the
trap. He was very sad that he lost his tail, but he was also very [(pause point)
proud.] When he went back to the pack, he said [(pause point), 'Look, every-
body, I cut off my tail. Life is great without a tail.'] All of the other foxes . . .

   This activity doesn't take much preparation and the students like it because
they all get to participate. (I have to set rules like not shouting out your prediction, of course.) And at the end I play the whole story, and this gives the
students a feeling of satisfaction.

Shireen Farouk, English teacher, member of Society of Pakistan English Language
Teachers), Lahore, Pakistan

9.7   Autonomous listening

Autonomous listening refers to a self-directed listening activity in which learners choose what to listen to, seek feedback on their comprehension, respond in ways they choose, and monitor their own progress. In effect, all **natural language acquisition** – acquisition that does not involve teachers or classrooms or online course – is autonomous listening. Within the autonomous listening paradigm, however, teachers can still influence the success of their students, particularly through instruction in a range of listening and learning strategies.

Concept 9.6   **Autonomous listening**

Autonomous listening refers to independent listening, without the direct guidance of an instructor. Autonomous listening can include all of the types of listening discussed – intensive, selective, extensive, interactive, responsive. The key is that the learner is in control of input selection, task completion, and assessment.

Ideas from practitioners

Promoting autonomy

At the core of autonomy lies the idea of control. However, since there are several ways in which learners can take control of their learning, the idea of autonomy is necessarily complex, involving both attitudes and skills internal to the learner and situational factors conducive to their development ... The idea of autonomy involves five hypotheses:

- Autonomy in learning is natural and available to all.
- Autonomous learning is more effective than non-autonomous learning.
- Autonomy is exhibited to different degrees by different individuals in different situations.
- Learners who lack autonomy are capable of developing it given appropriate conditions and preparation.
- The ways in which we organise teaching and learning exercise an important influence on the development of autonomy among our learners.

(See Benson, 2010, for elaboration on these ideas.)

Philip Benson, author, Hong Kong

For teaching purposes, two distinctions seem most important to make. First, if strategies are decisions that the user (the learner) makes, the mental decision or mental action that the learner undertakes must be psychologic-ally valid, that is, it must be clear to the learner when he or she is and is not engaging the strategy. Only psychologically valid strategies need to be con-sidered for instruction. Second, strategies that are associated with improved, or expert, performance are those that need to be identified, modelled and practised. Only success strategies need to be taught. Success strategies can be found through research of successful listeners – listeners who have made and are making progress in their listening ability (cf. Vandergrift, 2007). Where evidence of successful applications can be found, it is possible to teach strategies by way of indicating what the learner does (or should attempt to do) and what the teacher does to promote use of a particular strategy.

Ideas from practitioners

Developing lessons for autonomous listening

Films are obviously a rich source of listening materials for learners to use as they develop autonomous listening. Extension activities from interesting films – such as discussion or role play – usually work well, but I know students eas-ily get lost in the film when they're actually watching it. They need assistance and structure in order to stay involved in the story and learn language through it. For each movie I recommend for self-access, I include a transcript from selected scenes and develop a bank of exercises that students can use. Here are some from *What's eating Gilbert Grape?*

Selective listening: informational input to tasks

- Identify the characters: name, relationships, age, description, personality.
- Identify locations.

Global listening: thematic input to tasks

- Watch a scene silently and predict some of the language.
- Match script to specific scenes.
- Listening with questions to answer.
- Identify main topic of a scene.
- Speaking turn reorder.
- Occurrence of events reorder.
- Dialog gap. (Listen twice, then fill in the gap while watching with no sound.)
- Translate from native language subtitles to English.
- B only listens. A watches and listens and describes to B.
- Retell.

Brett Reynolds, teacher, Toronto, Canada

Within studies of strategy training (see Rost, 2006, for a review), there is broad agreement on the kinds of strategies that are frequently associated with successful listening. (This list is somewhat more general than the Block and Duffy, 2008, provided earlier in the chapter.) Five commonly recognised successful strategies are: (1) **predicting** information or ideas prior to listening (2) **making inferences** from incomplete information based on prior knowledge (3) **monitoring** one's own listening processes and relative success while listening (4) **clarifying** areas of confusion and (5) **responding** to what one has understood.

Ideas from practitioners

Exploring new ways of teaching

It seems clear that the methodology of teaching listening needs to change in a number of ways, in order to provide students with some opportunity to play an active role in their learning of the listening skill, and to engage with listening materials which interest and motivate them. Many of the problems associated with the traditional model of teaching listening can be lessened if teachers can find ways of allowing students to:

- Choose what they listen to.
- Make their own listening texts.
- Control the equipment (being in charge of replaying difficult parts of the listening text, for example).
- Give the instructions.
- Design their own listening tasks.
- Reflect on their problems in listening.

Goodith White, teacher trainer, author, London, UK

Summary: fresh instructional design

This chapter has outlined six types of listening practice, ranging from the most controlled to the most open. All six types are considered useful for language learning and acquisition, and some combination of the six types is likely to be most suitable for a given instructional context. Instructors need to consider variables such as age of learners, level of proficiency, cultural learning styles and expectations, class size and number of contact hours, and access to sources of listening input.

Many teachers who consult this chapter are likely to be working with assigned textbooks and course materials. Even when potentially constrained by assigned materials, teachers can find a multitude of ways to adapt the materials to include the types of listening practice outlined in this chapter (cf. Tomlinson, 2003).

The sampling of practitioner ideas in this chapter shows the variety of ideas that teachers come up with every day in the teaching of listening. Fresh ideas, particularly when situated within a principled framework of language learning, can be very motivating for students, and may help them find 'the right stuff' for their own language learning.

Chapter 10

Listening assessment

Assessment is an integral part of language teaching for three central reasons. First of all, assessment gives teachers appropriate starting and continuation points for planning instruction. Secondly, assessment provides an explicit means of feedback on learner performance and assists in goal setting for learners. Thirdly, assessment forms part of program evaluation, keeping the curriculum and teacher development on track.

In the area of listening, assessment is particularly important because receiving adequate feedback is essential for increasing the learner's confidence and for designing instruction that addresses learners' apparent weaknesses – or the weaknesses in the curriculum. This chapter offers guidance for integrating assessment into listening instruction, covering the following topics:

- types of listening assessment;
- factors that contribute to difficulty and influence performance;
- uses of oral interviews for assessing interactive listening;
- uses of descriptive scales to describe levels of listening proficiency;
- uses of portfolio style assessments for listening.

10.1 Defining the social and educational context for assessment

Our descriptions to this point have characterised listening as a complex ability with receptive, constructive, interactive, and transformative aspects. If we intend to assess listening in a comprehensive way, we need some means of describing a person's ability that reflects all of these aspects.

The inherent difficulty with assessing listening, of course, is that it is primarily a cognitive activity and is not readily observable by objective measures.

> **Quote 10.1** David Graddol on new forms of assessment
>
> In recent years, several developments in the practice of ELT have started to take ELT in new directions. The European language portfolio, for example, attempts to record a learner's experience and achievement in non-traditional ways. The Common European Framework of Reference for languages (CEFR) which attempts to provide a uniform approach to attainment levels across all languages, employs the concept of 'can do' statements rather than focusing on aspects of failure. Such developments illustrate the way that ELT practices are evolving to meet new social, political and economic expectations and I believe significantly depart from the traditional EFL model, even where that term is still employed.
>
> Graddol (2006)

This difficulty of direct access means that any assessment of listening must employ indirect measures, always at some degree removed from the actual psycholinguistic processes we wish to describe. The primary means of assessing listening is therefore to observe the various language activities that the learner is engaged in while listening, and to create qualitative descriptors and quantitative measures that have an acceptable degree of **validity** (cf. O'Sullivan *et al.*, 2002).

The concept of validity refers to an agreement on what is being assessed, both in broad and narrow terms. A starting point for considering validity is constructing a broad, contextual model for what is being assessed. Table 10.1 displays key variables in constructing a model for learning English, particularly factors that most impact choices of assessment.

When preparing forms of assessment and means of reporting, and making use of the results of assessment, it is important to understand the context in which the language is being learned, the goals of students in learning, and the potential social and political impact that any kind of **high-stakes assessment** will have on the students (Hamp-Lyons and Davies, 2008; 1997; Shohamy, 2001).

Table 10.1 **Models for learning English and choices of assessment**

EFL	ESL	EYL (ENGLISH FOR YOUNG LEARNERS)	GLOBAL ENGLISH/ENGLISH AS A LINGUA FRANCA (ELF)
Native speaker, usually American British, Australian	Native speaker– host country	*Target variety of English* Typically claims to use native speaker variety as target, but problems of teacher supply often make this unrealistic	Focus on international intelligibility rather than a specific variety; carry-over of some L1 characteristics; expected to maintain national identity through English; need for receptive skills in a range of international varieties
Focus on oral communication; emphasis on communication strategies for interaction with speakers of the TL	Equal focus on all skills, including literacy	*Skill focus* Young learners may not have L1 literacy skills, so emphasis is on speaking and listening	All skills including literacy; translation and interpretation skills often required; emphasis also on intercultural communication strategies
To communicate with native speakers of the TL, primarily; to satisfy entrance requirements for jobs, universities	To function in host country; sometimes to acquire a new nationality	*Primary purposes* To develop language awareness and prepare for higher levels of proficiency in later years	To get jobs in own country; to communicate with non-native speakers from other countries
Classroom focused; timetabled subject; occasional visits to English-speaking country	Host society provides immersion experience; some family members may provide model	*Learning environment* Often informal in kindergarten, pre-school or primary classroom; affective factors are important	Classroom is a key context but is insufficient. Private and home tutoring often used
Either local exams *or* international (IELTS, Cambridge ESOL, TOEFL, TOEIC)	Citizenship or visa exams	*Assessment* Usually local testing or informal assessment, though international exams are available	Existing exams often not appropriate; assessment often via assessment of ability to carry out tasks in English or by assessing knowledge taught through English (as in CEF framework)

Quote 10.2 Hamp-Lyons on contexts for assessment

The contexts and needs of classrooms and teachers are not the same as those of large scale testing. The large scale needs to discriminate, to separate, to categorise and label. It seeks the general, the common, the group identifier, the scaleable, the replicable, the predictable, the consistent, and the characteristic. The teacher, the classroom, seeks the special, the individual, the changing, the changeable, the surprising, the subtle, the textured, and the unique. Neither is better but they are different. We have only started to realise the extent of the difference in recent years. They grow from different epistemologies and we should not be surprised that they take us to different places...

Hamp-Lyons (1997)

10.2   Developing criteria and constructs

What is to be assessed can refer to both a **criterion** that represents a correlation with some standard of success and a **construct** that represents the underlying quality or trait that the assessment intends to measure. Criteria and constructs are related, but they do not technically refer to the same thing. The attempt to reconcile criterion-referenced assessment and construct-referenced assessment approaches has long been a source of concern in language assessment circles (cf. Weir, 2005; Fulchur and Davidson, 2007; Shohamy, 2001).

Concept 10.1   **Criterion and construct**

A **criterion-referenced test** is one that equates test scores with a statement about the behaviour to be expected of a person with that score to a specified subject matter. Most tests and quizzes written by instructors for their own students are criterion-referenced tests. The objective is simply to see whether or not the student has learned the material. Often criterion-referenced tests have a 'cut score': anyone scoring above this mark is said to have 'mastered' the material being tested. This 'cut score' can be called the 'criterion'.

In educational assessment, a construct is a specific aspect of intelligence, or competence, that a test purports to measure. If we believe that 'understanding conversational speech' is a construct, we are claiming that it is a unique characteristic of intelligence or ability that can be measured.

Work in psychometric testing in the 1950s instigated an investigation into the validity of psychological tests, and language tests can be considered as a kind of such psychological tests. Cronbach, regarded as the father of **construct validity**, argued that there are no absolutely valid tests of human abilities, only tests that have stronger or weaker inferential arguments about what is being tested (McNamara and Roever, 2006). In defining validity for language tests, two main types of arguments have been used: **criterion-referenced** or **construct-referenced**. (A third type, **consequential validity**, now increasingly important, first introduced by Messick – see Messick, 1995, for a review – concerns the effects of assessment on the learner's future learning path, which we discuss later in this chapter as 'washback'.)

Criterion-referencing arguments aim to predict that if a student does well on a given test (passes the criterion cut-off point), he or she will also exhibit the abilities and skills necessary to perform successfully on specific tasks outside of the specific test context, in the wider target domain. For language testing, this is the **Target Language Use**, or **TLU, domain**. An example of criterion referencing is the prediction that a person who performs well on the TOEFL listening test will *subsequently* perform well in listening to academic lectures at an English-medium university (Sawaki and Nissan, 2009). This type of criterion-referenced validity has come to be emphasised as part of a movement toward a more socially relevant **evidence-centred assessment** design (Mislevy and Risconscente, 2006).

Quote 10.3   William Hill on evidence-based assessment

I want us to begin to think about assessment in the same way as psychologists evaluate evidence-based therapy... Let's think about what we're doing in assessment as evidence-based teaching and learning – that we want to know we're accomplishing what we're intending to accomplish, and we're basing that on evidence.... Conceptualising classroom assessment in this way represents a departure from solely using student course evaluations or subjectively given grades to measure the effectiveness of a particular course. Gathering and using evidence of student learning is more valid than asking students if they're pleased with a course or a program of study as a whole.

Although these course exit surveys often include self-reports of learning, that doesn't objectively answer the question of whether they really learned anything. Students can be happy and not learn anything. We need a model of quality benchmarks... and begin to evaluate our own teaching and our own teaching programs in the same way as we assess our students... as underdeveloped, developing, effective or distinguished.

William Hill, Center for Excellence in Teaching and Learning, Kansas State University, Manhattan, KS, US

While criterion-referenced validity is mainly concerned with external measures and standards, **construct-referenced validity** is most concerned with direct evidence that a particular ability has been successfully demonstrated. (For example, if we believe that phonological discrimination is a valid construct, then we would want to design test items that allow the learner to demonstrate mastery of this ability.

Quote 10.4 Douglas Brown on the construct of listening

… listening is not simply a linear process of recording strings of language as they are transmitted to our brains. Consider the following list of what makes listening difficult:

- Clustering: attending to appropriate 'chunks' of language – phrases, clauses, constituents
- Redundancy: recognising the kinds of repetitions, rephrasing, elaborations, and insertions that unrehearsed spoken language often contains, and benefiting from that recognition
- Performance variables: being able to 'weed out' hesitations, false starts, pauses, and corrections in natural speech
- Colloquial language: comprehending idioms, slang, reduced forms, shared cultural knowledge
- Rate of delivery: keeping up with the speed of delivery, processing automatically as the speaker continues
- Stress, rhythm, and intonation: understanding the prosodic elements of spoken language
- Interaction: managing the interactive flow of language

Brown and Abewickrama (2010)

With any form of language testing, including testing of listening ability, we need to consider a combination of these approaches in order to claim validity. Any listening test will to some extent measure a learner's general language knowledge and general comprehension ability, in addition to the listening ability we seek to measure. This principle of necessary overlap in listening between **top-level (general) abilities** and **bottom-level (skill-specific) abilities** has been established in the language testing field, perhaps most clearly by Buck *et al.* (1998) and Tatsuoka (2009).

> **Concept 10.2 Rule space methodology**
>
> In psychometrics, the field concerned with the theory and technique of educational assessment, **Item Response Theory (IRT)** is a paradigm for designing and analysing scores on tests and questionnaires. IRT is based on the idea that the probability of a correct response to an item is a mathematical function of the test taker's parameters (true ability) and item parameters (difficulty and discrimination value of the item). **Rule-space methodology** is a statistical technique within IRT for identifying patterns of responses among test takers and defining traits or abilities that are measured by clusters of items.

Using a procedure called **Rule-Space Methodology (RSM)**, a statistical method for classifying examinees' test item responses on a test that are aimed at measuring different cognitive skills) Buck and Tatsuoka were able to isolate fifteen attributes for TOEFL test takers that accounted for virtually all of the **variance** in test takers' performance.

The **top-level attributes** (i.e. generalisable to all language skills) included:

- the ability to recognise the task by deciding what constitutes task-relevant information;
- the ability to use previous items to locate information;
- the ability to identify relevant information without explicit markers;
- the ability to make inferences and to incorporate background knowledge into text processing;
- the ability to draw on one's grammatical knowledge, lexical knowledge, sociopragmatic knowledge.

The **bottom-level attributes** (i.e. specific to listening) included:

- the ability to scan fast spoken text automatically and in real time;
- the ability to process dense information;
- the ability to understand and utilise prosodic stress;
- the ability to recognise and use redundancy.

Although this procedure of inferring underlying cognitive skills is not without problems (cf. Gierl *et al.*, 2005), it does help in identifying categories of skills that contribute to mastery of listening. Rost (2005) surveyed a range of published listening tests to identify categories of attributes that the tests were aiming to measure.

- *IELTS* (*Cambridge, British Council*). The International English Language Testing System is designed to assess the language ability of candidates who need to study or work where English is used as the language of communication.

- *TOEFL®* (*ETS*). The Test of English as a Foreign Language measures the ability of non-native speakers of English to use and understand North American English as it is used in college and university settings.
- *TOEIC®* (*ETS*). The Test of English for International Communication is produced by the Educational Testing Service. TOEIC test questions are based on real-life work settings in an international environment (meetings, travel, telephone conversations, etc.).
- *CPE* (*Cambridge*). The Cambridge Proficiency Examination for non-native speakers of English who aim to teach English to others or to study at a British university. Over 45,000 people in more than eighty countries.
- *CAE* (*Cambridge*). The Cambridge Certificate in Advanced English assesses communication ability for work or study purposes.
- *FCE* (*Cambridge*). The First Certificate in English is the most widely used of the Cambridge exams. It is used to measure the candidate's level of English for business or social contexts.
- *PET* (*Cambridge*). The Preliminary English Test is designed for learners at an intermediate level of English. It consists of reading, writing, listening and interview components.
- *KET* (*Cambridge*). The Key English Test is the easiest of the Cambridge exams. It measures a basic knowledge of reading, writing, speaking and listening.
- *ECCE* (*Michigan*). The Examination for the Certificate of Competency in English (ECCE) is a high intermediate-level general EFL exam. The ECCE emphasises communicative use of English rather than formal knowledge of English.
- *ECPE* (*Michigan*). The Examination for the Certificate of Proficiency in English is an advanced (C2) academic EFL exam. It is a test of advanced English language proficiency, reflecting skills and content typically used in university or professional contexts.
- *PTE General* (*Pearson*). The Pearson Test of English Academic is a computer-based academic English language test aimed at non-native English-speakers wanting to study abroad.

The survey identified five attributes that are commonly claimed to represent listening-specific attributes of language ability:

- *Phonological knowledge* of the sound system of the language, including phonemes, phonological rules, prosodic elements; ability to process speech quickly

- *Syntactic knowledge* of sentence- and discourse-level rules, structures, and cohesion; ability to perform accurate parsing quickly
- *Semantic knowledge* of words, lexical phrases, word categories, semantic relationships between lexical items; ability to perform semantic calculations (e.g. identifying synonyms and superordinate relationships between words) quickly
- *Pragmatic knowledge* of how fluent users of the language communicate, including use of formulaic expressions, gambits, indirectness, and ellipsis (omission of mutually understood information)
- *General knowledge* of commonly discussed topics and common human relationships, and the general knowledge of the world (history, geography, science, math), knowledge of how to utilise one's knowledge in testing situation
- (For the interview portion of tests) *interactive pragmatic knowledge*, including activation of phonological, syntactic, semantic knowledge in real-time interactions, real-time inferencing and updating representations; responding to interlocutor questions and feedback without lengthy pauses, employing **repair strategies for misunderstandings**.

10.3 Formulating a model of listening for assessment

Based on our description of components of listening involved in valid assessments, it is helpful to formulate a map to guide discussions of listening assessment. Figure 10.1 provides a general map of listening ability and shows its overlap with general language ability. Figures 10.2–6 provide additional detail for the components in the model.

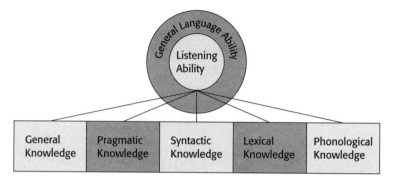

Figure 10.1 *General language ability and listening ability*. Listening ability is a sub-set of general language ability. Any assessment of listening ability will also be assessing general language ability

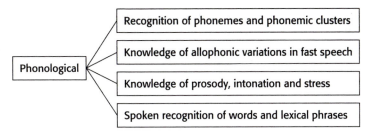

Figure 10.2 *Phonological knowledge* consists of knowledge of phonemes, allophonic variation, prosody, intonation, and stress. It also includes the application of this knowledge to recognise words in the stream of speech

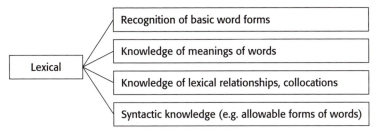

Figure 10.3 *Lexical knowledge* encompasses knowing the means of words and their relationships to other words and collocations

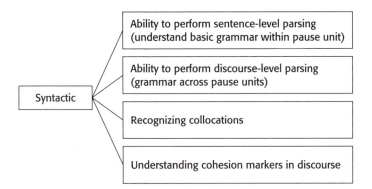

Figure 10.4 *Syntactic knowledge* is based on ability to parse speech at sentence and discourse levels

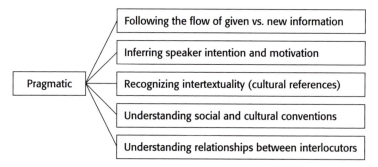

Figure 10.5   *Pragmatic knowledge* includes recognition of social dimensions in speech

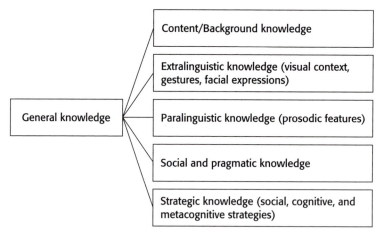

Figure 10.6   *General knowledge* includes knowledge about the world, including the ways that people communicate

10.4   Creating forms of assessment

Much as we developed the specifics of instructional design for listening (Chapter 9) based on research principles underlying language acquisition (Chapters 7 and 8), we need to describe forms of assessment based on principles of assessment of the underlying listening ability (sections 10.1–3). **Form of assessment** refers to the materials, including any media (audio, video, text), the general procedures and rubric for taking the test or participating in the assessment, and the means of scoring the assessment. Commonly used forms of assessment include the following:

Discrete item tests

- Multiple-choice questions following a listening text (scoring response right or wrong). An example (from Pearson Test of English) is shown in Figure 10.7.
- Open questions following presentation of a listening text (scoring questions on a scale of 'correctness' and 'completeness').

Task-based tests

- Tasks involving making an appropriate non-verbal action in response to a listening text.
- Closed task involving single response: An example (from UCLA, Korean Department) is shown in Figure 10.8.
- Open tasks involving multiple responses:
  - Tasks involving making an appropriate non-verbal action in response to a listening text. A sample (from Examenglish.com) is shown in Figure 10.9.

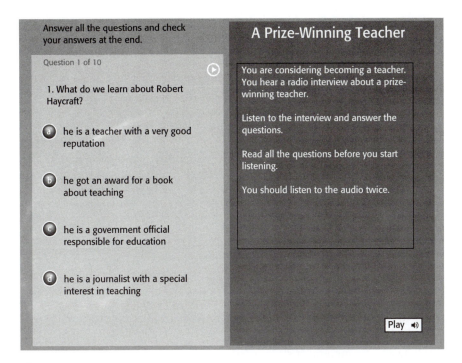

Figure 10.7   *Multiple-choice items following a listening text.*
Source. From the Pearson Test of English (© 2010 Pearson Education Ltd)

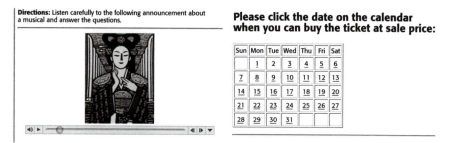

Directions: Listen carefully to the following announcement about a musical and answer the questions.

Please click the date on the calendar when you can buy the ticket at sale price:

Sun	Mon	Tue	Wed	Thu	Fri	Sat
	1	2	3	4	5	6
7	8	9	10	11	12	13
14	15	16	17	18	19	20
21	22	23	24	25	26	27
28	29	30	31			

Figure 10.8   *A closed task following a listening passage.*

Susan is telephoning a travel agency. Before listening to the conversation read the enquiry form carefully. Then listen and complete each gap with no more than three words.   **LISTEN ◄))**

Worldbridges Travel Agency Ltd. Enquiry form

Enquiry regarding holiday in

Number of people:

Kind of accommodation needed: Select ▼

Requirements

Price (£):

Location:

Customer's name:

Enquiry made in: Select ▼

When would Susan and her friends travel cheaper?

How far from the beach is the accommodation offered?

Who has already visited Greece?

What will Susan have to do before phoning Arnold again?

Figure 10.9   *An open task following a listening passage.*
Source. www.examenglish.com

Integrative tests

- Memory test following or during listening to an extract, e.g. taking notes or summarising of a lecture (scoring on a scale of accuracy and inclusion of facts and ideas).

- Dictation, complete or partial (scoring based on correct suppliance of missing words). A sample (from examenglish.com) is shown in Figure 10.10. This test simulates a listening portion in the CAE.)

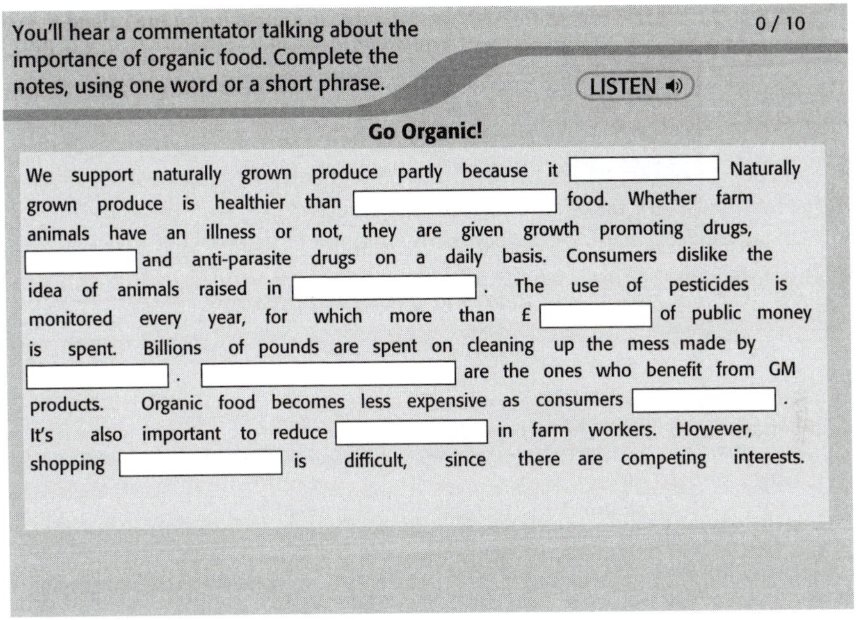

You'll hear a commentator talking about the importance of organic food. Complete the notes, using one word or a short phrase.

0 / 10

(LISTEN ◄»)

Go Organic!

We support naturally grown produce partly because it [＿＿＿＿＿] Naturally grown produce is healthier than [＿＿＿＿＿] food. Whether farm animals have an illness or not, they are given growth promoting drugs, [＿＿＿＿＿] and anti-parasite drugs on a daily basis. Consumers dislike the idea of animals raised in [＿＿＿＿＿]. The use of pesticides is monitored every year, for which more than £ [＿＿＿＿＿] of public money is spent. Billions of pounds are spent on cleaning up the mess made by [＿＿＿＿＿]. [＿＿＿＿＿] are the ones who benefit from GM products. Organic food becomes less expensive as consumers [＿＿＿＿＿]. It's also important to reduce [＿＿＿＿＿] in farm workers. However, shopping [＿＿＿＿＿] is difficult, since there are competing interests.

Figure 10.10 *An integrative test of listening.*
Source. englishexam.com (© 2010 englishexam.com)

- Communicative tests:
  - Written communicative tasks involving listening (scoring on the basis of successful completion of a task, such as writing a complaint letter after hearing a description of a problem).
  - Oral tasks involving listening (scoring on the basis of successful completion of the task, such as following directions on a map).

Interview tests

- Face-to-face performances with the teacher or another student (scoring based on a checklist of items, such as appropriate response to questions, appropriate use of clarification questions).
- Extended oral interviews (scoring keyed to a scale of 'native-like' behaviours, such as the Foreign Service Institute scale).

Self-assessment

- Learner rates self on given criteria, via questionnaires or checklists, during or following listening activities.

- Learner provides holistic assessment of own abilities via oral or written journal entries.

Portfolio assessment

- Learner is observed and evaluated periodically throughout course on performance in tasks and other class activities (see illustration box: Contemporary Topics); observations may be audio or video recorded.
- Portfolio may include any or all of the above types of objective and subjective measures.

Ideas from practitioners

Portfolio assessment

I have moved toward a portfolio style assessment in my academic listening courses. At one point I had used just objective tests at the end of each lecture as a measure of their progress, since I thought this would be more realistic preparation for when they entered actual university courses. Over time, I saw how this approach was demotivating: students were not engaging in class activities, only exerting any energy for studying for the test. In order to show that classroom activities did contribute to their success, I started using the activities as part of the assessment. Now I give the objective test about 40 per cent of the total score, but I use 'the portfolio' for 60 per cent of the student's grade. This includes a variety of things: participation in (and summaries of) group discussion, completion of notes, and follow up projects as part of the assessment. Since I've moved to this more rounded approach to assessment, I get much more participation in all activities, and I think the students get better overall results this way.

Cynthia Lennox, teacher and author, Pittsburgh, US

10.5 Adjusting factors that influence test performance

Assessment researchers have identified several factors that tend to influence listening test performance. Wagner (2010), Alderson *et al.* (2006), Brindley and Slatyer (2002) and others have demonstrated how the nature of the input (video versus audio, speech rate, complexity of input) and response type (item type and openness of response options) are likely to influence performance and interpretation of test results. Table 10.2 is a summary of findings in this area.

Table 10.2 **Factors influencing test performance**

FACTOR	DESCRIPTION	PREDICTION
Medium of the input	Video or audio-only presentation; accompaniment with graphics or text enhancements	Enhancements tend to improve test taker performance, such as video presentation, graphic cues, text subtitling or selective captioning
Nature of the input	Dialect, speech rate, length, background, propositional density, amount of redundancy	Unfamiliar dialect, faster speech rate, increased length and proposition density, decreased redundancy will influence test performance negatively
Nature of the assessment task	Use of visual context, amount of context given, clarity of instructions, availability of question preview, type of thinking processes involved	Lack of visual context, lessening of contextual information, ambiguous instructions, absence of question preview, requirement for higher-order thinking processes will influence test performance negatively
Individual listener factors	Memory, interest, background knowledge, motivation, readiness to take the test	Test taker with limited memory skills, limited interest in test topics or the test itself, limited background knowledge with test topics or the test itself, limited motivation to perform well, will negatively impact test performance

10.5.1 Modelling listener processes during assessment

Just as language comprehension involves integration of various 'stages' of processing, performance on tests involves an integration of stage-like processes. In a protocol analysis of test takers of the lecture portion of the TOEFL listening test, Jamieson *et al.* (2000) discovered various decision-making processes that test takers were able to monitor. For each stage, the researchers proposed underlying goal and cognitive processes that the test takers used.

Stage 1. Listening to the stimulus

- *Goal.* Listen to the stimulus (i.e. the two-minute mini-talk) and remember information in order to answer each question following the stimulus. (ETS now allows note-taking during the lecture.)
- *Process.* Represent in working memory any information in the stimulus that seems to be important.

- Variables that may affect this process:
  - ○ *Stimulus variables*. Length of lecture, syntactic complexity, density of information, lexical difficulty.
  - ○ *Listener variables*. Knowledge of the context of the task, knowledge of the language, attention, working memory capacity, background knowledge.

Stage 2. Listening to or reading each question

- *Goal*. Understand the questions and what is required for a response.
- *Process*. Identify the given and requested information in the question and represent in working memory the requested information.
- Variables that may affect this process:
  - ○ *Item variables*. Lexical difficulty, syntactic complexity, length.
  - ○ *Listener variables*. Knowledge of the context of the task, knowledge of the language, attention, working memory capacity, background knowledge.

Stage 3. Searching for the correct answer

- *Goal*. Retrieve information from stimulus that answers the question.
- *Process*. Search working memory for information in the stimulus that matches the information requested in the questions.
- Variables that may affect this process:
  - ○ *Stimulus variables*. Length of lecture, syntactic complexity, density of information, lexical difficulty.
  - ○ *Item variables*. Type of information, type of match, explicitness, main/supporting idea redundancy.
  - ○ *Listener variables*. Knowledge of the context of the task, knowledge of the language, attention, working memory capacity, background knowledge.

Stage 4. Identifying the correct answer

- *Goal*. Select the correct answer from the options given.
- *Process*. Identify an answer to the question by finding a match with the appropriate information from working memory and verifying that none of the other options is a better match.
- Variables that may affect this process:
  - ○ *Stimulus variables*. Length of lecture, syntactic complexity, density of information, lexical difficulty.
  - ○ *Item variables*. Type of information, type of match, explicitness, main/supporting idea redundancy, plausibility of distractors.

- *Listener variables*. Knowledge of the context of the task, knowledge of the language, attention, working memory capacity, background knowledge.

10.6   Listener preparation for listening tests

Because individual factors, such as motivation and familiarity with test formats, do affect test performance, a number of instructional approaches and even testing institutions are preparing guidelines to help students perform well on tests.

Educational Testing Service (ETS) publishes their own tips for students preparing to take the TOEFL test. Following is an extract related to preparation for the Listening portion. The purpose of providing this type of preparation for teachers is to allow teachers to expand their repertoire of teaching skills. Preparing students for high-stakes tests involves three major factors:

- *Self management*. An understanding of how to build and conserve mental, emotional, and physical energy and when to use this energy; the use of strategies for dealing with difficult, pressurised, or ambiguous situations.
- *Test-wiseness*. An understanding of the testing process and the underlying aims of each part of a test and each item within a test; strategies for answering questions efficiently.
- *Mastery of knowledge base*. An acquisition of the knowledge and skills required to perform well on the test.

Teachers and coaches of test takers can assist their students in all three of these areas. Although the content teacher's primary responsibility is in developing the learners' mastery of knowledge, the emotional and strategic components of test performance cannot be treated lightly. (I have been amazed on visits to testing seminars, in EFL contexts particularly, at the overwhelmingly high proportion of training that is dedicated to test-wiseness and self-management, seemingly at the expense of developing real knowledge in the area to be tested!)

10.6.1   Helping students prepare for the computer-based TOEFL Listening Test

What the section measures

Ability to understand conversations and talks in North American English.

About the section

- Section includes dialogues, short conversations, academic discussions and talks (mini-lectures).
- Points tested: main idea, supporting ideas, important details, inferences, order of a process, categorisation of topics/objects.

Test-taking strategies for each section

Use visuals accompanying test questions effectively. Two types of visuals:

- *Context-setting* visuals focus on what is said, not the visual.
- *Content-based* visuals may contain important content, therefore examinee should look at these visuals when listening.

Skill-building ideas for the classroom

Practise listening skills.

Focus on overall understanding, not analysis of sentences or word-by-word meaning:

- Practise inferencing (drawing a conclusion from evidence or reasoning based on information presented).
- Listen to non-academic material, such as radio, television and movies.
- Develop own questions and have discussions about the material.
- Summarise the material orally or in writing.
- Become accustomed to colloquial English.

Help students become familiar with different types of rhetorical patterns (e.g. steps in a process, categorising of topics).

- Teach textual cues (order – now, next, etc.; opposing ideas – conversely, however, etc.).
- Teach oral cues (stress, intonation, pauses).
- Listen to short excerpts from academic material:
  - Listen for main ideas and important details with and without taking notes.
  - *Beginning-level students.* Write what they hear and connect those ideas to formulate sentences.
  - *Intermediate to advanced students.* After listening to the material, break into groups and predict possible test questions.
  - *Advanced students.* Use notes to write short summaries.
  - *Very advanced students.* Summarise the material orally, exchange questions with other groups, and answer the questions, make this into an enjoyable activity, such as a game show.

Ideas from practitioners

Helping students prepare for tests

Students often experience anxiety in taking tests and as a result do not give their best performance. In order to help students do their best on tests, and to create a positive **washback effect** in instruction, it is useful to do four things: (1) allow the students to become familiar with the format of the tests they will take, including all subsections of the test; (2) simulate test conditions with a full current-version test administered as the actual test will be (e.g. via computer if computer-based), with actual time constraints; (3) go over the test results with the students, pointing out strategies for improving their performance; and (4) respond to any questions or concerns that students have about the test, scoring, and how the results are used. These steps tend to alleviate anxieties that students feel about tests.

In order to prepare test takers for either computer-based or paper-based tests, it is best to have a trial run, particularly in the case of listening tests involving video, in order to help the learner become familiar with the test format and the potential distractions involved in having to listen, view the computer screen, and respond more or less simultaneously.

David Conium, teacher trainer, Hong Kong

Ideas from practitioners

Helping students develop strategies for taking listening tests

Here are some strategies that I teach students for taking listening tests.

- *Read and predict*. Read the questions before listening. Predict answers based on what you know.
- *Get ready*. Have your pen ready to write before the recording starts.
- *Answer immediately*. As soon as you know the answer, write it down. Don't hesitate.
- *Be word-wise*. Listen for words in the questions and synonyms in the answers.
- *Focus your listening*. Don't listen for the gist. Focus on specific information for the test item.
- *Don't give up*. If you get lost, keep listening. You can get back on track.
- *Listen for pauses*. Pauses always mean something. They may tell us there's a change in topic or that the speaker is building up to an important moment.
- *Notes first*. If you have to take notes, just write key words. After you're done listening, review your notes right away and write full ideas from them.
- *Guess*. If you don't know, make a guess using the context.

JJ Wilson, teacher trainer and author, New Mexico, US

10.7   Assessing listening proficiency in oral interview tests

An essential element in assessing second language listening performance is evaluating a learner's ability in interactive settings in which goal-oriented oral communication is required. Because these settings often cannot be readily replicated for testing purposes, evaluators typically rely on some form of oral interview as a sample of the learner's oral and interaction ability. In an oral interview test (often called OPI, for Oral Proficiency Interview), the test candidate is placed in the role of the listener and is expected to respond (as quickly and completely as possible) to the interviewer's prompts, which are usually questions (e.g. *What kind of work do you do?*) or open-ended invitations to talk about suggested topics (e.g. *Tell me more about your job.*).

Although this provides an appropriate setting to test interactive speaking and listening, the notion of construct validity in these tests has been challenged. While the OPI ostensibly resembles natural conversation, it has been shown that such interviews lack the prototypical aspects of conversation, such as features of conversational involvement and symmetry. (See O'Loughlin, 2001, for a detailed comparison of direct, semi-direct, and indirect speaking tests.)

A. Brown (2004) described oral interview test interaction as a process of elicitation of specific output and compliance with more explicit routines than a normal interactive conversation would have. Increasingly, interview tests are being designed as testing tasks with the tasks being closely associated with specific situations and goal-oriented, and involving active participation of the language user.

May (2009) studied the features of accommodation and control used in oral interviews. In investigating the potential threats to validity of OPI testing, she found that key features of the interaction are perceived by the raters as mutual achievements, and it further suggests that the awarding of shared scores for interactional competence is one way of acknowledging the inherently co-constructed nature of interaction in a paired speaking test.

It is widely noted in OPI training that the interviewer-rater may not initially be aware of the constraints his or her own cultural background and expectations of normal, symmetrical discourse may impose on the sample of speech produced by interviewees. Specifically, critics point out that OPIs, as instances of cross-cultural interactions, often produce miscommunication due to misfits between politeness systems, which are deployed to assert or maintain face (House and Kasper, 1989; Nakatushara, 2008).

10.7.1   Accommodation and control features in oral proficiency interviews

As a means of raising awareness of discourse moves that contribute to perceptions of well formed oral discourse, Berwick and Ross (1996) have developed a descriptive system for the accommodation and control features that are observed in the OPI.

Accommodation

- *Display question.* The interviewer asks for information which is already known to the interviewer or which the interviewer believes the interviewee ought to know.
- *Comprehension check.* The interviewer checks on the interviewee's current understanding of the topic or of the interviewer's immediately preceding utterance.
- *Clarification request.* The interviewer asks for a restatement of an immediately preceding utterance produced by the interviewee.
- *Or-question.* The interviewer asks a question and immediately provides one or more options from which the interviewee may choose an answer.
- *Fronting.* The interviewer provides one or more utterances to foreground a topic and set the stage for the interviewee's response.
- *Grammatical.* The interviewer modifies the syntactic or simplification semantic structure of an utterance so as to facilitate comprehension.
- *Slowdown.* The interviewer reduces the speed of an utterance.
- *Over-articulation.* The interviewer exaggerates the pronunciation of words and phrases.
- *Other-expansion.* The interviewer draws on the perceived meaning of the interviewee's utterance and elaborates on words or phrases within the utterance.
- *Lexical simplification.* The interviewer chooses what is assumed to be a simpler form of a word or phrase which the interviewer believes the interviewee is unable to comprehend.

Control

- *Topic nomination.* The interviewer proposes a new topic by foregrounding information not previously introduced in the discourse. This typically leads to a question which may be introduced by informative statements and which requires no link to previous topic development.

- *Topic abandonment.* The interviewer unilaterally ends a current topic even though the interviewee may still show evidence of interest in further development.

- *Self-expansion.* The interviewer extends and alters the content of the interviewer's immediately preceding utterance so as to accomplish interview objectives.

- *Propositional.* The interviewer refocuses the interviewee's reformulation attention on a previously nominated topic or issue which has not produced enough language to confirm a rating for the interviewee.

10.8   Describing listening proficiency

An important consideration in assessment be it for quantitatively scored tests or qualitative evaluations of performance, is finding a way to describe and report a listener's current stage of ability in a manner that is comprehensive and comprehensible to teacher and learner alike – and to an administrator who may view or act on this assessment.

Holistic assessments are typically scales, often at five levels, with *plus* or *minus* at each level, creating fifteen discrete holistic ratings (e.g. 3–, 3, 3+). Each band on the scale consists of descriptors that depict some criterion on a target behaviour that the learner exhibits.

Proficiency scales can be very useful as part of a portfolio assessment. Scales have a built-in feedback mechanism in order to suggest to the learner the kinds of skills needed to graduate to the next level.

Proficiency scales for listening have been established by various educational foundations, including the Council of Europe (2010) the Centre for Applied Linguistics (2010) and DIALANG (see Alderson, 2005) in order to guide teaching and assessment across a wide range of educational contexts.

Table 10.3 displays working models of these proficiency scales, based on ongoing validation. The proficiency level descriptions in the scale provide relative criteria for comprehension of the spoken language. Each of the six base levels implies *control* of any *functions* and *accuracy standards* from the previous base levels. A 'plus level' designation (e.g. A1+ or B2+) is assigned when proficiency substantially exceeds one base skill level and does not fully meet the criteria for the next base level. The plus-level descriptions are therefore supplementary to the base-level descriptions.

A skill level is assigned to a person through a language examination or series of examinations or a series of long-term observations. Examiners assign a level on a variety of performance criteria exemplified in the descriptive statements. Therefore, the examples are intended to illustrate, but not to exhaustively describe, either the skills a person may possess or situations in which he or she may function effectively.

Statements describing accuracy refer to typical stages in the development of competence in the most commonly taught languages in formal courses. In other languages, emerging competence parallels these systems, but often with different details.

The term *native listener* refers to native speakers and listeners of a standard dialect. *Well educated*, in the context of these proficiency descriptions, does not necessarily imply possessing formal higher education. However, in cultures where formal higher education is common, the language-use abilities of persons who have had such education is considered the standard. That is, such a person meets contemporary expectations for the formal, careful style of the language, as well as a range of less formal varieties of the language.

Summary: fairness in assessment

This chapter has outlined the role of assessment in the teaching of listening, from the perspective of providing feedback to learners on their development of listening ability. The chapter considers notions of validity, objective testing of listening ability, interactive listening ability, and ways of describing listening proficiency holistically.

We first looked at ways of describing the social and educational contexts in which assessment is used, since assessment always influences the goals of instruction, and learner motivation, by way of the **washback effect**. We then looked at the notion of validity and how criteria referencing and construct definition can be used to establish an acceptable level of validity.

At the core of this chapter is the construction of a model of the listening construct that is used for assessment. We propose five strands – phonological, lexical, syntactic, pragmatic, and general – that should be considered in constructing listening assessments. We next considered types of items that are constructed for objective listening tests. Following this, we examined some of the issues involved in assessment of interactive listening.

The overarching intent of the chapter has been to show that assessing listening fully is not easy. It is at least as difficult as describing listening fully. We are most often describing and assessing just one aspect of this complex ability, and knowing this, we should be cautious in making claims about what listening assessments are actually measuring or describing. Portfolio-style assessments of listening, including measures of listening integrated with other skills (interviews, collaborative tasks, and interactive presentations in particular) and into larger tasks and projects (involving reading especially), are recommended because they provide evidence of performance in a wider range of contexts.

Table 10.3 Council of Europe scale

LEVEL   DESCRIPTOR

Proficient user

C1   Can understand with ease virtually everything heard or read. Can
        summarise information from different spoken and written sources,
        reconstructing arguments and accounts in a coherent presentation.
        Can express him/herself spontaneously, very fluently and precisely,
        differentiating finer shades of meaning even in more complex situations

C2   Can understand a wide range of demanding, longer texts, and recognise
        implicit meaning. Can express him/herself fluently and spontaneously
        without much obvious searching for expressions. Can use language flexibly
        and effectively for social, academic and professional purposes. Can
        produce clear, well structured, detailed text on complex subjects, showing
        controlled use of organisational patterns, connectors and cohesive devices

Independent user

B2   Can understand the main ideas of complex text on both concrete
        and abstract topics, including technical discussions in his/her field of
        specialisation. Can interact with a degree of fluency and spontaneity that
        makes regular interaction with native speakers quite possible without strain
        for either party. Can produce clear, detailed text on a wide range of
        subjects and explain a viewpoint on a topical issue giving the advantages
        and disadvantages of various options

B1   Can understand the main points of clear standard input on familiar matters
        regularly encountered in work, school, leisure, etc. Can deal with most
        situations likely to arise whilst travelling in an area where the language is
        spoken. Can produce simple connected text on topics which are familiar or
        of personal interest. Can describe experiences and events, dreams, hopes
        and ambitions and briefly give reasons and explanations for opinions

Basic user

A2   Can understand sentences and frequently used expressions related to
        areas of most immediate relevance (e.g. very basic personal and family
        information, shopping, local geography, employment). Can communicate
        in simple and routine tasks requiring a simple and direct exchange of
        information on familiar and routine matters. Can describe in simple terms
        aspects of his/her background, immediate environment and matters in
        areas of immediate need

A1   Can understand sentences and frequently used expressions related to areas of
        most immediate relevance (e.g. very basic personal and family information,
        shopping, local geography, employment). Can communicate in simple and
        routine tasks requiring a simple and direct exchange of information on familiar
        and routine matters. Can describe in simple terms aspects of his/her background,
        immediate environment and matters in areas of immediate need

Source. Table 10.3 from Council of Europe (2010), http://www.coe.int/T/DG4/Portfolio/?M=/
main_pages/levels.html, http://www.ealta.eu.org/, © Council of Europe

Table 10.4 Listening: self-assessment grid

A1	A2	B1	B2	C1	C2
I can recognise familiar words and very basic phrases concerning myself, my family and immediate concrete surroundings when people speak slowly and clearly	I can understand phrases and the highest frequency vocabulary related to areas of most immediate personal relevance (e.g. very basic personal and family information, shopping, local area, employment). I can catch the main point in short, clear, simple messages and announcements	I can understand the main points of clear standard speech on familiar matters regularly encountered in work, school, leisure, etc. I can understand the main point of many radio or television programmes on current affairs or topics of personal or professional interest when the delivery is relatively slow and clear	I can understand extended speech and lectures and follow even complex lines of argument, provided the topic is reasonably familiar. I can understand most television news and current affairs programmes. I can understand the majority of films in standard dialect	I can understand extended speech even when it is not clearly structured and when relationships are only implied and not signalled explicitly. I can understand television programmes and films without too much effort	I have no difficulty in understanding any kind of spoken language, whether live or broadcast, even when delivered at fast native speed, provided I have some time to get familiar with the accent

Section

III Researching listening

Section Introduction: Direct insight

The first two sections of this volume have aimed to define listening and describe effective approaches to teaching listening. This third section explores avenues of research for refining our definitions of listening and for personalising approaches to teaching listening. This section sets out frameworks for a range of exploratory research projects that can be carried out by readers directly. The central purpose of the projects in this section is to promote direct experience and insight concerning listener attitudes, behaviours, abilities, constraints, choices, and means of development.

Because some of the projects entail data gathering, collaboration with colleagues, and longitudinal perspectives, many readers will not be able to carry out these projects completely. However, even if the reader does not carry out the full steps in any research project, reflection on the project framework and procedures, and examination of sample data provided, is still likely to yield valuable insights.

Each of the project types starts with an overview and a series of initial questions for exploring the project topic. Following this series of questions are sample data or other resources that provide an overview of what is involved in conducting the project. Next, there is a set of specific steps and options for implementing the project. Finally, a concept related to the goal of the research is presented. It is important to note that the projects in this section emphasise concepts and applications rather than data analysis and computations. Additional resources for conducting research, performing quantitative and qualitative analyses, and for disseminating findings are provided in Chapter 14.

The projects in this section are organised according to orientation:

Chapter 11. Sociolinguistic orientations
11.1   Listener perspective
11.2   Listener participation

A key to conducting successful research is taking on a questioning orientation, asking progressively more precise questions. As Wicks *et al.* (2008) note, the process of inquiry requires, above all, a commitment to having a questioning perspective, and then *improving the questions* we wish to ask – *before* rushing to address them. Improving questions often means posing a simpler *series of sub-questions*, attempting to identify the simplest possible questions and hypotheses before proceeding with a research design.

Choice of methodology is of course a key concern in conducting any type of research. Cresswell (2009) points out the utility, particularly in language use and language education research, of employing mixed methods of inquiry. Combining quantitative and qualitative measures allows for triangulation, the possibility of seeing consistencies in observation. The goal of research then is not attempting to prove or disprove a particular hypothesis, but to enrich the inquiry process by seeing issues from complementary perspectives.

Sociolinguistic orientations

A sociolinguistic orientation to listening research is primarily concerned with the listener's role in any language use situation. What exactly is the listener doing? Does the listener have goals and plans? How is the listener formulating and enacting these goals and plans during the interaction? How are the participants influencing the listener? These are key questions that arise in a sociolinguistic orientation to research.

Because sociolinguistics is concerned with the relationship between language use and social factors, the projects in this section will explore such factors as setting, function and relationships between participants. Researching listening from a sociolinguistic perspective also concerns ways in which our cultural background influence how we listen. Specifically, we will want to ask how do listeners attend to, select, amplify, clarify, and possibly distort aspects of events as they listen and recall what they have heard.

The projects in this section explore (11.1) **listener perspective**, the notion that our cultural background provides certain schematic overlays that influence how we comprehend events and how we internally structure and report those events; (11.2) **listener participation**, the ways in which conversational encounters are co-created with listeners, who display various patterns of participation; (11.3) **listener response**, the options the listener chooses from during a listening event and how these responses shape the event, give meaning to it, and contribute to the listener's competence; (11.4) **listeners in cross-cultural interactions**, an exploration of ways in which L1–L1 interactions parallel and differ from L1–L2 and L2–L2 interactions.

11.1   Listener perspective

The purpose of this project is to explore the notion of listener perspective, which we have defined as the cognitive, cultural, and emotional influences on the way the a person listens: senses the world, categorises and codifies experiences. As was discussed in Chapters 3 and 4, a listener's perspective – which is formed through a personal history of background experiences – will strongly influence the way he or she attends to the input, participates, recalls what has transpired, and reports his or her version of events.

11.1.1   Initial questions

- Do we listen in different ways – with differing attention, focus, or effort – depending on the topic, the content, or the speakers involved?

- How do our life experiences and current interests affect the way we listen?

- How do we report what we have listened to? Do we attempt to depict our understanding accurately and completely, or do we reduce or embellish our understanding? Do we consciously or unconsciously distort what we have recalled?

- How is our way of reporting of our understanding affected by the audience?

11.1.2   Data sample: story recountings: *The Pear Stories*

The *Pear Stories* research is an ongoing project that explores ways that individuals comprehend and recall a story, a simple non-verbal narrative involving a bushel of pears (Chafe, 1980). This piece of data is a recall protocol of a subject who watched the short film *The Pear Story* and recounted what she saw. This sample is from Erbaugh (2010), focusing on comparisons among Chinese speakers.

In this data, notice the organisation: the shortness of each pause unit, the **paratactic sequencing**, and the number of false starts and self-corrections that occur in this kind of unplanned, spontaneous discourse. Also notice the style of editorialising of the speaker. She goes into descriptions of the story sequence, followed by interpretations, and evaluations of the way the story is presented. As we discussed in Chapters 3 and 4, we can see that the listener typically reports what was heard by weaving together different strands of information, interpretation, and judgements.

> Identity code: M12.
> Age: 22.
> Sex: female.
> Education level: university year 3.
> Spoken language during childhood: Chiu Chau.
> Spoken language during adolescence: Cantonese.
> Family language: Guilin Mandarin.

Abbreviations. BA, object marker; BEI, passive marker; BEI, passive marker; PFV, perfective verb aspect; CL, specific noun classifier.

Note. Following the researcher's conventions, there are four numeric indications of tone: (1) tone 1, high level, (2) tone 2, high rising, (3) tone 3, low dipping, (4) tone 4, high falling. There is **sandhi** in Chinese intonation – tone shifts depending on phonological context – but these are not indicated here.

1.1 開始是……我……
kai1shi3shi4 . . . wo3 . . .
it starts out . . . I . . .

1.2 開始是一在摘那個番石榴（=芭樂）
kai1shi4shi4zai4zhai na4ge4 fan1shi2liu4(=ba1le4)
starts out [someone] is picking those guavas

1.3 這樣我覺得拍得很好。
zhe4yang4wo3jue2de2pai1de2hen3hao3
this way I think was staged very well

1.4 那個光線……嗯，
na4ge4guang1xian4 . . . en
that light . . . um

射過來那種像發射出來那種光線。
she4guo4lai2na4zhong3xiang4fa1she4chu1lai2na4zhong3guang1xian4
shining over those kinds of rays of that kind of light

1.5 給人家那種很明朗，
gei3ren2jia1na4zhong3hen3ming2lang2
gives people that kind of very clear brightness

很快……感覺那種。
hen3kuai4 . . . gan3jue2na4zhong3
very quickly . . . feel that kind of

1.6 好像農人收獲以後，
hao3xiang4nong2ren2shou1huo4yi3hou4]
it looks like a farmer after picking the crop

他那種愉快的心情在摘。
ta1na4zhong3yu2kuai4dexin1qing2zaizhai
he has that kind of happiness in his heart while he's picking

1.7 然後，他就……把……
ran2hou4, ta1jiu4 . . . ba3 . . .
and then, he just . . . BA passive . . .

摘過的放下來，倒出來。
zhai1guo4defang4xia4lai2, dao4chu1lai2
what he's picked he sets down, pours out

1.8   後來, 就⋯⋯遠遠聽到⋯⋯
　　　hou45lai2, jiu4 . . . yuan2yuanting1dao4 . . .
　　　and then, just . . . from a distance we hear . . .

　　　有一種聲音, 好像是鳴⋯⋯鳴叫聲。
　　　you3yi4zhong3sheng1yuin, hao3xiang4shi4ming2 . . . ming2jiao4sheng1
　　　there's a kind of sound, it sound's like birdsong . . . sounds of birdsong

1.9   叫不久了, 在⋯⋯不⋯⋯不遠的地方,
　　　jiao4bu4jiu3le, zai4 . . . bu4 . . . bu4yuan2dedi4fang
　　　[the birds] sing not very long, and from . . . not . . . not far away

　　　就有一個人牽著一頭小牛出來。
　　　jiu4you3yi2ge4ren2qian1zheyi45tou2xiao3niu2chu1lai2
　　　there's a man leading CL little calf comes by

1.10   他就把牛⋯⋯牛走過去。
　　　ta1jiu4ba3niu2 . . . niu2zou3guo4qu4
　　　he just BA calf . . . calf walks on by

1.11   不過, 牛看到那個水果,
　　　bu2guo4, niu2kan4dao4na4ge4shui3guo3
　　　but still, the calf sees that fruit

　　　牠就很想吃。
　　　ta1jiu4hen3xiang3chi1
　　　it really wants to eat it

1.12   牠一直回頭要吃。
　　　ta1yi4zhi2hui2tou2yao4chi1.
　　　it keeps turning its head back, wanting to eat

1.13   那個人就不給牠吃。
　　　na4ge4ren2jiu4bu4gei3ta1 chi1
　　　that man just won't let it eat

1.14   把牠拉過去了。
　　　ba3ta1laguo4qu4le
　　　BA it pull over go PFV

1.15   嗯, 那個人就把東西倒上去繼續摘呀。
　　　en, na4ge4ren2jiu4ba3dong1xidao4shang4qu4ji4xu4zhai1ya
　　　um, that man just BA things pour out and keeps on picking

1.16   結果, 我覺得它音響效果很好呀。
　　　jie2guo3, wo3jue2deta1deyin1xiang3xiao4guo3hen3hao3ya
　　　and so, I think, the sound effects were really good

1.17   他上那個樓梯的聲音都很清楚。
　　　ta1shang4na4ge4lou2ti1desheng1yin1dou1hen3qing1chu3
　　　the sound of him going up that ladder is very clear

1.18   再後來, 有一個小孩子騎單車來。
　　　zai4hou4lai2, you3yi2ge4xiao3hai2qi2dan1che1lai2
　　　and later, there's a little boy who comes in riding a bike

1.19 嗯，他騎單車來。
en, ta1qi2dan1che1lai2
um, he comes riding a bike

1.20 他就看到有人在摘。
ta1jiu4kan4dao4you3ren2zai4zhai1
he just sees that there's a man picking [fruit]

1.21 他覺得那個人不會注意到他，
ta1jue2dena4ge4ren2bu2hui4zhu4yi4dao4ta1
he thinks that man won't notice him

就聽下來。
jiu4ting1xia4lai2
just hear him

1.22 要......嗯，大概想要那個番石榴。
yao4 . . . en, da4gai4xiang3yao4na4ge4fan1shi2liu4
wants . . . um, probably wants those guavas . . .

(Protocol continues for forty-four turns; see Erbaugh, 2010, for full transcript.)

11.1.3 Project plan

You will be working with audio or video-recordings of individuals recalling a story or event, similar to the 'pear stories' narrative in the data sample. After you record the data, you will be examining the recall protocol for evidence of listener perspective: framing (how they present the event), organisation, comparisons, editorial opinions, emphases.

- Obtain a clear audio or video recording of an event, such as a story being enacted or news report, or a short narrative film. For initial research purposes, it is preferable to use a film with minimal spoken language. In fact, in this project you are not testing verbal comprehension or retention, so you may wish to use a silent film as input, such as *The Pear Story* (referenced above and available on line: search 'Pear Stories' video.). Aim to have at least a three-minute segment for listener to hear, and no longer than six or seven minutes.

- Find two or more listeners who are willing to watch or listen to the recording and report what they saw or heard. They need not **take notes**, and should not feel under any particular pressure to **recall** details or conform to particular standards of correctness. Before you play the extract, give only a short description of what the listener will see and hear, or just a brief introduction. (For example, *This is a story about a man who's picking pears.*)

- Play the recording of the extract just one time. When the extract is over, ask your listener one or two **open-ended questions** such as *Tell me what* *the story is about* or *What do you remember about the story?* Avoid asking specific probing questions about content, as this provides too much structuring by the interviewer, and may signal your preferences for **framing** the listener's **perspective**. Record what each listener says, either by written notes, or preferably by audio and video recording so that you can go back to analyse later.

- Compare transcriptions. Are there differences in what the two listeners noticed in the story or what they emphasised and chose to report? Are there differences in organisation? What evaluative statements did the listeners make? How did the listeners differ in their listening styles or reporting styles?

- To what extent can you see evidence of a listener perspective? (If you have multiple listeners from a similar linguistic or cultural or personal background) Are you able to see any patterns of common perspectives among listeners?

- Based on your subjects' responses, what evidence do you see of listener perspective? What cues in the language itself indicate internal processing by the listener? What role does cultural or educational or language background seem to play in the listener's responses?

Research technique   Coding of introspection protocols

An interview protocol is a term used in social sciences for the spoken language data that is collected as part of a study. It is called a protocol because it is intended to follow specific replicable procedures, to improve the validity of the information collected. Interviews should be conducted only with the clear consent and voluntary participation of the subjects. (See the sample consent form.)

After we record our interviews, it is important to transcribe and analyse them. When we analyse a recall protocol from a listener, we can do a systematic coding, line by line (or according to whatever units we are interested in) in order to identify the subject's discourse choices. We can begin with an established system of **discourse coding**, and then modify the system as needed. For the coding of a story recall protocol, here is an initial list (based on Norrick, 2008):

- F reporting a fact or event (from the story).
- R reporting emotion or showing rapport or conflict (with characters in the story).
- A analysing how the story was told or how the events took place.
- C monitoring cognitive and affective states.
- E elaborating on something tangential (that was cued by an event in the story).

Listening research tool   Research consent form

This is a sample oral consent form that is used in social research interviews. It contains maximum detail about purpose of the research, nature of volunteering, and protections for the interviewee. For L2 research, the consent instructions should be given in the interviewee's L1.

Oral consent script

Thank you for expressing interest in my work. Before we can get into the interview, I need to go over some things as mandated by . . .

Everyone who does research involving people, instead of books, or films, has to follow some rules so that . . . can be sure that the researcher is conducting research in a responsible way . . . has established these rules so that the people who are involved in the research understand what the researcher is doing, and why and what any possible risks and benefits to them might be. These rules arose from concerns regarding work which might harm or manipulate people.

As such, I want to let you know some very specific things about my work. As you know, my name is . . . and I am . . . As you also know, I would very much appreciate it if you would be willing to take part in my research.

I want you to know that involvement in the study is voluntary. If, at any time, you no longer wish to continue, you have the right to withdraw from the study, without penalty, at any time up until the study has ended. Also, please let me know if you have any questions at any point in the interview about what we are doing here and I will be happy to explain anything in greater detail if you wish.

My research is about . . . I am interested in learning more about . . . You will be asked to take part in a . . . time . . . interview. All information will be kept confidential. This means that I will assign a number to your responses, and only I will have the key to indicate which number belongs to which participant. In any articles or books I write, if I refer to you or your information I will either use a number or a made up name for you. I will make every effort to change or generalise details so no one reading the work can identify you from your remarks or the stories you tell me about your practice.

For anyone who wants to be identified by name, I will list people's names in an acknowledgement section of any article or book I write. For those who do not want to be identified at all I will simply say something like 'and thank you to all of the other people who participated in this research.' Please let me know by the end of this interview if you want me to list your name in the acknowledgement section or not. Please note that you can change your mind, either about being listed or not listed, up until the final draft of any manuscript I write.

The benefit of this research is . . . This is also an opportunity to share and learn about. . . . You may also learn something new about . . . as part of the interview. The research we are doing should help us to . . .

There are a few risks, as well. You may learn something about yourself that is a surprise. You may think that I have understood you incorrectly. In order to minimise this possibility, and to support work that is a collaborative undertaking between respondent and researcher, I will send each respondent a copy of my final . . . and ask for your thoughts and feedback. If you are not interested, there will be no obligation to read or respond to the . . . The final results will be made into a book and articles which will be generally available.

I will make sure everyone who has participated has a copy of . . . I will be recording these interviews so that I can transcribe them and be sure I really understood everything that you said correctly. Is that all right with you? I will keep the recordings until . . . and then they will be . . .

If you want to reach me my phone number is . . . and my email is . . . Do you have any questions at this point? For the sake of the recording and . . . could you tell me if all of your questions have been answered and if you wish to participate in this research study?

Interview protocol example procedure, based on *The Pear Story*

I am going to play a recording for you. It's a story of a man who is picking some fruit from a fruit tree. There is no language, only actions. The story is about seven minutes long. I'd like you to watch the film one time. Don't take notes and don't ask any questions or stop the film. At the end of the film I will ask you a few general questions about the film. Are you ready?

[Play the recording. Turn the recording device on.]

Now I'll ask you a few questions.

Can you describe what happened in the film? Use as much detail as you can.

What do you think is the point of the film?

If you had to give the film a title, what title would you give it?

Thank you. That's all for now.

11.2   Listener participation

The purpose of this project is to investigate patterns and tendencies of listener participation. As we outlined in Chapter 4, conversation is essentially co-created by speakers and listeners. Listeners use a range of devices to show participation and shape the course and meaning of the discourse. When we understand these participation styles, we develop a richer concept of discourse and the ability to listen interactively.

11.2.1   Initial questions

• What role does the listener play in listening to a speaker in narrating an event, in a face-to-face conversation?

- How does the listener guide the story, assist in prompting, provide feedback?
- How does the listener deal with any ambiguities or understanding problems that come up? How does the listener deal with any interpretation conflicts with the speaker?

11.2.2   Data sample: parent–child interaction

A fertile source of data for sociolinguistic analysis is family interactions, particularly parents and children, since this type of intimate interaction often contains detail not found in public discourse. This piece of data is from interactive storytelling extracts, gathered by Minami (2002) among families in Tokyo, Japan. Minami's analysis focuses on how the mother (ostensibly the listener) and the daughter interactively construct events and their meaning. The setting is at home, with Sachi and Mother seated at a table.

Mother. Tanjoobi kai de obake yashiki shite?
   At the birthday party, you played haunted house?
Sachi. Ehtto, ne . . .
   Um, you know . . .
Mother. Un?
   Uh-huh?
Sachi. Sensei ga, ne . . .
   The teacher, you know . . .
Mother. Un?
   Uh-huh?
Sachi. Omen kabutte, koo shite, ne . . .
   Put on a mask, and did this, you know . . .
Mother. Un?
   Uh-huh?
Sachi. Date sensei, ne . . .
   Because the teacher, you know . . .
Mother. Un?
   Uh-huh?
Sachi. Kumagumi san no heya e itta toki, ne . . .
   When we went into the 'bear' classroom, you know . . .
Mother. Un?
   Uh-huh?
Sachi. Konna kao data mon . . .
   (We saw her face) was like this . . .
Mother. Ah so!
   Oh, really?

Sachi. Obake no kao data mon.
  (It) was a spooky face.

Mother. Obake no kao dattan, heee!
  (It) was a spooky face? Oh my!

11.2.3 Project plan

You will be recording a dyad, one person telling a story and one listening. You will then be analysing the recording or transcript, identifying specific ways in which the listener participates: backchannelling, asking clarification questions, prompting, eliciting expansions, etc.

- Record a sample of a person telling a story – or simply recounting an event – in a face to face interaction. Two-way phone recordings or internet-based voice chats can also be used. (You can be the storyteller yourself, and find a willing listener who agrees to be recorded.) You can do this with either L1 or L2 speakers and listeners.

- After you have made the recording of a person telling a story to a live listener, play it back and identify an extended interactive segment of a minute or more that you can use for your analysis. (Participants do not need to be present for this selection process, but their input on what is interesting to them about the extract can be useful as **triangulation**, which adds depth to your research.)

- Transcribe the segment, using as much detail as possible. Add paralinguistic features: words or phrases with particular emphasis (loudness, duration, or rise in pitch), indicating places that have notably faster or slower pace. If you are using a video recording, include salient gestures and body language, as outlined in Chapter 4. (See Chapter 14 for resources on transcribing and encoding discourse.)

- In your analysis, pay special attention to the listener's linguistic and non-linguistic behaviour. What actions is the listener performing: backchannelling, asking for clarifications, providing comments or judgements or endorsements or objections, redirecting, etc.? What non-verbal actions (body position, head movements, gaze) seem to indicate an interaction with the speaker?

- Based on your analysis, what patterns or styles do you see in the listener's behaviour?
  - How much of this behaviour is linguistic?
  - How much is non-linguistic?
  - How would you evaluate your listener's effectiveness?
  - How would you assess the listener's impact on the story-telling?

To what degree are the speaker and listener interdependent?

Listening research tool   Transcription of complex recordings

To develop a feel for spoken language and to provide stability and reliability in analysis, it is necessary to transcribe extracts from conversations. This is seldom an easy task, so the transcriber aims to do the best job possible. Extracts that contain overlaps, false starts, interruptions, and incompletions are often 'messy' to transcribe and analyse, but the effort required to portray them accurately provides additional insight to the richness of language (see Cauldwell, 2004 for discussion).

11.2.4   Basic transcription conventions

[ ]	Brackets indicate overlapping utterances.
=	Equal marks indicate contiguous utterances, or continuation of the same utterance to the next line.
(.)	Period within parentheses indicates micropause.
(2.0)	Number within parentheses indicates pause of length in approximate seconds.
ye:s	Colon indicates stretching of sound it follows.
<u>yes</u>	Underlining indicates emphasis.
YES	Capital letters indicate increased volume.
°yes°	Degree marks indicate decreased volume of materials between.
hhh	h's indicate audible aspiration, possibly laughter.
·hhh	Raised large period indicates inbreath audible aspiration, possibly laughter.
ye(hh)s	h's within parentheses indicate within-speech aspiration, possibly laughter.
((cough))	Items within double parentheses indicate some sound or feature of the talk which is not easily transcribable, e.g. '((in falsetto))'.
(yes)	Parentheses indicate transcriber doubt about hearing of passage.
↑yes, ↓yes	Arrows indicate upward or downward intonation on the sound they precede

11.2.5   Common problems in transcription, with examples

Dealing with silence

Suggestions:

- Use dashes for tenths of seconds with a plus for the one that makes up a full second.
- Give the duration numerically in brackets.

If you cannot time the pause, write a *pause* in double brackets if it occurs within a speaker's turn, and *gap* within double brackets if it occurs between different speakers' turns.

> *A.* What she said to me ((pause)) I can't repeat that.
>
> *B.* You sure you don't want to tell me?
> ((gap))
>
> *A.* Yes, I'm sure.

Dealing with overlaps

Suggestions:

- Where one person begins when someone else is already speaking, use a single opening square bracket before the new speaker's words, aligned vertically with another at the appropriate point.

> *A.* So we didn't have to   [wait long
>
> *B.*   [No, we didn't.

- If it is already the end of a line, but you want to show that the same speaker has continued, although someone intervened during the line, use the latching symbol.

Dealing with obscurity

Suggestions:

- If it really is impossible to decipher the utterance, put empty brackets, or write 'indecipherable' in brackets, or insert an asterisk for each indecipherable syllable.
- If you can guess what the obscure part is, but you have some doubt about it, put your guess in parentheses:

> *A.* There's no way (in hell) I'm going back there.
>
> *B.* Look, I'm not asking you (indecipherable) there if you don't want to.

Dealing with volume

Suggestions:

- Use capital letters to show loudness.
- Use degree signs (superscript circles) on both sides of a quiet utterance.

> *A.* He told me °he was letting me go°.
>
> *B.* He told you WHAT?

Dealing with multiple channels of information (non-verbal, semi-verbal, breath patterns (e.g. laughter; cf. Chafe, 2007)

Suggestions:

- Voiced exhalation ^ (exhaled laughter: ^^^^^):

    Great. Just what I wanted to hear ^^^

- Lengthened exhalation ᵥ:

    Oh, well ᵥᵥᵥᵥ I guess this means we just have to start over.

- Example spoken with a smile (~example~):

    Sure. ~Let's go~

- Example spoken with tremolo (rapid repetition):

    What kind of stupid <u>law</u> is that?

11.3   Listener response

The purpose of this project is to observe the range of responses listeners make, and to frame this as a series of choices that influence the outcome of an interaction or a 'take away' from the listening event (if it is not inter-active, as in watching a television show). As outlined in Chapter 4, listener responses are always subjective: each response reflects what is important to the listener at a particular point in the discourse, and indicates an attempt to direct the discourse in a way that better satisfies the listener's needs or goals at that time. In this sense, listener response is also evaluative: any response includes a judgement about what is happening in the discourse and what the listener may prefer.

An interesting source of data for this type of investigation is professional service settings. These settings produce examples of institutional discourse – discourse in which one person who represents an institution encounters another who is seeking its services. In these settings, skill in verbal inter-action is almost always critical to the outcomes – both **transactional** (what is accomplished) and **affective** (how the participants feel about each other and the institution). In many professional contexts, listening ability is a key component of competence; therefore, institutional discourse research can serve a vital training function.

11.3.1   Initial questions

- Can you think of particular professing settings in which the spoken language serves an important function? Can you access a specific pro-fessional site that is of interest you? Why is that site of interest to you? What relationships or interactions do you find particularly compelling?

Examples include: *hospital:* doctor–patient, doctor–nurse, nurse–patient, receptionist–patient; *business office:* boss–assistant, co-worker–co-worker, receptionist–client; *school:* teacher–student, student–student, teacher–administrator, teacher–teacher.

- What transpires in these relationships and interactions? What topics are covered? What decisions are made? How do the participants evaluate each other?

- What aspects of these interactions typically goes well? What, if anything, is or can be problematic about these interactions? What aspects of discourse may be contributing to these problems?

11.3.2   Data sample: doctor–patient interaction, medical workplace

We often think of professional settings, such as business offices, schools, government agencies, and hospitals as places where the interactions are important. The interactions may have strong personal, familial, social, financial, or medical consequences, and therefore tend to be underpinned with strong emotion.

The following extracts come from a medical case file at a fertility clinic in Australia. This particular case involves a female client (AF2) in her forties who attends the clinic together with her husband (MP). This is an Appointment 1 session, which follows a Preliminary session in which the client has confirmed that they want to go ahead and discuss the fertility testing procedure further. The genetic counsellor (GC) is a middle-aged woman and a genetic nurse is also present. The first extract occurs approximately two-thirds of the way through the appointment. The second extract occurs near the end. Pay particular attention to the professional (GC). We can view the conversation as guided by her decisions: probing for information, asking for clarification, reminding the client of goals, querying motives, prompting, and so on. We can also see displays of GC's attitudes, such as showing tolerance or showing support or showing aggravation. Note that the extracts are somewhat long, but it is necessary to have an extended section in order to detect patterns and decisions.

Extract 1

01   *GC.* = I must say that you you seem much (.) sort of more settled in, actually, since we saw you in May.

02   *MP.* Well, as I say, we've (.) we got a new house [living in a new house] =

03   *AF2.* [Living in a new house]

04   *MP.* = We haven't got our noisy neighbours any more [and it's a better =

05   *AF2.* [(We ^^^^)]

06   *MP.* = house] and we can actually sit now in the living room and sleep in our own bedroom because we haven't got the noisy neighbours (.) which has taken a lot and we've just moved in the house and we're all settled

and it's a better house, it's just (.) better part (.) same estate but just better neighbours, it's just (.) generally that's made life a lot better (.) 'cause
g-g-given us chance to actually sit back and have a bit of peace and quiet
and think [(.)] and just be able to sit there and listen to =

07 *GC.* [Yeah]

08 *MP.* = nothing (.) and not next door and to be able to think (.) and talk
things over without being wound up by the neighbours it's (.) oh it's
been so much better (.) this last few months since we've moved.

09 *GC.* Yes, you seem (.) much [different] to me from when we saw you in =

10 *MP.* [Mm]

11 *GC.* = [May], so I think even though it has been a delay *I sort of sort of =

12 *MP.* [Yes]

13 *GC.* = [you seem]*

14 *AF2.* [We're getting there]

15 *MP.* Yeah. we are (.) [well]

Extract 2

01 *GC.* the other (.) issue talked that we talked a (.) a bit about last time (.)
um (.) was (.) having children ((coughs)) (.) Your feelings or both of your
feelings about that has (.) has that still been something that you sort of
been (.) talking about or something that you've been [(.) thinking about?]

02 MP. [Funnily enough] we had er (.) a conversation about it in the kitchen
(.) the other day, when I turned around and said that (.) there's probably
a lot of people out there who think that (.) not have that having children
is (.) is an important thing but (.) I'm one of those people that (.) the way
the world is believes that er (.) it's probably better off (.) I'm glad I didn't
in, in a lot of ways so (.) I think we've come to accept it now (.) haven't
we? It's (.) ten years down the line, and she was more worried for me (.)
her because she's got two girls by the previous marriage and it was like
me (.) but I've just come to accept it now and accept the two girls I mean
I've been bringing them up for the best part of ten years it counts for a
lot ·hh (.) AND as for bringing a small child into the world we live in
now I couldn't be so heartless (.) I really don't think I could (.) because
it's not exactly the (.) the (.) most ideal world to (.) to bring children in
to, so (.) gives me a little bit of peace of mind (0.5) at the end of the day.

03 *GC.* How – and how do you feel about it?

04 *AF2.* I a lot of it was worried the fact that he hasn't got children (.) but
(.) I've always wanted three (.) three children I it's something about it (.)
[always wanted three] and (.) but (.) looking on it no (.) because =

05 *MP.* [Yeah, always said that.]

06 *AF2.* = (.) I'm too old and (.) everything but (.) if I could have gone
back yes I would have love loved another child (.) but it's STILL it's still
like when I see babies there's still hurt there (.) but (.) you never know
I might become a grandmother (.) in a couple of years.

07   *GC.* Um, so you sound like you're feeling (.) little bit sort of (.) sort of more settled about things (.) and I think I think you're right that (.) y- you know you always will feel that if you see a little baby and I think [(.)] even people who've decided actually they're going to finish =

08   *AF2.* [Y:::eah]

09   *GC.* = their family when they see their last ones growing up you think [that, you know, everyone does] (.) feel that.

10   *AF2.* [Well, my friend, now] my friend now just gone sterile (.) and I tried talking her out of it she was a single parent with three children (.) and I said to her, don't do it (.) and erm (.) behold, she had it done (.) A year down the line now she's with a new (.) partner and she's going through this (.) he've got children by his marriage (.) she've got children (.) but she wants one with him [(.)] S:o

11   *GC.* [Mm] (1.0)

12   *AF2.* But I I wouldn't advise anyone or anything like that I had it done to me (.) under protest [(.)] but this is why I'm going ahead (.) with =

13   *GC.* [Yeah]

14   *AF2.* = this because (.) I've got two girls (.) and I don't want it happen-ing to them.

15   *GC.* *Right* (.) 'cause last time we talked part of the reason that you were (.) wanting to go through for the test was [(.)] because you were =

16   *AF2.* [*Yes*]

17   *GC.* = hoping that you yourself might want to have children but (.) now you're thinking it's (.) because of the girls

18   *AF2.* The girls more than anything 'cause like I said I was sterilised (.) at eighteen (.) they wanted to sterilise me at sixteen (.) I didn't even sign the consent forms. My (.) (^^^) and my ex-husband signed the forms (.) and (.) I woke up from giving birth to (.) ((daughter)) (.) and went straight into theatre (.) having it taken away, you know (.) and (.) from that day I felt like (.) my womanhood had been taken (.) away from me under protest [(.)] so but I don't want my girls going =

19   *GC.* [Mm]

20   *AF2.* = through it (.) if they want six children (.) let them have six children with the knowledge that, no, they're not going to have Huntington's.

(Data from Sarangi and Brookes-Howell, 2006)

11.3.3   Project plan

You will be obtaining (with permission of the participants) long extracts, on audio or video, of participants in a professional setting. You will be analysing the interactions for examples of listener responses, or choices of how they evaluate and guide the interaction.

- Record or obtain multiple samples of interaction in a work setting or other professional setting. The samples should have common features:

same participants, or same roles of participants (e.g. boss–employee), or same type of interactions, or same setting, etc.

- What interesting or problematic aspects do you notice in the encounters? Can you identify some response ranges for the participants? For example, is one party showing a range of tolerant–intolerant attitudes or responses? Sympathetic–unsympathetic, etc.? Choose two or three descriptive ranges that can be graded on a scale. These are referred to as **Likert scales** for measuring attitudes, and are often used in social research. (See Chapter 14 for resources for constructing this type of scale and for statistical procedures for analysing results.)

- Identify specific places in the recording or transcript that reveals a particular attitude of a participant. What is the evidence – linguistic and non-linguistic – for your judgement? What other options did the participant have in that discourse moment? What might that option appear as in the discourse?

- Identify some places where the participants were making choices in how to respond to other participants? Were the participants aware of the choices they were making? How do you know? Did any of these choices lead to a congenial or desired outcome? Did any of these choices lead to a misunderstanding, or breakdown, or undesired outcome? How would you evaluate the discourse competence of the participant in the professional role?

Research principle   Identify choices among response options

Verbal messages are an important part of communication, but emotional meanings are often encoded, or perceived, using paralinguistic information and non-verbal information (see Chapter 2). In order to get a sense of what sources of information are used in communication, we can identify a range of emotional responses to a message and ask listeners to give their emotional impression, or to identify the emotional component of the message. Below are some ranges that have been used in evaluating the emotional components of messages in social research.

responsive–unresponsive
patient–impatient
interested–uninterested
attentive–inattentive
trusting–suspicious
warm–cool
accepting–rejecting
sincere–insincere
direct–indirect
friendly–unfriendly
involved–detached

personal–impersonal
considerate–inconsiderate
sensitive–insensitive
receptive–unreceptive
calm–nervous
sympathetic–unsympathetic
tolerant–intolerant
encouraging–discouraging

On a questionnaire the range would be laid out like this:
Circle one number

[1]	[2]	[3]	[4]	[5]
Calm				Nervous

11.4   Listeners in cross-cultural interactions

The purpose of this project is to explore the nature of listening in cross-cultural interactions. Specifically, we wish to explore the ways in which L1–L1 interaction is similar to and different from cross-cultural (L1–L2 and L2–L2) interactions, again from the perspective of the listener's role. As we discussed in Chapters 8 and 9, interaction for an L2 listener often presents asymmetries that must be addressed for positive **affective outcomes** (how the participants feel during and after the interaction) and successful **transactional outcomes** (what was actually accomplished as a result of the interaction).

Partial communication and miscommunication can often be attributed to differences in communicative style and, violations of expected discourse structures, as well as to limited command of the linguistic code.

11.4.1   Initial questions

- Do you take part in regular L1–L2 interactions in which you are the L1 user? Do you have frequent interactions in which you are the L2 user? What do you recall most vividly about a recent interaction of this sort?

- What seems most different to you about the two types of interactions (L1–L1 and L1–L2)? The style of interaction itself? The feelings of the participant? The length or outcome of the interactions?

- What additional work is required for the L1 or L2 user in these interactions?

11.4.2   Data sample: cross-cultural exchanges

Short discourse samples are often all that researchers have access to in investigating cross-cultural interactions. Short interactions are often all that is recorded or recalled, and often L2 interactions are brief. Still, we can learn a great deal about L1–L2 **communication strategies** from short inter-actions. The following extracts present a variety of types of L2 interactions.

Sample 1

Bilingual researcher (Spanish–English) talking with partially bilingual child (Spanish–English). The researcher uses only English, the child's L2, and the child is not aware that the researcher also speaks Spanish. We can see how the child uses **code switching** to tease the interviewer.

> *Child.* Know what's wrong with your teeth?
> *Experimenter.* What about my teeth?
> *Child.* Look at this one.
> *Experimenter.* What about it?
> *Child* (giggling). Es cheuco. (It's crooked.)
> *Experimenter.* It's what?
> *Child.* Es chueco.
> *Experimenter.* What's that in English? I don't understand what you're saying.
> *Child.* Es chueco.
>
> (From Liceras *et al.*, 2008)

Sample 2

An Australian researcher is interviewing an Aboriginal woman, a native speaker of Ngaanyatjarra, in Western Australia. We can see how the interviewer adjusts her questioning strategies – asking questions without inverting word order – in order to better accommodate the woman's pre-ferred discourse patterns for friendly conversation.

> *Australian interviewer.* Were you very young then?
> *Aboriginal woman.* Eh?
> *Australian interviewer.* You were very young?
> *Aboriginal woman.* Yes, I was about fourteen.
>
> (From Eades, 2000)

Sample 3

In this sample (which preserves the transcription style used by the researcher), we see the L1 speaker (NSE) having a social conversation with the L2 speaker (NNS 9–2). Here the L1 speaker supports the L2s in keep-ing the floor through shows of interest (*Oh, really!?*), indirect signals to keep talking and/or tolerating ambiguity (*Um . . .*), emotional support (laughing), asking elaboration questions (*Did you want to . . . ?*).

NSE 8	NNS 9–2
Is English your major?	No, I'm majoring in law.
Oh, really?	Yes, but law is not so interesting to me now.
Um	Before entering this university I really interested in law and, I wanted to change social, social Japan! (*Laughs.*)
Great! (*Laughing.*)	Ah, but, it's not reality! So (*laughing*) I'm not interested in law now.
Uh, did you want to become a lawyer?	I used to be, but now (*looks down*), um, uhm, now (*speaking softly and slowly*) (*brings hand up under chin and looks down*) (*looks back up at [NSE 8], speaking more loudly*) now I don't want to have some job.
Um	Because I want to study a lot of things
Um-hum	during my life, so . . .
That's great. That's great!	Um. How about you?

11.4.3   Project plan

You will be recording (audio or video) conversations involving an L1 and an L2 speaker or two L2 speakers. You will be identifying instances of communication strategies, in which one or both participations utilise strategies to extend their own conversational competence or that of their partner.

- Record one extended conversation involving an L1 and L2 speaker or two L2 speakers, or use multiple short conversations with the same participants. The conversations can be interview formats, with one speaker asking a series of questions and recording responses, or an open-ended conversation in which the participants discuss a particular topic or set of topics.

- Listen to or watch the recording at least three times. What do you notice?
  ○ Which speaker does the most speaking? Are the speaking turns symmetrical?
  ○ Do the participants experience any communication difficulties? What are these difficulties? What are the apparent causes?

- What tactics do they use to deal with communication difficulties? What code switching do you observe? Are there any apparent rules for code switching?

- Is the transactional goal of the communication (exchanged information and any desired effects) achieved? If not, what has impeded this goal?

- What are the affective outcomes of the interaction – do the speakers experience any negative emotion (anxiety, upset, anger, confusion) or positive emotion (cheerfulness, intimacy, humour, agreement) during the interaction? Are these affective outcomes linked to particular behaviours in the interaction?

- What specific strategy tokens do you notice in the discourse (request for clarification by L1S? by L2S? appeal for assistance? Do any discourse tokens seem particularly frequent to you? If you wish to test statistical significance of particular discourse moves or tokens, you can use a **chi-square** statistical procedure. (See Chapter 14 for resources.)
- Reflect back on the initial questions of the project. What kind of 'work' do the participants need to do in cross-cultural interaction in order to have successful interactions?

Listening research tool   Identifying cues to listener difficulties

Discourse research has shown that listeners experience a range of particular problems in interactions involving their L2. It's useful in research to learn to identify areas and cues that signal the onset of a problem – the specific verbal and non-verbal signals in the interaction. The following problems have been identified by a number of researchers:

Sample interaction	Listener problem
L1S. You'll need to file this claim before we can process your payment.	
L2S. Sorry, again please?	Not fully hearing what the speaker has said
L1S. You'll need to file this claim before we can process your payment.	
L2S. Umm…	Not having adequate background or cultural knowledge to respond fully
	Not having linguistic resources to respond fully
L2S. Aha, I see. [L2S later admits she did not understand.]	Feigning comprehension or delaying full comprehension until later
L1S. You'll need to file this claim before we can process your payment.	
L2S. What does this claim mean?	Asking for clarification
L1S. You'll need to file this claim before we can process your payment.	
L2S. I don't want any claim. Can I speak to the director?	Changing topic
L1S. You'll need to file this claim before we can process your payment.	
L2S. This is so complicated. Can you help me?	Appealing to speaker for support

Research principle   Ethics in research

The technology available to capture and edit high-quality audio and video recordings is constantly improving. The main issue of recording and using discourse samples concerns ethics. Generally, it is advisable *never* to make surreptitious recordings. All recordings of individuals that are to be used for research should be cleared with all parties appearing on the recording. For informal research, a verbal agreement that a recording is being made is acceptable, but for formal published research, signed releases are needed from participants. Contrary to what many people believe, participants usually warm up to recording devices and give typical, natural performances even when they are being recorded.

Use of recordings gained from others sources, such as the Internet, radio or television, runs into this same ethical issue. Copyright law is very well defined with respect to utilising a third party recording, despite the movement toward downloading virtually everything from the Internet. The current copyright law document that covers this most stringently is the Digital Millennium Copyright Act (DMCA). The Electronic Frontier Foundation (EFF) claims to fight for digital freedom and is generally against the DMCA. The World Intellectual Property Organisation (WIPO) is a section of the United Nations and its web site has many resources on copyright law. Educause, a non-profit association whose mission is to advance higher education by promoting the intelligent use of information technology, has a useful site with DMCA resources. (See Chapter 14 for links to resources.)

Summary: the social dimension of language

In this chapter we outlined four types of projects for investigating listener attitudes and behaviour. In these projects we are adopting primarily a sociolinguistic perspective, that is, an orientation toward the role of the listener, the listener's relationship with the participants, the language they use, and the adjustments and accommodations they make to each other.

The projects in this section provided broad outlines for researching listener roles, perspectives, expectations, and patterns of participation. The types of explorations of roles and interactions in this chapter can be extended to other social groups or settings as well. For instance, studies of male–female interaction and cultural and racial group interactions can be conducted in similar fashion. The keys to informative research in this domain are using a reliable system for gathering data, rich sources of interaction, a reliable way of capturing and analysing the data, and a way of triangulating findings.

The theme of this chapter has been emphasising the social dimension of language. Particularly when researching listening, the social dimension is often ignored. However, as explorations in this chapter have shown, the listener plays a vital role in creating the meaning in all discourse situations – whether directly, as in the **two-way discourse** of face-to-face interaction, or indirectly, as in **audience design** used in preparing one-way discourse such as media programmes.

Chapter 12

Psycholinguistic orientations

A psycholinguistic orientation to listening research focuses on the listener's cognitive processing. What types of knowledge must the listener have? How is the listener decoding the input, comprehending messages, building meaning, encoding meaning in memory? These are the types of questions that come up in this orientation to research.

Because psycholinguistics is concerned with cognitive processing, we will present projects to explore aural perception and the ways in which listeners process for deficient or missing parts of the input, comprehension. We will also propose projects for examining the encoding processes in memory – how we store what we have understood for later retrieval – and also recall processes for reactivating what was previously understood. Finally, we will present a project for exploring listening strategies, which are ways of compensatory for distorted and partially encoded input.

The projects in this section are (12.1) listener processing of speech, the ways in which the speech signal itself is perceived (12.2) listener memory, the process by which listeners draw on long-term memory, including cultural schemata, to interpret speech; (12.3) listener misunderstandings, the types of mishearings and misinterpretations that the listener and speaker create; and (12.4) listener strategies, the options the listener chooses from during a listening event and how these responses shape the event, give meaning to it, and contribute to the listener's competence.

12.1 Listener processing

The purpose of this project is to examine the detail of speech processing, particularly when the listener encounters unfamiliar words, or blurs, of speech. As we described in Chapter 2, **bottom–up speech processing** involves accurate perception of the speech signal, so that the listener can decode what was said into words and grammatical units. Because bottom-up perception is never entirely accurate or complete – even for L1 listeners – developing confidence in one's ability at oral perception is a persistent challenge for L2 learners. Habitual patterns in phonological perception, due to one's L1, and lack of familiarity with L2 prosodic patterns often lead to mishearings.

12.1.1 Initial questions

- How do we process unfamiliar segments of speech?
- What speech elements does an L2 listener have most difficulty processing?
- What is the L2 listener actually taking in from the spoken input when he or she experiences difficulties?
- Is there a developmental pattern for L2 listeners? (Do less proficient listeners make the same type of processing errors?)
- What do errors in perception suggest about the nature of the listening process? How do listeners compensate for errors in perception?

12.1.2 Data sample: transcriptions from a dictation

In a study of aural perception (Field, 2008), fourteen L2 listeners were presented with a series of short spoken inputs, and were asked to transcribe what they heard. In this extract from the study, the presentation sentence was:

> I found out that the thud was the cat.

Table 12.1 shows what fourteen listeners in the study reported hearing.

12.1.3 Project plan

For this project, you will be setting up a basic experimental design in which you will present input and elicit reconstruction of the input. The goal is to find out how listeners use phonological, lexical, and grammatical knowledge as they listen.

- Identify or compose a text that has a clear theme and a set of facts. The text should be accessible to the students, but should have parts that are beyond the students' ability to comprehend fully. The text should be long enough that the students cannot try to memorise it, but short enough to allow them to remember the main idea and some key facts without note-taking.
- Prepare two versions of the text. One version is the full version. This will be used for the idea-reconstruction phase of the task. The other version has words gapped out. This version will be used to evaluate what

Table 12.1   What listeners reported hearing

SUBJECT	I	FOUND OUT	THAT	THE THUD	WAS	THE CAT
1				the sound	was	the cat
2	I	found out		where	was	the cat
3	I	found out	that	the front	was	the cat
4				the thing	was	the cat
5				the fog	of	the cat
6	I	found out	that	the sun	in	the cat
7	I	found out		the frog	and	the cat
8	I			thought it	was	a cat
9			in	the front	was	the cat
10			what	I thought	that	a cat
11	I	found out	and	the frod	is	the cat
12				the thrub	was	the cat
13	I	found out	that		is	a cat
14	I	found out	that		was	the cat

specific perception and word-recognition problems your students are experiencing. Gap out words of a particular class. For example, you may gap out all of the function words in one paragraph and the content words in another paragraph.

- For the first phase of the task, ask the students to listen without taking notes. You may read the passage aloud once or twice. Following this, ask the students to attempt to reconstruct the main ideas of the text in writing. If the students work in groups they will collectively remember more and push each other to verbalise what they have understood. (This is the basic tenet of the *dictogloss method* developed by Swain, 1985.)

- For the second phase of the task, use the gapped version of the text, or simply have the students take dictation of selected portions of the text. Collect this version for compilation purposes. You can then distribute the full version of the text to the students as a follow-up.

- Compile the students' responses, using a baseline version of the text and adding a mark for each full word that was recognised by the students (see the data sample above for an example).

- From this analysis, draw conclusions about the kinds of word-recognition errors that your students are making most often.

Listening research tool Creating an implicational scale

An implicational scale is an ordinal (rank order) scale that shows relative frequency of occurrences of events, and implies that higher order events include lower order events. An implicational scale shows a hierarchy of patterns of occurrences, which may be patterns in the recognition or production of a particular linguistic feature (e.g. past tense markings) among a group of individuals. A typical scale, filled in with data from a perception experiment, looks like this:

- *Input*. After the mail is collected, it is taken to the post office and put through a machine for processing…
- *Output*. Subjects transcribe what they hear.
- *Scale*. + Demonstrated full perception of the feature. – Did not demonstrate full perception of the feature.

Based on the totals in Table 12.2 for just six subjects, we can see that feature 3 (a particular lexical item or the entire collocation) was the most difficult (least often perceived accurately) and feature 4 was the easiest (most often perceived accurately). An implicational scale based on this data might propose that 'prepositional phrases' are more easily perceived fully than 'passive verb phrases' and that acquisition of a higher order feature (in the scale) predict that lower order features have already been acquired. (See Rickford, 2004 for elaboration.)

Table 12.2 Typical implicational scale of perceived difficulty

SUBJECT	PERCEPTION OF DIFFICULTY OF FEATURE NO.				TOTAL
	1	2	3	4	
	AFTER THE MAIL	IS COLLECTED	IT IS TAKEN	TO THE POST OFFICE	
1	+	–	–	+	2
2	+	+	–	+	3
3	+	+	+	+	4
4	–	–	–	+	1
5	+	–	+	+	2
6	+	+	–	+	2
Total	5	3	2	6	

Research principle   Identifying stages of development

One goal of language acquisition research is to begin to detect stages of development in various skill and strategy areas that seem to apply to learners generally. In the case of speech processing, one such line of longitudinal research was undertaken by Kim (1995). Using two different forms of input (slow and normal), Kim was able to formulate an implicational scale for connected speech. This scale implicates that perception of clausal relationships (Phase 5) proceeds from perception of clause, and that this level of perception cannot be achieved until perception of clauses (Level 4) has been to some degree 'acquired.'

- *Phase 1. Pre-key word phase.* The listener cannot identify key words that bear phonetic prominence in speech (e.g. reporting *milk* or *meal* for *mail*).

- *Phase 2. Key words.* The listener identifies phonetically prominent words, and forms associative relationships between them to understand (e.g. hearing *mail, machine* and *stamps*).

- *Phase 3. Phrases.* The listener encodes not only key words but also less prominent surrounding elements that form a small grammatical unit (e.g. hearing *mail, put through a machine* and *cancelling stamps*).

- *Phase 4. Clauses.* The listener encodes grammatical relationships between lexical words, identifying semantic relationships between arguments and predicates in a clause (e.g. hearing *the mail is collected, taken to the post office, it is put through a machine*).

- *Phase 5. Clauses plus.* The listener encodes not only almost all clauses in the input but also the relationships among them (e.g. hearing *the mail goes through several steps before it is delivered*).

12.2   Listener memory

As we discussed in Chapter 3, comprehension and memory are inter-related. All comprehension draws upon memory – linguistic memory and semantic memory – so if memory does not serve the listener well, comprehension will be unstable. Similarly, because measures of comprehension entail both recalling what was understood and producing a representation in speech or writing, comprehension and production are interrelated. The purpose of this project is to explore ways in which we comprehend long texts, and how we report our understanding.

12.2.1   Initial questions

- After we listen to a long content-rich text, such as a classroom lecture, or attend to a lengthy complex input, such as a feature film, what kinds of images and information do we retain?

- Does our memory for that text or experience change over time?
- How does unfamiliar content or familiar content laden with unfamiliar cultural references influence the listener's comprehension processes?
- How does our cultural background or personal perspective influence what we comprehend and what we remember?
- Does the way that we are prompted to recall something influence what we actually remember?

12.2.2 Data sample: recall of a culturally rich story

The War of the Ghosts was one of the texts used by Mandler and Johnson (1977) in their classic story recall experiments. Subjects were asked to read a passage involving an unknown cultural ritual and then were tested on their recall at various intervals. This experiment provided support for the notion that our cultural background influences the ways we remember what we hear or read. We typically distort concepts and reconstruct events in order to make them fit with our own knowledge and expectations.

The War of the Ghosts

One night two young men from Egulac went down to the river to hunt seals, and while they were there it became foggy and calm. Then they heard war cries, and they thought: 'Maybe this is a war party.' They escaped to the shore and hid behind a log. Now canoes came up, and they heard the noise of paddles, and saw one canoe coming up to them. There were five men in the canoe, and they said:

'What do you think? We wish to take you along. We are going up the river to make war on the people.'

One of the young men said, 'I have no arrows.'

'Arrows are in the canoe,' they said.

'I will not go along. I might be killed. My relatives do not know where I have gone. But, you,' he said, turning to the other, 'may go with them.'

So one of the young men went, but the other returned home.

And the warrior went on up the river to a town on the other side of Kalama. The people came down to the water, and they began to fight, and many were killed. But presently the young man heard one of the warriors say, 'Quick, let us go home: the Indian has been hit.' Now he thought: 'Oh, they are ghosts.'

12.2.3 Data sample: recall protocol

RP (speaker 3) Portuguese-speaker, English L2, heard story in English, respond in English orally (transcribed by researcher).

Interviewer. What do you remember from the story?
Speaker 3.

1   I heard this:
2   there are two Indians
3   they are young
4   that was in . . .
5   a kind of (inaudible) hunting.
6   They had been close
7   to some water or some stream
8   in the night and (+ +)
9   and had waited
10   something.
11   I assuming that they
12   they are . . . were a long
13   stay there a long time . . .
14   when they . . . how you say? . . . startled
15   for some type of the group was coming
16   maybe they thought
17   they attacked at them. (+ +)
18   So . . . Or at first
19   they had thought that it was
20   was some type of the attackers.
21   They had hidden close
22   Close to the coast of the lake.
23   But the group has found them,
24   and I'm not sure
25   said them to come together with them,
26   come with us, ok.
27   So now
28   one of the hunters (+ +)
29   the boys said, No
30   no I cannot come with you
31   and another one said that he was . . .
32   (laughs) distrustful
33   that they could be . . . dead.
34   So I guess they are afraid.
35   Yes, of course of afraid.
36   They were trying really to prevent
37   you know to prevent to go with the group.
38   But they had finally decided one of them will go

39 (laughs) You go, not me,
40 and the other return to the village.
41 The group that was fighting
42 have many losses
43 deaths you say (+)
44 and then the boy who carried through
45 he thinks that they were ghosts
46 they are fighting ghosts (+ +)
47 so umm
48 that it was some type of
49 the challenge
50 spiritual challenge
51 we must assume.

12.2.4   Data sample: recall protocol 2

RP. Answer these questions about the story (elicited after oral summary was given). Spoken questions, spoken responses (transcribed by researcher).

* Where were the men from? *I'm not sure, sounds like Eagle Lake.*
* How many men went to the river? *There are two.*
* What were they hunting? *They are hunting animals.*
* What did they hear? *Some sounds or noise.*
* Why did they escape to the shore? *They are afraid.*
* Who was in the canoe? *Some warriors.*
* What did the men in the canoe say to the young men? *Come with us.*
* One young man said, 'I have no . . .' – what? *'I have no arrows, so I cannot fight.'*
* What did the young men decide to do? *One will go, one will stay back.*
* What did the young man think at the end? *These are ghosts, not warriors.*

12.2.5   Project plan

You will be conducting a listening and recall experiment. You will present an input (in person or pre-recorded) and elicit comprehension by way of an open task (recall) and a closed task (question answering).

* Gather some texts, such as stories, interviews or news reports that originated in cultures or sub-cultures that are not familiar to your students. There are many free sources, such as *YouTube* (use search words like: healing rituals, story-telling, oral history, cultural stories). Create a video

or audio recording about two minutes in length, preferably without using many visual cues.

- Present the story – verbatim – to a group, either through a pre-recorded listening on audio or video, or do an oral reading. (Note: different presentation modalities can be used for an additional experimental study of effects of presentation mode on comprehension). You may want to repeat the story two or three times. (*Avoid paraphrasing* the story as this can introduce your own distortions!)

- (A) Ask some of the listeners to reconstruct the story individually (not in a group), either in writing or orally. Record the recountings of the story. (B) Ask some of the listeners to respond individually to a series of specific questions about the story. Record their responses.

- For A subjects, compare the original version of the story with the retellings. What is different? How do your findings relate to schema theory? (See Chapter 3.) For B subjects, compare their responses to the actual events in the story. If you wish to test for statistical significance, which events were recalled most frequently by the subjects in your study, you can do an analysis of variance (ANOVA).

- Which group seemed to recall more of the story? How do the two types of tasks differ in terms of eliciting what the listeners understood? How do you relate your findings to schema theory? How do you relate your findings to theories of memory?

Research principle   Utilising alternative memory probes

When we conduct language experiments involving long-term memory, we have to be aware of the normal limitations of human memory, even for events that took place in our L1. Comprehension and memory are inextricably intertwined, and any probes of comprehension will involve memory limitations, decay, and distortions.

In Mandler and Johnson's prototypical study (1977), the researchers presented stories to subjects and asked them to remember the story – to reconstruct the story as closely as possible to the version they had just read. They then asked for subsequent recall of the same story – without rereading it – at various periods, one week, one month, three months. What Mandler and Johnson discovered is quite consistent with schema theory as discussed in Chapter 3: Subjects tended to recall the stories in terms of their own familiar schemata, and tended to use broad generalisations about what they remembered as the time from the event increased (as their actual memory decayed). Because these stories were typically foreign to the subjects, involving characters and events and outcomes that were quite different from the cultural schemata that the subjects were familiar with, the subjects had to depend upon more familiar schemata in their recounts, which inevitably 'distorted' the actual events they were trying to recall. Based on this type of evidence, we might conclude that our memories are faulty. However, cognitive psychologies view these distortions as signs of a healthy memory, as ways of preserving a stable cognitive functioning. These types of selective omissions and adjustment of the facts are seen as part of a healthy cognition.

Based on this type of evidence, Schacter (2001) has formulated a list of seven 'sins' of memory (though it is clear in his treatment that he does not consider these deficiencies):

- *Transience:* the decreasing accessibility of memory over time.
- *Absentmindedness:* lapses of attention and forgetting to do things.
- *Blocking:* temporary inaccessibility of stored information, such as tip-of-the-tongue syndrome.
- *Suggestibility:* incorporation of misinformation into memory due to leading questions, deception and other causes.
- *Bias:* retrospective distortions produced by current knowledge and beliefs.
- *Persistence:* unwanted recollections that people cannot forget, due to strong vividness or highly emotional content.
- *Misattribution:* attribution of memories to incorrect sources or believing that you have seen or heard something you actually have not.

12.3   Listener misunderstandings

Misunderstandings are a common feature of communication, and as we discussed in Chapters 3 and 4, most go undetected or are never addressed because they do not reach a critical level at which the communication breaks down. When breakdowns do occur, competent listeners know how to address misunderstandings strategically. Skilled listeners can address misunderstanding without loss of face to either the speaker or listener, which entails not attributing fault to either party, but rather focusing on the repair itself.

It is very common in analyses of communication problems to attribute a misunderstanding to the weaker or minority party – the child, the non-native speaker, the employee, the unpopular party in a dispute, etc. An important contribution of research on misunderstanding is its demonstration that *all* misunderstandings are co-constructed, rather than the responsibility of any one participant. However, the reality is that the minority participant is often saddled both with the blame for a misunderstanding and the responsibility for sorting it out.

The purpose of this particular project is to explore misunderstandings *from a psycholinguistic perspective*, even though sociolinguistic elements and issues are involved as well. From a psycholinguistic perspective we may ask: What cognitive process caused or triggered the misunderstanding? This type of causation does not refer to personal intention or responsibility. We are in effect asking: What aspects of cognitive processing or what assumptions, by both the speaker and the listener, are involved in creating the misunderstanding?

12.3.1 Initial questions

- Lyons (1995) has remarked that you could never understand if you had been understood, only when you had been misunderstood. To what extent do you find this to be true?

- Kerekes (2007) in a study of cross-cultural job interviews said that 'Misunderstandings are always co-constructed.' In what sense do you consider this statement to be true?

- What are some recent misunderstandings you have experienced in your L1? What are the causes? What are some recent misunderstandings you have experienced in your L2? What are the causes? Are they the same as those in the L1? What are some ways to repair misunderstandings? Are there ways to prevent them?

Here are several samples of misunderstandings, provided from different sources. Some are presented in list format in an attempt to account for relevant details, with additional notes attached. Some are presented as narrative accounts only. Some hypothesise about the cause of the misunderstanding, while others do not.

12.3.2 Data sample 1: let car

Date/time. n.a.

Location. A language school in London.

Event. Students are in a class practising for the Cambridge Certificate in Advanced English speaking exam. (Extract from eight hours of recorded material.)

Participants. Japanese female JF, Swiss male SM.

Verbal element (transcribed):

SM. I didn't understand the let cars. What do you mean with this?

JF. Let [let] car? Three red [red] cars. (Articulated very slowly.)

SM. Ah, red.

JF. Red.

SM. Now I'm understanding. I understood car to hire, to let. Ah, red. Yes, I see.

Physical elements present. Visual materials for language task.

Other notes. From researcher: We are examining dyads of learners to detect comprehensibility problems depending on whether interlocutors shared the same L1.

(From Jenkins, 2000)

12.3.3   Data sample 2: two or three questions

One evening in my Gothenburg (Sweden) hotel I (German male) approached the young man at the reception starting like this: 'I've two or three questions,' to which he replied by turning around to the board where all the room keys were hanging, repeating, 'Two, oh, three.'

'Two or three **ques**tions I have,' I replied. And he smiled and said, 'Ah, **ques**tions you have. I thought you wanted the **key**.'

The misunderstanding was verbal, in that 'two or three' sounds like 'two-oh-three'. And it was partially schematic, since guests usually just do routine things like ask for keys, not pose questions.

(Data from Hinnenkamp, 2009)

12.3.4   Data sample 3: 'Let's go to my place'

Date/time. Weekday after class (~5:00 p.m.).

Location. American language programme campus.

Event. Student reporting of an invitation by classmate to study together that evening.

Participants.

Verbal element (recalled by KF):

AM. Do you want to study for the test together?

KF. Sure, that's a good idea.

AM. Let's go to my place. We can study at my apartment.

KF. No, no, no, no.

Physical elements present. Books, notes

Other notes. Researcher: KF reports to researchers that she took this as an invitation for a date, and refused immediately, thinking AM was too aggressive, and was just interested in dating her, not in studying together. Cause of misunderstanding is not clear, as AM's intentions not known. But assuming AM did intend to invite KF to study, there is a difference in schema. AM's schema allows studying to be done at his residence; KF's schema allows studying to be done at a neutral location.

12.3.5 Data sample 4: Que haces?

Date. n.a.
Event. Buying grocery in a supermarket
Location. Barcelona, Spain
Participants. American male (~20), Spanish female (~25), Spanish male (~50)
Verbal element. SM: 'Que haces? Son mis bolsillas, no?'
Physical elements present. BM had picked up bags on counter for his own groceries that were brought by SM, behind him in line
Other notes. To researcher from BM (from oral report):

When I was living in Barcelona one summer, the first time I went to the grocery store, I gathered my groceries and went to the checkout counter. After scanning half of my goods, the checkout lady reached the vegetables. She sighed, looked up, and ordered me to go weigh and price the vegetables myself, much to the frustration of those behind me in line. After I had paid, I looked around but could not find any plastic bags. A few moments later, the checkout lady threw some bags toward me, so I began filling them with my groceries. When I was nearly finished, the man behind me yelled at me, 'Que haces? Son mis bolsillas, no?' which means 'What are you doing? Aren't those my bags?' Apparently the bags that the lady threw my way were bags that the man had purchased. She had assumed they were mine.

12.3.6 Data sample 5: Blick auf die Narren

I was standing at an empty intersection in Munich, with no cars in the horizon. I stood and waited for a green light together with a pack of other people, presumably most were local Germans. Assessing correctly that there was absolutely no danger in crossing, I took a step off the kerb. Seemingly to be acting in unison, the pack of Germans erupted in profanities and condemnation. I heard things like 'Blick auf die Narren', which I think is something like 'Look at that fool', and 'Das ist sehr gefährlich', 'That's very dangerous', and 'Was zum Teufel macht er?' 'What the hell is he doing?'). Taken together, I think I got the message: they were scolding me for being a dysfunctional member of society. The cause of the misunderstanding was that I, as the outsider, did not understand the custom. You simply don't violate certain social customs or laws in Germany, no matter how innocuous you may think the rule is.

12.3.7 Project plan

You will be collecting multiple examples of misunderstandings, from a variety of sources. By compiling the examples in a uniform format, you will better be able to compare them, and share your sources with others. Excellent project! Really likely to produce some interesting data

• Over a period of one week, collect examples of verbal misunderstandings. These can be from your own experience, or from reports of others. Record each misunderstanding on a card set up like Figure 12.1. Try to record the data as soon as possible after it happens in order to reflect the facts as closely as possible.

• Analyse the misunderstandings. Is the cause linguistic (phonological, syntactic, lexical) or conceptual (based on differing schematic knowledge or lack of common ground)?

• Based on your examples of misunderstandings, what could you teach to L2 speakers about misunderstanding? How to prevent them? How to deal with misunderstandings when they arise? Based on these examples, what could you teach to L1 speakers about ways of dealing with misunderstandings?

Date

Event

Participants

Verbal element

Physical elements present

Other notes:

Figure 12.1   *Misunderstanding card.*

Research principle   Multiple causes of misunderstanding

Susan Dunn, an American psychologist who works with clients trying to develop their emotional intelligence tells them that 'The first law of communication is: assume you have been misunderstood.' Though most of us coast through our everyday interactions with an assumption that everyone is more or less tuned in to us and we to them, we all have more misunderstandings than we apprehend.

Because we all need to operate on a **'good enough' comprehension strategy** (Ferreira and Patson, 2007) in our everyday language use, we seldom detect, much less feel the need to call out or repair, small misunderstandings. We typically will not notice a misunderstanding unless there is an adverse effect on us, and only then might we attempt to examine or repair it and try again for better understanding.

When we are in the position of an L2 listener though, we often *do* notice more misunderstandings because of more frequent adverse effects: We may not get what we want, if only in the way of a desired response from our interlocutors. In L2 situations, understanding difficulties in conversation arise not only because of the L2 listener's incomplete command of the language code, but also from a number of other non-linguistic sources.

12.3.8 Possible causes of misunderstandings

- *Ambiguity*. I'll see you <u>soon</u>.
- *Substitution*. I think <u>so</u>.
- *Ellipsis*. Where is he? _____ in the bathroom.
- *Inaccessible lexical item*. You'll have to be <u>examined</u>./I'll <u>catch</u> you later.
- *Mismatch of schema*. <u>We can study at my place</u>.
- *Unfamiliar routine*. <u>Can I help you?</u>
- *Mishearing*. He's very <u>elegant</u> (<u>arrogant</u>?)
- *'Difficult' construction*. <u>Not only is it</u> important for you to be here on time . . .
- *Acoustic problems*. I'll pick you up at <u>@#%*&@.</u>
- *Complex utterance*. A signed report will be needed by your physician before we can allow your son to participate.
- *Indirectness*. We close at midnight.
- *False cognates*. The <u>service</u> wasn't very good.
- *Inadequate elaboration*. Entry is prohibited.
- *False assumption about shared knowledge*. The pen is <u>in the drawer</u>.
- *False assumption about speaker's intention*. Let's hang out together sometime.
- *Wilful failure* (unwillingness to understand) (at a museum entrance, at 4:45 p.m.). *A*. Can we please go in for a few minutes? We've come all this way and we didn't know closing time was 5:00 p.m.! *B*. The museum is closed.
- *Psychiatric disturbance* (on a train). *A*. Would you mind moving over so I can sit down? *B*. I'm Albert. I live here.

12.4   Listener strategies

The purpose of this project is to identify ways in which listeners monitor their own cognitive processes while listening. As listeners, we all have the capability of monitoring our own comprehension and making decisions about how to adjust our attention. However, there appear to be constraints on this process and limits to its effectiveness.

12.4.1   Initial questions

- When listening to an engaging talk or interview or when watching an engaging film or performance, how do you adjust your attention, concentration, and desire to analyse or comprehend more fully?
- What kinds of strategy do you use when you encounter a difficult or incomprehensible stretch of the talk or performance?
- If there is a pause in the talk or film, what kind of predictions do you typically make?
- In listening to a second language, do you utilise the same kinds of adjustments and strategies? Do you make the same kind of predictions during pauses?

12.4.2   Data sample: English-speakers learning French

The researcher played audio samples to students of French, and paused the recordings after each chunk of text. He asked the students – in one on one interview settings – what they were thinking at the time. One student, Paula, had tested at an intermediate level; the other student, Tom, had tested at a beginning level.

(*Background noises*.) Bonjour, Sylvain. Salut, Philippe! Salut, Christine! Ça va, toi? Plus au moins. Pourquoi? Tu n'as pas passé une bonne fin de semaine? Oh oui! C'est là le problème.

Paula. There's, there's friends talking and, uh, they're talking about, so I guess that a weekend. Doesn't sound like what, the guy had a good weekend. He's about to tell the girl why.

Interviewer. What makes you think that way?

Tom. Ah, didn't hear much there. I heard a problem, this guy's got a problem because, um, by the tone of his voice, he sounds very depressed. Ah . . .

Interviewer. Anything else going on in your mind?

Researcher's note. Both listeners make effective use of voice and extra-linguistic inferencing (tone of voice and background noises) along with word inferencing (*problème, fin de semaine*) to elaborate on the topic of this text. Both are creating a conceptual framework (friends talking about a weekend and something happened) within which they will interpret the upcoming language input. However, only the effective listener (Paula) gives evidence that she is anticipating what she might hear next.

> Tu sais, mon frère Francis, le grand de vingt ans, il a loue un appartement avec sa blonde. Il est parti de chez nous en fin de semaine et je l'ai aidé à déménager.

Paula. He helped his friend do something. I don't know what it was, but I heard him say helping his friend. Whatever happened, it was with his friend.	*Tom.* Just that I heard 'blonde', so must be something to be associated with a girlfriend because well, she wouldn't talk about another guy, so I mean, usually, probably, it's probably another girl, so they're, they're probably having a fight or some, some, something like that.

Researcher's note. Even though both listeners had difficulty with this excerpt, their protocols demonstrate a distinct difference in how they are handling this new input. Paula is using the framework she created earlier, along with a key verb (*aider*) to venture that 'he helped his friend do something' (problem identification), something she will continue to listen for. On the other hand, Tom has missed everything except 'blonde,' which he tries to tie in with what he learned earlier. Because he has missed so much new information, Tom appears to be in a 'deficit position' already with regard to interpreting upcoming linguistic input.

(Data from Vandergrift, 1998)

12.4.3   Research sample: using paused texts

A study by Rost and Ross (1991) presented listeners with paused texts (delivered in a one-to-one setting) and had them ask clarification questions. The researchers found that more proficient listeners tended to use more hypothesis-testing (asking about specific information in the story) rather than lexical push-downs (asking about word meanings) and global reprises (asking for general repetition). However, they also discovered that after training sessions, listeners at all levels could ask more hypothesis-testing questions and that their comprehension (measured by written summaries) improved as a result.

12.4.4   Research sample: using retrospective self-reports

Vandergrift (2007) reported on an extensive study involving retrospective self-report, in which learners report in an interview the techniques they used to comprehend recorded L2 (French) texts and their teacher while in class, as well as any out-of-class listening in French. Elaborating on O'Malley and Chamot's (1990) strategy classifications, Vandergrift found explicit examples of learner use of both metacognitive strategies such as planning and monitoring (e.g. 'I read over what we have to do first'), cognitive strategies such as linguistic inferencing and elaborating (e.g. 'I used other words in the sentence and guessed'), and socio-affective strategies such as questioning for clarification and self-encouragement (e.g. 'I ask the teacher to repeat'; 'I tell myself everyone else is probably having the same problem'). He found a greater reported use of metacognitive strategies at higher proficiency levels. Based on these findings, some researchers have proposed a pedagogy for encouraging use of metacognitive strategies at *all* levels of proficiency: a recommendation consistent with that of others advocating a metacognitive approach to language learning (See also: Goh, 2008; Cross, 2009; O'Malley, Chamot and Kupper 1989, Oxford 2010 for examples of retrospective listening reports.)

12.4.5 Project plan

In this project you will be comparing introspections of listeners to the same input. You can compare: two L1 listeners, one L1 and 1 L2 listener, or two L2 listeners.

- Preparation: Identify a pre-recorded audio or video input, such as a lecture segment or a scene from a film. Alternatively, you can pre-record your own audio or video for this purpose. Prepare a unit of text, at least a few minutes long, to present to your subjects. Prepare several pauses for the listeners to introspect.

- Identify the prompt, or probe, that you will use to elicit the listeners' reaction or response. If a student is unsure of what to say or how to continue, you can use non-cueing probes to encourage the listener to report what he or she was thinking: *What are you thinking now? What's going on in your mind? What makes you think that?* It is best not to ask specific text-related questions in order to avoid the question–answer type of interview. Also avoid having the introspection session become the listener asking you for clarification.

- Play the extract for the listeners. To increase the validity of this methodology, the system you use should be replicable. If you wish to examine and compare the listeners' protocols in detail, you will need to administer this procedure in a controlled way: with one listener at a time, pausing only at the pre-set points, using the same probes, etc. However, if you wish only to get a feel for this kind of research and its potential applications, you can use the methodology with a larger group, having the subjects write, rather than verbalise, their responses. Or it could be done in a language lab-type setting with individual microphones and audio recorders.

- After you have recorded your introspection reports, analyse the data. Can you label the types of responses you are getting. For example: talks about words, talks about ideas, asks about words, asks about ideas, predicts, makes an inference.

- Reflect on the protocols you have collected. Do you see any patterns in the protocols? What are the differences between L1 and L2 protocols? What are the differences among your L1 and L2 listeners?

Listening research tool   Think-aloud protocol

Strategy use has been studied through **retrospection** (asking the listener how he or she solved various problems while listening), through **online tasks** (particularly with 'problem texts' that force a listener to invoke a strategy for understanding), or through **reflection** (with paused listening activities, asking the listener what he or she is attending to at a particular moment).

Listening is impossible to observe directly, so researchers must utilise indirect means of accessing the listening process. One social research method, developed by Faerch and Kasper (1984) for L2 use, and elaborated by Vandergrift (1997; 1998) for listening is the **think-aloud protocol**.

Subjects are asked to listen to an audio extract or view a video extract. The extract is paused at pre-set points, usually corresponding to idea units or transitions in the text, or to plausible chunking units for short-term memory (approximately twenty to thirty seconds). At each pause point, the subject is asked to state what he or she is thinking, or produce some other protocol that can be analysed later.

Summary: access to psycholinguistic processes

The projects in this chapter included practical ways of gaining access to psycholinguistic processing. Though there are a range of experimental tasks that also reveal underlying psycholinguistic processing (see Chapters 2 and 3 for examples), most of these tasks and required presentation and measurement systems are impractical for most teachers and researchers to carry out.

The first project explored listener perception of speech, and the processing of the speech signal itself. In particular, the project is intended to demonstrate how, for competent listeners, it is possible to compensate for incomplete input and arrive at a comprehensible representation of what was said, even if the input contained unknown lexical items or grammatical structures. For less competent listeners, when processing goes awry, meaning building is often seriously disrupted.

The second project explored the complex topic of listener memory, and showed how comprehension and memory are interrelated. (Indeed, most tests of comprehension, as we saw in Chapter 10, are involved with probing memory.) We saw that different probes – open versus closed – are likely to yield different views of what the listener has understood and remembered. Closed probes (such as direct questions) often seem to indicate that the listener has understood and recalled a great deal more information than is indicated with open probes (such as summarising).

The third project concerned listener misunderstandings, with an emphasis on the notion that all misunderstandings have multiple causes, and these causes can be attributed to assumptions made by both the speaker and the listener.

The fourth project concerned listener strategies, or listener monitoring of plans for understanding. This project employed introspection protocols for gaining access to decisions about how to process unknown information, and about how much background knowledge to utilise when building meaning.

Chapter 13

Developmental orientations

A developmental orientation to listening research concerns both sociolinguistic and psycholinguistic aspects of listening, and focuses on how the person's listening ability develops over time. What aspects of listening ability are developing most quickly? Which are developing least effectively? Is there regression in any area? What factors seem to promote development? What factors seem to retard development?

Section II of this volume described approaches and methods for developing listening in a range of contexts, and recommended principles to apply in teaching, curriculum development, and assessment. This chapter does not aim to provide further recommendations, but rather attempts to outline approaches for researching learner development.

Three of the projects in this section explore ways of selecting designing tasks, activities, and courses for language learners (13.1) academic listening, (13.2) designing a listening course for autonomous learning, (13.3) evaluating listening materials. The fourth project in this section outlines a research project for teacher trainers: (13.4) conducting a teacher training module on listening.

13.1 Academic listening

Academic listening was discussed in Chapter 10 as a type of extensive listening, although it has some characteristics which make it unique. In academic listening contexts, primarily school and university settings, the listener (the student) is expected to interact with multiple sources of knowledge and to form collaborative relationship with other students. The listener is expected to use multiple sources of knowledge, only some of which are lecture situations, to help build mastery of a set of concepts in a particular domain and to demonstrate a degree of mastery of that content (cf. Benson, 1994; Flowerdew and Miller, 2009).

Specifically, academic listening, in its prototypical setting, entails the learner being responsible not only for listening to lectures, but also participating in discussion groups, interactions with tutors, collaborating with classmates on research and projects, and taking tests.

The purpose of this project is to trial different combinations of **interventions** in academic listening, in order to observe effects on learners' motivation, learning strategies, and listening performance. Interventions are defined here as particular instructional actions that the teacher takes during the course of a lesson to draw learners' attention to opportunities for learning that they are missing or to bring learners back on task if they have been overwhelmed or distracted (Clement, 2007).

13.1.1 Initial questions

- How does academic listening differ from social listening? In terms of listener role? In terms of interaction with others? In terms of preparation? In terms of accountability?

- In an academic lecture, how do we know the extent to which the typical listener is understanding the lecture content, fully or partially?

- How do we know when an L2 listener is distracted or 'off message'? An early study in this area by Candlin and Murphy (1976) explored how L2 listeners in engineering lectures were attending to the 'core message' (what Candlin and Murphy called the 'gen'), and to what extent they were listening and attending to 'off focus' comments by the lecturer (signalled by distinct prosody and pacing, gestures, physical positioning). To what extent do you think L2 listeners might be able to distinguish 'core' messages' from 'tangential' or 'off focus' messages?

- How does a listener gauge his or her own understanding? How do listeners come to understand content that they don't initially understand?

- What can lecturers do to improve understanding by listeners?

- What factors improve listener performance? Preparation, note-taking prompts, class participation, note-taking review, repeated listenings, tests?

- What are valid measurements of lecture comprehension?

13.1.2 Data sample: interventions

Clement *et al.* (2009) prepared an intervention model of instruction in an academic listening class using pre-recorded lectures on video. They attempted to measure perceived effects of the following interventions on learner performance:

- Explicit instruction on strategies for attention focusing and note-taking.
- Use of 'pop-up instructional tips' that provided note-taking tips (twelve different tips were provided) and attention reminders (three different reminders: prediction, guessing, and reflective summarising) on the video screen at fixed intervals.
- Multiple listenings and three re-trials of note-taking after feedback.
- Use of guided discussion to review notes, by native speaker models. The researchers had pre-recorded native speaker models of students discussing their notes, along with a list of nine specific discussion strategies that students were encouraged to try in their own groups.

At the end of the course, learners were asked to evaluate these interventions in terms of their perceived value in making progress in the course. Learner questionnaires were compiled and a relative weighting of perceived importance of these interventions was calculated:

Test taking practice, 30 per cent.

Discussion groups, 20 per cent.

Note-taking practice and tips, 20 per cent.

Group projects, 10 per cent.

Vocabulary instruction, 10 per cent.

Guided summarisation of lectures, 10 per cent.

Based on this evidence of learner evaluating, and triangulating with other objective measures of learner progress, the researchers concluded that test-taking practice and guided discussion groups were key activities that should be emphasised in courses dealing with academic listening. They also concluded that the 'pop-up interventions' during the video, while reported as helpful by some, were not perceived as more helpful than more traditional, non-technical interventions such as vocabulary and summarisation practice.

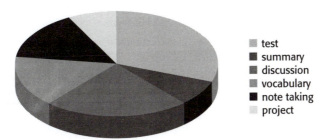

Figure 13.1 *Student perceptions of value in various interventions.*
A graphic depiction of the perceived importance of various instructional activities provides useful feedback to the teacher

13.1.3   Project plan

- Choose one or more **interventions** that you will systematically use in your teaching of listening. If you are teaching an academic listening class, you can choose interventions such as pre-listening **note-taking tips** (**reductive** or **elaborative**) **simplifications** during the lectures or repetitions of the lectures, addition of a group discussion step following each lecture or lecture segment, or previews of tests before lectures.

- Choose an observable measurement for assessing whether the intervention is having any effect on learner improvement or motivation. (Keep in mind that the effect may not be in the predicted direction.) The measurement might be increase in some form of participation from students, change in note-taking density or style, performance on tests or written assignments, or self-reflective comments from the learners.

- Repeat the treatment or intervention for a number of trials (classes). Keep track of leaner performance or attitudes over time. If you wish to test for significance of correlations between subjects' reports of which interventions they rated as most valuable and their (rank-order) progress on objective measures in the course, you will need to use Spearman rho (correlations). (See Chapter 14 for resources.)

- Reflect on the role of instruction and the role of specific interventions on student learning. Is progress due mainly to 'time on task', that is, the time that students spend actually engaged in the target situation and

---

Listening research tool   Use quasi-experimental designs in educational settings

A true experiment seeks to compare treatments or interventions in order to arrive, and it usually implies a controlled experiment in which individuals are randomly assigned to one of two or more treatment groups. At the end of a treatment period, average results are compared for the groups.

While it is useful to compare treatments (such as, instructional plans) and interventions (such as, specific instructional techniques), these types of controlled experiments are typically not plausible in language education. In normal educational settings, it is seldom possible to conduct a randomised, controlled experiment, and it is often unethical to withhold a potentially beneficial treatment from some students for the sake of experimentation. The alternative is to use a quasi-experimental design, which uses natural groupings of individuals (e.g. already meeting as part of a class-based curriculum), and does not seek to compare treatments with another group, but to compare the value of treatments *with itself* over time, from one session to the next. This is called a time-series analysis, and is very useful for educational settings. (See Chapter 14 for resources on using this type of design.)

trying to excel in it? How much of the progress is due to specific instructional interventions and feedback from the instructor? How much of the progress is due to guidance given in advance?

13.2   Listening materials

The purpose of this project is to generate criteria for evaluation of listening materials. As we outlined in Chapter 9, listening materials include the input materials, accompanying tasks and means of assessment and feedback. This project is designed to be of use when materials for a course or for learners are already assigned, including text, audio, video, and online components. By conducting a valid materials evaluation project, teachers and curriculum planners can arrive at practical solutions for selecting and adapting and supplementing materials.

13.2.1   Initial questions

- Are published materials (books, prepared audio and video materials) needed for listening instruction or are naturally occurring materials (found sources on public media or from internet sources from academic institutions) sufficient for teaching academic listening?
- What are the essential criteria for selecting materials? Authenticity? (See Chapter 8 for a discussion.) Relevance to student interests? Length? Type of pedagogic support?
- If materials are already assigned for a learner or class (including text, media, online components), which of the components should be used? Which components can be skipped or adapted? How should the materials be best exploited?
- What is the value of making collaborative decisions between teacher and learners on which materials to use, how to use them, and how to supplement them?

Teaching materials for listening consist of some form of input and some form of a task or a sequence of tasks. Tasks play an important part in language pedagogy. Candlin (1987), in a seminal work on task design, provided a working definition of a language learning task as a 'problem-posing, social, and interdependent activity which involves the application of existing knowledge to attain a goal'. Ellis (2002), Richards (2008), Wilson (2008) and others, defining **listening tasks**, have elaborated this notion to include **task-as-workplan** (with a definable external goal) or **task-as-process** (with targeted psycholinguistic processes) (cf. Samuda and Bygate, 2008; Breen, 2001). The former, task-as-workplan, aligns with 'listening to comprehend', while the latter, task-as-process, aligns with 'listening to learn.'

13.2.2 Sample questionnaires: materials evaluation frameworks

Framework 1

When selecting, adapting or designing materials for listening, curriculum planners and teacher groups often develop explicit educational criteria, based on principles of listening and effective instruction, to guide their decisions. (These criteria are intended to neutralise emotional and political criteria that often underpin selection decisions.) Two examples are given below. Alamri (2008), preparing criteria for selection of materials for students in Saudi Arabia, and Thein (2006), evaluating materials for Thailand, used the following categories (synthesised here):

- *General appearance.* Is it modern and up to date with current trends?
- *Design and illustration.* Are they attractive?
- *Objectives.* Are they clearly stated, aligned with current theory?
- *Topic content.* Is the content thorough and ordered sensibly?
- *Listening content.* Is it naturally recorded? Is it sufficient? Are there a variety of speakers?
- *Multimedia content.* Is it varied, state-of-the-art, engaging?
- *Language content.* Is it complete? Does it cover items in syllabus?
- *Social and cultural context.* Is it varied? Does it convey appropriate cultural values?
- *Language skills.* Are skills balanced? Is there appropriate focus on all four skills?
- *Teachability.* Is it easy for teachers to know what to do?
- *Flexibility.* Is it easy to supplement?
- *Practice.* Does it have ample practice?
- *Testing.* Does it have abundant testing? Are the tests fair?

This list of categories is adapted from Alamri (2008), preparing criteria for selection of materials for students in Saudi Arabia, and from Thein (2006), evaluating materials for Thailand.

Framework 2

Skierso (1991) has proposed less structured, more reflective questions for materials evaluation:

- Do the materials teach what you want to teach – specific skills, strategies, general abilities to deal with certain inputs?

- What classroom procedures will you be using when you employ these materials?
- Is the material at the right level for your students?
- Are the procedures easy to figure out – for you? For the students?
- Are there appropriate visuals – charts, illustrations, etc., to engage students and guide learning?
- Is it reasonably up to date?
- Are the exercises varied? (Too varied?)
- What kind of supplementation will be necessary?
- Does the material allow for learners at multiple levels to use it?
- Is the material readily available?
- Is it reasonably priced for the students?
- What kind of supplementation will be needed in class and out of class?

13.2.3   Project plan

In this project you will be examining multiple sets of materials for adoption for a particular learner or group of learners. To carry out the project you need a set of materials for consideration, and a target group of learners for whom the materials are intended.

- Survey the materials currently used in your plan for teaching listening. Develop a questionnaire like that of Skierso (1991) or a checklist of categories like that of Almari (2008) and Thein (2006). Consider developing a separate checklist for each component: textbook, audio, video, online resources, other technologies.
- Using your checklist, go through each set of materials you are using (textbooks, media, teacher's guides) thoroughly and answer each question explicitly. If possible, have a colleague do the same, either independently, or collaboratively with you.
- Compile the results of the survey in a raw form. Discuss the results with a colleague before deciding how to present them. Consider a statistical computation of frequencies of responses, and check for correlations of responses, among teachers.
- If possible, have some students participate in the evaluation. Incorporate their responses into the overall data.
- Compile the survey data and present the data in a way that is clear to everyone who is involved in the rating and the decision-making.
- How does the presentation of survey findings assist you in making decisions about the utility of materials? In what areas is there most clarity?

In what areas is there most ambiguity? Are some categories weighted more heavily than others? Does a negative in one particular category outweigh other positives?

- If you can design your own materials or supplement the course materials, what are the top priorities for you?

13.3 Autonomous listening

Increasing learner autonomy, even in small ways, is generally a positive goal for teaching learners of all ages. The purpose of this project is to create an autonomous listening course, one in which learners perform some or most of the work in the course by themselves, without direct instruction or supervision from the teacher. This project provides three sets of resources to use as guidelines for developing an initial proposal.

13.3.1 Initial questions

- What role does self-access play in developing listening skills?
- What are the relative strengths and weaknesses of self-access learning centres?
- What would the ideal self-access centre be like? Would your students use it?
- What 'help options' are needed to keep learners involved and on track?
- What types of guidance or advice tips are needed to help assure success in an autonomous listening course?

Self-access listening centres are an important resource for language teaching. Here are some principles that successful centres have followed:

- Have an ample amount of oral material, on a variety of topics, in different modalities.
- Prepare exercises to accompany at least some of the materials.
- Require learner logs or journals to report what they have listened to and their reactions to it.
- Keep tape scripts available for reference for at least some of the material.
- Provide a means of ongoing teacher support for learners who use the listening centre.
- Give guidance to students on how to use the centre.
- Give advice for long-term learning strategies.

(Cf. Miller *et al.*, 2007)

13.3.2   Sample resources

Resource 1: general guidelines for setting up a self-access language centre (SALC)

- *Self-access learning should be truly self-access.* Many institutions *require* students to use their self-access centre as part of a course of study. Cooker believes that self-access learning, to be sustainable, should be truly self-access. Although all learners in a programme should be given a thorough orientation and a 'pitch' about the value of self-access learning, the learners should not be required to use the facility. Cooker (2004, 2008) reports that in the SALC at the Kanda Institute of Foreign Studies in Chiba, Japan, use of the centre is completely optional. Despite this, she notes, the centre is extremely popular.

- *Students should have an integral role in the running of the centre.* Students should take on a guiding role in the development of the SALC. Students can become part-time administrators, and play an important role not just in staffing the SALC but also in selecting and trialling materials and in promoting the centre to other students. At a remarkable SALC at Kin-ki University Osaka, Japan, called E-cube, faculty claim that student involvement and student promotion are the keys to its success.

- *Language learning should be fun.* If a self-access centre is truly self-access, then learners need to be enticed into the centre, and the most effective way of doing this is to make language learning fun. The SALC is stocked with materials which aim to engage learners in ways which are fun and entertaining, and not available in their regular classroom courses. In many EFL contexts in which English language classes are traditionally very teacher-centred, encouraging learners to understand that language learning can be enjoyable *and* worth while has been a persistent challenge.

- *The self-access centre should aim to be a place where learners choose to be.* The SALC should aim to create an environment which does not feel like a typical classroom or library. Through careful choice of decorative schemes, furniture, physical layout and displays it is possible to create a space that feels 'different'. Cooker notes that her students at Kanda University of International Studies have commented that the SALC felt like a 'little piece of America' or that it was like a 'reverse home stay'. The relaxed ambience provides a place where students would choose to hang out, and thereby encourage them to use the facilities and materials.

(Adapted from Cooker, 2008)

Resource 2: checklist for activity and task support

In addition to the global features that support successful SALCs (cf. Cooker, 2008; Gardner and Miller, 1999), it is important to investigate the effectiveness of the learning materials themselves, and the kinds of support provided to allow learners to maximise the use of the materials. Rost (2007) surveyed online learning materials and available 'help options' to see which of these options were being used and valued by learners as they interacted with media and tasks. A list of the options appears below:

- Annotations: textual (translation or L2).
- Background information.
- Vocabulary look ups.
- Pause.
- Replay options.
- Bookmarking.
- Coaching comment, interventions during the viewing or listening experience.
- Record own comment (record file).
- Opportunity to repeat (record button).
- Send question (oral or written) to teacher.
- Post comment to discussion board, social network.
- Check answers immediately.
- Get cue for incorrect answers.
- Internet links directly related to tasks.
- Track own progress (time on tasks, scores).
- Self-assessment tools.

(Rost, 2007)

Resource 3: material selection

The actual design of a self-access listening centre, whether it is a physical facility or an online resource network, will involve general design principles (such as those suggested by Cooker, 2008), selection of input materials and tasks, and insurance of task support. The following example, from McVeigh (2010) presents a 'top ten' list of ideas that have been successful for his SALC in selecting materials and designing tasks.

Here's my Top Ten list of what makes our self-access learning center work:

- *Recommended films.* I keep only a small selection of films for the center. In addition to *When Harry Met Sally* and *Clueless*, the films that I have had the most success with are *Butch Cassidy and the Sundance Kid*, *Dead Poets Society*, *The Graduate*, *The Princess Bride* and *A River Runs through It*. Using a small number of recommended resources – in several categories like comedies, dramas, serial television shows, etc. – works better for us than just having a bunch of unclassified resources that we aren't sure will be successful.

- *Transcripts.* Generally, I use screenplays – or preferably transcripts – together with the movie or television show or video clip, to help students grasp the language, which is often quite idiomatic. You can find lists of published scripts at the larger internet booksellers. A search on the web for screenplays will also reveal a number of sites that have full texts.

- *Caption decoder* (provides captioning at the bottom of the screen). This reinforces listening with reading.

- *Comprehension questions.* We have found that including comprehension checks keeps learners on track. Just having a few comprehension questions helps focus students' attention on specific aspects of a film or video. I usually have students work on these in a small group team format.

- *Dictations* or modified dictations, at least for parts of the film or video, help develop intensive listening ability. And learners who think they understand everything are very surprised when they try to do close dictations of parts of the films.

- *Vocabulary round-tables.* Vocabulary learning is always a motivator for our students, and they will use the SALC if they think it's helping them improve their vocab. Invite students to identify new words and expressions in the script, try to come up with their meanings and share their word lists with other students.

- *Sequencing activities.* This is sort of game-like, and it helps loosen up the atmosphere. We prepare one-sentence summaries of the key events in the film. We then cut them into pieces or put them on a page or screen in random order. Have students rearrange or number them to reconstruct the chronological story of the film.

- *Acting out.* Because SALCs tend to have a reputation for being too passive, we try to include more active tasks. Have students select a small portion of the film and act it out with fellow students. I would suggest recommending specific scenes which would lend themselves to this.

- *Student-developed quizzes.* Have students come up with their own questions about the film and then face off in teams in a quiz-show format.

- *Sportscasting.* Turn down the sound. Students in pairs take turns describing the action on the screen.

Joe McVeigh
www.joemcveigh.com

13.3.3 Project plan

In this project you will be creating a self-access listening resource centre (which may or may not be a physical place) for a group of learners. You can use guidelines provided in the resource set, or develop your own.

- Identify a single learner or a group of learners who may benefit from an autonomous listening course, or a supplemental listening component to an existing language or content course. If possible, survey them on what content, methodology and technologies they would like to use.

- Gather available resources that can be used for the course. If the learners are going to be meeting at a specific facility, you can start small, with perhaps a few music MP3 files, a dozen films or television shows in a computer database (these should be obtained legally, of course), or using DVD media, five or six recorded interviews as MP3 files, a few computers with internet access, and a list of free or subscribed web sites you recommend. (See Chapter 14 for recommendations.) By 'starting small' you can get the SALC operating, and add materials and links and subscriptions as needed.

- Develop some kind of task or collaborative activity to go with each listening input. These can be open-ended questions, brief reports, self-reflection questionnaires or team discussion questions. You can revise these tasks on an ongoing basis.

- Develop some form of learner logs. Learners should record what they listened to or watched or participated in and their evaluation of the experience. Learner logs can be done in teams, along the lines of 'listening buddies' recommended by Goh (2010).

- At the end of a given period, prepare a 'top ten' list. What resources or sites or particular activities did the learners use most? Which received the highest evaluations? Why?

- Post your updated top-ten lists and other comments, perhaps using a course management system like Moodle (www.moodle.com). Elicit comments from the students and encourage the creation of discussion boards. (Establish firm rules and appoint student monitors for any discussion boards.)

- After a period of time, prepare some tips for other teachers on developing an autonomous listening course.

13.4 Teacher training

This entire book has focused on concepts, practices, and attitudes that contribute to better research and teaching in the area of listening. Section II (Chapters 7–10) in particular dealt with principles of curriculum design, instruction, and assessment. Many readers of this volume will be responsible for teacher training, and may be using this book as part of their research on conducting training modules for teachers. The purpose of this project is to provide a structure for researching concepts and resources to be included in a condensed course on the teaching of listening.

13.4.1   Initial questions

- Of the teachers you know, who are the best at teaching listening? Why are they successful? What do they do differently from other teachers?
- What does every language teacher need to know about the nature of listening – L1 and L2 listening – in order to teach listening well? Can you think of five topics or concepts that teachers should be familiar with?
- Which listening experts – teachers, authors, applied linguists, other educators – have influenced you, and may be able to have a positive impact on other teachers in the area of listening?
- If you were to design a short course for teaching listening, what readings, lectures, and activities would you include?

Resource 1: Teacher Development Interactive: Listening

An introductory online course designed by Rost (2009) prepares new teachers to teach listening, and to provide a refresher course for practicing teachers. Consider the coverage and structure of the course, as outlined below. The course consists of short lessons featuring:

- Short lecture clips of experts in English language teaching and teacher training who present material through video lectures and slide presentations.
- Written texts and glosses to help explain key concepts.
- Frequent concept checks and practice tasks provide immediate feedback on key concepts.
- Video clips of actual classroom lessons in which listening is being taught, demonstrating the concepts in action.
- Podcasts with expert interviews give important additional information about the concepts.
- Application tasks and discussion questions to put concepts into practice.
- Writing assignments with opportunities for reflection, materials design, and classroom research.
- Assessment through 'concept checks' and quizzes in each lesson and a final module test.

Table 13.1 **Plan for a short teacher-training module on listening**

LESSON	SESSION A	SESSION B	SESSION C
1 Understanding listening	Listening processes	Listening skills and strategies	Listening problems
2 Preparing a three-stage listening lesson	Before listening	While listening	After listening
3 Selecting listening materials	Finding sources of listening input	Using different types of listening	Using multimedia for listening
4 Designing tasks	Recognising four modes of listening	Devising tasks	Promoting self-access
5 Assessing listening	Designing your own tests	Reviewing standard tests	Self-assessment

Resource 2: How to Teach Listening *(Wilson, 2008)*

Wilson's *How to Teach Listening* is intended to be very practical: it provides a multitude of examples of published activities and includes a CD-ROM that provides sample audio in addition to textbook illustrations. The book is organised around these chapters:

1 *Listening in the world of language learning* includes a discussion of why listening is difficult and the role of listening in communicative language teaching.

2 *Listening texts and listening strategies* includes a short discussion of 'authentic' versus 'pedagogic' texts and an overview of twelve strategies that 'good listeners' use.

3 *Listening sources, listening tasks* discusses benefits of different sources of listening (teacher talk, student talk, guest speakers, textbook recordings, media – television, video, DVD, radio – songs, internet), including a breakdown of popular genres (news, film clips, advertisements, documentaries, comedy episodes, animation, interviews, game shows) and benefits of using them for listening practice, and types of comprehension exercises in the form of 'listen and . . .' (e.g. 'listen and take notes').

4 *Pre-listening skills and activities* includes a general discussion of activating schemata and establishing reasons for listening, comprehension questions, and the value pre-teaching vocabulary.

5 *While-listening skills and activities* includes a discussion of listening for gist versus listening for detail, inferring, and participating.

6 *Post-listening skills and activities* includes a discussion of reflection and types of responses.

Resource 3: Teaching ESL/EFL Listening and Speaking *(Nation and Newton, 2009)*

This teacher training volume by Nation and Newton presents an integrated approach to teaching listening and speaking. The course is based on the notion of incorporating speaking and listening within a balanced language course that consists of four strands:

- Learning through meaning-focused input: listening and reading.
- Learning through meaning-focused output: speaking and writing for an audience.
- Learning through deliberate attention to language items and language features.
- Developing fluent use of known language items and features over the four skills.

Within this framework, the course deals with models of listening (as an active process), types of listening (one-way versus two-way), and listening processes (bottom-up and top-down). The course then discusses a range of activities for meaning-focused listening. In addition, there is a full chapter on language-focused learning through dictation and related intensive listening activities.

13.4.2   Project plan

This project involves outlining a teacher training course or module on the topic of listening, based on what you consider to be the most important elements to include. It is best done if you have a group of teachers or trainees in mind.

- Create an initial assessment instrument for your teachers. What do they already know about teaching listening? What are their current practices? What do they feel they need to know? What do you feel they need to know?

- Survey at least three training oriented books or online courses related to listening. You can use the three resources sampled above, or others that are available to you. Aim for a range of resources, rather than ones that emphasise the same topics or approaches. What are the key concepts in each course? What concepts seem to be made overly complex? Which seem overly simplified? Are some concepts ignored or misrepresented in any of the courses?

- Locate at least five extracts (readings or audio or video recordings of lectures) from different teachers or researchers in the area of listening that you would like to include in your course. Give each extract a title, showing the reason you have included it.

- Present your course outline to colleagues and ask for their feedback: How relevant is your course? How thorough is it? How up to date is it? How user-friendly is it? How will you assess whether users have benefited from your course?

Summary: mixed methods of research

This chapter has presented outlines for four research projects that focus on developmental goals for learners and for teachers. The first three projects were aimed at researching learners in the process of developing their listening skills and strategies.

The fourth project was designed to place the reader in the role of teacher trainer, providing a framework for researching what elements would constitute a valuable course on listening for language teachers.

IV Exploring listening

Chapter 14

Resources for further exploration

14.1 Resources for teaching listening

Materials for teaching listening include sources of audio and video input, as well as opportunities for spoken interaction, and structured tasks and activities that develop comprehension and learning strategies. Commercial educational publishers provide a steady stream of new materials, and countless internet sites provide an abundance of free and affordable resources for teaching listening. In this part of the chapter, which supplements Section II, only a small sampling of this array of resources can be indicated, along with guidelines for making sensible selections. (See also section 13.3 for guidelines on evaluating materials.)

While there are several major publishers who offer commercially available listening materials, there are numerous small publishers and local publishers to supplement the offerings of the major ones. In order to stay current on the offerings of publishers, it is advisable to survey online catalogues for new publications. Below are a few of the online catalogues that can be checked periodically for updates. Most sites allow for online viewing of samples of student and teacher materials, including any electronic versions of products and companion web sites (which may offer supplementary listening or viewing resources), and auditing of audio and video clips.

14.1.1 Published sources

Because published resources are updated continuously, it is best to view current catalogues – online versions are preferable because it is easier to search for key words (such as *new*, *listening*, *multimedia*, etc.). Here are some of the many sources of published material to begin a review. At each publisher site, the first step is to search 'catalogue' and then enter additional search terms. Some search terms are suggested below.

Cambridge University Press, www.cambridge.org/us/esl/catalog/. Search: skills, listening, academic listening, coursebooks.

Cengage Learning, www.cengage.com. Search: catalogue, skills, listening, academic listening, coursebooks, online learning.

Macmillan English, www.macmillanenglish.com. Search: catalogue, skills, listening, coursebooks, multimedia, onestopenglish.

Oxford University Press, www.oup.com. Search: catalogue, skills, listening and speaking.

Pearson Education, www.pearsonlongman.com/index.html. Search: skills, listening, academic, coursebooks, assessment, e-learning, multimedia, myEnglishlab, SIOP (Sheltered Instruction Observation Protocol).

An alternative to visiting global publisher sites is to visit a local publisher site, a local teacher training site or local bookseller site to view the published resources that they have available.

14.1.2 Internet sources

Internet sources for listening, particularly in English or other major languages, are also abundant. The key to selection on the internet is not popularity, or ease of access to the site, or even ease of navigability on the site. The keys to selection are: appropriateness and relevance of content, length of extracts (shorter is generally preferable), linking of extracts (interrelated are preferable), support material for comprehension (graphic and textual), possibilities of networking with other users and availability of help menus, as well as transparency of navigation. Below are selected examples:

Awesome stories, www.awesomestories.com. A resources site that allows users to access information about films, famous trials, disasters, history and biography. Includes text, audio and video clips on a range of subjects. Also includes lesson plans, designed for native speakers, that can be adapted to EFL/ESL audiences.

Brain Pop, www.brainpop.com. A subscription site that includes academic topics presented in a **sheltered instruction** style: science, health, reading and writing, social studies, mathematics, arts and technology. Includes two additional sites: Brain Pop Junior for younger learners and Brain Pop ESL for L2 learners.

Learn Out Loud, www.learnoutloud.com. Offers a large directory of audio and video learning resources. Access to 10,000 available titles, including audio books, MP3 downloads, podcasts and free educational audio and video.

Story Corps, www.storycorps.org. An independent non-profit project whose stated mission is to honour and celebrate one another's lives through listening. The Story Corps audio archive contains over 50,000 stories told by family and friends. Story Corps is one of the largest oral history projects of its kind, and millions listen to its broadcasts on public radio and the web. Stories are generally told interactively to an interviewer, and presented in short segments, less than five minutes each, for easy accessibility. Site also includes ways for users to add their own stories.

Lingual Net, www.lingual.net. Includes a variety of genres of short films, including drama, animation, comedy, travel, music and short serial stories presented in an interactive game format. Includes transcripts, subtitles, comprehension checks and interactive coaching for some films.

English Language Listening Library Online, www.elllo.org. A popular free site features hundreds of short interview and monologue audio clips conducted in natural English, with notes and quizzes. Produced at an international university in Japan, elllo features a range of language varieties and accents, and contains a number of game-like activities.

Stone Soup, www.stonesoup.com/listen. For elementary age students, fictional stories told by young authors.

TED (Technology, Entertainment, Design), www.ted.com. Video recordings from global TED events where the world's leading thinkers and doers in a variety of fields, from science to politics, gather to find and share inspiration. Generally advanced in conceptual and linguistic level, themes are related to technology.

14.1.3   Online listening sources

Games

The American Speech–Hearing Association (ASHA) www.asha.org provides therapeutic listening activities, which can be used to help a person recovering from auditory aphasia: www.mnsu.edu/comdis/kuster4/part88.html. This site is co-ordinated by Judith Kuster of Minnesota State University, Mankato, MN.

The Baby Center provides an abundance of language activities and games involving listening for very young children: www.babycenter.com/kids-activities.

The EFL playhouse offers a large menu of language learning games for children, many of which involve listening: www.esl4kids.net/games.html.

The Experiential Learning Group offers listening games oriented for adults: www.experiential-learning-games.com/listeninggames.html.

Learn English Kids, a British Council-supported site, offers links to a variety of listening games: www.britishcouncil.org/kids-listen-up.htm.

Podcasts and videocasts

The following sites provide resources for developing your own podcasts, as well as directories to a range of ready to use podcasts, videocasts and audio and video links.

Podbean.com, www.podbean.com. Provides a range of high-quality content, including 'The Medical Minute', several exercise, dance, and yoga instructional video series, video game reviews and 'Mondo Mini' shows (comedy).

ESLpod.com, www.eslpod.com. Provides a variety of short pedagogic podcasts (simplified or slowed-down presentations, with lists of vocabulary) many for free download.

ESLstudentpublications.com, www.eslstudentpublications.com. Provides a range of student-produced podcasts, usually in the form of interviews or demonstration-slide shows. Topics include a variety of 'how-to' demonstrations and talks about current events.

listen-to-english.com, www.listen-to-english.com. Focuses on short pedagogic podcasts and vocabulary building.

Short films

Various sites show short films that are suitable for language learning. Many contain subtitles and offer some interactivity with viewers: www.video.about.com/, www.yappr.com, www.jokeroo.com/, shorts. futurethought.tv.

Commercial television

Hulu, www.hulu.com. Free showings of selected commercial television from American networks, including talk shows and comic series.

Public broadcasts

BBC, www.bbc.co/uk/worldservice/BBC_English/progs.htm. A range of audio and video broadcasts available for online streaming.

BBC, www.bbc.co.uk/podcasts/series/tae. Downloadable podcasts.

CNN, www.cnn.com/video. Streaming video of current news stories.

Radio broadcasts

Live 365, www.live365.com/index.live. Links to live internet radio stations from around the world, including global varieties of music and talk radio shows.

Shoutcast, www.shoutcast.com/radio/Spoken.

Internet radio guide, www.internet-radio-guide.net/en/web-radio/220-comedy.html\.

14.1.4   Online courses

There are countless online courses available for English and other major languages, and the number increases constantly. This is a selected review of a few courses that are listening based.

Aurolog, us.tellmemore.com. Emphasises interaction and use of language skills in real-world situations. Video-based, using authentic contexts. Uses speech-recognition technology and feedback.

LiveMocha, www.livemocha.com. Social network site that includes interaction with other members, peer correction. A range of optional online courses, including Active English, a version of Longman English Interactive.

Tactical language, www.tacticallanguage.com. Developed by the US Defense Language Institute, students play immersive, interactive 3-D video games that simulate real life communication by role playing with animated 'socially intelligent virtual humans'. If students speak and behave correctly, the virtual humans become trustful and co-operative, and provide information that trainees need to advance. Storylines provide a wide range of game-play paths, interactive dialogs and action options.

Testing resources

Cambridge ESL, www.cambridgeesol.org/exams/index.html. Publishers of KET (Key English Test) PET (Preliminary English Test), FCE (First Certificate in English), CAE (Certificate in Advanced English), YLE (Young Learners Exam) and other exams.

Educational Testing Services, http://ets.org/portal/site/ets/. Publishers of TOEFL®, TOEIC® and many other exams. Contains test analyses and samples.

English Online, www.english-online.org.uk/exam.htm. Contains practice tests, including listening extracts for major exams, including PET, FCE, CAE, CPE, TOEFL, IELTS.

Oxford English Testing, www.oxfordenglishtesting.com. Features the Oxford Online Placement Test and online practice tests for the KET, PET, FCE, CAE, IELTS, TOEIC® and TOEFL® iBT exams.

Pearson Longman Exams, www.pearsonlongman.com/exams/. A portal for information and practice on numerous exams, including the Pearson

Test of English (PTE), Cambridge ESOL, IELTS, TOEIC,® TOEFL,® London Tests of English, University of Cambridge Local Examinations Syndicate (UCLES), Michigan Tests, Trinity ESOL Business Language Testing Service (BULATS), the European Languages Certificate (TELC).

14.1.5 Directories

A number of web sites now serve as directories for aiding teachers in finding online resources. Here are a few of them:

California Distant Learning Project, www.cdlponline.org. Adult learning activities, linked to audio and video resources. Oriented toward practical topics for immigrants to the U.S., including working, law and government, family, school, housing. Each topic area contains up to fifty audio or video 'stories', with learning activities.

Outreach and technical assistance network, www.otan.us. Web-based activities, teacher-developed courses uses authentic audio and video.

Community Learning Network, www.cln.org/themes/listening.html. Collection of themes for teaching listening using online resources.

14.2 Resources for researching listening

Section III (Chapters 11–13) presented projects for researching listening. This section offers additional resources for carrying out those projects and other related projects, for finding published projects of similar types, and for disseminating one's own research.

14.2.1 Research networks

Research networks are groups of individuals and institutions engaged in similar research plans. Many of these networks are open, and provide resources and support freely.

I Teach, I Learn, iteachilearn.com. Participates in multiple levels of educational research and design, particularly focusing on bilingual education. Serves as a portal to a number of other informative and interactive sites.

Method Space, www.methodspace.com. Methodspace claims to be the home of 'the research methods community' from across the world. Contains forums, groups, resources and live chats.

National Clearinghouse for English Language Acquisition, www.ncela.gwu.edu/webinars/. The (US) National Clearinghouse for English Language

Acquisition collects, co-ordinates and conveys a broad range of research and resources in support of an inclusive approach to high quality education for ELLs.

UACES Student Forum, www.uacesstudentforum.org. The UACES Student Forum is the student branch of the University Association for Contemporary European Studies (UACES), which aims to provide students with useful resources and networks for their research. The aim of the Student Forum is to provide a voice for graduate students within UACES and to facilitate dialogue and the exchange of information between students at different institutions.

14.2.2   Research tools

As discussed in Section 3 (Chapters 11, 12, 13), carrying out a project in a thorough and replicable fashion requires using specific qualitative and quantitative tools, such as surveys, correlations and group comparisons. This sub-section of the chapter provides links to obtaining and developing these resources.

Research Methods Knowledge Base, www.socialresearchmethods.net/kb/. The Research Methods Knowledge Base is a free web-based textbook offering an introductory course in applied social research methods, created by Bill Trochim, a professor at Cornell University. It covers the theory and practice of research, and topics such as defining a research question, sampling, measurement, research design and data analysis.

ESRC National Centre for Research Methods, www.ncrm.ac.uk/. The centre works in collaboration with the ESRC Research Methods Programme to provide a focal point for the identification, development and delivery of a national training programme for research methods. Details of publications and training events are available from the site.

COPAC, www.copac.ac.uk/. A good starting point for literature searches on a variety of educational topics, COPAC is a freely available bibliographic catalogue of 24 of the major university research libraries in the UK as well as the British Library, National Library of Wales and National Library of Scotland. Users can connect to the web interface or connect directly to the database using bibliographic management software to download references directly to their computers.

Qualitative Report, www.nova.edu/ssss/QR/. *The Qualitative Report* (TQR) is a peer-reviewed online journal dedicated to qualitative research and critical enquiry which also serves as a forum and sounding board for researchers.

Internet for Social Research Methods, www.vts.intute.ac.uk/tutorial/social-research-methods/. Free online tutorials designed to help students, lecturers and researchers improve their internet information literacy and IT skills.

Qual-software, www.jiscmail.ac.uk/lists/qual-software.html. A discussion list to increase awareness and debate about Computer Assisted Qualitative Data Analysis Software. The list provides an instant forum for users and developers to air problems, offer opinions, argument and advice on the variety of software packages in use.

Qualitative-research, www.jiscmail.ac.uk /lists/qualitative-research.html. A list devoted to all aspects of qualitative research: methodological; theoretical and practical and is also intended to facilitate discussion of diverse qualitative research: interviewing; ethnography; participation observation; focus groups; biographical and life history studies.

Center for Advanced Research on Language Acquisition, www.carla.umn.edu/resources/teaching/chinese_mn.html. The Center for Advanced Research on Language Acquisition at the University of Minnesota offers resources on research for instruction and assessment.

Center for Applied Linguistics, www.cal.org/research/. CAL funds and publishes applied linguistics research as a foundation for the development of pragmatic solutions to a variety of issues related to language and culture.

Experimental Designs, www.mantex.co.uk/2009/09/29/how-to-solve-research-problems/. Tutorials in selecting appropriate experimental designs.

Quantitative Design and Statistics tutorials, www.statpages.org. The Interactive Statistical Pages project represents an ongoing effort to develop and disseminate statistical analysis software in the form of web pages. Utilising HTML forms, CGI and Perl scripts, Java, JavaScript and other browser-based technologies, each web page contains within it (or invokes) all the programming needed to perform a particular computation or analysis.

Statistical Consulting, www.dkstatisticalconsulting.com/statistics-resources/. Includes a number of resources for statistics students. Has information and resources on Pearson's correlation coefficient or Pearson's r, chi-square, t-tests, including the one-sample t-test, the independent samples t-test and the dependent samples t-test, and the ANOVA, or Analysis of Variance.

SticiGui (pronounced 'sticky gooey'), statistics.berkeley.edu/~stark/SticiGui/. An introductory class in statistics for business, social science, taught by Philip Stark.

Sample release forms for researchers. Free Management Library, managementhelp.org/evaluatn/consent.htm; Stories for Change, storiesforchange.net/resource/sample_release_form_full.

Techniques. A list of techniques, with examples, from John Dubois and the International Pragmatics Association, http://elanguage.net/journals/index.php/pragmatics/article/view/464/396.

Transcription conventions. Global Autonomous Language Exploitation (GALE), University of Pennsylvania, http://projects.ldc.upenn.edu/gale/Transcription/English_BC_QTR_Outsource_V1.0.pdf.

14.2.3   Research sources and avenues for dissemination

A major asset in conducting research is familiarity with 'the literature', what has already been done, published, disseminated and discussed in one's area of interest. This sub-section provides short descriptions of a number of journals, both print and online, that publish research in the areas of defining, teaching and researching listening that have been covered in this volume. These same journals, of course, can also serve as avenues of dissemination for relevant research conducted by the reader. While there are literally hundreds of print and online journals that deal with issues involving listening in cognitive science, language education, language acquisition and linguistics, this short review highlights some of the most relevant ones. (To find the contact information for any of these journals, use any standard internet search engine, such as Google, and enter 'Journal: [name of the journal]').

Print journals

Note. Most print journals also have online subscription options.

Annual Review of Applied Linguistics. Reviews research in key areas in the broad field of applied linguistics. Each issue is thematic, covering the topic by means of critical summaries, overviews and bibliographic citations. Every fourth or fifth issue surveys applied linguistics broadly, offering timely essays on language learning and pedagogy, discourse analysis, teaching innovations, second-language acquisition, computer-assisted instruction, language use in professional contexts, sociolinguistics, language policy and language assessment.

Brain and Language. An interdisciplinary journal that focuses on the neuro-biological mechanisms underlying human language. The journal covers the large variety of modern techniques in cognitive neuroscience, including lesion-based approaches as well as functional and structural brain imaging, electrophysiology, cellular and molecular neurobiology, genetics and computational modelling.

CALICO Journal. A quarterly publication devoted to the exploration of the new technologies as applied to language learning. This journal also provides timely information on events of interest to the technology inclined language professional.

Canadian Modern Language Review. Publishes articles of interest to teachers and researchers of French as a second language, English as a second language, and other foreign languages at all levels of instruction. Other features beyond articles and reviews: practical tips for the classroom, readers' opinions and reactions, calendar of forthcoming events, annual list of recently published Canadian materials.

Communication Studies. A peer-reviewed scientific journal; it publishes theoretical and empirical papers and essays and book reviews that advance an understanding of interpersonal, intercultural or organisational communication processes and effects. Submissions may have a psychological, social or cultural orientation.

Computer Speech and Language. Speech and language sciences have a long history, but it is only relatively recently that large-scale implementation of and experimentation with complex models of speech and language processing has become feasible. This journal publishes research that is carried out somewhat by practitioners of artificial intelligence, computer science, electronic engineering, information retrieval, linguistics, phonetics or psychology.

Critical Inquiry in Language Studies. A peer-reviewed journal publishing articles in the overlapping fields of applied linguistics, language policy, language planning, modern languages and literatures, education, anthropology, sociology, psychology and cultural studies. This journal focuses on critical discourse and research in language matters that is generated from qualitative, critical pedagogical and emerging paradigms.

Discourse Processes. A multidisciplinary journal providing a forum for crossfertilisation of ideas from diverse disciplines sharing a common interest in discourse – prose comprehension and recall, dialogue analysis, text grammar construction, computer simulation of natural language, crosscultural comparisons of communicative competence or related topics. The problems posed by multi-sentence contexts and the methods required to investigate them are of specific interest.

ELT Journal. Publishes for all those who are professionally involved in the field of teaching English as a second or foreign language internationally. It is concerned with the fundamental practice factors that influence the evaluation of the profession as well as with the theoretical issues that are everyday concerns of teachers in their classrooms.

English for Specific Purposes. Publishes articles, research notes and book reviews on specialised varieties of English and ESP methodology. Topics of articles include: discourse analysis, second language acquisition in ESP contexts, needs assessment, curriculum development and evaluation, materials preparation, teaching and testing techniques and the effectiveness of various research and pedagogical approaches in ESP contexts.

Foreign Language Annals. The official journal of the American Council on the Teaching of Foreign Languages and publishes bimonthly. This journal serves the professional interests of classroom instructors, researchers and administrators concerned with the teaching of foreign languages at all levels of instruction. Preference is given to articles that report educational research or experimentation, that describe innovative and successful practice and methods and/or that are relevant to the concerns and issues of the profession.

International Journal of Applied Linguistics. Publishes articles that focus on the mediation between expertise about language and experience of language. This journal seeks to develop an awareness of the way language works, how it affects peoples' lives and what interventions are desirable and feasible to make in differing domains of language use and learning.

International Journal of Listening. Publishes articles that focus on listening in daily life and professional settings, as well as in educational environments. Topics include childhood listening development, impact of vocal cues on judgements of the speaker, training methods for active listening in professional settings and therapy for individuals with language deficits. Articles are a mix of theoretical and practical.

International Journal of the Sociology of Language. Seeks to attract readers and contributors from all parts of the world and from all disciplines that pertain to the study of language use in social behaviour.

International Review of Applied Linguistics in Language Teaching (IRAL). Publishes articles in areas of research which concern first and second language acquisition, including naturalistic and instructed language learning, language loss, bilingualism, language contact, pidgins and creoles, language for specific purposes, language technology, mother-tongue education, lexicology, terminology and translation.

Journal of Applied Linguistics and Professional Practice. Aims to build bridges between communication and discourse studies and professional, organisational and workplace sites by providing authoritative analyses of real-life practice in collaborative, informed and explanatory ways.

Journal of Child Language. Publishes articles on all aspects of the scientific study of language behaviour in children, the principles which underlie it and the theories which may account for it. The international range of authors and breadth of coverage allow the journal to forge links between many different areas of research including psychology, linguistics, cognitive science and anthropology. This interdisciplinary approach spans a wide range of interests: phonology, phonetics, morphology, syntax, vocabulary, semantics, pragmatics, sociolinguistics or any other recognised facet of language study.

Journal of English for Academic Purposes. A forum for the dissemination of information and views which enables practitioners of and researchers in EAP to keep current with developments in their field and to contribute to its continued updating. The journal publishes articles, book reviews, conference reports and academic exchanges in the linguistic, sociolinguistic and psycholinguistic description of English as it occurs in the contexts of academic study and scholarly exchange itself. Topics include classroom language, teaching methodology, teacher education, assessment of language, needs analysis; materials development and evaluation, discourse analysis, acquisition studies in EAP contexts, research writing and speaking at all academic levels, the sociopolitics of English in academic uses and language planning.

Journal of Language and Social Psychology. Explores the social dimensions of language and the linguistic implications of social life. Articles are drawn from a wide range of disciplines including linguistics, cognitive science, sociology, communication, psychology, education and anthropology.

Journal of Memory and Language. Aims to contribute to the formulation of scientific issues and theories in the areas of memory, language comprehension and production, and cognitive processes. Special emphasis is given to research articles that provide new theoretical insights based on a carefully laid empirical foundation.

Journal of Pragmatics. Linguistic pragmatics has been able to formulate a number of questions over the years that are essential to our understanding of language as people's main instrument of 'natural' and 'societal' interaction. By providing possible theoretical foundations for the study of linguistic practice, linguistic pragmatics has helped to increase our knowledge of the forms, functions and foundations, of human interaction. The journal identifies with this general scope and aims of pragmatics.

Language Acquisition. A Journal of Developmental Linguistics. Offers explanatory insights into and advance our knowledge of how language is acquired. Focusing primarily on experimental, linguistic and computational approaches, the journal discusses the syntax, semantics, pragmatics and phonology of language acquisition – merging the data of developmental psycholinguistics with recent discoveries in linguistic theory to yield a more adequate understanding of the growth of language.

Language and Education. Published work with immediate bearing upon thought and practice in education. Articles draw from their subject matter important and well-communicated implications for one or more of the following: curriculum, pedagogy or evaluation in education. Articles are welcomed concerning all aspects of mother tongue and second language education.

Language Learning. A Journal of Research in Language Studies. A scientific journal concerned with theoretical issues in language learning. It publishes articles on a broad range of topics including child, second and foreign language acquisition, language education, literacy, language representation in mind and brain, culture, cognition, pragmatics, sociolinguistics and inter-group relations.

Language in Society. An international journal of sociolinguistics concerned with language and discourse as aspects of social life. The journal publishes empirical articles of general theoretical, comparative or methodological interest to students and scholars in sociolinguistics, linguistic anthropology and related fields.

Language and Speech. Provides an international forum for communication among researchers in the disciplines that contribute to our understanding of the production, perception, processing, learning, use, and disorders of speech and language.

Language Teaching Research. Supports and develops investigation and research within the area of second or foreign language teaching. It covers a wide range of topics in the area of language teaching: programme, syllabus, materials design, methodology, teaching of specific skills and language for specific purposes.

Mind and Language. The phenomena of mind and language are currently studied by researchers in linguistics, philosophy, psychology, artificial intelligence and cognitive anthropology. This journal aims to bring this work together in a interdisciplinary way.

Modern Language Journal. Focuses on questions and concerns about learning and teaching foreign and second languages. It publishes articles, research studies, editorials, reports, book reviews and professional news and announcements pertaining to modern languages, including TESL.

Music Perception. Though not directly related to listening in the linguistic domain, this journal deals with issues of perception and cognition that parallel language understanding. The broad range of disciplines covered in the journal includes psychology, psychophysics, linguistics, neurology, artificial intelligence, computer technology and music theory.

RELC Journal. A Journal of Language Teaching and Research in Southeast Asia. Published in Singapore, presents information and ideas on theories, research, methods and materials related to language learning and teaching, especially, although not exclusively, in Southeast Asia. The journal publishes articles in such areas of current enquiry as first and second language learning and teaching, language and culture, discourse analysis, language planning, language testing, multilingual education, stylistics and translation.

Sage Annual Reviews of Communication Research Second Language Research. Publishes theoretical and experimental papers on second language acquisition and second language performance. Each volume includes one special guest-edited article focusing on a current theme and specially commissioned review articles addressing major issues in the field, forming a useful resource for the research community.

Speech Communication. An interdisciplinary journal whose primary objective is to fulfill the need for the rapid dissemination and thorough discussion of basic and applied research results. In order to establish frameworks to inter-relate results from the various areas of the field, emphasis will be placed on viewpoints and topics of a transdisciplinary nature.

Studies in Language and Communication. Aims to consolidate and extend the major themes and issues in communication studies in accessible ways. It reflects new areas of theoretical, ethical and methodological significance while maintaining the practical relevance of the field.

Studies in Second Language Acquisition. Provides a scientific discussion of issues in second and foreign language acquisition of any language. Each volume contains four issues, one of which is devoted to a current topic in the field. The other three issues contain articles dealing with theoretical topics, some of which have broad pedagogical implications and reports of quantitative and qualitative empirical research.

System. A Journal for Educational Technology and Language Learning Systems. An international journal devoted to the applications of educational technology and applied linguistics to problems of foreign language teaching and learning. Attention is paid to all languages and to problems associated with the study and teaching of English as a second or foreign language.

TESOL Journal. A publication of teaching and classroom research. It publishes articles that discuss teaching English as a second, foreign or additional language to learners of all ages, in any setting. *TESOL Journal* invites manuscripts on a wide range of topics, including, but not limited to, current TESOL methodology, curriculum materials and design, teacher development, literacy, bilingual education and classroom inquiry and research.

Text and Talk. An internationally recognised forum for interdisciplinary research in language, discourse and communication studies, focusing, among other things, on the situational and historical nature of text/talk production; the cognitive and sociocultural processes of language practice and action; and participant-based structures of meaning negotiation and multimodal alignment. The journal encourages critical debates on these and other relevant issues.

Online journals

Asian EFL Journal, www.asian-efl-journal.com. A refereed online journal for teaching and learning English as a foreign language. This online journal examines issues within the Asian EFL linguistic scene, and considers how traditional educational approaches are integrated with or contrasted against what is arguably a very specialised and relatively new field of study.

ELT Newsletter, www.eltnewsletter.com. Publishes a new article every week on English language teaching. It covers a wide variety of topics – young learners, adults, general English, business English, exam classes, modern concepts and ideas such as Multiple Intelligences. It also provides ELT discussion forum for English teachers to share and exchange their thoughts.

English Teaching Forum, www.exchanges.state.gov/forum/. A practical refereed quarterly journal published by the US Department of State for teachers of English as a foreign or second language. This journal publishes articles from English teachers, teacher trainers and programme administrators on a wide variety of topics in second/foreign language education, including principles and methods of language teaching; activities and techniques for teaching the language skills; classroom-based studies and action research; needs analysis, curriculum and syllabus design; assessment, testing and evaluation; teacher training and development; materials writing; and English for Specific Purposes.

ESL Magazine, www.eslmag.com. A bi-monthly colour print magazine serving English language educators and other professionals. *ESL Magazine* combines practical, informative articles by recognised leaders in the field, information about the latest ESL/EFL products and services. It provides latest news, trends, methods, products and services that matter to ESL/EFL professionals.

Internet TESL Journal, www.iteslj.org. A monthly which includes articles and research papers, teaching techniques and web-based lessons and projects in teaching and learning English as a second language.

Language Learning and Technology, www.llt.msu.edu. A refereed online journal with an editorial board of scholars in the fields of second language acquisition and computer-assisted language learning. The focus of this publication is not technology per se, but rather issues related to language learning and language teaching, and how they are affected or enhanced by the use of technologies.

Teaching English with Technology, www.iatefl.org.pl/call/callnl.htm. A quarterly refereed electronic journal published by IATEFL Poland Computer Special Interest Group. This journal deals mainly with issues of using computers, the internet, computer software in teaching and learning languages.

TEFL NET Magazine, www.tefl.net/magazine/index.htm. Provides latest news, articles, book reviews, lesson plans, resources and job listings for ESL/EFL teachers and schools worldwide.

TESL-EJ, www.writing.berkeley.edu/tesl-ej/index.html. A refereed electronic journal that has become an internationally recognised source of ESL and EFL information. TESL-EJ publishes original articles in the research and practice of English as a second or foreign language, including studies in ESL/EFL pedagogy, second language acquisition, language assessment, applied socio- and psycholinguistics, and other related areas.

Exploring, researching, teaching

This volume has explored the notion of listening, from neurological, psychological, sociological and education perspectives, with a focus on considering listening as an expandable skill. Although we often think of listening as a fixed ability, listening in first or a second language can be expanded through focus, practice, organisation – and inspiration. Although I have attempted to offer vigorous and thorough guidance through these various perspectives, I consider this volume an invitation to the reader – whether a teacher, student, or interested observer – to continue to explore listening further. This chapter in particular has provided a number of resources and pathways that may assist you in this exploration, with the hope that one or more of these suggestions will inspire you to become a better listener, a better learner, and a better teacher.

Glossary

This glossary contains short contextual definitions or explanations of terms in *Teaching and Researching Listening* that are highlighted in the text in **bold** type, *except for* bold-faced words that appear in tables or lists with an explanation given.

abandoned structure A type of **false start** in which the speaker does not complete the full grammatical structure.

academic listening (also known as **listening for academic purposes**) Listening in an academic context, usually involving the integration of listening with content learning, classroom interaction, note-taking, discussion with peers, reports and presentations, and test-taking.

accentuated input A type of modified input that aims to draw attention to particular features in the text.

acceptable understanding A listener representation of understanding that is effective, that accomplishes the listener's goal.

accommodation (*psycholinguistics*) The process changing a current cognitive structure to make sense of the environment.

accommodation (*sociolinguistics*) The tendency for both parties in an interaction to compromise toward the norms of the other.

acculturation Degree of understanding of, sympathy for, and integration with target culture norms and values.

acknowledgement A discourse move by the listener that shows neutral evaluation of what the speaker has communicated.

acoustic mishearing Hearing a different sound or sequence from the one that was spoken, which is the most common type of mishearing (cf. **blended mishearing**).

acoustic snapshot The unit of phonological analysis in speech recognition.

activation cost The mental energy used to bring a concept into working memory.

activation space In connectionism, a spreading activation model of memory contends that over time the activation of one unit spreads to all the other units connected to it; this is called the activation space.

activation (*psycholinguistics*) Engagement of neurological and cognitive processes needed for understanding.

active information Information that is being used in working memory.

activity frame The social activity that the speaker and listener are engaged in, as understood by the participants.

activity level In connectionist views of memory, different nodes in a memory network have varying activity levels according to how frequently they are activated.

addressee The intended **recipient** of the speaker's utterance.

addressor The speaker of an utterance that is intended for an addressee.

adjudicator A person has additional power in the transaction to reach an outcome.

affective elements The emotional, moral, social, spiritual, aesthetic and motivational aspects of an experience or understanding of an event.

affective filter In language acquisition theory, part of the internal processing system that subconsciously screens incoming language based on affect: the learner's motives, needs, attitudes and emotional states.

affective involvement The emotional, moral, social, spiritual, aesthetic and motivational aspects of participants that are affected by the interaction.

affective level A level of analysis of discourse that focuses on how the participants feel about each other, their mutual actions, and any contextual (e.g. institutional) influences on the discourse.

affective outcomes How the participants feel about their interlocutor during and after the interaction.

affective In descriptions of learning strategies, affective strategies refer to focusing awareness of one's emotional states and ways of regulating emotion in learning situations.

after-image An optical or auditory (or other sensory) illusion that refers to an image continuing to appear in one's visual or auditory (or other sensory) loop in working memory after the exposure to the original image has ceased.

allophonic variations Context-dependent variations in sounds, usually consonants. In English, the variations are a function of the principle that in fluent speech, articulation of successive consonants within a phrase will overlap substantially.

analysis by synthesis A form of audio signal processing that uses approximation techniques (mathematical algorithms) to identify spoken words.

anaphoric/anaphora An anaphoric reference refers to something within a text that has been previously mentioned.

aphasia An impairment in any one area of the brain.

arousal The first stage of attention in which the brain becomes reactive to stimuli. Arousal involves the activation of the reticular activating system in the brain stem, the autonomic nervous system and the endocrine system, leading to increased sensory alertness and readiness to respond.

articulatory causes A means by which the listener perceives sounds based on presumed articulation.

Artificial Conversational Entity (ACE) A computer program designed to simulate an intelligent conversation with one or more human users via auditory or textual methods.

automated speech recognition (ASR) Computer processing of spoken language.

assimilation The interpretation of events in terms of existing cognitive structure.

attention The cognitive process of selectively concentrating on one aspect of the environment while ignoring other things; the allocation of processing resources; includes three stages (**arousal, orientation, focus**).

audience design A sociolinguistic model which proposes that linguistic style-shifting occurs primarily in response to a speaker's audience. According to this model, speakers adjust their speech style towards that of their audience in order to express solidarity or intimacy with them.

audience Any **overhearers** of an utterance in addition to the primary recipient, the **addressee.**

audition (*neurolinguistics*) The physical process of perceiving sound.

auditory cortex The region of the brain that is responsible for processing of sound, located in the temporal lobe of the brain.

authentic language Topics, language style and concept complexity that represents natural usage.

authentic lectures Academic talks that have not been shortened or simplified in presentation.

authenticity A concept in instructional design relating the relative role of the source of L2, which may include local and international sources.

autonomous listening A form of listening practice in which the learner selects own extracts and tasks, monitors own progress; decides on own patterns of interaction with others.

backchannelling Short verbal and non-verbal messages sent by the listener back during the partner's speaking turn or immediately following the speaking turn to indicate the listener's mental state.

background information Information needed to interpret part of the input.

baton signals Hand, arm, torso, and head movements which are typically associated with emphasis and prosodic cadence.

benchmarks Criteria against which interactions can be evaluated and through which effective listening may be modelled and learned.

binary logic A form of logic that utilises the semantic principle of bivalence, which states that every meaningful proposition is either true or false.

blended mishearing A mishearing that is influenced by a perception from a different modality, usually based on a mismatch from audio and visual perception.

blended mishearing A misperception of input in which part of the input is taken from an audio source and part from another sensory source, usually visual, such as environmental co-text or gestures from speakers or the written form of a word, especially in a pictographic language, such as Chinese.

bottom-level attributes Skills identified in a listening test that are specific to listening.

bottom-up information Information that is conveyed directly by the speech signal.

bottom-up processing A form of information processing that is guided by input in real time, and proceeds in subsequent stages.

bottom-up speech processing A form of speech processing that is guided by the speech signal in real time, and proceeds in subsequent stages.

bottom-up strategies Text-based strategies for comprehension, focusing on combinations of sounds, words, and grammar.

Broca's area A part of the brain, in the inferior front gyrus of the brain (above the left temple) which is involved in comprehension and responses to language-related tasks.

built-in syllabus An internal system of learning which governs both when learners acquire particular grammatical features and also how they learn them.

case grammar A system of linguistic analysis used in frame semantics which focuses on the link between the valence, or number of subjects, objects, etc., of a verb and the grammatical context it requires.

case relations A system of marking lexical items for the type of relationship they bear to a verb.

cataphoric/cataphora A cataphoric reference refers to something within a text that has not yet been identified.

categorical perception The capacity to discriminate speech sound contrasts in their native language in a number of different phonetic dimensions.

challenge A discourse move that requires the speaker to give more information about or support for his intention.

characteristic frequency (CF) The maximum rate of compression in a waveform (sound) that pass a given point in a second; the unit of frequency is the hertz (Hz); each auditory nerve fibre has different set of characteristic frequencies (CF) to which it responds.

chatterbot (also known as **chatbot** or **artificial conversational entity**) A computer program designed to simulate an intelligent conversation with one or more human users via auditory or textual methods.

chi square A statistical test commonly used to compare observed data with data we would expect to obtain according to a specific hypothesis.

child-directed speech (CDS) A register of language often used by adults when addressing children, involving increased volume and pitch span, repetition, and frequent backchannelling.

citation form The pure phonological form of a word, when, uttered in isolation.

claim A direct or indirect assertion that a statement is true.

claim A statement that the speaker wants the listener to believe is true.

clitic group A lexical item that consists of one core word and other grammaticalising words.

close activity A kind of learning activity involving intensive listening, with written text provided with gaps, also called gap filling.

co-articulation Processes of **assimilation**, vowel **reduction** and **elision** when two or more sounds are uttered in rapid succession or simultaneously.

co-articulatory effects Phonological variations caused by sounds being articulated together.

cocktail party effect The ability to focus one's listening attention on a single talker among a mixture of conversations and background noises, ignoring other conversations.

code-switching Changing from use of one language to another during the course of communication.

cognates Words that have a common etymological origin. For example, *night* in English and *nuit* in French have a common origin in Proto-European.

cognitive anchor In cognitive psychology, a bias toward interpreting new input and evidence based on one's initial belief.

cognitive commitment An affective response by the listener to the input which influences depth of processing.

cognitive difficulty The intrinsic complexity of the content in a text.

cognitive load An estimation of difficulty of a text for a listener based on analysis of length, genre, text components, required inferences and overall structure.

cognitive map Cognitive maps, **mental maps**, **mind maps**, **cognitive models**, or **mental models** all refer to a type of mental processing presumed to be composed of a series of psychological transformations by which an individual can acquire and use information about phenomena in their real or metaphorical environment.

cognitive structures Patterns of physical or mental action that underlie specific acts of development of intelligence.

cognitive transfer Shifting of a learned skill or competence from one domain (such as first language use) to another domain (such as second language use).

cognitive In descriptions of learning strategies, cognitive strategies refer to altering or enhancing thinking processes.

coherence The 'deep' (semantic) level of co-ordination of concepts related to linguistic elements in input.

cohesion The surface level co-ordination of linguistic elements.

collocation A sequence of words or terms which co-occur more often than would be expected by chance. Collocation defines the restrictions on how words can be used together, for example which prepositions are used with particular verbs, or which verbs and nouns are used together.

common ground The mutual knowledge, mutual beliefs, and mutual assumptions that are essential for communication between two people.

communication strategies Plans for identifying perceived barriers and perceived benefits of behaviour or attitude change in order to alter communication processes or outcomes.

communicative insincerity Deceptive behaviour and use of communicative devices to mislead a listener.

communicative state In systems theory, a communicative state is the level of knowledge obtained by a participant in an interaction.

communicative task An interaction focused on a tangible outcome.

compensatory strategies Thinking strategies that enable the listener to adopt a cognitive perspective to improve comprehension or interaction.

competition model A psycholinguistic theory of language acquisition and sentence processing which claims that the meaning of language is interpreted by comparing a number of linguistic cues within a sentence, and that language is learned through the competition of basic cognitive mechanisms in the presence of a rich linguistic environment.

competitors In word recognition theory, a competitor is a similar word (i.e. has similar phonological form) that must be ruled out before the target word is fully recognised.

comprehensible input Input that can be understood by a learner with only minimal effort due to its familiarity or high degree of contextual support.

comprehensible output A language development activity in which the learner is compelled to formulate and express ideas in the target language, in order to 'force negotiation', that is, leading the learner to come to express more precisely whatever was not initially understood.

comprehension strategy Instruction a form of reading or listening instruction that focuses explicitly on development awareness of processing difficulties and identifying and practicing 'attack strategies' for dealing with difficult texts, such as prediction based on prior knowledge activation, seeking clarification when confused, and summarisation.

concept maps A diagram showing the hierarchical relationships among concepts. The relationship between concepts can be articulated in linking phrases such as 'gives rise to' or 'results in'.

conceptual schema (or **conceptual data model**) A map of concepts and their relationships. This describes the semantics of an organisation of concepts and represents a series of assertions about its nature. Specifically, it describes the things of significance to an organisation (entity classes), about which it is inclined to collect information, and characteristics of (attributes) and associations between pairs of those things of significance (relationships).

concession A discourse move by the listener that show negative evaluation of what the speaker has communicated.

confirmation check An act of explicitly checking with the listener to see if the prior message or intention has been understood.

consciousness The neurological-cognitive bridge between individual and universal perception and personal experience.

consequential validity The effects of assessment on the learner's future learning path.

constative In speech act theory, any speech act that has truth value, that is, can be evaluated in terms of being true or false; includes speech acts such as announcing, denying, insisting, or predicting.

construct validity (or **construct-referenced validity**) The extent to which a test actually measures what it claims to be assessing.

construct A representation of the underlying quality or trait that the assessment intends to measure.

construction grammar A model of grammar used in cognitive linguistics which is based on the idea that the primary unit of grammar is the grammatical construction which exists in a taxonomy.

contact situation The actual context of instruction or learning.

Contemporary Topics system A method of note-taking review involving group collaboration and reconstruction of content using questioning strategies.

content schemata Organisation of knowledge in the listener's mind that is relevant to understanding the topic domain of the input.

content words Nouns, verbs, adjectives, adverbs, question words that carry the lexical meaning of the utterance.

context of situation The totality of extralinguistic features having relevance to a communicative act.

context The relevant constraints on input that influence the way it is processed. (Includes **external context** and **internal context**.)

context-sensitive paraphrases A rephrasing of a lexical item or proposition, that explains or clarifies the text that is being cited.

contextual language routines Highly comprehensible routines that integrate action and language, such as eating, getting dressed, playing with toys, taking a bath, going to bed. In these situations, salient features of the context as well as habituated routines help the child understand the role of language in the routines and the amplificatory meaning of the language used.

continuous perception The ability to hear continuous speech as combinations of sound sequences.

contrast Any differentiation at phonemic, morphological, lexical, semantic, pragmatic levels which changes meaning.

conversational adjustments Modifications made by a speaker to improve comprehensibility or intelligibility.

conversational maxims Principles of co-operation that allow for smooth understanding of conversation.

Cornell method A method of academic note-taking, involving spacing and charting information in a way that facilitates review.

co-text The text that surrounds a passage, i.e. the words or sentences coming before and after it.

crisp logic A form of logic that utilises defined categories and mathematical symbols, > (greater than), < (less than), = (equal).

criterion A standard for judging a performance.

criterion-referenced test A test that equates test scores with a statement about the behaviour to be expected of a person with that score.

cultural schema theory A theory that explains the familiar and pre-acquainted knowledge one uses when entering a familiar situation in his or her own culture.

decibel (dB) A logarithmic unit of measurement that expresses the magnitude of sound intensity relative to a reference level.

deduction Reasoning which constructs or evaluates conclusions. In logic, an argument is deductive when its conclusion is a logical consequence of the premises. A deductive argument is valid if and only if the conclusion follows from the premises.

deictic reference A reference to something or someone in the physical environment.

deictic Relating to the physical context, the actual people and things present in the communication event.

detecting In language acquisition, noticing differences between what one has previously understood in the TL input and what one now understands.

dialogic interaction A form of learning emphasising intersubjective processes in acquisition of language.

dichotic listening A procedure commonly used to investigate selective attention in which two different auditory stimuli are presented to the participant simultaneously, one to each ear.

dicto-comp An activity involving long oral texts and learners working in groups to reconstruct the texts.

differentiation Separation of a word from a whole event and start to use it as a label for a specific object or event.

direct evidence A goal of assessment, in which the testing procedure allows the learner to demonstrate an ability directly or holistically.

directional changes in perception Perceptual adjustments to tune into the sounds of the language.

directional gaze Eye movement and focusing used to direct the listener or audience to an **exophoric reference** or to refer to a particular moment in an event.

directness–indirectness A continuum of stylistic choices for expressing an intention in speech; directness tends to clarify meaning, though it may be face-threatening, while indirectness tends to be face-saving, though it may obfuscate intended meaning.

disclosure pattern In systems theory, the sequence of discourse moves that reveals necessary information in a transaction.

discourse coding In discourse analysis, the technique of identifying discourse moves associated with utterances.

discourse level The scale of analysis that focuses on coherence of communication and is not confined by grammatical units, such as the sentence.

disfluency A break or irregularity of an utterance that is not consistent with any specific grammatical construction and occur within the flow of otherwise fluent speech.

dispreferred response A response not expected by the speaker which requires additional effort to complete a transaction.

distal mode (of consciousness) The orientation of consciousness that attends to non-present, abstract, or imaginary references and concepts.

DRAGON Family of speech recognition software, with three primary areas of functionality: dictation, text-to-speech and command input.

dual coding A type of storage of knowledge in long-term memory that has separate access by L1 and L2 cues.

duration The time that a sound endures, measured in milliseconds.

echoic memory The auditory version of sensory memory, referring to the phenomenon in which there is a brief mental echo that continues to sound after an auditory stimulus has been heard.

efficiency principle A principle of language in which the most frequently used words tend to be the shortest ones in a language and communication patterns develop to allow for a maximum of **ellipsis.**

elaborative simplification A type of text simplification strategy which helps to make content more comprehensible to the listener by adding complexity to the grammatical and lexical system.

elided sounds Sounds that are omitted, usually as the result of fast articulation or co-articulation.

ellipsis The omission of sounds or words or structures presumed to be understood by the listener.

ellipsis/ellipted propositions Missing parts of a text or textual structure (such as a logical argument) that the listener is able to provide.

embedded level In ASR parsing, the embedded level is interpreted in relation to the larger, superordinate level.

empathy A listener state that can be signalled by backchannelling.

empathy Show of understanding speaker's emotional states and shifts in emotion during the conversation.

endorsement A discourse move by the listener that show positive evaluation of what the speaker has communicated.

engagement The pragmatic notion of engagement encompasses the listener's relationship with the speaker, including awareness of emotional shifts in the speaker's state, and allows for pragmatic processing of the speaker's meaning.

enhancement A cognitive process in which attention is deliberately focused toward a particular semantic network.

enriched input In instructional design, the manipulation of input to add features that will increase the likelihood of learner processing particular concepts or noticing particular text features.

enriching speaker input Part of the listening process in which the listener enhances the speaker's message: through inferring speaker emotion and elaborating speaker meaning.

equality position Acknowledged status in which both parties in an interaction consider themselves as sharing common ground.

et cetera principle A sociolinguistic principle which contends that all communication makes use of an assumption that, though not everything has been strictly defined for some uttered statement, there is a recoverable area of relevance which is supposed to be the same for each participant.

evaluating In communication theory, the acts of judging, weighing evidence, or deciding on degree of agreement with the speaker.

evidence-centred assessment A form of assessment synthesising evidence across multiple tasks or from different performances.

evocative expressions Short words and phrases, including expletives, that are inserted to show intensity of emotion or to evoke emotion in the listener.

excitation pattern The distribution of the neural activity in the cochlea

exophoric/exophora An exophoric reference refers to language outside of the text (extralingualistic) in which the reference is found.

expectation What the listener considers the most likely to happen; in psychological modelling of language it is an assumption about what will be true in the future.

extensive listening A form of listening practice in which the learner listens to longer extracts and performs meaning oriented tasks.

external context All of the perceptible information provided by perceptual contact with an external stimulus.

extraction patterns In NLP an analysis of co-occurrences of entities in a text (such as lexical phrases), according to given ontologies, or hierarchies of information.

extraction A process in speech perception of finding recurring temporal units in speech that are bounded by silence.

face validity A form of validity emphasising transparency of the value of activity.

face-threatening act An act in a discourse that upsets the participation frame by challenging or demoting one interlocutor's rights or power.

fallacies of reasoning Incorrect or incomplete reasoning that results in a lack of understanding or a misunderstanding.

false start The start of an utterance that is abandoned and left incomplete.

feature analysis A process involved in word recognition through incremental recognition of phonological features of the word.

feature inhibitor A part of word recognition in which phonological features are ruled out by context, thus narrowing the search for the target word.

feature Phonological phenomena created by articulatory movements, such as glides, obstruents, and sonorants.

feedback The process of obtaining information about success or failure of reaching a communicative goal.

felicity In speech act theory, the felicity conditions for a speech act, such as promising, to be performed successfully are the states of awareness and capability for both the speaker and listener.

fillers Sounds and words that are used to fill silences during a speaking turn, which do not carry specific semantic meaning.

first listening The initial time an input is heard.

first pass In syntactic processing, the identification by the listener of syntactic categories in a sentence.

first-order goal The most important goal in a hierarchy of goals.

Flesch–Kincaid A readability test designed to show how easy or difficult a text is to read. It uses a formula based on average number of words in sentences and average number of syllables per word.

flouting The intentional violation of a conversational maxim for special effect, may include: **infringing**, ignoring, subverting, or **opting out** of a maxim for a particular effect.

flowing chunks A concept in psycholinguistics referring to integrating of smaller chunks of text into larger chunks of text, in order to increase the functioning of **short-term memory**.

focal centre of attention The most prominent word inside an intonational unit.

focal information Information in the input that the speaker draws attention to through phonological or gestural cueing.

focus on form A type of instructional focus encouraging learners to notice syntactic features while processing texts for meaning.

focus The third stage of attention involving selection of attention and intention to extract information.

foot (F) In phonology, a strong-weak syllable sequence.

form of assessment Materials, media, and procedures for taking a test and the means of scoring.

formal operations stage In Piagetan psychology, the stage (twelve to fifteen years), in which the child's thinking can deal with abstractions.

formal schemata Organisation of knowledge in the listener's mind that is relevant to understanding rhetorical devices and general properties of the social and technical genres in the input.

formulaic language Strings of language that are often interpreted as having a single meaning, e.g. idioms, collocations, turns of phrase, preferred ways of saying things, routines, set phrases, rhymes, songs, prayers, proverbs.

fossilised In language acquisition, stalled in development, usually due to lack of need for additional progress in a skill or competence.

fragment grammar A method for understanding fluent speech by generating a collection of fragments, each representing a set of syntactically and semantically similar phrases.

frame (frame semantics) A further development of case grammar, relates linguistic semantics to encyclopaedic knowledge. The basic idea is that a listener cannot understand the meaning of a word without access to the essential knowledge that relates to that word.

frame relationships The syntactic and semantic relationships that are associated with a word.

frame In speech recognition, a sequence of acoustic snapshots that is used to analyse speech.

framing In discourse analysis, the action of establishing a conceptual framework from which the listener is expected to interpret the discourse.

frequency A measurement of vibrations, expressed as hertz (Hz). The relationship between the fundamental frequency (f_0) of a sound and its other audible harmonic frequencies (f_1, f_2, f_3) determines the identity of a sound.

function/functional words (grammatical words) Particles, prepositions, pro-forms, articles, *be* verbs, auxiliary verbs, conjunctions that carry relational meaning rather than lexical meaning.

fuzzy set theory Fuzzy sets are sets whose elements have degrees of membership; fuzzy set theory is used in speech recognition programming to allow for recognition of words on a graded scale rather than an absolute (right–wrong) scale.

gairaigo Japanese for loan word or borrowed word, and indicates a transliteration (or transvocalisation) into Japanese, for example, *sabisu* is gairaigo for 'service', borrowed from English.

gap filling The language acquisition process in which the child does not yet know the right term for an object and then uses another label for it.

gatekeeping In communication theory, the process through which ideas and information are protected and filtered.

genderlect A sociolect (speech variety) denoting the difference in interactional styles between males and females.

generalisation In language acquisition, the process of the child labelling numerous things and situations with the same words.

genuineness A characteristic of having features of colloquial style of spontaneous planning that are characteristic of everyday spoken discourse.

given information Information assumed to be known or easily recalled by the listener.

goal In communication theory, the goal of an interaction is a combination of what the speaker and listener intend to accomplish.

goal-directed communication The pattern of communication in a purpose-driven task.

'good enough' comprehension strategy A proposal that the human language comprehension system creates syntactic and semantic representations that are merely 'good enough' (GE) given the task that the comprehender needs to perform.

good enough recognition A threshold at which mishearings or missed parts of input do not influence message recognition.

graded texts Spoken or written texts that are controlled, usually by simplifying lexis and syntax, to make them easier to listen to or to read.

grammar-discovery approach A way of combining listening and grammar instruction, providing learners with data to illustrate a particular grammatical point and getting them to analyse it in order to reach an awareness of how the feature works.

graphical user interface (GUI) A type of user interface item that allows people to interact with programs in more ways than typing such as computers; hand-held devices such as MP3 Players, portable media players or gaming devices.

grounds Evidence or a belief that supports a claim.

grounds The reason that the speaker holds for wanting the listener to believe a claim is true.

guide signals The systematic gestures and movements of any part of the body used to guide interpretation of the discourse; may include **emblems**:

direct replacements for words; **illustrators**: shaping what is being said; **affect displays**, shows of emotion; **regulators**: for controlling the flow of conversation.

harmonic tones The relationship of formant frequencies which assist the listener in perception; A **harmonic** of a wave is a component frequency of the signal that is a multiple of the fundamental frequency (f_0, f_1, f_2, f_3).

HARPY A speech recognition system developed in the 1980s at Carnegie Mellon University, using large vocabularies, served as a prototype for future research.

head word The central lexical item in an utterance to which other constituents are related.

hearing The physical process that allows for reception and conversion of sound waves to electrochemical impulses.

HEARSAY An approach to ASR that attempts to recover the speaker's intention from the sound and resolve ambiguities and uncertainties in real time.

heuristic In computer science a technique designed to solve a problem that ignores whether the solution is practical or can be proven to be correct.

hidden Markov models (HMMs) Statistical probabilities that represent the grammatical, lexical, and phonological aspects of speech as snapshots or frames.

high-stakes assessment A test or other form of assessment with important consequences for the test taker; passing may result in significant benefits, such as a diploma or a promotion.

humour In communication theory, the tendency of particular cognitive experiences to provoke laughter and provide amusement.

hypotaxis/hypotactic organisation A style of speaking, more often associated with writing, that uses complex structures, subordinating conjunctions, and involves non-sequential time order.

i + 1 level A level of input slightly above the learner's current level of competence in terms of vocabulary, syntax, discourse features, length and complexity.

immediate mode (of consciousness) The orientation of consciousness that deals with present, tangible references.

implicational scale A set of items that are in the same constituent category (such as lexical items or grammatical structure), and ordered in terms of a value (such as frequency of occurrence).

implicature What is suggested in an utterance, even though not expressed or strictly entailed by the utterance.

implicit grounds Unstated facts or evidence that the listener is able to infer.

inactive information Information that is accessible to the listener, but is not currently being used in working memory.

incomplete structures Structures in speech that are not fully formed.

incomplete utterances Utterances that are not complete or abandoned during speech.

induction A type of reasoning that involves moving from a set of specific facts to a general conclusion. It uses premises from objects that have been examined to establish a conclusion about an object that has not been examined.

inferencing/making inferences Filling in missing parts of a text or adding reasoning processes to make sense of a text.

information extraction (IE) A type of information retrieval whose goal is to automatically extract structured information from unstructured machine-readable documents, generally human language texts by means of natural language processing.

information gap task A type of interaction in which each party has information the other does not have.

information manipulation theory A way of looking at the interpersonal communication process that deals with the way in which information packages (in the form of messages) are put together in order to give an impression that is false from the perspective of the sender.

information-processing model In language acquisition, a five-stage acquisitional procedure involving comparing and adjusting semantic representations.

infringing Exceeding the limits of a conversational maxim.

initiating act The opening move in a discourse sequence.

inner ear The innermost part of the ear consisting of the bony labyrinth, a system of passages that has two main functional parts: the cochlea which is dedicated to hearing and the vestibular system which is dedicated to balance.

inner speech In Vygoskyian psychology, the means by which the child mediates and regulates their activity through their thoughts.

input hypothesis In language acquisition theory, a hypothesis claiming that second languages are acquired by understanding messages or by receiving **comprehensible input**.

input-processing model In language acquisition, an information processing model of language acquisition that posits that progressive noticing of new features (phonological, lexical, syntactic, and pragmatic) in the input is the fundamental way of acquiring an L2.

intake The cognitive representation that a learner finally understands or remembers from an experience or text.

integration A central process in comprehension in which the information conveyed by the text is combined with information and concepts already known by the listener.

intelligible/intelligibility A measure of how understandable speech is, or the degree to which speech can be understood. Intelligibility is affected by spoken clarity, explicitness, comprehensibility, and precision.

intensity (phonology) The loudness of a sound, measured in decibels (dB).

intensity A concept in instructional design relating to how intensive a learning experience should be in relation to other activities in the learner's life.

intensive listening A form of listening practice in which the learner pays close attention to what is actually said.

intention The interactive goal of the speaker, what the speaker intends the listener to do as the result of speaking, often called the **perlocutionary force**. *In NLP*, an analysis of the response that the user is seeking.

interaction adaptation Display of involvement with the speaker, particularly when the speaker is attempting to persuade the listener.

interactional competence Knowing and using the mostly-unwritten rules for interaction in various communication situations within a given speech community and culture.

interactional dance Verbal and non-verbal interplay between speaker and listener, requiring mutual co-ordination.

interactional level A level of analysis of discourse that focuses on relationship perceptions and shifts between participants.

interactional work Effort required by a participant to keep the interaction on track, moving toward a desired outcome.

interactive listening A form of listening practice in which the learner interacts verbally with others, in collaborative tasks, to discover information or negotiate solutions.

interactive markers Short words and phrases (such as 'You know') that are inserted in speech to show connection with the listener.

internal context The subjective experience brought about by interaction with input, influenced by recent events and related memories.

international phonetic alphabet (IPA) A system of phonetic notation based primarily on the Latin alphabet, widely used as a standardised representation of the sounds of spoken language form, organised by **phonetic features**.

interoception The monitoring of sensate data for our internal bodily systems.

interpersonal deception theory A way of explaining the manner in which individuals deal with actual or perceived deception on the conscious and subconscious levels while engaged in face-to-face communication.

interpreter role A listener perspective in which the listener is perceived as a participant.

interpreting In communication theory, the act of arriving at an understanding.

interpretive community A group that shares common contexts and experiences and uses those commonalities in interpreting events.

intersubjective rules Guidelines for interaction and interpretation that are mutually negotiated by participants.

intersubjectivity A term used in philosophy and psychology to describe a condition somewhere between subjectivity and objectivity, one in which a phenomenon is personally experienced (subjectively) but by more than one subject.

intertextual competence The ability to make sense of complex texts that contain numerous references to other texts, particularly popular texts in a target culture.

intertextual/intertextuality The shaping of text meaning by other texts.

intervention An instructional act designed to alter the learner's normal way of thinking or processing of information.

intonation unit (IU)/phonological phrase (P-phrase) A phonological unit consisting of a lexically stressed item plus supporting grammatical elements, uttered in a single pause.

intonation unit A unit of speech, defined by the presence of one primary intonational prominence.

intonational bracketing Tonal grouping of more than one intonational unit to show that the units are conceptually connected, in which falling tones at the end of intonational units go progressively lower.

involvement The deliberate nature of attention which differentiates listening from hearing.

irony The use of words to convey a meaning that is the opposite of the literal meaning of the words themselves.

islands of expertise A notion in language development that the learner develops language through focused areas of interest.

item response theory (IRT) A paradigm for designing and analysing scores on tests and questionnaires.

jigsaw listening A learning activity in which students hear different parts or versions of a text and then pair up to exchange their information.

key word method A method of academic note-taking focusing on key words, sequencing, and abbreviations.

kinesic signals The body movements, including posture, head movements, and facial signals.

kinesic Relating to the interpretation of body language such as facial expressions and gestures.

knowledge representations In ASR, the linking of entities in the input with relational ordering.

knowledge superior (K+), knowledge equal (K=) or knowledge inferior (K−) An attribution to participants within the participant frame of an interaction, identifying which participants are expected to display superiority of knowledge or authority in conducting the interaction.

labelling In language acquisition, the first of three related tasks a child has to perform during the acquisition for any new word. Children have to discover that sequences of sound can be used as names for things.

language-focused learning An emphasis on language instruction that focuses on language form in addition to language processing skills.

language-general capacity In child language acquisition, a reference to the capacity of an infant for discriminating potential phonetic contrasts in any of the world's languages.

learning-by-selection A neural modal of learning that takes advantage of species-specific capacities pre-wired into the cortex, and requires only minimal triggering.

lemma In linguistics, a **lemma** (plural lemmas or lemmata) is either of two things: In lexicography, the **canonical form**, **dictionary form**, or **citation form** of a word, or in psycholinguistics, the abstract conceptual form of an utterance in the early stages of speech production.

lexical phrase A formulaic element consisting of frequently used **clitic groups** and **phonological words**, interpreted together, contributing to a single lexical meaning.

lexical segmentation strategy A means for identifying word boundaries in a stream of speech based on phonological principles.

lexical transfer Use of knowledge of one's L1 to acquire new L2 lexical items, including the use of **cognates**.

lexicalised conditioning In ASR, a learning algorithm that enables the software to add new collocations to its data based on input from users.

lexis–first comprehension principle Understanding messages through focusing primarily on lexis and ignoring syntax.

Likert scale A graded scale for measuring subjective responses and attitudes of participants.

limited capacity A measure of the restrictive nature of attention and processing resources; in speech processing, the limitation of a person is the ability to process only one stream of information or one bundled set of features.

linguistic environment The ambient or natural environment surrounding a listener in everyday life, which provides sources of input.

linguistic intentions A theory of word recognition which characterise the listener as utilising knowledge of the language to estimate the speaker's intended utterance.

linguistic processing Sound perception, word recognition, syntactic parsing.

linguistic representations In ASR, a string of elements derived from the input.

listenability indexes Estimations of the ease of listening to a particular text, based on textual factors such as word complexity, delivery factors such as pace, cognitive factors, such as inherent difficulty and familiarity.

listener enrichment A concept in pragmatics which describes the role of the listener in filling in missing parts of the input, and adding imagery and background knowledge while listening.

listener messages Responses from the listener that are incorporated into the speaker's subsequent messages.

listener perspective Interpreting discourse from the vantage point of the listener, including actions the listener makes to construct and transform meaning.

listenership cues An array of verbal and non-verbal signals given by the listener to show that he or she is attending to the speaker.

listening for acquisition A learning strategy in which the learner utilises spoken input for purposes of analysis and long-term acquisition.

listening for comprehension A communication strategy in which the learner aims to understand what was said without additional intention to learn more about the language that was spoken.

listening strategies Techniques or plans that contribute directly to the comprehension and recall of listening input. Listening strategies can be classified by how the listener processes the input.

listening task An activity the listener performs while listening or immediately after listening, utilising knowledge gained from an aural input.

listening The intentional process of trying to make sense of input, usually input that has an oral component.

logical inference The process of drawing a conclusion by applying clues of logic (induction and deduction) to observations or hypotheses or by interpolating the next logical step in a pattern.

logogen A word recognition unit in memory with a threshold for activation, triggered by context.

long-term learning Sustained learning and retention beyond the immediate experience.

long-term memory A set of related neural pathways that can be activated at will; long term memory pathways are formed through the process of long-term potentiation, which involves a physical change in the structure of neurons.

loudness (*phonology*) The intensity of a sound, measured in decibels (dB).

low action orientation A listener perspective in which the listener expects to have little or no participation in the discourse.

magnetic tuning A neural process to focus on prototypical sounds in a language; involves, **enhancement**, **attenuation**, **sharpening**, **broadening** and **realignment** of **sound prototypes**.

manner of delivery The style of the speaker, including pacing, pausing, and pattern of **disfluencies**.

mathemagenic models Methods of instruction that aim to aid learners in defining strategies and enhancing retention of learned material.

maxim of quality One of the Gricean **maxims of communication**; a way to explain the link between utterances and what is understood from them. This maxim states in its original form: Be truthful. Do not say what you believe to be false. Do not say that for which you lack adequate evidence.

McGurk effect A perceptual phenomenon which demonstrates an interaction between hearing and vision in speech perception.

memory node A proposed identification point in a memory network which is composed of a set of nodes connected by links. The nodes may represent concepts, words, perceptual features.

mental representation A way of explaining how a listener holds ideas and concepts in memory while listening.

metacognitive In descriptions of learning strategies, metacognitive strategies refer to enhancing awareness of language use conditions and processes.

metapragmatic Relating to an awareness of pragmatic forces, what speech *does* in a particular context.

metrical segmentation strategy A way of identifying words in the stream of speech by applying a metrical strategy, such as 'every strong syllable is likely to be the onset of a new content word'.

mind maps scheme A method of note-taking involving creation of personalised graphic imagery and connectives.

mishearing In ASR, a mismatch of input to analysis.

mismatch A difference at the conceptual level between the speaker's intention and the listener's understanding.

mismatched interpretation A phenomenon in which the listener arrives at an acceptable interpretation which differs from the speaker's intention, often due to differences in **activity frames** or **participant frames**.

misunderstanding A listener interpretation that differs markedly with the speaker's intention.

mixed initiative system A language understanding system in which the actions of the user and an agent (the computer), working on a joint task, are interleaved.

modified input Input modification is a way of making input comprehensible: one way is by pre-modifying input before it is offered to the learner, (pre-modified input), another way is to negotiate the input through interaction (interactionally modified input).

monitoring A cognitive activity of noting the progress of a transaction toward its goal.

memory organisational packets (MOPs) In information science, a network of generalised knowledge about events, containing linkages to specific events.

mora (symbolised as μ) A half-syllable or unit of syllable weight, used in some languages, such as Japanese and Hawaiian.

multidimensional model A psycholinguistic theory of language acquisition based on developmental sequences that may be enhanced or disrupted by individual differences (e.g. motivation).

multi-time resolution A process involved in word recognition through proactive and retroactive analysis, using context.

mutual exclusivity strategy A strategy for learning new lexical items, in which the learner seeks a new word to name a newly identified concept.

mutuality of development A notion in language and cognitive development that both child and caretaker undergo a common form of development.

narrow listening A learning technique focusing on seeking abundant input on the same topic from different perspectives.

natural language acquisition Acquisition that does not involve teachers or classrooms or formal courses.

natural order hypothesis In language acquisition theory, a hypothesis stating *if* there is a natural order of acquisition for all language learners, there must be a consistent way to map and guide progress for all learners.

negotiate meaning Engage in active interaction in order to understand what has been initially not understood or misunderstood.

negotiation for meaning (NfM) Interaction for the purpose of clarifying meaning.

neighbourhood density A concept in psycholinguistics relating to activation of semantic memory networks; when related concepts have been activated in memory, density of 'neighbouring' concepts is considered greater, and more readily accessible.

network-building task A part of lexical acquisition in which the child develops an understanding of relations between words and concepts.

neural commitment The process of using progressively smaller areas of neural tissue to process a familiar or recurring input.

neural commitment The process of using progressively smaller areas of neural tissue to process a recurring input, in order to make processing more efficient.

neural net models (NNs) Computational models in ASR that rely on simultaneous processing at multiple layers: phonetic, lexical and syntactic to calculate the best fit.

neurones Individual nerve cells that make up the nerve fibres, and form interactive networks (also known as **neurons**).

new information Information assumed to be unknown or not easily recalled by the listener.

Nijssen's information analysis method (NIAM) A method of conceptual modelling. In which the designer of a database builds a formal model of the application area or **universe of discourse (UoD)**; can be used as a tool for information and rules analysis; simplifies the design process by using natural language, as well as intuitive diagrams which can be populated with real-world examples.

NNS accents Ways of speaking characteristic of L2 speakers of particular L1 backgrounds.

non-understanding Absence of any listener interpretation for an utterance.

note-taking tips Specific instructional guidance for taking notes during a lecture, and for calling attention to rhetorical devices used by the lecturer to structure information.

noticing In language acquisition, the process of detecting occurrences and regularities in speech events.

Occam's razor The metatheoretical principle based on the axiom that 'entities must not be multiplied beyond necessity' and the conclusion of this principle, that the simplest solution is usually the correct one.

online tasks Tasks the listener performs while listening.

ontology In information science, an ontology is a formal representation of the knowledge by a set of concepts within a domain and the relationships between those concepts.

open-ended question A question that has an open set of answers, which can be answered in a variety of ways.

operating principles Cognitive strategies that underlie our innate ability to acquire language.

operational stage In Piagetan psychology, the stage (eight to eleven years) in which the child develops logic, but depends largely upon concrete referents.

opinion gap task A type of interaction in which each party has to find out the opinion of the others, which they do not know in advance.

opting out Choosing not to participate in the observance of a specific conversational maxim.

oracy A concept in instructional design relating to the relative role of the spoken language in L2 instruction, including listening.

orientation The second stage of attention, involving awareness of dimensions of time, place and active agents (people or things).

ostensive signals Perceptible signs, such as audible words and visible gestures, made for a communicative purpose.

ostensive–inferential process A theory of communication in which the speaker offers receivable signals (ostension) from which the listener makes inferences.

outer ear The external portion of the ear, which consists of the pinna, concha, and auditory meatus. It gathers sound energy and focuses it on the eardrum.

out-of-vocabulary words Words that are outside of one's vocabulary knowledge, either nonsense words or words that have not yet been acquired.

overextension In language acquisition, the process learner applying labels to too wide a range of concepts.

overexuberance of connections In child language acquisition, the notion that all possible phonetic contrasts are available to the child, the child learns to pare down this innumerable set of possibilities into only those realised by the language(s) the child is learning.

overhearer A listener for whom the speech was not directly intended.

pacing The speed and timing of the speaker in articulating an utterance.

packaging task A part of lexical acquisition in which the learner apply a label to a wider range of objects of the same type but simultaneously to restrict the label when appropriate.

paradigmatic structure A concept in semiotics, the analysis of semantic meaning of words, meaning relationships between words, and deep structure of the word meanings themselves.

paralinguistic features A suprasegmental aspect of language (applying across words), such as tone of voice, stress and intonation that colour the meaning of the speaker.

parallel processing The simultaneous processing of different types of information.

paratactic sequencing Sequencing of events in temporal order.

parataxis/paratactic organisation A style of speaking that favours short, simple sentences, without the use subordinating conjunctions, usually delivered in a direct time sequence (first, then, after that, etc.).

parse A hierarchical order of sentence constituents.

parsimony principle Use of the simplest or most frugal route of explanation available, using the fewest assumptions.

parsing The process of analysing input, made of a sequence of tokens (phonological words) to determine its grammatical structure.

participant frame The role that each person is playing within that activity, as understood by the participants.

participatory status The recognised right (or denial of this right) of a person to take part in a discourse or to direct it or decide its outcome.

pascal The measurement of pressure pulses that are exerted by sound waves (Force over an Area: $p = F/A$).

pause unit A unit of speech, defined by the presence of pauses at the start and end of the burst of speech.

paused task A listening task in which the audio or video input is paused for the listeners to complete a task or to generate questions.

pausing Temporary stopping of speech.

perceived social distance The relative intimacy and power that a participant experiences in an interaction, *vis-à-vis* the other participants.

perception The initial neurological response to any source of sensory stimulation, such as sound waves; auditory sensations are considered to reach perception only if they are received and processed by a cortical area in the brain.

perceptual constancy The ability to tolerate acoustic variability and still recognise target sounds.

perceptual goodness When perceiving a speech signal, our decision about what we actually hear is based on the relative match or constancy (also called 'goodness') between the stimulus information and values of particular prototypes.

perceptual magnet effect The psychological process by which the child learns to recognise sound variations according to a prototype for each phoneme in the language.

performatives In speech act theory, any speech act that the speaker uses to achieve a particular action and effect, such as apologising, inviting, complaining, or congratulating.

permission In conversational analysis, acknowledgement by speaker that listener may participate.

phonetic contrast A perceptible difference in sound quality that is used for meaning distinctions.

phonetic features Specific variables in articulation that affect production of sounds. For consonants, these variables include point of articulation (labial, labiodential, dental, alveolar, palatal, velar, glottal) and type of articulatory movement (plosive, nasal, fricative, lateral). For vowel sounds, these variables include position of the tongue and shaping of the lips.

phonological hierarchy A series of increasingly smaller regions of a phonological utterance.

phonological reduction The reduction of articulatory effort needed to produce a sound.

phonological rehearsal loop A memory process that links the auditory processing in the temporal lobe with motor processing from the prefrontal cortex.

phonological tagging A method of access to knowledge through language-specific (L1 or L2) cues.

phonological word or **prosodic word** (symbolised as ω) A constituent in a phonological hierarchy higher than the syllable and the foot but lower than intonational phrase and the phonological phrase.

phonotactic knowledge Knowledge of allowable sounds and sequences in a language.

phonotactic system The system of sounds containing restrictions in a language on the permissible combinations of phonemes and tonal sequences.

pitch In phonology, represents the perceived **fundamental frequency** of a sound. It is one of the four major auditory attributes of sounds, along with loudness, timbre and sound source location.

plausible intention A necessary inferencing process by a listener, an assumption about what the speaker has intended to accomplish by what was said.

politeness strategies Ways of formulating messages in order to save the hearer's face when face-threatening acts are being used in the discourse.

politeness In pragmatics, the expression of the speaker's intention to alleviate threats to 'face', or positive social value.

pragmatic competence The general ability to understand another speaker's intentions; an understanding of a speaker's feelings and attitudes.

pragmatic comprehension A specific understanding of a speaker's intentions; an understanding of a speaker's feelings and attitudes.

pragmatic processing Awareness of and integrating of pragmatic components of an event as part of the meaning.

preferred discourse pattern A sequence of discourse turns with which a language user is most familiar and most comfortable.

preferred response A response expected by the speaker or listener which completes the transaction with the least effort.

pre-listening A phase of instruction designed to prepare students for listening.

preoperation stage In Piagetan psychology, the stage (three to seven years) in which the child's intelligence is dominated by intuitive thinking.

presentation cues Linguistic and paralinguistic signals that show the relative 'newness' of information.

primary focus on meaning An instructional strategy of guiding learners to focus on concepts and ideas rather than on language form.

priming effects Stimulation of short-term memory, creating a readiness to process certain kinds of information, due to activation of related concepts or routines.

priming A memory effect in which exposure to a stimulus influences response to a subsequent stimulus.

principle of least effort The principle of language production in which speakers minimise articulatory effort in order to maximise the amount of what can be said in the shortest possible time.

probabilistic context-free grammar (PCFG) The system of syntactic rules that is used in ASR to confirm that incoming speech is well formed.

problem-solving process A focused inferencing process aimed at solving a specific comprehension problem in a text.

processing instruction A form of instruction in which pedagogic tasks are designed based on predictions about features of grammar that learners need to notice and acquire.

projection Listener action that supports the speaker's next turn.

prominence The primary focus in an utterance, which may be indicated by lexical, grammatical, or phonological structuring decisions by the speaker.

proof listening A learning procedure designed to enable learners to go over transcripts of natural oral texts systematically, successively identifying particular features that they may otherwise not notice.

proposition In psycholinguistics, an idea unit in memory, consisting of two or more lexical concepts in a semantic relationship.

propositional model A computational psycholinguistic model of language comprehension; the processing mechanism is lexically driven and maps the relationship of lexical items in the input.

prototype theory A mode of graded categorisation in cognitive science, where some members of a category are more central than others.

prototype A mental model of a pure or ideal form (of a sound or image or idea) that serves as a reference for identifying variations.

prototypical settings Typical cases, based on the listener's personal experience, that are assumed to be the basis of a description.

proximal zone (also **zone of proximal development, ZPD**) The difference between what a learner can do without help and what he or she can do with help.

psychoacoustic effects The process of utilising perceived and expected sounds to process sounds and recognise words.

psychoacoustic elements Physical composition of sound waves that can be differentiated by the listener, specifically **frequency**, **tone**, **duration** and **intensity**.

psychological distance The gap between the learner and the target language culture.

psychological reality The perceived reality or believability of an experience, its relevance for the perceiver.

psychological validity A form of validity emphasising the learner's recognition of the underlying value of an activity or assessment.

psychologically valid Modelling actual human behaviour, and identifiable by language users as a part of their planning or decision-making process.

pure dictation A form of listening practice in which the learner transcribes the exact words that a speaker utters.

pushed output tasks Tasks that force learners to articulate in speech or writing exactly what they have heard.

pushed output The requirement to utilise structures learners have not yet acquired, under demanding conditions, in order to speed up developmental processes of acquisition.

rates of speaking The speed of articulation, which varies by speaker and part of utterance.

read–encode–annotate–ponder (REAP) A procedure for evaluating reading ability and learning strategies for reading difficult texts.

readability indexes (also called **readability tests**, **readability formulas**, or **readability metrics**) Formulas for evaluating the readability of text, usually by counting syllables, words, and sentences and computing grammatical complexity.

readiness A listener state of preparation in which attention is primed; in conversation analysis, this state can be signalled by backchannelling.

reading/listening for pleasure An approach to reading or listening instruction emphasising reading or listening that learners do of their own free will, anticipating the satisfaction that we will get from the act of reading or listening; typically involves materials that reflect their own choice.

real-time reasoning Logical processes used during comprehension, which are often faulty because the listener may take short cuts in reasoning due to time or processing constraints.

recall Bring attention back to an event or information in a text.

recasts Restating and emphasising a more correct or appropriate formulation.

receiver apprehension (also called **communication apprehension**) A psycholinguistic phenomenon in which a participant experiences anxiety due to expectations about what needs to be understood.

reception Overt signalling that a message has been received.

recognition vocabulary Lexical items that the listener can recognise and interpret readily without contextual cues.

reductive (restrictive) simplification A type of text simplification strategy that serves the purpose of achieving an optimal result in comprehension.

reference frame A set of elements that is needed to interpret input; this may be a syntactic reference frame, consisting of obligatory and optional grammatical components, or a semantic reference frame, consisting of physical, emotional, and cultural elements needed for interpretation.

reference In psycholinguistics, a memory node corresponding to a particular element in the input.

reflection A method of assessing listener understanding by pausing an input and asking the listener what he or she is thinking.

regional accents Identifiable variations in pronunciation of a standard language between various populations, usually deriving from the phoneme inventory of the local dialect.

regional NS accents Ways of speaking characteristic of particular regions.

relationships between entities In information science, the designated link between two items that allows them to be computed as a single unit.

relevance theory A proposal that seeks to explain communication in terms of the tendency of the human mind to instinctively react to information that it conceives to be relevant.

relevance A sense of how pertinent, connected, or applicable something is to a person for a given purpose.

relevant input Genres, topics, and styles that have immediate importance to the listener.

repair strategies for misunderstandings Ways of managing or rectifying difficulties in understanding.

resonance A memory process in which neural circuits successfully copy detected linguistic forms to temporary local buffers so that listener can focus on incoming, unprocessed material while still retaining the recognised material in local memory.

response processing In NLP processing of input in order to determine an appropriate response from a specific set of response types.

response In communication theory, the non-verbal feedback to show understanding, and verbal contributions, such as asking questions or paraphrasing.

responsive listening A form of listening practice in which the learner seeks opportunities to respond and convey her own opinions and ideas.

reticular activating system (RAS) The area of the brain (including the reticular formation and its connections) responsible for regulating arousal and sleep-wake transitions.

retrospection A method of assessing listener understanding by asking the listener to report what was understood or what cognitive processes the listener used.

rising tone (referring tone) Increase in pitch at the end of an utterance.

role-play A type of interaction in which participants take on roles in order to complete a hypothetical transaction.

rule space methodology (RSM) A statistical technique within IRT for identifying patterns of responses among test-takers and defining traits or abilities that are measured by clusters of items.

rules In conversation analysis, the rules for conducting an interaction include co-ordination of turns and routines, as well as rules for mutual inferences.

sampling A perceptual process in which only limited extracts of a signal are perceived, and extrapolated to produce the actual recognition of the signal.

sandhi A cover term for a wide variety of phonological processes that occur at morpheme or word boundaries, particularly the fusion and transformation of sounds.

save face Keep, protect or guard (a thing) from damage, loss, or destruction, particularly to prevent being humiliated, losing one's credit, good name, or reputation.

schema (plural: **schemata**) Structures which organise our knowledge and assumptions about something and are used for interpreting and processing information. *In psycholinguistics* the term is used in multiple senses: A mental structure that represents some aspect of the world, or a structured cluster of pre-conceived ideas, or an organised pattern of thought or behaviour, or a mental framework centring round a specific theme, that helps us to organise social information.

schematic slot A component part of the schema that the listener assumes to exist in the speaker's model and the listener will fill in slots 'by default' unless given evidence to do otherwise.

script Prototypical knowledge about an event and sequences within it; Scripts contain our generalised knowledge about the temporal sequence of events which occur within an event. A **prototype** is an abstraction of a particular class of objects, while an exemplar is a specific instance that is considered representative of a set of objects.

second pass In syntactic processing, the integration by the listener of sentence-level parsing with discourse-level parsing.

segment Individual phonemes that make up syllables and word, e.g. [k], [æ] and [t] in *cat*.

segmentation A process in speech perception of breaking off pieces of extracted units to make internal comparisons.

selective attention A cognitive process that occurs whenever multiple sources, or streams, of information are present; involves a decision, a commitment of processing resources.

selective listening A form of listening practice in which the learner attempts to extract key information and construct or utilise information in a meaningful way.

semantic cues Processing hints based on meaning of surrounding context that help readers decode and comprehend input; semantic cues may include animacy, word order and case markings.

semantic operator *In NLP*, a 'movement trigger' that converts a proposition into a specific set of relationships that the computer can act upon.

semantic processing Linking of words to concepts and access of schemata in memory.

semantic role labelling In computer science, the designation of entities to meaningful roles, such as agent, destination, time.

semantically contingent Related to objects and events to which the child is already paying attention.

semi-active state A state of attention in which information has been previously activated, but has receded from working memory.

semi-verbal utterances Utterances that consist of partial words or non-words, such as *uh-huh, hmm*.

sensing In communication theory, the act of taking in messages.

sensorimotor stage In Piagetan psychology, the stage (birth to two years) during which the child's intelligence takes the form of motor actions.

sentence level The scale of analysis that is confined to a single sentence, that is a verb and other constituents.

sheltered language instruction An approach to teaching language that integrates language and content instruction. The dual goals of sheltered instruction are: to provide access to mainstream, grade-level content, and to promote the development of L2 proficiency.

short-term memory (STM) The capacity for holding a small amount of information in mind in an active, readily available state for a short period of time (also called primary memory or active memory).

short-term memory In neurobiology, a short-term memory is a temporary potentiation of neural connections that can become long-term memory through the process of rehearsal and meaningful association.

simplified lectures Academic talks that have been shortened or simplified in presentation to make them easier to follow.

single coding A type of storage of knowledge in long-term memory that has the same access channel in both L1 and L2 use.

single initiative system A language understanding system in which the actions of the user and an agent (the computer), working on a joint task, are fixed.

sinusoidal stimulation The process of the internal membranes inside the cochlea, which contains thousands of nerve fibres surrounded by a fluid, responding to movements.

situated presence A characterisation of the mind as physically grounded in its present context, which contributes to the meaning of any event or language the person encounters.

situational model (also called **mental model**) A model of memory and learning in which learning involves a referential mental world of what the text is about. The situation model contains temporal, spatial, and causal chains of events or relationships in a text.

social accommodation A social psychology term that refers to mutual movements of interlocutors toward the language and behaviour standards of the other.

social framework The underlying structure that connects and supports the various members and parts of a community or human organisation.

social In descriptions of learning strategies, social strategies refer to enhancing awareness of interlocutors and ways of interacting to increase learning effectiveness.

sociocultural theories (SCT) of language acquisition posit that language learning is a complex activity, a socially situated phenomenon. Within SCT, the goals and motives of the learner are of paramount importance, as are the learners' perception of themselves within their social environment.

sociocultural theory of mind The original theory of Vygotsky which explored the uniqueness of human development unique and the ways that higher psychological functions be studied and operationalised.

solidarity A benchmark for communication effectiveness referring to the listener's demonstration of affinity for and empathy with the speaker.

sound formants The distinguishing frequency components of human speech; sound formants are determined by articulatory movements of the speakers.

spectral information Data conveyed through electronic mapping of speech (mapping of **duration, loudness, pitch**). A **spectrogram** is an image that shows how the spectral density of a signal varies with time. Also known as **sonograms, voiceprints,** or **voicegrams,** spectrograms are used to identify phonetic sounds, to analyse sounds for speech processing. The instrument that generates a spectrogram is called a **spectrograph** or **sonograph.**

spectral processing A form of processing that detects harmony and melody and integrates sound with other forms of input.

speech recognition (also known as **automated speech recognition (ASR), human speech recognition (HSR),** and **computer speech recognition**) A process of converting spoken words to text.

stages of development A model of development that defines criteria and thresholds through which all learners must pass before they reach the subsequent stage.

statistical calculations A statistical pattern-matching technique in ASR in which incoming speech segments are matched to closest templates in the data base.

strategies for current use A category of learning strategies aimed at maximising learning in context; including retrieval strategies, rehearsal strategies, covert strategies (to exert control), and communication strategies (to convey or receive a message).

strategy A plan of action for a complex task.

Strathcylde A readability formula that heavily weights lexical items and relevance.

structure building framework A figurative procedure by which a listener constructs comprehension by interlinking concepts.

structure building A perspective on comprehension in which the listener relates language to concepts in memory and to references in the real world in a way that aims to find coherence and relevance.

sub-net A part of a grammatical parsing network in ASR that defines allowable syntactic forms to express specific semantic content.

superior olivary complex The initial area of the brain contacted by the auditory nerves, which plays a co-ordinating role in listening. The medial superior olive (MSO) is a specialised nucleus that measures the timing and frequency differences of sounds; the lateral superior olive (LSO) measures the difference in sound intensity.

superior position (superiority position) Status of an interaction in which one party claims to have knowledge or rights that the other party does not have.

superordinate level In ASR input parsing, the primary frame of the sentence, which may also contain embedded levels.

supporting grounds The factual or evidentiary basis of an argument, on which a conclusion is based, which may or may not be explicit in what the speaker says and are therefore assumed by the listener to be true.

suppression A cognitive process in which attention is deliberately focused away from a particular semantic network.

syllable A unit of organisation for a sequence of speech sounds; a syllable consists of the following segments: onset (obligatory in some languages, optional or restricted in others), plus a rime, which consists of nucleus (usually an open vowel sound, obligatory in most languages) and a coda (usually a consonant sound, optional in some languages, restricted or prohibited in others).

symbolisation In language acquisition, the process in which a child can understand the connection between sound, object and meaning.

syntactic accent A tendency to overuse L1 grammatical structures and patterns when speaking in an L2.

syntactic accent In sentence interpretation, a tendency to maintain L1 syntactic settings in both reception and production of the L2.

syntactic reference map Memory traces of the syntax that was used by the speaker after decoding an utterance.

syntagmatic structure A concept in semiotics, the analysis of surface structure.

syntonic Solidarity seeking by the listener, responding in a way that is in harmony with the speaker's belief system.

systemic grammar A model of grammar used in sociolinguistics which views language as 'a network of systems, or interrelated sets of options for creating meaning'.

tags In ASR parsing, tags are indicators of how constituents are related to the head words.

take notes Actively noting in written form cues from the text to aid in later recall and reconstruction.

target language use (TLU) domain The set of specific language use tasks that the learner is to be engaged in outside of the test that the test claims to approximate.

task-as-process A task designed with targeted psycholinguistic processes.

task-as-workplan A learning task with a definable external goal.

template In language acquisition, a neural sequence for particular forms (sounds, words, syntactic patterns) that is hard-wired into the brain to facilitate learning.

template-matching In ASR, a procedure for matching frames. A template contains a sequence of frames corresponding to a typical utterance of each word. When a sequence of speech is uttered, frame patterns are matched to measure the least difference or distance between the input and plausible words and sequences of words.

temporal lobe A major part of the brain that lies in the back half of the superior temporal gyrus (STG) and also enters into the transverse temporal gyri (also called Heschl's gyri). This is the first brain structure to process incoming auditory information.

temporal processing A form of sensory processing that sequences input, including sounds.

text linguistics A branch of linguistics that deals with texts as communication systems. Text linguistics takes into account the form of a text, but also its setting, i.e. the way in which it is situated in an interactional, communicative context.

textbase model A model of memory and learning in which learning involves representing explicit propositions in the text in a stripped-down form that captures the semantic meaning but loses details of the surface code.

think-aloud protocol A research tool in which the researcher asks the subject to talk spontaneously during performance of a task, with the intent of using this verbal report as evidence of cognitive processes.

tone Pattern of sound waves created by a vibration; the purity or complexity of this pattern determines the clarity of a sound.

tonic prominence The primary stress in an intonational unit.

tonotopic organisation A theory of the functioning of the auditory cortex in which the perceived tone is related to the area of the cortex that is stimulated; fibres with high **characteristic frequencies (CF)** are found in the outside periphery of the nerve bundle, with an orderly decrease in CF toward the centre of the nerve bundle.

top down processing Information processing guided by higher level mental processes as we construct representations, drawing on our experiences and expectations.

top-down strategies Listener based strategies for understanding; the listener taps into background knowledge of the topic, the situation or context, the type of text, and the language. This background knowledge activates a set of expectations that help the listener to interpret what is heard and anticipate what will come next.

topic shift Changing the subject of a conversation or monologue.

topic–comment structure A characteristic of language in which the topic is mentioned first, followed by information relating to it.

top-level (general) abilities Abilities within a construct that influence or interact with more specific abilities; in the case of listening, vocabulary recognition is a top-level ability that influences listening for specific words, a bottom-level ability, or skill-specific ability.

top-level attributes Skills identified in a listening test that are generalisable to all language skills.

training data In ASR, the body of spoken and written language structures that the software uses for matching incoming speech.

training of the database In speech recognition software, providing spoken data to use as template for matching incoming speech.

transactional level A level of analysis of discourse that focuses on what was achieved, or transacted, in the discourse.

transactional outcome What was actually accomplished as a result of an interaction.

transduce/transduction The process of converting one form of energy into a different form, in the case of listening, the converting of the mechanical movements of the fluid in the cochlea into nerve activity.

transitional elements Linguistic devices that signal a shift in time or perspective or organisation.

transliteration Converting a text from one writing system into another in a systematic way.

transverse temporal gyri The cortical structure that first processes incoming auditory information.

transverse temporal gyri The first cortical structure to process incoming auditory information; part of the superior temporal gyrus of the brain.

transvocalisation Converting a text from one phonological system into another in a systematic way, using only the phonotactic system from the borrowed-into language.

triangulation A research process of obtaining multiple perspectives on the same data in order to add depth to analysis.

trigger In NLP, a target word or phrase or interaction pattern that identifies a category for the input and prompts a particular response.

trochaically timed language A language, such as English, whose prosody is marked primarily by metrical feet consisting of one long or stressed syllable followed by one short or unstressed syllable.

two-way collaborative task An interaction focused on a tangible outcome, in which two or more learners collaborate to reach the outcome.

two-way discourse Conversation in which two or more interlocutors are participating.

uncertainty management theory A theory of communication that accounts for the role of anxiety, uncertainty, and mindfulness in face-to-face communication.

underextension In language acquisition, the process of the child over-simplifying concepts and failing to apply them to more than only one case.

universe of discourse (UoD) A term referring to the collection of objects being discussed in a specific discourse. In model-theoretical semantics, a universe of discourse is the set of entities on which a model is based.

unplanned discourse Spoken language that is unprepared, delivered spontaneously, without explicit rehearsal or use of written prompts.

updating The cognitive process of elaborating a particular memory network based on current experience or recent input.

uptake What the listener actually understands or 'takes away' from an interaction or event.

utterance A grammatical unit, consisting of an intonation unit, plus surrounding grammatical elements needed for its interpretation.

validity The degree to which a process or outcome is justifiable, effective, logical, and fair.

variance In statistical analysis, the variance of a measurement (such as a test score) or distribution is the expectation, or mean, of the deviation of that variable from its expected value or mean.

variation The principle that the same target word or sound may be uttered in different ways, all of which are intelligible.

vestibular nerve One of the two branches of the vestibulocochlear nerve, used for balance and orientation; the cochlear nerve is the other branch of this nerve.

vestibular nerve (*continued*) The nerve responsible for balance, it is intertwined with the auditory nerve.

vocal tract configurations Size, density, and position of parts of the vocal apparatus, including lungs, bones of the torso, neck, head, jaws, teeth, tongue, nasal passages.

vowel reduction The term in phonetics that refers to various changes in the acoustic quality of vowels, which are related to changes in stress, sonority, duration, loudness, articulation, or position in the word and which are perceived as weakening.

washback effect The consequences of an action on subsequent attitudes of participants; in educational settings, the tendency of teaching goals to mirror testing goals.

weakening A decrease in articulatory precision, stress, duration, or loudness in the process of articulation.

weight In connectionist views of memory, different nodes in a network have different weights, based on their frequency of use or centrality of position in the network.

Wernicke's area A part of the brain, located as the posterior section of the superior temporal gyrus (STG) in the left (or dominant) cerebral hemisphere (behind left ear), which is responsible for speech recognition, lexical and syntactic comprehension.

word recognition The cognitive process of identifying what word was spoken, and activating word meanings associated with it.

working memory The attentional aspect of short-term memory involved in the integration, processing, disposal, and retrieval of information. Working memory tasks include the active monitoring or manipulation of information.

References

Aboitiz, F., Aboitiz, S. and García, R. (2010) The phonological loop: a key innovation in human evolution. *Current Anthropology*, **51** (1), pp. 55–65.

Ackerman, P., Beier, M., and Boyle, M. (2002) Individual differences in working memory within a nomological network of cognition and perceptual speed abilities. *Journal of Experimental Psychology*, **131**, pp. 567–89.

Adams, C., Smith, M., Pasupathi, M., and Vitolo, L. (2002) Social context effects on story recall in older and younger women: does the listener make a difference? *Journal of Gerontology: Psychological Sciences*, **57**, pp. 28–40.

Adank, P., Evans, B., Stuart-Smith, J., and Scott, S. (2009) Comprehension of familiar and unfamiliar native accents under adverse listening conditions. *Journal of Experimental Psychology: Human Perception and Performance* **35**, pp. 520–9.

Agar, M. (1985) Institutional discourse. *Text: Interdisciplinary Journal for the Study of Discourse*, **5**, pp. 147–68.

Aist, G., Allen, J., Campana, E., Galescu, L., Gomez Gallo, C. A., Stoness, S., Swift, M., and Tanenhaus, M. (2006) Software architectures for incremental understanding of human speech. *Proceedings of the International Conference on Spoken Language Processing (ICSLP)*. Pittsburgh, PA: ICSLP.

Aist, G., Campana, E., Allen, J., Rotondo, M., Swift, M., and Tanenhaus, M. (2005) Variations along the contextual continuum in task-oriented speech. *Scientific Commons*, www.scientificcommons.org/42374621.

Aitchison, J. (2003) *Words in the mind: an introduction to the mental lexicon*, 3rd edn. New York: Wiley.

Alamri, A. (2008) An Evaluation of the Sixth Grade English Language Textbook for Saudi Boys' Schools. M.A. thesis, Jeddah: King Saud University.

Alderson, C., Figueras, N., Kuijper, H., Nold, G., Takala, S., and Tardieu, C. (2006) Analysing tests of reading and listening in relation to the Common European Framework of Reference: the experience of the Dutch CEFR construct project. *Language Assessment Quarterly*, **3** (1), pp. 3–30.

Alderson, J. C. (2005) *Diagnosing foreign language proficiency: the interface between learning and assessment*. London: Continuum.

Alea, N., and Bluck, S. (2003) Why are you telling me that? A conceptual model of the social function of autobiographical memory. *Memory*, **11**, pp. 165–78.

Alexandrov, Y., and Sams, M. (2005) Emotion and consciousness: ends of a continuum. *Cognitive Brain Research*, **25**, pp. 387–405.

Al-Khanji, R., El-Shiyab, S., and Hussein, R. (2000) On the use of compensatory strategies in simultaneous interpretation, in *Report 45*. Paris: Centre national de la recherche scientifique, pp. 548–60.

Allwood, J. (2002) in B. Granström, D. House, and I. Karlsson (eds) Bodily communication dimensions of expression and content, in B. Granström *et al.* (eds) *Multimodality in language and speech systems*, pp. 7–26. The Hague: Kluwer.

Allwood, J. (2006) Consciousness, thought and language, in K. Brown (ed.) *Encyclopedia of language and linguistics*, 2nd edn. Oxford: Elsevier.

Alptekin, C. (2006) Cultural familiarity in inferential and literal comprehension in L2 reading system, *System*, **34** (4), pp. 494–508.

Al-Seghayer, K. (2001) The effect of multimedia annotation modes on L2 vocabulary acquisition: a comparative study. *Language Learning and Technology*, **5**, pp. 202–32. http://llt.msu.edu/.

Altenberg, E. (2005) The perception of word boundaries in a second language. *Second Language Research*, **21**, pp. 325–58.

Amoretti, M. S., Mendonça, A., and Santos, C. (2007) Evaluation of oral comprehension of Amazonian tales: making a diagnosis of conceptual maps with PIPA software, in T. Bastiaens and S. Carliner (eds) *Proceedings of World Conference on E-learning in Corporate, Government, Healthcare, and Higher Education*. Chesapeake, VA: Association for the Advancement of Computing in Education, pp. 374–78.

Anderson, A. (2006) Achieving understanding in face-to-face and video-mediated multiparty interactions. *Discourse Processes*, **41** (3), pp. 251–87.

Anderson, R. (1996) The primacy aspect of first and second language acquisition: the pidgin–creole connection, in W. Ritchie and T. Bhatia (eds) *Handbook of second language acquisition*. San Diego, CA: Academic Press.

Anderson, R., and Shirai, Y. (1994) Discourse motivations for some cognitive acquisition principles. *Studies in Second Language Acquisition*, **16**, pp. 133–56.

Anderson, R., Baxter, K., and Cissna, N. (2003) *Dialogue: theorizing difference in communication studies*. New York: Sage.

Aniero, S. (1990) The Influence of Receiver Apprehension among Puerto Rican College Students. PhD thesis, New York University. *Dissertation Abstracts International*, **50**, p. 2300A.

Appel, R., and Muysken, P. (2006) *Language contact and bilingualism*. Amsterdam: Amsterdam University Press.

Arasaratnam, L. A. (2007) Empirical research in intercultural communication competence: a review and recommendation. *Australian Journal of Communication*, **34**, pp. 105–17.

Arasaratnam, L. A. (2009) The development of a new instrument of intercultural communication competence. *Journal of Intercultural Communication*, **20**.

Archibald, J. (2000) *Second language acquisition and linguistic theory*. New York: Wiley.

Arciuli, J., and Cupples, L. (2004) Effects of stress typicality during spoken word recognition by native and nonnative speakers of English: evidence from onset gating. *Memory and Cognition*, **32**, pp. 21–30.

Arnold, J. E., Kam, C., and Tanenhaus, M. (2007) 'If you say thee uh you are describing something hard': the online attribution of disfluency during reference comprehension. *Journal of Experimental Psychology: Learning, Memory, and Cognition*, **33**, pp. 914–30.

Ash, D. (2003) Dialogic inquiry in life science conversations of family groups in a museum. *Journal of Research in Science Teaching*, **40**, pp. 138–62.

Aslin, R., Jusczyk, P., and Pisoni, D. (1998) Speech and auditory processing during infancy: constraints on and precursors to language, in R. Seigler (ed.) *Mussen's handbook of child psychology*. New York: Wiley.

Au, K. (1979) Using the experience–text relationship method with minority children. *The Reading Teacher*, **32** (6), pp. 677–9

Auer, P., Couper-Kuhlen, E., and Muller, F. (1999) *Language in time: the rhythm and tempo of spoken interaction*. Oxford: Oxford University Press.

Auer, P., and Kern, F. (2001) Three ways of analysing communication between East and West Germans as intercultural communication, in A. di Luzio, S. Günthner and F. Orletti (eds) *Culture in communication*. Amsterdam: Benjamins.

Austin, J. H. (1998) *Zen and the brain*. Cambridge MA: MIT Press.

Austin, J. H. (2006) *Zen-brain reflections*. Cambridge, MA: MIT Press.

Austin, J. L. (1962) *How to do things with words*. Oxford: Oxford University Press.

Ausubel, D. (1978) In defense of advance organizers: a reply to the critics. *Review of Educational Research*, **48**, pp. 251–7.

Aylett, M., and Turk, A. (2006) Language redundancy predicts syllable duration and the spectral characteristics of vocalic syllable nuclei. *Journal of the Acoustical Society of America*, **119**, pp. 3048–58.

Baars, B., Banks, W., and Newman, J. (2003) *Essential sources in the scientific study of consciousness*. Boston, MA: MIT Press.

Bachman, L. F. (2007) What is the construct? The dialectic of abilities and contexts in defining constructs in language assessment, in J. Fox, M. Wesche, and D. Bayliss (eds) *What are we measuring? Language testing reconsidered*. Ottawa: University of Ottawa Press.

Bachman, L., and Palmer, A. (2009) *Language assessment in practice*, 2nd edn. Oxford: Oxford University Press.

Baddeley, A. (1997) *Human memory: theory and practice*, rev. edn. New York: Psychology Press.

Baddeley, A. (2001) Is working memory still working? *American Psychologist*, **56**, pp. 851–7.

Baddeley, A. (2003) Working memory and language: an overview. *Journal of Communication Disorders*, **36** (3), pp. 189–208.

Baddeley, A., and Larsen, J. (2007) The phonological loop: some answers and some questions. *Quarterly Journal of Experimental Psychology*, **60**, pp. 512–18.

Baggio, G. (2008) Processing temporal constraints: an ERP study, *Language Learning*, **58**, pp. 35–55.

Baltova, I. (1999) Multisensory language teaching in a multidimensional curriculum: the use of authentic bimodal video in core French. *Canadian Modern Language Review*, **56**, pp. 31–48.

Banda, F. (2007) Radio listening clubs in Malawi and Zambia: towards a participatory model of broadcasting: research article, *Sabinet*, **26**, pp. 130–48.

Barbey, A., and Barsalou, L. (2009) *Encyclopedia of neuroscience*, **8**, pp. 35–43.

Bard, E. G., Anderson, A. H., Sotillo, C., Aylett, M., Doherty-Sneddon, G., and Newlands, A. (2000) Controlling the intelligibility of referring expressions in dialogue. *Journal of Memory and Language*, **42**, pp. 1–22.

Bardovi-Harlig, K. (2006) On the role of formulas in the acquisition of L2 pragmatics, in Bardovi-Harlig, K., Félix-Brasdefer, C., and Omar, A. (2006) *Pragmatics and Language Learning*, **11**, pp. 1–28.

Barker, J., Ma, N., Coy, A., and Cooke, M. (2010) Speech fragment decoding techniques for simultaneous speaker identification and speech recognition. *Computer Speech and Language*, **24** (1), pp. 94–111.

Barr, D., and Keysar, B. (2002) Anchoring comprehension in linguistic precedents. *Journal of Memory and Language*, **46**, pp. 391–418.

Barret, L., Tugate, M., and Engle, R. (2004) Individual differences in working memory capacity and dual-process theories of the mind. *Psychological Bulletin*, **130**, pp. 553–73.

Barron, B. (2004) Learning ecologies for technological fluency: gender and experience differences. *Journal of Educational Computing Research*, **31**, pp. 1–36.

Bartlett, C. (1932) *Remembering*. Cambridge: Cambridge University Press.

Barzilay, R., and Lapata, M. (2008) Modeling local coherence: an entity-based approach. *Computational Linguistics*, **34** (1), pp. 1–34.

Batstone, R. (2002) Contexts of engagement: a discourse perspective on 'intake' and 'pushed output'. *System*, **30**, pp. 1–14.

Baxter, L., and Braithwaite, D. (2008) *Engaging theories of communication: multiple perspectives*. New York: Sage.

Beach, C. (1991) The interpretation of prosodic patterns at points of syntactic structure ambiguity: evidence for cue trading relations. *Journal of Memory and Language*, **30**, pp. 644–63.

Beach, W. (2000) Inviting collaboration in stories. *Language in Society*, **29**, pp. 379–407.

Beale, A. (2009) *Reading the hidden communications around you: a guide to reading body*. Bloomington, IN: iUniverse.

Beebe, L. (1985) Input: choosing the right stuff, in S. Gass, and C. Madden (eds) *Input in second language acquisition*. New York: Newbury House.

Behrman, M., and Patterson, K. (2004) *Words and things*. Hove: Psychology Press.

Belin, P., Van Eeckhout, P., Zilbovicius, M., Remy, P., Francois, C., Guillaume, S., Chain, F., Rancurel, G., and Samson, Y. (1996) Recovery from nonfluent aphasia after melodic intonation therapy: a PET study. *Neurology*, **47**, pp. 1504–11.

Bell, A. 2005. *You can't talk to me that way! Stopping toxic language in the workplace*. Franklin Lakes, NJ: Career Press.

Bella, A., Brenierc, J., Gregoryd, M., Girande, C., and Jurafsky, D. (2009) Predictability effects on durations of content and function words in conversational English. *Journal of Memory and Language*, **60**, pp. 92–111.

Benasich, A., and Tallal, P. (2002) Infant discrimination of rapid auditory cues predicts later language impairment. *Behavioural Brain Research*, **136**, pp. 31–49.

Bennett, D. (2003) *Logic made easy: how to know when language deceives you*. New York: Norton.

Benson, M. (1989) The academic listening task: a case study. *TESOL Quarterly*, **23**, pp. 421–45.

Benson, M. (1994) Lecture listening in an ethnographic perspective, in J. Flowerdew (ed.) *Academic listening: research perspectives*. Cambridge: Cambridge University Press.

Benson, P. (2007) Autonomy in language learning and teaching. *Language Teaching*, **40**, pp. 21–40.

Benson, P. (2010) *Autonomy in language learning*, 2nd edn. Applied Linguistics in Action series. Harlow: Longman.

Berlo, D. (1960) *The Process of Communication*. New York: Holt.

Berwick, R., and Ross, S. (1996) Cross-cultural pragmatics in oral proficiency interview strategies, in M. Milanovic and N. Saville (eds) *Performance testing, cognition and assessment*. Cambridge: Cambridge University Press.

Bezuidenhout, A., and Morris, R. (2004) Implicature, relevance and default pragmatic inference, in I. A. Noveck and D. Sperber (eds) *Experimental pragmatic*. Basingstoke: Palgrave Macmillan.

Bialystok, E. (1990) *Communication strategies: a psycholinguistic analysis of second language use*. Oxford: Blackwell.

Bialystok, E. (2007) Acquisition of literacy in bilingual children: a framework for research. *Language Learning*, **57**, pp. 45–77.

Biemiller, A. (2009) Teaching vocabulary: early, direct and sequential, in M. Graves (ed.) *Essential readings on vocabulary instruction*. Newark, DE: International Reading Association.

Bilmes, J. (1988) The concept of preference in conversation analysis. *Language in Society*, **17**, pp. 161–81.

Birdwhistell, R. (1970) *Kinesics and context: essays in body motion communication*. Philadelphia, PA: University of Pennsylvania Press.

Birnie, J., and Johnson, I. (1965) Developments in language laboratory materials. *ELT Journal*, **20**, pp. 29–35.

Bisanz, G., LaPorte, R., Vesonder, G., and Voss, J. (1981) Contextual prerequisites for understanding: some investigations of comprehension and recall. *Journal of Verbal Learning and Verbal Behaviour*, **17**, pp. 3337–57.

Bishop, D. (2000) Pragmatic language impairment: a correlate of SLI, a distinct sub-group, or part of the autistic continuum? In D. Bishop and L. Leonard (eds) *Speech and language impairments in children: causes, characteristics, intervention and outcome*. Hove: Psychology Press.

Blevins, J. (2007) Interpreting misperception: beauty is in the ear of the beholder, in M. Solé, P. Beddor and M. Ohalavb (eds) *Experimental approaches to phonology*. Oxford: Oxford University Press.

Bley-Vroman, R. (1990) The logical problem of foreign language learning. *Linguistic Analysis*, **20**, pp. 3–49.

Block, C., and Duffy, G. (2008) Research on comprehension instruction: where we've been and where we're going, in C. Block and S. Parris (eds) *Comprehension instruction: research-based best practices*. New York: Guilford Press.

Block, C., and Parris, S. (2008) *Comprehension instruction: research-based best practices*, 2nd edn. New York: Guilford Press.

Block, D. (2003) *The social turn in second language acquisition*. Edinburgh: Edinburgh University Press.

Blum-Kulka, S., House, J., and Kasper, G., eds (1989) The CCSARP coding manual (appendix), in *Cross-cultural pragmatics: requests and apologies*. Norwood, NJ: Ablex.

Bodrova, D., and Leong, D. (2007) *Tools of the mind: the Vygotskian approach to early childhood development*. New York: Prentice-Hall.

Bobrow, D., Kaplan, R., Kay, M., Norman, D., Thompson, H., and Winograd, T. (1977) GUS, a frame-driven dialog system. *Artificial Intelligence*, **8** (2), pp. 155–73.

Boersma, P. (1998) *Functional phonology: formalizing the interactions between articulatory and perceptual drives*. The Hague: Holland Academic Graphics.

Boland, J., and Blodgett, A. (2001) Understanding the constraints on syntactic generation: lexical bias and discourse congruity effects on eye movements. *Journal of Memory and Language*, **45**, pp. 395–411.

Bolter, J., MacIntrye, B., Gangy, M., and Schweitzer, P. (2006) New media and the permanent crisis of aura. *Convergence: the International Journal of Research into new Media Technologies*, **12**, pp. 21–39.

Bonk, W. (2000) Second language lexical knowledge and listening comprehension, *International Journal of Listening*, **14**, pp. 14–31.

Bosco, F., Bucciarelli, M., and Bara, B. (2004) The fundamental context categories in understanding communicative intention. *Journal of Pragmatics*, **36** (3), pp. 467–88.

Bosco, F., Bucciarelli, M., and Bara, B. (2006) Recognition and repair of communicative failures: a developmental perspective. *Journal of Pragmatics*, **38**, pp. 1398–429.

Bostrom, R. (1990) *Listening behaviour: measurement and application*. New York: Guilford Press.

Bowe, H., and Martin, K. (2007) *Communication across cultures: mutual understanding in a global world*. Cambridge: Cambridge University Press.

Bradac, J. (2001) Theory comparison: uncertainty reduction, problematic integration. *Journal of Communication*, **3**, pp. 456–76.

Braidi, S. (1998) *The acquisition of second language syntax*. London: Arnold.

Braine, M., and O'Brien, D. (1998) *Mental logic*. Abingdon: Routledge.

Brainerd, C. (1978) *Piaget's theory of intelligence*. Englewood Cliffs, NJ: Prentice-Hall.

Brainerd, C. (1978) The stage question in cognitive developmental theory. *Behavioral and Brain Sciences*, **1**, pp. 173–82.

Bransford, J. (2003) *How people learn: brain, mind, experience, and school*. Washington, DC: National Academies.

Bransford, J., and Johnson, M. (2004) Contextual prerequisites for understanding: some investigations of comprehension and recall, in D. Balota and E. Marsh (eds) *Cognitive psychology: key readings*. New York: Psychology Press.

Brazil, D. (1995) *A grammar of speech*. Oxford: Oxford University Press.

Breen, M. (1985) Authenticity in the language classroom. *Applied Linguistics*, **6**, pp. 60–70.

Breen, M. (2001) *Learner contributions to language learning: new directions in research*. Harlow: Pearson.

Bremer, K., Roberts, C., Vasseur, M., Simonot, M., and Broeder, P. (1996) *Achieving understanding: discourse in intercultural encounters*. Language in Social Life series. Harlow: Longman.

Briggs, C., and Bauman, R. (2009) Genre, intertextuality, and social power, in A. Duranti (ed.) *Linguistic anthropology: a reader*. New York: Wiley.

Brindley, G. (1998) Assessing listening abilities. *Annual Review of Applied Linguistics*, **18**, pp. 178–98.

Brindley, G. (2002) Exploring task difficulty in ESL listening assessment. *Language Testing*, **19**, pp. 369–94.

Brindley, G., and Slayter, H. (2002) Exploring task difficulty in ESL listening assessment, *Language Testing*, **19**, pp. 369–94.

Brinton, D., Snow, M., and Wesche, M. (1989) *Content-based second language instruction*. New York: Newbury.

Brisard, F., Östman, J-O., and Verschueren, J. (2009) Theories of grammar, in *Grammar, meaning and pragmatics*. Amsterdam: Benjamins.

Brown, A. (2003) Interviewer variation and the co-construction of speaking proficiency. *Language Testing*, **20**, pp. 1–25.

Brown, C. (2000) The interrelation between speech perception and phonological acquisition from infant to adult, in J. Archibald (ed.) *Second language acquisition and linguistic theory*. Oxford: Blackwell.

Brown, G. (1977) *Listening to spoken English*. London: Longman.

Brown, G. (1994) Dimensions of difficulty in listening comprehension, in D. Mendelsohn and J. Rubin (eds) *A guide for the teaching of second language listening*. San Diego, CA: Dominie Press.

Brown, G. (1995) *Speakers, listeners and communication: explorations in discourse analysis*. Cambridge: Cambridge University Press.

Brown, H. D., and Abewickrama, P. (2010) *Language assessment: principles and classroom practices*, 2nd edn. White Plains, NY: Pearson Longman.

Brown, J. D., and Rodgers, T. (2002) *Doing educational research*. Oxford: Oxford University Press.

Brown, J., and Palmer, A. (1987) *The listening approach: methods and materials for applying Krashen's input hypothesis*. New York: Longman.

Brown, R., Waring, R., and Donkaewbua, S. (2008) Incidental vocabulary acquisition from reading, reading-while-listening, and listening to stories. *Reading in a Foreign Language*, **20**, pp. 136–63.

Brownell, J. (1996) *Listening: attitudes, principles and skills*. New York: Allyn & Bacon.

Bruner, J. (1983) *Child's talk: learning to use language*. New York: Norton.

Bruner, J. (1986) *Actual minds, possible worlds*. Cambridge, MA: Harvard University Press.

Bruner, J. (1990) *Acts of meaning*. Cambridge, MA: Harvard University Press.

Buchweitz, A., Mason, R., Tomitch, L., and Just, M. (2009) Brain activation for reading and listening comprehension: an fMRI study of modality effects and individual differences in language comprehension. *Psychology and Neuroscience*, **2**, pp. 111–23.

Buck, G. (1992) Listening comprehension: construct validity and trait characteristics. *Language Learning*, **42** (3), pp. 313–57.

Buck, G. (2001) *Assessing listening*. Cambridge: Cambridge University Press.

Buck, G., Tatsuoka, K., Kostin, I., and Phelps, M. (1997) The sub-skills of listening: rule-space analysis of a multiple-choice test of second-language listening comprehension, in A. Huhta, V. Kohonen, L. Kurki-Sonio and S. Luoma (eds) *Current developments and alternatives in language assessment. Proceedings of LTRC*, **96**, pp. 599–624.

Burger, J., Cardie, C., Chaudhri, V., Gaizauskas, R., Harabagiu, S., Israel, D., Jacquemin, C., Lin, C.-Y., Maiorano, S., Miller, G., Moldovan, D., Ogden, B., Prager, J., Rilo, E., Singhal, A., Shrihari, R., Strzalkowski, T., Voorhees, E., and Weischedel, R. (2002) *Issues, tasks and program structures to roadmap research in question and answering (Q&A)*. Available at www-nlpir.nist.gov/projects/duc/roadmapping.html.

Burgoon, J. K., and Qin, T. (2006) The dynamic nature of deceptive verbal communication. *Journal of Language and Social Psychology*, **25** (1), pp. 76–96.

Burgoon, J., and White, C. (1997) Researching non-verbal message production: a view from interaction adaptation theory, in J. Greene (ed.) *Message production: advances in communication theory*. Mahwah, NJ: Erlbaum.

Burman, E. (2007) *Deconstructing developmental psychology*. London: Routledge.

Burns, A. (2005) Action research: an evolving paradigm? *Language Teaching*, **38**, pp. 57–74.

Burt, C., Kemp, S., and Conway, M. (2003) Themes, events, and episodes in autobiographical memory. *Memory and Cognition*, **31**, pp. 317–25.

Burton-Roberts, N., Carr, P., and Docherty, G. (2000) *Phonological knowledge: conceptual and empirical issues*. Oxford: Oxford University Press.

Burzio, L. (2007) Phonology and phonetics of English stress and vowel reduction. *Language Sciences*, **29**, pp. 154–76.

Byrnes, H. (2005) Content-based instruction, in C. Sanz (ed.) *Mind and context in adult second language acquisition: methods, theory, and practice*. Washington, DC: Georgetown University Press.

Caillies, S., Denhiere, G., and Kintsch, W. (2002) The effect of prior knowledge on understanding from text: evidence from primed recognition. *European Journal of Cognitive Psychology*, **14**, pp. 267–86.

Cameron-Faulkner, T., Lieven, E., and Tomasello, M. (2003) A construction based analysis of child directed speech. *Cognitive Science*, **27**, pp. 843–73.

Camiciottoli, B. (2007) *The language of business studies lectures: a corpus-assisted analysis*. Amsterdam: Benjamins.

Campbell, D. (2008) *Sound spirit: pathway to faith*. Los Angeles, CA: Hay House.

Campbell, D., McDonnell, C., Meinardi, M., and Richardson, B. (2007) The need for a speech corpus. *ReCALL*, **19**, pp. 3–20.

Campion, N., Martins, D., and Wilhelm, A. (2009) Contradictions and predictions: two sources of uncertainty that raise the cognitive interest of readers. *Discourse Processes*, **46**, pp. 341–68.

Candlin, C. (1987) *Language learning tasks*. New York: Prentice-Hall.

Candlin, C., and Mercer, N. (2000) English language teaching in its social context. *Course materials for LING 937*. Sydney: Macquarie University.

Candlin, C., and Mercer, N. (2001) *English language teaching in its social context: a reader*. London: Routledge, pp. 323–44.

Candlin, C., and Murphy, D. (1976) *Engineering lecture discourse and listening comprehension*. KAAU project: Lancaster Practical Papers in English Language Education. Lancaster: University of Lancaster.

Cárdenas-Claros, M., and Gruba, P. (2009) Help options in CALL: a systematic review. *CALICO Journal*, **27** (1), pp. 69–90.

Carpenter, P., Miyake, A., and Just, M. (1994) Working memory constraints in comprehension: evidence from individual differences, aphasia and aging, in *Handbook of psycholinguistics*. New York: Academic Press.

Carr, T., and Curran, T. (1994) Cognitive processes in learning about structure: applications to syntax in second language acquisition. *Studies in Second Language Acquisition*, **16**, pp. 221–35.

Carrier, K. (1999) The social environment of second language listening: does status play a role in comprehension? *Modern Language Journal*, **83**, pp. 65–79.

Carroll, S. (2006) Salience, awareness and SLA, in M. Grantham, C. O'Brien and J. Archibald (eds) *Generative Approaches to Second Language Acquisition conference (GASLA) proceedings*. Somerville, MA: Cascadilla Proceedings Project, pp. 17–24.

Carstensen, L., Pasupathi, M., Mayr, U., and Nesselroade, J. (2000) Emotional experience in everyday life across the adult life span. *Journal of Personality and Social Psychology*, **79**, pp. 644–55.

Carter, R. (2003) *Exploring consciousness*. Berkeley, CA: University of California Press.

Carter, R., and McCarthy, M. (2004) Talking, creating: interactional language, creativity, and context. *Applied Linguistics*, **25**, pp. 62–8.

Carver, R. (2003) The highly lawful relationships among pseudoword decoding, word identification, spelling, listening, and reading. *Scientific Studies of Reading*, **7**, pp. 127–54.

Carver, R., and David, A. (2001) Investigating reading achievement using a causal model. *Scientific Studies of Reading*, **5**, pp. 107–40.

Cauldwell, R. (2002) Grasping the nettle: the importance of perception work in listening comprehension. Retrieved from www.developingteachers.com/.

Cauldwell, R. (2004) Review. L. Shockey, *Sound patterns of spoken English* (2003). *Journal of the International Phonetics Association*, **34** (1), pp. 101–4.

Cauldwell, R. (2004) Speech in action: teaching listening with the help of ICT, in A. Chambers, J. Conacher and J. Littlemore (eds) *ICT and language learning: integrating pedagogy and practice*. London: Continuum.

Center for Applied Linguistics (2010) www.cal.org/topics/ta/.

Cevasco, J., and van den Broek, P. (2008) The importance of causal connections in the comprehension of spontaneous spoken discourse. *Psicothema*, **20**, pp. 801–6.

Chafe, W. (1980) The pear stories: cognitive, cultural, and linguistic aspects of narrative production, in R. Freedle (ed.) *Advances in discourse process*, Norwood, NJ: Ablex.

Chafe, W. (1994) *Discourse, consciousness, and time: the flow and displacement of consciousness in speaking and writing*. Chicago: University of Chicago Press.

Chafe, W. (2000) Loci of diversity and convergence in thought and language, in M. Pütz and M. Verspoor (eds) *Explorations in linguistic relativity*, Amsterdam: Benjamins, pp. 101–23.

Chafe, W. (2007) *The importance of not being earnest: the feeling behind laughter and humor*. Amsterdam: Benjamins.

Chafe, W., and Tannen, D. (1987) The relation between written and spoken language. *Annual Review of Anthropology*, **16**, pp. 383–407.

Chalmers, D. J. (1996) *The conscious mind: in search of a fundamental theory*. New York: Oxford University Press.

Chalmers, D. J. (2002) Consciousness and its place in nature, in *Philosophy of mind: classical and contemporary readings*. Oxford: Oxford University Press.

Chambers, C., Tanenhaus, M., Eberhard, K., Hana, F., and Carlson, G. (2002) Circumscribing referential domains during real-time language comprehension. *Journal of Memory and Language*, **47**, pp. 30–49.

Chamot, A. (2005) Language learning strategy instruction: current issues and research. *Annual Review of Applied Linguistics*, **25**, pp. 112–30.

Chamot, A. U., Barnhardt, S., El Dinary, P. B., and Robbins, J. (1999) *The learning strategies handbook*. White Plains, NY: Addison-Wesley Longman.

Chan, S., Cheung, L., and Chong, M. (2010) A machine learning parser using an un-lexicalized distituent model. *Computational Linguistics and Intelligent Text Processing: Lecture Notes in Computer Science*, **6008**, pp. 121–36.

Chandler, D. (2007) *Semiotics: the basics*, 2nd edn. Oxford: Routledge.

Chandler-Olcott, K., and Mahar, D. (2003) Tech-savviness meets multiliteracies: exploring adolescent girls' technology-mediated literacy practices. *Reading Research Quarterly*, **38** (3), pp. 356–85.

Chang, A. (2009) Gains to L2 listeners from reading while listening versus listening only in comprehending short stories. *System*, **37**, pp. 652–63.

Chang, A., and Read, J. (2006) The effects of listening support on the listening performance of EFL learners, *TESOL Quarterly*, **40**, pp. 375–97.

Changeues, J., Heidmann, T., and Patte, P. (1984) Learning by selection, in P. Marler and H. Terrace (eds) *The biology of learning*. Berlin: Springer.

Chater, N., and Manning, C. (2006) Probabilistic models of language processing and acquisition. *Trends in Cognitive Sciences*, **10** (7), pp. 335–44.

Chaudron, C. (1983) A method for examining the input/intake distinction, in S. Gass and C. Madden (eds) *Input and second language acquisition*. Boston. MA: Heinle & Heinle.

Chaudron, C. (1988) *Second language classrooms: research on teaching and learning*. Cambridge: Cambridge University Press.

Chaudron, C. (1995) Academic listening, in D. Mendelsohn and J. Rubin (eds) *A guide for the teaching of second language listening*. San Diego, CA: Dominie Press.

Chaudron, C. (2006) Some reflections on the development of (meta-analytic) synthesis in second language research, in J. Norris and L. Ortega (eds) *Synthesizing research on language learning and teaching*. Amsterdam: Benjamins.

Chella, A., and Mazotti, R. (2007) *Artificial consciousness*. Exeter: Imprint Academic Press.

Chen, Y. (2007) Learning to learn: the impact of strategy training. *ELT Journal*, **61**, pp. 20–9.

Cheng, W., Greaves, C., and Warren, M. (2005). The creation of a prosodically transcribed intercultural corpus: the Hong Kong Corpus of Spoken English (prosodic). *ICAME Journal: Computers in English Linguistics*, **29**, pp. 47–68.

Cherry, E. (1953) Some experiments on the recognition of speech, with one and with two ears. *Journal of the Acoustical Society of America*, **25**, pp. 975–9.

Cheung, H. (2007) The role of phonological awareness in mediating between reading and listening to speech. *Language and Cognitive Processes*, **22**, pp. 130–54.

Cheung, H., and Wooltorton, L. (2002) Verbal short-term memory as an articulatory system: evidence from an alternative paradigm. *Quarterly Journal of Experimental Psychology*, **55**, pp. 195–223.

Chiaro, D., and Nocella, G. (2004) Interpreters' perceptions of linguistic and non-linguistic factors affecting quality. *Meta*, **49**, pp. 278–93.

Chikalanga, I. (1992) Exploring inferencing ability of ESL readers: a suggested taxonomy of inferences for the reading teacher. *Reading in a Foreign Language*, **8**, pp. 697–709.

Ching-Shyang, A., Chang, H., and Read, J. (2008) Reducing listening test anxiety through various forms of listening support. *TESL-EJ*, **12** (PDF).

Chorost, M. (2005) *Rebuilt: how becoming part computer made me more human*. New York: Houghton Mifflin.

Christison, M. A. (2006) *Multiple intelligences and language learning*. Burlingame, CA: Alta.

Chun, D. (2002) *Discourse intonation in L2: from theory and research to practice*. Amsterdam: Benjamins.

Chun, D., and Plass, J. (1997) Research on text comprehension in multimedia environments. *Language Learning and Technology*, **1**, pp. 60–81. Retrieved 17 October 2001 from http://llt.msu.edu/.

Churchland, P. (2006) *Neurophilosophy at work*. Cambridge: Cambridge University Press.

Churchland, P. M. (1999) Learning and conceptual change: the view from the neurons, in A. Clark and P. Millican (eds) *Connectionism, concepts and folk psychology*. Oxford: Oxford University Press.

Churchland, P. M. (2005) Functionalism at forty: a critical perspective. *Journal of Philosophy*, **102**, pp. 33–50.

Churchland, P. S. (2002). *Brain-wise: studies in neurophilosophy*. Cambridge, MA: MIT Press.

Churchland, P. S., and Churchland, P. M. (2002) Neural worlds and real worlds. *Science*, **296** (5566), pp. 308–10.

Cicourel, A. (1999) Interpretive procedures, in A. Jaworski and N. Coupland, (eds) *The discourse reader*. London: Routledge.

Clark, A., and Millican, P., eds (1999) *Connectionism, concepts and folk psychology*. Oxford: Oxford University Press.

Clark, H. (2006) Common ground. *Encyclopedia of language and linguistics*, 2nd edn. Oxford: Elsevier.

Clark, H., and Krych, M. A. (2004) Speaking while monitoring addressees for understanding. *Journal of Memory and Language*, **50**, pp. 62–81.

Clark, J. M., and Paivio, A. (1991) Dual coding theory and education. *Educational Psychology Review*, **3**, pp. 149–70.

Clark, R., Nguyen, F., and Swellen, J. (2006) *Efficiency in learning: evidence-based guidelines to manage cognitive load*. San Francisco: Wiley.

Clement, J. (2007) The Impact of Teaching Explicit Listening Strategies to Adult Intermediate and Advanced-level ESL University Students. Ed.D. dissertation. Pittsburgh, PA: Dusquesne University.

Clement, J., Lennox, C., Frazier, L., Solorzano, H., Kisslinger, E., Beglar, D., and Murray, N. (2009) *Contemporary topics*, 3rd edn. White Plains, NY: Longman.

Coates, J. (2008) *Men talk: stories in the making of masculinities*. Oxford: Blackwell.

Cohen, A. (2008) Teaching and assessing L2 pragmatics: what can we expect from learners? *Language Teaching*, **41**, pp. 213–35.

Cohen, A., and Macaro, E., eds (2007) *Language learner strategies: thirty years of research and practice*. Oxford: Oxford University Press.

Cohen, M., and Grossberg, S. (1987) Masking fields: a massively parallel neural architecture for learning, recognizing, and predicting multiple groupings of patterned data. *Applied Optics*, **26**, pp. 1866–91.

Colston, H. (2007) On necessary conditions for verbal irony comprehension, in R. Gibbs and H. Colston (eds) *Irony in language and thought: a cognitive science reader*. Abingdon: Routledge.

Coniam, D. (2001) The use of audio or video comprehension as an assessment instrument in the certification of English language teachers: a case study. *System*, **29**, pp. 1–14.

Coniam, D. (2006) Evaluating computer-based and paper-based versions of an English-language listening test. *ReCALL*, **18** (2), pp. 193–211.

Cook, V. (2007) The nature of the L2 users. *EUROSLA Yearbook*, **7** (1), pp. 205–22.

Cooke, S., and Bliss, T. (2006) Plasticity in the human central nervous system. *Brain*, **129** (7), pp. 1659–73.

Cooker, L. (2004) Towards independence in the management of one's own learning. *Working Papers in Language Education*, **1**, pp. 13–25.

Cooker, L. (2008) Some self-access principles. *Independence* (IATEFL Learner Autonomy SIG), spring, pp. 20–1.

Cooney, J., and Gazzaniga, M. (2003) Neurological disorders and the structure of human consciousness. *Trends in Cognitive Sciences*, 7, pp. 161–5.

Corder, S. P. (1967) The significance of learners' errors. *International Review of Applied Linguistics*, **4**, pp. 161–70.

Corder, S. P. (1974) Error analysis, in J. Allen and S. P. Corder (eds.), *The Edinburgh Course in Applied Linguistics*, Vol. III, *Techniques in applied linguistics*. London: Oxford University Press.

Corley, M., MacGregor, L., and Donaldson, D. (2007) 'It's the way that you, er, say it': hesitations in speech affect language comprehension. *Cognition*, **105**, pp. 658–68.

Corsaro, W. (1985) *Friendship and peer culture in the early years: language and learning for human service professions*. Norwood, NJ: Ablex.

Council of Europe (2010) www.coe.int/T/DG4/Portfolio/?M=/main_pages/levels.html, www.ealta.eu.org/.

Coupland, N. (2007) *Style: language variation and identity*. Cambridge: Cambridge University Press.

Cowan, A. (2005) *Working memory capacity: essays in cognitive psychology*. New York: Taylor & Francis.

Cowan, N. (1998) *Attention and memory: an integrated framework*. Oxford: Oxford University Press.

Cowan, N. (2000) The magical number 4 in short-term memory: a reconsideration of mental storage capacity. *Behavioral and Brain Sciences*, **24**, pp. 87–185.

Coyne, M., Zipoli, R., Chard, D., Faggella-Luby, M., Ruby, M., Santoro, L., and Baker, C. (2009) Direct instruction of comprehension: instructional examples from intervention research in listening and reading comprehension. *Reading and Writing Quarterly*, **25**, pp. 221–45.

Craik, F. (2002) Levels of processing: past, present . . . and future? *Memory*, **10**, pp. 305–18.

Craik, F., and Salthouse, T. (2000) *The handbook of aging and cognition*. Mahwah, NJ: Erlbaum.

Cresswell, J. (2007) *Qualitative inquiry and research design: choosing among five approaches*. Thousand Oaks, CA: Sage.

Cresswell, J. (2009) *Research design: qualitative, quantitative, and mixed methods approaches*. Thousand Oaks, CA: Sage.

Croft, W. (2007) Phonological development: toward a 'radical' templatic phonology. *Linguistics*, **45**, pp. 683–725.

Cross, J. (2009a) Effects of listening strategy instruction on news videotext comprehension. *Language Teaching Research*, **13**, pp. 151–76.

Cross, J. (2009b) The Development of Metacognition of L2 Listening in Joint Activity. Ph.D. thesis, University of Melbourne.

Crowley, K., and Jacobs, M. (2002) Building islands of expertise in everyday family activity, in G. Leinhardt, K. Crowley and K. Knutson (eds) *Learning conversations in museums*. Mahwah, NJ: Erlbaum.

Crystal, D., ed. (1995) *The Cambridge encyclopedia of the English language*. Cambridge: Cambridge University Press.

Cullen, T. (2008) Teaching grammar as a liberating force. *ELT Journal*, **62**, 221–30.

Cumming, A. (2009) Language assessment in educations: tests, curriculum, and teaching. *Annual Review of Applied Linguistics*, **29**, pp. 90–100.

Cummins, J. (2009) Bilingual and immersion programs, in M. Long and C. Doughty (eds) *The handbook of language teaching*. Oxford: Blackwell.

Cutler, A. (1997) The comparative perspective on spoken language processing. *Speech Communication*, **21**, pp. 3–15.

Cutler, A., ed. (2005) *Twenty-first century psycholinguistics: four cornerstones*. Mahwah, NJ: Erlbaum.

Cutler, A., and Broersma, M. (2005) Phonetic precision in listening, in W. Hardcastle and J. Beck (eds) *A figure of speech: a festschrift for John Laver*. Mahwah, NJ: Erlbaum.

Cutler, A., and Butterfield, S. (1992) Rhythmic cues to speech segmentation: evidence from juncture misperception. *Journal of Memory and Language*, **31**: 218–36.

Cutting, J. (2002) *Pragmatics and discourse*. London: Routledge.

Czikszentmihalyi, M., and Czikszentmihalyi, I. (1992) *Optimal experience: psychological studies of flow in consciousness*. Cambridge: Cambridge University Press.

Dahan, D., Magnuson, J., and Tanenhaous, M. (2001) Time course of frequency effects in spoken-word recognition. *Cognitive Psychology*, **42**, pp. 317–67.

Dalmau, M., and Gotor, H. (2007) From 'Sorry very much' to 'I'm ever so sorry': acquisitional patterns in L2 apologies by Catalan learners of English. *Intercultural Pragmatics*, **4** (2), pp. 287–315.

Damer, T. (2001) *Attacking faulty reasoning*, 4th edn. Belmont, CA: Wadsworth.

Danan, M. (2004) Captioning and subtitling: undervalued language learning strategies. *Meta: journal des traducteurs*. Retrieved 14 April 2008 from www.erudit.org/revue/meta/2004/v49/n1/009021ar.html.

Daniels, H. (2005) *An introduction to Vygotsky*. Oxford: Routledge.

Daulton, F. (2008) *Japan's built-in lexicon of English-based loan words*. Clevedon: Multilingual Matters.

Davies, A. (2006) What do learners really want from their EFL courses? *ELT Journal*, **60**, 3–12.

Davies, K. H., Biddulph, R., and Balashek, S. (1952) Automatic speech recognition of spoken digits. *Journal of the Acoustic Society of America*, **24**, pp. 637–42.

Davis, M., Marslen-Wislon, W., and Gaskell, M. (2002) Leading up the lexical garden path: segmentation and ambiguity in spoken word recognition. *Journal of Experimental Psychology*, **28**, pp. 218–44.

Davis, P., and Rinvolucri, M. (1988) *Dictation: new methods, new possibilities*. Cambridge: Cambridge University Press.

Day, R., Yamanaka, J., and Shaules, J. (2009) *Impact Issues 1–3*, 2nd edn. Hong Kong: Pearson.

De Jong, N. (2005) Can second language grammar be learned through listening? An experimental study. *Studies of Second Language Acquisition*, **27**, pp. 205–34.

DeCarrico, J., and Nattinger, J. (1988) Lexical phrases for the comprehension of academic lectures. *English for Specific Purposes*, **7**, pp. 91–102.

Delogu, F., Lampis, G., and Belardinelli, M. (2010) From melody to lexical tone: musical ability enhances specific aspects of foreign language perception. *European Journal of Cognitive Psychology*, **22**, pp. 46–61.

Denes, P., and Pinson, E. (1993) *The speech chain: the physics and biology of spoken language*, 2nd edn. New York: Freeman.

Denzin, N. (2001) *Interpretive interactionism.* Thousand Oaks, CA: Sage.

DePaulo, B., Lindsay, J., Malone, B., Muhlenbruck, L., Charlton, K., and Cooper, H. (2003) Cues to deception. *Psychological Bulletin*, **129**, pp. 74–118.

Desmet, T., De Baecke, C., and Brysbaert, M. (2002) The influence of referential discourse context on modifier attachment in Dutch. *Memory and Cognition*, **30**, pp. 150–7.

Deutsch, J. A., and Deutsch, D. (1963) Attention: some theoretical considerations, *Psychological Review*, **70**, pp. 80–90.

Dietrich, A. (2004) Neurocognitive mechanisms underlying the experience of flow. *Consciousness and Cognition*, **13**, pp. 746–61.

Donkaewbua, S. (2008) Incidental vocabulary acquisition from reading, reading-while-listening, and listening to stories. *Reading in a Foreign Language*, **20**, 2, pp. 232–35.

Donnell, P., Lloyd, J., and Dreher, T. (2009) Listening, pathbuilding and continuations: a research agenda for the analysis of listening. *Continuum: Journal of Media and Cultural Studies*, **23**, pp. 423–39.

Dörnyei, Z. (2001) *Applied linguistics in action: teaching and researching motivation.* Harlow: Longman.

Dörnyei, Z., and Ushioda, E. (2009) *Motivation, language identity and the L2 self.* Clevedon: Multilingual Matters.

Doughty, C., and Long, M. H. (2003) Optimal psycholinguistic environments for distance foreign language learning. *Language Learning and Technology*, **7**, pp. 50–80.

Driver, J. (2001) A selective review of selective attention research from the past century. *British Journal of Psychology*, **92**, pp. 53–78.

Du, X. (2009) The affective filter in second language teaching. *Asian Social Science*, **5** (8).

Duff, P. (2007) Second language socialization as sociocultural theory: insights and issues. *Language Teaching*, **40**, pp. 309–19.

Duff, S. and Logie, R. (2001) Processing and storage in working memory span. *Quarterly Journal of Experimental Psychology*, **54A**, pp. 31–48.

Duffy, G., Miller, S., Howerton, S., and William, J. (2010) Comprehension instruction: merging two historically antithetical perspectives, in D. Wyse, R. Andrews and J. Hoffman (eds) *The Routledge international handbook of English, language and literacy training*. Abingdon: Routledge.

Dulay, H., and Burt, M. (1977) Remarks on creativity in language acquisition, in M. Burt, H. Dulay and M. Finnochiaro (eds) *Viewpoints on English as a second language*. New York: Regents.

Dumay, N., Frauenfelder, H., and Content, A. (2002) The role of the syllable in lexical segmentation in French: word-spotting data. *Brain and Language*, **81**, pp. 144–61.

Dunn, W., and Lantolf, J. (1998) Vygotsky's zone of proximal development and Krashen's i + 1: immeasurable constructs, incommensurable theories. *Language Learning*, **48**, pp. 411–42.

Dunning, D., and Perretta, S. (2002) Automaticity and eyewitness accuracy: a ten- to twelve-second rule for distinguishing accurate from inaccurate positive identification. *Journal of Experimental Psychology*, **29**, pp. 813–25.

Duranti, A., and Goodwin, C., eds (1992) *Rethinking context: language as an interactive phenomenon*. Cambridge: Cambridge University Press.

Eades, D. (2000) 'I don't think it's an answer to the question': silencing Aboriginal witnesses in court. *Language in Society*, **29**, pp. 161–95.

Echevarria, J., Vogt, M., and Short, D. (2008) *Making content comprehensible for English learners: the SIOP model*, 3rd edn. Paris: Lavoisier.

Eckert, P. (1989) Gender and sociolinguistic variation, in J. Coates (ed.) *Language and gender: a reader*. New York: Wiley.

Eckert, P., and McConnell-Ginet, S. (2003) *Language and gender*. Cambridge: Cambridge University Press.

Ekman, P., Friesen, W., O'Sullivan, M., and Chan, A. (1987) Universals and cultural differences in the judgments of facial expressions of emotion. *Journal of Personality and Social Psychology*, **53**, pp. 712–17.

Elgin, S. (1993) *Genderspeak: men, women, and the gentle art of verbal self-defense*. New York: Wiley.

Elgin, S. (2000) *The gentle art of verbal self-defense at work*. New York: Wiley.

Ellis, N. (2002) Frequency effects in language processing. *Studies in Second Language Acquisition*, **24**, pp. 143–88.

Ellis, R. (2006) The methodology of task-based teaching. *Asian EFL Journal*, **8**, 19–45.

Ellis, R. (2009) Educational settings and second language learning. *Asian EFL Journal*, **9** (4), *Conference Proceedings*, pp. 11–27.

Ellis, R. (2010) Second language acquisition research and language-teaching materials, in N. Harwood (ed.) *English language teaching materials: theory and practice*. Cambridge: Cambridge University Press.

Ellis, R., and Chang Jiang (2007) Educational settings and second language learning. *Asia EFL Journal*, **9** (4), www.asian-efl-journal.com/ Dec_2007_re.php.

Ellis, R., and Gaies, S. (1999) *Impact grammar*. Hong Kong: Longman.

Ellis, R., and Heimbach, R. (1997) Bugs and birds: children's acquisition of second language vocabulary through interaction. *System*, **25**, pp. 247–59.

Erbaugh, M. (2010) The Chinese Pear stories: narratives across seven Chinese dialects. Retrieved from http://pearstories.org/.

Erman, L., Hayes-Roth, F., Less, V., and Reddy, D. (1980) The Hearsay-II speech understanding system: integrating knowledge to resolve uncertainty. *Computing Surveys*, **12**, pp. 213–53.

Ervin, S., and Osgood, C. (1954) Second language learning and bilingualism. *Journal of Abnormal and Social Psychology*, **49**, pp. 139–46.

Ethofer, T., Kreifelts, B., Wiethoff, S., Wolf, J., Grodd, W., Vuilleumier, P., and Wildgruber, D. (2009) Differential influences of emotion, task, and novelty on brain regions underlying the processing of speech melody. *Journal of Cognitive Neuroscience*, **21**, pp. 1255–68.

Eykyn, L. (1993) The Effects of Listening Guides on the Comprehension of Authentic Texts by Novice Learners of French as a Second Language. Ph.D. thesis, University of South Carolina. *Dissertation Abstracts International*, 53: 3863A.

Faerch, C., and Kasper, G. (1987) *Introspection in second language research*. Clevedon: Multilingual Matters.

Feldman, J. (2003) The simplicity principle in human concept learning. *Current Directions in Psychological Science*, **12**, pp. 227–32.

Feldman, J. (2006) *From molecule to metaphor: a neural theory of language*. Cambridge, MA: MIT Press.

Fernandez, R., Ginzburg, J., and Lappin, S. (2004) Classifying Ellipsis in Dialogue: a Machine Learning Approach. International Conference on Computational Linguistics (CoLing), Geneva, *Proceedings*, pp. 240–6.

Ferreira, F. (2003) The misinterpretation of noncanonical sentences. *Cognitive Psychology*, **47**, pp. 164–203.

Ferreira, F., and Patson, N. (2007) The 'good enough' approach to language comprehension. *Language and Linguistics Compass*, **1**, pp. 71–83.

Ferreira, F., Bailey, K., and Ferraro, V. (2002) Good-enough representations in language comprehension. *Current Directions in Psychological Science*, **11**, pp. 11–15.

Ferri, G. (2007) Narrating machines and interactive matrices: a semiotic common ground for game studies. *Situated Play* (University of Tokyo journal), pp. 466–73.

Fiebach, C. M., Schlesewsky, M., and Friederici, A. (2001) Syntactic working memory and the establishment of filler-gap dependencies: insights from ERPs and fMRI. *Journal of Psycholinguistic Research*, **30** (3), pp. 321–38.

Field, J. (2002) The changing face of listening, in J. Richards and W. Renandya (eds) *Methodology in language teaching*. Cambridge: Cambridge University Press.

Field, J. (2003) Promoting perception: lexical segmentation in L2 listening. *ELT Journal*, **57**, pp. 325–333.

Field, J. (2004) An insight into listeners' problems: too much bottom-up or too much top-down. *System*, **32**, pp. 363–77.

Field, J. (2008) Bricks or mortar: which parts of the input does a second language listener rely on? *TESOL Quarterly* **42**, pp. 411–32.

Fillmore, C. (1968) The case for case, in E. Bach and T. Harms (eds) *Universals of linguistic theory*. New York: Holt.

Finardi, K. (2007) Working Memory Capacity and the Acquisition of Syntactic Structure in L2 Speech. Departmental MS. Florionopolis, Brazil: Universidade federal de Santa Catarina.

Finardi, K. (2008) Effects of task repetition on L2 oral performance. *Trabalhos em linguística aplicada*, **47**, pp. 31–43.

Finardi, K., and Weissheimer, J. (2008) On the relationship between working memory capacity and L2 speech development. *Signótica*, **20** (2), pp. 367–91.

Finch, A. (2001) The non-threatening learning environment. *Korea TESOL Journal*, **1**, pp. 1–19.

Firth, C., and Firth, U. (2006) The neural basis of mentalizing. *Neuron*, **50**, pp. 531–4.

Fisher, J. W., III, and Darrell, T. (2002) Informative subspaces for audio-visual processing: high-level function from low-level fusion, in *Proceedings of the International Conference on Acoustics, Speech and Signal Processing*. New York: ACM.

Flavell, J. (1999) Cognitive development: children's knowledge about the mind. *Annual Review of Psychology*, **50**, pp. 21–45.

Fletcher, C., and Chrysler, S. (1990) Surface forms, textbases, and situation models: recognition memory for three types of textual information. *Discourse Processes*, **13**, pp. 175–90.

Florit, E., Roch, M., and Levorato, C. (2010) Follow-up study on reading comprehension in Down's syndrome: the role of reading skills and listening comprehension. *International Journal of Language and Communication Disorders*. DOI 10.3109/13682822.2010.487882.

Florit, E., Roch, M., Altoè, G., and Levorato, M. C. (2009) Listening comprehension in pre-schoolers: the role of memory. *British Journal of Developmental Psychology*, **27** (4), pp. 935–51.

Flowerdew, J., and Miller, L. (2005) *Second language listening: theory and Practice*. New York: Cambridge University Press.

Flowerdew, J., and Miller, L. (2009) Listening in a second language, in A. Wolvin (ed.) *Listening and human communication in the twenty-first century*. Oxford: Wiley-Blackwell.

Fodor, J. (2002) Pyscholinguistics cannot escape prosody. Aix-en-Provence: ISCA Archive, 83–90.

Fodor, J., Bever, T., and Garrett, M. (1975) The psychological reality of semantic representations. *Linguistic Inquiry*, **6**, pp. 515–31.

Fox, C. (1997) Authenticity in intercultural communication. *International Journal of Intercultural Relations*, **21**, pp. 5–103.

Fox Tree, J. E. (1995) The effects of false starts and repetitions on the processing of subsequent words in spontaneous speech. *Journal of Memory and Language*, **34**, pp. 709–38.

Fox Tree, J. E. (2001) Listeners' uses of *um* and *uh* in speech comprehension. *Memory and Cognition*, **29**, pp. 320–6.

Fox Tree, J. E. (2002) Interpretations of pauses and *ums* at turn exchanges. *Discourse Processes*, **34**, pp. 37–55.

Frazier, L. (2008) Processing ellipsis: a processing solution to the undergeneration problem? *Syntax*, **4**, pp. 1–19.

Freedle, R., and Kostin, I. (1996) The prediction of TOEFL listening comprehension item difficulty for minitalk passages: implications for construct validity. TOEFL Research Report No. RR-96-20. Princeton, NJ: Educational Testing Service.

Freeman, D., and Johnson, K. E. (1998) Reconceptualizing the knowledge base of language teacher education. *TESOL Quarterly*, **32**, pp. 397–417.

Frenck-Mestre, C. (2002) An online look at sentence processing in a second language, in R. Heredia and J. Altarriba (eds) *Bilingual sentence processing*. Oxford: Elsevier.

Fritz, J., Elhilali, M., David, S., and Shamma, S. (2007) Auditory attention: focusing the searchlight on sound. *Current Opinion in Neurobiology*, **17**, pp. 437–55.

Fujisaki, H. (2005) Communication of Intention and Modeling the Minds: Lessons from a Study on Human–Machine Dialogue Systems. International Symposium on Communication Skills of Intention, Fukuoka, Japan.

Fukumura, K., van Gompel, R., and Pickering, M. (2010) The use of visual context during the production of referring expressions. *Quarterly Journal of Experimental Psychology*, **63**, pp. 1–16.

Fulchur, G. and Davidson, F. (2007) *Language testing and assessment: an advanced resource book*. Abingdon: Routledge.

Furness, E. (1957) Listening: a case of terminological confusion. *Journal of Educational Psychology*, **48**, pp. 477–82.

Gabay, D., Netzer, Y., Meni Adler, M., Goldberg, Y., and Elhadad, M. (2010) *Advances in web and network technologies and information management: lecture notes in computer science*, **5731**/2010, pp. 210–21. DOI: 10.1007/978-3-642-03996-6_20.

Gallese, V., and Lakoff, G. (2005) The brain's concepts: the role of the sensory-motor system in conceptual knowledge. *Cognitive Neuropsychology*, **22**, pp. 455–79.

Gamble, T., and Gamble, M. (1998) *Contacts: communicating interpersonally*. Boston: Allyn & Bacon.

Gambrill, E. (2006) *Critical thinking in clinical practice: improving the quality of judgments and decisions*, 2nd edn. New York: Wiley.

García, O., and Baker, C. (2007) *Bilingual education: an introductory reader*. Clevedon: Multilingual Matters.

Garcıa, O., Skuttnab-Kangas, T., and Torres-Guzman, M. (2006) *Imagining multilingual schools: languages in education and globalization*. Clevedon: Multilingual Matters.

Gardner, D., and Miller, L. (eds) (1999) *Establishing self-access: from theory to practice*. Cambridge: Cambridge University Press.

Gardner, H. (1993) *Multiple intelligences: the theory in practice*. New York: Basic Books.

Gardner, K. (1990) *Sounding the inner landscape*. Rockport, MA: Element Books.

Gardner, R. (1998) Between speaking and listening: the vocalisation of understandings. *Applied Linguistics*, **19**, pp. 204–24.

Gardner, R., and Macintyre, P. (1992) A student's contribution to second language learning, Part II, Affective variables. *Language Teaching*, **26**, pp. 1–11.

Garis, E. (1997) Movies in the language classroom: dealing with problematic content. *TESOL Quarterly*, **6**, pp. 20–3.

Garvuseva, L. (1995) Positioning and framing: constructing interactional asymmetry in employer–employee discourse. *Discourse Processes*, **20**, pp. 325–45.

Gass, S. (1996) Second language acquisition and second language theory: the role of language transfer, in W. Ritchine and T. Bhatia (eds) *Handbook of second language acquisition*. San Diego, CA: Academic Press.

Gass, S., and Mackey, A. (2006) Input, interaction, and output: an overview. *AILA Review*, **19** (1), pp. 3–17.

Gass, S., and Selinker, L. (2008) *Second language acquisition: an introductory course*, 3rd edn. New York: Routledge.

Gathercole, Susan E., Adams, Anne-Marie, and Hitch, Graham J. (1994) Do young children rehearse? An individual differences analysis. *Memory and Cognition*, **22**, pp. 201–7.

Gay, G. (2000) *Culturally responsive teaching: theory, research, and practice*. New York: Teachers College Press.

Geeraerts, D. (2006) Prospects and problems of prototype theory, in D. Geeraerts (ed.) *Cognitive linguistics: basic readings*. The Hague: Mouton, pp. 141–66.

Genesse, F. (1987) *Learning through two languages*. New York: Newbury House.

Gernsbacher, M., and Shroyer, S. (1989) The cataphoric use of the indefinite 'this' in spoken narratives. *Memory and Cognition*, **17**, pp. 536–40.

Gierl, M., Leighton, J., and Hunka, S. (2005) An NCME instructional module on exploring the logic of Tatsuoka's rule-space model for test development and analysis. *Educational Measurement: Issues and Practice*, **19**, pp. 34–44.

Giles, H. (2009) The process of communication accommodation, in N. Coupland and A. Jaworski (eds) *The new sociolinguistics reader*. New York: Palgrave Macmillan.

Giles, H., and Smith, P. (1979) Accommodation theory: optimal levels of convergence, in H. Giles and R. St Clair (eds) *Language and social psychology*. Oxford: Blackwell.

Gitterman, M., and Datta, H. (2007) Neural aspects of bilingualism, in J. Centeno and R. Anderson (eds) *Communication disorders in Spanish speakers: theoretical, research and clinical aspects*. Clevedon: Multilingual Matters.

Glennie, E. (2010) How to listen, www.ted.com/talks/lang/eng/evelyn_glennie_shows_how_to_listen.html.

Glisan, E. (1988) A plan for teaching listening comprehension: adaptation of an instructional reading model. *Foreign Language Annals*, **21**, pp. 9–16.

Gobl, C., and Chasaide, A. (2010) Voice source variation and its communicative functions, in W. Hardcastle, J. Laver and F. Gibbon (eds) *Handbook of phonetic sciences*, 2nd edn. Oxford: Wiley.

Goddard, C., and Wierzbicka, A. (2004) Cultural scripts: what are they and what are they good for? *Intercultural Pragmatics*, **1**, pp. 153–66.

Goetz, E., Anderson, R., and Schallert, D. (1981) The representation of sentences in memory. *Journal of Verbal Learning and Verbal Behaviour*, **20**, pp. 369–81.

Goffman, E. (1974) *Frame analysis*. New York: Harper & Row.

Goh, C. (1997) Metacognitive awareness and second language listeners. *ELT Journal*, **51**, pp. 361–9.

Goh, C. (2002) Exploring listening comprehension tactics and their interaction patterns. *System*, **30** (2), pp. 85–206.

Goh, C. (2002) *Teaching listening in the language classroom*. Singapore: SEAMEO Regional Language Centre.

Goh, C. (2008) Metacognitive instruction for second language listening development: theory, practice and research implications. *RELC Journal*, **39**, pp. 188–213.

Goh, T. (2010) Listening as process: learning activities for self-appraisal and self-regulation, in N. Harwood (ed.) *English language teaching materials: theory and practice*. Cambridge: Cambridge University Press.

Golding, J., Graesser, A., and Hauselt, J. (1996) The process of answering direction-giving questions when someone is lost on a university campus: the role of pragmatics. *Applied Cognitive Psychology*, **10**, pp. 23–39.

Goldwater, S., Jurafsky, D., and Manning, C. (2010) Which words are hard to recognize? Prosodic, lexical, and disfluency factors that increase speech recognition error rates. *Speech Communication*, **52**, pp. 181–200.

Gollan, T., and Acenas, L. (2004) What is a TOT? Cognate and translation effects on tip-of-the-tongue states in Spanish–English and Tagalog–English bilinguals. *Journal of Experimental Psychology: Learning, Memory, and Cognition*, **30**, pp. 246–69.

Goodman, S., and Graddol, D. (1996) *Redesigning English: new texts, new identities*. London: Routledge.

Goodwin, C., and Duranti, A. (1992) Rethinking context: an introduction, in A. Duranti and C. Goodwin (eds) *Rethinking context: language as an interactive phenomenon*. Cambridge: Cambridge University Press.

Goodwin, M. (1997) Children's linguistic and social worlds. *Anthopology Newsletter, American Anthtropological Association*, **38** (4), pp. 1–4.

Gottron, T., and Martin, L. (2009) Estimating web site readability using content extraction. International World Wide Web Conference Proceedings, pp. 1169–70.

Graddol, D. (2006) *English next: why global English may mean the end of 'English as a Foreign Language'*. London: British Council.

Graddol, D., Leith, D., Swann, J., Rhys, M., and Gillen, J., eds (2007) *Changing English*. London: Routledge.

Graham, S. (2003) Learner strategies and advanced level listening comprehension. *Language Learning Journal*, **28**, pp. 64–9.

Graham, S., Santos, D., and Vanderplank, R. (2007) Listening comprehension and strategy use: a longitudinal exploration. *System*, **36**, pp. 52–68.

Granena, G. (2008) Elaboration and simplification in Spanish discourse. *IRAL: International Review of Applied Linguistics in Language Teaching*, **46**, pp. 137–66.

Graves, M. (2009) *Essential readings on vocabulary instruction*. Newark, DE: International Reading Association.

Greene, J., and Burleson, B. (2003) *Handbook of communication and interaction skills*. Mahwah, NJ: Erlbaum.

Grenfell, M., and Macaro, E. (2007) Language learner strategies: claims and critiques, in E. Macaro and A. Cohen (eds) *Language learner strategies: thirty years of research and practice*. Oxford: Oxford University Press.

Grice, P. (1969) Utterer's meaning and intentions. *Philosophical Review*, **78**, pp. 147–77.

Grossberg, S. (2003) Resonant neural dynamics of speech perception. *Journal of Phonetics*, **31**, pp. 423–45.

Gruba, P. (2004) Understanding digitized second language videotext. *Computer Assisted Language Learning*, **17**, pp. 51–82.

Gruba, P. (2005) *Developing media literacy in the L2 classroom*. Sydney: National Centre for English Teaching and Research, Macquarie University.

Gruber, Helmut (2001) Questions and strategic orientation in verbal conflict sequences. *Journal of Pragmatics*, **33**, pp. 1815–57.

Gudykunst, W. (1995) The uncertainty reduction and anxiety–uncertainty reduction theories of Berger, Gudykunst, and associates, in D. Cushman and B. Kovacic (eds) *Watershed research traditional in human communication theory*. New York: NYU Press.

Gudykunst, W. (2003) Intercultural communication theories, in W. Gudykunst (ed.) *Cross-Cultural and Intercultural Communication*. Thousand Oaks, CA: Sage.

Gudykunst, W. (2005) An anxiety/uncertainty management theory of strangers' intercultural adjustment, in W. Gudykunst (ed.) *Theorizing about intercultural communication*. London: Sage.

Gudykunst, W. (2009) *Communication yearbook*. Paris: Lavoisier.

Gudykunst, W., and Kim, Y. (2003) *Communicating with strangers: an approach to intercultural communication*. New York: McGraw-Hill.

Gullberg, M. (2006) Some reasons for studying gesture and second language acquisition: hommage à Adam Kendon. *IRAL, International Review of Applied Linguistics in Language Teaching*, **44**, pp. 103–24.

Gumperz, J. (1990) The conversational analysis of interethnic communication, in R. Scarcella, E. Anderson and S. Krashen (eds) *Developing communicative competence in a second language*. New York: Heinle & Heinle.

Gurian, M. (2008) *Strategies for teaching boys and girls: elementary level*. San Francisco: Wiley.

Hadley, A. O. (2001) *Teaching language in context*. Boston, MA: Heinle & Heinle.

Hafez, O. (1991) Turn-taking in Egyptian Arabic: spontaneous speech versus drama dialogue. *Journal of Pragmatics*, **15**, pp. 59–81.

Hall, E. (1980) Giving away psychology in the 80s: George Miller interview. *Psychology Today*, **14**, p. 82.

Hall, T. A. (1999) The phonological word: a review, in T. Hall and U. Kleinhenz (eds) *Studies on the Phonological Word*. Amsterdam: Benjamins.

Halliday, M., and Hasan, R. (1983) *Cohesion in English*. Harlow: Longman.

Halliday, M., and Webster, J., eds (2009) *Continuum companion to systemic functional linguistics*. London: Continuum.

Halone, K., and Pecchioni, L. (2001) Relational listening: a grounded theoretical mode. *Communication Reports*, **14** (1), pp. 59–71.

Hamamura, T., Heine, S., and Paulhus, D. L. (2008) Cultural differences in response styles: the role of dialectical thinking. *Personality and Individual Differences*, **44**, pp. 932–42.

Hammer, M. R., Bennett, M. J., and Wiseman, R. (2003) Measuring intercultural sensitivity: The intercultural development inventory, *international Journal of Intercultural Relations*, 27, 421–443.

Hamp-Lyons, L. (1997) Washback, impact and validity: ethical concerns. *Language Testing*, **14**, pp. 295–303.

Hamp-Lyons, L., and Davies, A. (2008) The Englishes of English tests: bias revisited. *World Englishes*, **27** (14), pp. 26–39.

Handel, S. (1993) *Listening: an introduction to the perception of auditory events*. Cambridge, MA: MIT Press.

Handel, S. (2006) *Perceptual coherence: hearing and seeing*. Oxford: Oxford University Press.

Hanna, J., Tanenhaus, M. K., and Trueswell, J. C. (2003). The effects of common ground and perspective on domains of referential interpretation. *Journal of Memory and Language*, **49** (1), pp. 43–61.

Hansen, M., and Rubin, B. (2009) Audio art, http://www.earstudio.com/projects/listeningpost.html.

Harnad, Stevan (2005) To cognize is to categorize: cognition is categorization, in C. Lefebvre and H. Cohen (eds) *Handbook of categorization in cognitive science*, New York: Elsevier Press.

Harpaz, Y., Levkovitz, Y., and Lavidor, M. (2009) Lexical ambiguity resolution in Wernicke's area and its right homologue. *Cortex*, **45**, pp. 1097–103.

Harrigan, J., Rosenthal, R., and Scherer, K. (2007) *New Handbook of Methods in Nonverbal Behavior Research*. Oxford: Oxford University Press.

Harris, T. (2008) Listening with your eyes: the importance of speech-related gestures in the language. *Foreign Language Annals*, **36**, pp. 80–187.

Hartup, W. (1996) The company they keep: friendships and their developmental significance. *Child Development*, **67**, pp. 1–13.

Hatim, B. (2001) *Teaching and researching translation*. Harlow, UK: Longman.

Havas, D., Glenberg, A., and Rinck, M. (2007) Emotion simulation during language comprehension. *Psychonomic Bulletin and Review*, **14** (3), pp. 436–41.

Hayes, B. (2004) Phonological acquistion in optimality theory: the early stages, in R. Kager, J. Pater and W. Zonneveld (eds) *Constraints in phonological acquisition*. Cambridge: Cambridge University Press.

Hayes, B., and Wilson, C. (2008) A maximum entropy model of phonotactics and phonotactic learning. *Linguistic Inquiry*, **39**, pp. 379–440.

Haynes, J. D., and Rees, G. (2005) Predicting the stream of consciousness from activity in human visual cortex. *Current Biology*, **15**, pp. 1301–7.

Haynes, J. D., and Rees, G. (2006) Decoding mental states from brain activity in humans. *Nature Reviews Neuroscience*, **7**, pp. 523–534.

Higuera, C. (2010) *Grammatical inference: learning automata and grammars*. Cambridge: Cambridge University Press.

Hinds, J. (1985) Misinterpretations and common knowledge in Japanese. *Journal of Pragmatics*, **9**, pp. 7–19.

Hinnenkamp, V. (2009) Intercultural communication, in G. Senft, J. Östman and J. Verschueren (eds) *Culture and language use*. Amsterdam: Benjamins.

Hirai, A. (1999) The relationship between listening and reading rates of Japanese EFL learners. *Modern Language Journal*, **83**, pp. 367–84.

Hirschman, L., and Gaizauskas, R (2001) Natural language question answering: the view from here. *Natural Language Engineering*, **7**, pp. 275–300.

Hoey, M. (2005) *Lexical priming: a new theory of words and language*. New York: Routledge.

Holmes, J. (2006) Sharing a laugh: pragmatic aspects of humor and gender in the workplace, *Journal of Pragmatics*, **38**, pp. 126–50.

Holmqvist, K., and Holsanova, J. (2007) Embodied communication and gestural contrast, in J. Allwood and E. Ahlsén (eds) *Communication, action, meaning: a festschrift to J. Allwood*. Göteborg: Department of Linguistics, University of Göteborg.

Horwitz, E. (2001) Language anxiety and achievement. *Annual Review of Applied Linguistics*, **21**, pp. 112–26.

House, J. (2009) Introduction. The pragmatics of English as a lingua franca. *Intercultural Pragmatics*, **6** (2), pp. 141–5.

Houston, S. (2004) The archaeology of communication technologies. *Annual Review of Anthropology*, **33**, pp. 223–25.

Hughes, R. (2010) *Teaching and researching: speaking*, 2nd edn. Harlow: Longman.

Hulstijn, J. (2002) Towards a unified account of the representation, processing and acquisition of second language knowledge. *Second Language Research*, **18**, pp. 193–223.

Hulstijn, J. (2003) Connectionist models of language processing and the training of listening skills with the aid of multimedia software. *Computer Assisted Language Learning*, 1744–3210, **16**, pp. 413–25.

Hulstijn, J. (2007) Fundamental issues in the study of second language acquisition. *EUROSLA Yearbook*, **7**, pp. 191–203 (13).

Hutchby, I., and Wooffitt, R. (2008) *Conversation analysis*. Temple Hills, MD: Stafford.

Hwang, M.-H. (2003) Listening Comprehension Problems and Strategy Use by Second Learners of English (FL) in Korea. M.A. dissertation, Colchester: University of Essex.

Hymes, D. (1964) Toward ethnographies of communicative events, in P. Giglioli (ed.) *Language and social context*. Harmondsworth: Penguin.

Hymes, D. (1972) *Towards communicative competence*. Philadelphia, PA: University of Pennsylvania Press.

Hymes, D. (2001) On communicative competence, in A. Duranti (ed.) *Linguistic anthropology: a reader*. Malden, MA: Blackwell, pp. 53–73. (First published in R. Huxly and E. Ingram (eds) *Mechanisms of language development*. London: Centre for Advanced Study in Developmental Science. Article first appeared in 1967.)

Hymes, D. (2009) Ways of speaking, in A. Duranti (ed.) *Linguistic anthropology: a reader*.

Ihde, D. (2007) *Listening and voice: phenomenologies of sound* 2nd edn. New York: State University of New York Press.

Indefrey, P., and Cutler, A. (2004) Prelexical and lexical processing in listening, in M. S. Gazzaniga (ed.) *The cognitive neurosciences*, 3rd edn. Cambridge, MA: MIT Press, pp. 759–74.

Ioup, G. (2008) Exploring the role of age in L2 phonology, in J. Edwards and M. Zampini (eds) *Phonology and second language acquisition*. Amsterdam: Benjamins.

Iskold, L. (2008) Research-based listening tasks for video comprehension, in F. Zhang and B. Barber (eds) *Handbook of research on computer-enhanced language acquisition and learning*. London: IGI Global.

Ittycheriah, A., and Roukos, S. (2006) IBM's Statistical Question Answering System: TREC-11. *Science Commons*, http://handle.dtic.mil/100.2/ADA456310.

Iverson, J., and Goldin-Meadow, S. (2005) Gesture paves the way for language development. *Cognitive Development*, **6**, pp. 315–42.

Iverson, P., Kuhl, P. K., Akahane-Yamada, R. C., Diesch, E. D., Yohich Tohkura, Y., Kettermann, A., and Siebert, C. (2003) A perceptual interference account of acquisition difficulties for non-native phonemes. *Cognition*, **87**, pp. 47–57.

Izumi, S. (2002) Output, input enhancement, and the noticing hypothesis. *Studies in Second Language Acquisition*, **24**, pp. 541–77.

Jackson, C., and Dussias, P. (2009) Cross-linguistic differences and their impact on L2 sentence processing. *Bilingualism: Language and Cognition*, **12**, pp. 65–82.

James, W. (1890) *The principles of psychology*. New York: Holt; repr. New York: Dover Publications, 1950.

Jamieson, J., Jones, S., Kirsch, I., Mosenthal, P., and Taylor, C. (2000) *TOEFL 2000 framework: a working paper*. TOEFL Monograph Series Report No. 16. Princeton, NJ: ETS.

Janusik, L. (2004) *Researching listening from the inside out: the relationship between conversational listening span and perceived communicative competence*. College Park, MD: University of Maryland.

Janusik, L. (2007) Building listening theory: the validation of the conversational listening span. *Communication Studies*, **58**, pp. 139–56.

Jayarajan, V., Nandi, R., and Caldicott, B. (2005) An innovation in insert visual reinforcement audiometry in children. *Journal of Laryngology and Otology*, **119** (2), pp. 132–3.

Jenkins, J. (2000) *The phonology of English as an international language*. Oxford: Oxford University Press.

Jeon, J. (2007) A Study of Listening Comprehension of Academic Lectures within a Construction–Integration Model. Ph.D. dissertation. Columbus, OH: Ohio State University.

Jhangiani, S., and Vadeboncoeur, J. (2010) Health care 'as usual': the insertion of positive psychology in Canadian mental health discourse. *Mind, Culture, and Activity*, **17**, pp. 169–84.

Jiang. H., Li, X., and Liu, C. (2006) Large margin hidden Markov models for speech recognition. *Audio, Speech, and Language Processing: IEEE Transactions*, **14** (5), pp. 1584–95.

Johnson, J. (2005) *MELAB: descriptive statistics and reliability estimates*. Ann Arbor, MI: University of Michigan.

Johnson, K. (2006) A step forward: investigating expertise in materials evaluation. *ELT Journal*, **60** (3), pp. 1–7.

Johnson, M. (2007) *The meaning of the body: aesthetics of human understanding*. Chicago: University of Chicago Press.

Johnson, M., Weaver, J., Watson, K., and Barker, L. (2000) Listening styles: biological or psychological differences? *International Journal of Listening*, **14**, pp. 32–46.

Johnson-Laird, P. (1984) *Mental models*. Cambridge: Cambridge University Press.

Johnson-Pynn, J., Fragaszy, D. M., and Cummins-Sebree, S. (2003) Common territories in comparative and developmental psychology: the quest for shared means and meaning in behavioral investigations. *International Journal of Comparative Psychology*, **16**, pp. 1–27.

Joiner, M. (1996) 'Just girls': literacy and allegiance in junior high school. *Written Communication*, **13**, pp. 93–129.

Jonassen, D., and Hernandez-Serrano, J. (2002) Case-based reasoning and instructional design: using stories to support problem solving. *Educational Technology Research and Development*, **50**, pp. 65–77.

Jones, L., and Plass, J. (2002) Supporting listening comprehension and vocabulary acquisition with multimedia annotations. *Modern Language Journal*, **86**, pp. 546–61.

Jones, M. N., Kintsch, W., and Mewhort, D. J. K. (2006) High dimensional semantic space accounts of priming. *Journal of Memory and Language*, **55**, pp. 534–52.

Juang, B., and Rabiner, L. (2004) *Automatic speech recognition: a brief history of the technology development*. Oxford: Elsevier.

Jung, H. K. (2006) Misunderstanding of academic monologues by nonnative speakers of English. *Journal of Pragmatics*, 38 (5), pp. 1928–42.

Jurafsky, D., and Martin, J. (2009) *Speech and language processing: an introduction to natural language processing*. New York: Prentice-Hall.

Jusczyk, P. (1997) *The discovery of spoken language*. Cambridge, MA: MIT Press.

Jusczyk, P. (2003) How infants begin to extract words from speech, in G. Altmann (ed.) *Psycholinguistics: critical concepts in psychology*, Vol. 4. London: Routledge.

Juslin, P., and Laukka, Petri (2001) Impact of intended emotion intensity on cue utilization and decoding accuracy in vocal expression of emotion. *Emotion*, **1**, pp. 381–412.

Kaan, E., and Swaab, T. (2002) The brain circuitry of syntactic comprehension. *Trends in Cognitive Sciences*, **6**, pp. 350–6.

Kaivanpanah, S., and Alavi, S. (2008) The role of linguistic knowledge in word–meaning inferencing. *System*, **36**, pp. 172–95.

Kam, K., Kim, M.-S., and Koyama, T. (2003) The truth may not set you free . . . San Diego, CA: International Communication Association, www.allacademic.com/meta/p111453_index.html (accessed 20 February 2010).

Kanaoka, Y. (2009) *Academic listening encounters*. New York: Cambridge University Press.

Karat, C., Vergo, J., and Nahamoo, D. (2007) Conversational interface technologies, in A. Sears and J. A. Jacko (eds) *The human–computer interaction handbook: fundamentals, evolving technologies, and emerging applications*. Human Factors and Ergonomics. Mahwah, NJ: Erlbaum.

Kasper, G. (2006a) Pragmatic comprehension in learner-native speaker discourse. *Language Learning*, **34**, pp. 1–20.

Kasper, G. (2006b) Speech acts in interaction: towards discursive pragmatics, in K. Bardovi-Harlig, J. Félix-Brasdefer and A. Omar (eds) *Pragmatics and language learning*. Honolulu, HI: University of Hawaii Press.

Kasper, G., and Kellerman, E., eds (1997) *Communication strategies: psycholinguistic and sociolinguistic perspectives*, Harlow: Longman.

Kasper, G., and Ross, S. (2007) Multiple questions in oral proficiency interviews. *Journal of Pragmatics*, **39**, pp. 2045–70.

Kearsly, G. (2001) Media and learning, hagar.up.ac.za/catts/learner/2001.

Kellett, P. M. (2007) *Conflict dialogue*. London: Sage.

Kelter, S., Kaup, B., and Claus, B. (2004) Representing a described sequence of events: a dynamic view of narrative comprehension. *Journal of Experimental Psychology: Learning, Memory, and Cognition*, **30**, pp. 451–64.

Kemmis, S., and McTaggart, R. (1988) *The action research planner*. ECT 432/732 Action Research in Curriculum. Geelong, Vic.: Deakin University.

Kerekes, J. (2007) The co-construction of a gatekeeping encounter: an inventory of verbal actions. *Journal of Pragmatics*, **39**, pp. 1942–73.

Kesselring, T., and Müller, U. (2010) *The concept of egocentrism in the context of Piaget's theory: new ideas in psychology*. Oxford: Elsevier.

Key, M. (1975) *Paralanguage and kinesics*. Metuchen, NJ: Scarecrow Press.

Khafaji, A. (2004) An Evaluation of the Materials used for Teaching English to the second Secondary Level in male Public High School in Saudi Arabia. Unpublished M.A. thesis, University of Exeter.

Kiesling, S., and Johnson, E. (2009) Four forms of interactional indirection. *Journal of Pragmatics*, **42**, pp. 292–306.

Kim, H. (1995) Intake from the speech stream: speech elements that learners attend to, in R. Schmidt (ed.) *Attention and awareness in foreign language learning*. Honolulu, HI: University of Hawaii Press.

Kim, J., and Davis. C. (2003) Hearing foreign voices: does knowing what is said affect masked visual speech detection? *Perception*, **32**, pp. 111–20.

Kim, Y.-H. (2009) An investigation into native and non-native teachers' judgments of oral English performance: a mixed methods approach. *Language Testing*, **26**, pp. 187–217.

Kintsch, W. (1998) *Comprehension: a paradigm for cognition*. New York: Cambridge University Press.

Kintsch, W. (2000) Metaphor comprehension: a computational theory. *Psychonomic Bulletin and Review*, **7**, pp. 257–66.

Kintsch, W. (2001) Predication. *Cognitive Science*, **25**, pp. 173–202.

Kintsch, W. (2007) Meaning in context, in T. K. Landauer, D. McNamara, S. Dennis and W. Kintsch (eds) *Handbook of latent semantic analysis*. Mahwah, NJ: Erlbaum.

Kisley, M., Noecker, T., and Guinthe, P. (2004) Comparison of sensory gating to mismatch negativity and self-reported perceptual phenomena in healthy adults. *Psychophysiology*, **41**, pp. 604–12.

Kobayashi, K. (2006) Combined effects of note-taking/reviewing on learning and the enhancement through interventions: a meta-analytic review. *Educational Psychology*, **26**, pp. 459–77.

Koch, C. (2004) *The quest for consciousness: a neuroscientific approach*. Englewood, CO: Roberts.

Koda, K. (1996) L2 word recognition research: a critical review, *Modern Language Journal*, **80**, pp. 450–60.

Kokubo, H., Hataoka, N., Lee, A., Kawahara, T., and Shikano, K. (2006) Embedded Julius: continuous speech recognition software for microprocessor multimedia signal processing, San Diego, CA: IEEE Conference Proceedings, pp. 378–81.

Konieczny, L., and Voelker, N. (2000) Referential biases in syntactic attachment, in B. Hemforth and L. Konieczny (eds) *German sentence processing*. Dordrecht: Kluwer.

Kowal, M., and Swain, M. (1997) From semantic to syntactic processing: how can we promote it in the immersion classroom? in R. Johnson and M. Swain (eds) *Immersion education: international perspectives*. New York: Cambridge University Press.

Kramsch, C. (1997) Rhetorical models of understanding, in T. Miller (ed.) *Functional approaches to written text: classroom applications*. Washington, DC: USIA.

Kramsch, C.; and Whiteside, A. (2008) Language ecology: towards a theory of symbolic competence in multilingual settings. *Applied Linguistics* **29**, pp. 645–71.

Kranowitz, K. (2005). *Recognizing and coping with sensory processing disorder*, rev. edn. New York: Penguin.

Krashen, S. (1982) *Principles and practice in second language acquisition*. New York: Pergamon Press.

Krashen, S. (1985) *The input hypothesis: issues and implications*. Harlow: Longman.

Kroll, J., and Tokowitz, N. (2005) Models of bilingual representation and processing: looking back and to the future, in J. Kroll and A. de Groot (eds) *Handbook of bilingualism: psycholinguistic approaches*. Oxford: Oxford University Press.

Kuhl, P. (2000) A new view of language acquisition. *Proceedings from the National Academy of Sciences of the United States*, **97**, pp. 11850–7.

Kuhl, P. (2004) Early language acquisition: cracking the speech code. *Nature Reviews Neuroscience*, **5**, pp. 831–43.

Kuhl, P., Conboy, P., Coffey-Corina, S., Padden, D., Rivera-Gaxiola, M., and Nelson, T. (2008) Phonetic learning as a pathway to language: new data and native language magnet theory expanded. *Philosophical Transactions of the Royal Society*, **363**, pp. 979–1000.

Kuiken, F., and Vedder, I. (2001) Focus on form and the role of interaction in promoting language learning. (Handout.) St Louis, MO: American Association of Applied Linguistics.

Kumaravadivelu, B. (1994) The postmethod condition. *TESOL Quarterly*, **28**, pp. 27–48.

Kumaravadivelu, B. (2006) *Understanding language teaching: from method to post-method* London: Routledge; Mahwah, NJ: Erlbaum.

Lachmann, T., and van Leeuwen, C. (2007) Goodness takes effort: perceptual organization in dual-task settings. *Psychological Research*, **71**, pp. 152–69.

Lakoff, R. (2000) *The language war*. Berkeley, CA: University of California Press.

Lambert, W., and Tucker, G. (1972) *Bilingual education of children: the St Lambert experiment*. New York: Newbury House.

Lambert, W., Havelka, J., and Crosby, C. (1958) The influence of language acquisition contexts on bilingualism. *Journal of Abnormal and Social Psychology*, **56**, pp. 239–44.

Lantolf, J., ed. (2000) *Sociocultural theory and second language learning*. Oxford: Oxford University Press.

Lantolf, J. (2006) Sociocultural theory and L2: state of the art. *Studies in Second Language Acquisition*, **28**, pp. 67–109.

Lantolf, J., and Thorne, S. (2006) *Sociocultural theory and the genesis of second language development*. New York: Oxford University Press.

Larson, G., and Jacobsen, K. (2008) *Theory and practice of yoga*, 2nd edn. Leiden, Netherlands: Brill.

Lau, E., and Ferreira, F. (2005) Lingering effects of disfluent material on comprehension of garden path sentences. *Language and Cognitive Processes*, **20**, pp. 633–66.

Laufer, B. (1990) 'Sequence' and 'order' in the development of L2 lexis: some evidence from lexical confusions. *Applied Linguistics*, **11**, pp. 281–96.

Laufer, B., and Hulstijn, J. (2001) Incidental vocabulary acquisition in a second language: the construct of task-induced involvement. *Applied Linguistics*, **22**, pp. 1–26.

Lavy, M. (2001) Emotion and the Experience of Listening to Music: A Framework for Empirical Research. Ph.D. thesis, University of Cambridge.

Leaper, C., Carsonn, M., Baker, C., Holliday, H., and Myers, S. (1995) Self-disclosure and listener verbal support in same-gender and cross-gender friends' conversations. *Sex Roles*, **33**, pp. 387–404.

Lee, N. (2004) The neurology of procedural memory, in J. Schumann, S. Crowell, N. Jones, N. Lee, S. Schuchert and L. Wood (eds) *Neurobiology of learning: perspectives from second language acquisition*. Mahwah, NJ: Erlbaum.

Lee, T.-H. (2006) A comparison of simultaneous interpretation and delayed simultaneous interpretation from English into Korean. *Meta: journal des traducteurs*, **51**, pp. 202–14.

Leech, G. (2003) Towards an anatomy of politeness in communication. *International Journal of Pragmatics*, **14**, pp. 101–23.

Lehnert, W., Dyer, M., Johnson, P., and Yang, C. (1983) BORIS: an experiment in in-depth understanding of narratives. *Artificial Intelligence*, **20**, pp. 15–62.

Lenneberg, E. (1967) *Biological foundations of language*. New York: Wiley.

Leow, R. (2007) Input in the L2 classroom: an attentional perspective on receptive practice, in R. DeKyeser (ed.) *Practice in a second language*. Cambridge: Cambridge University Press.

Levelt, W. (1989) *Speaking: from intention to articulation*. Cambridge, MA: MIT Press.

Levine, T., Asada, K., and Lindsey, L. (2003). The relative impact of violation type and lie severity on judgments of message deceitfulness. *Communication Research Reports*, **20**, pp. 208–18.

Levinson, S. (1983) *Pragmatics*. Cambridge: Cambridge University Press.

Levinson, S. (2000) Presumptive meanings: the theory of generalized conversational implicature. Cambridge, MA: MIT Press.

Lewis, D. (1970) General semantics. *Synthèse*, **22**, pp. 16–67.

Lewis, T. (1958) Listening: review of educational research. *Review of Educational Research*, **28** (2), pp. 89–95.

Liceras, J., Perales, R., Pérez-Tattam, R., and Spradlin, K. (2008) Gender and gender agreement in bilingual native and non-native grammars: a view from child and adult functional–lexical mixings. *Lingua*, **118**, pp. 827–51.

Lieven, E. (2005) Language development: an overview, in K. Brown (ed.) *The Encyclopedia of Language and Linguistics*, 2nd edn, Vol. 6. Oxford: Elsevier.

Lieven, E., and Tomasello, M. (2008) Children's first language acquisition from a usage-based perspective, in P. Robinson and N. Ellis (eds) *Handbook of cognitive linguistics and second language acquisition*. London: Routledge.

Lin, H., and Chen, T. (2006) Decreasing cognitive load for novice EFL learners: effects of question and descriptive advance organizers in facilitating EFL learners' comprehension of an animation-based content lesson. *System*, **34**, pp. 416–31.

Linde, C., and Labov, W. (1975) Spatial networks as a site for study of language and thought. *Language*, **51**, pp. 924–39.

Lingard, L., Espin, S., Whyte, S., Regehr, G., Baker, G., Reznick, R., Bohnen, J., Orser, B., Doran, D., and Grober, E. (2004) Communication failures in the operating room: an observational classification of recurrent types and effect. *Qualitative Safe Health Care*, **13**, pp. 330–4.

Liu, H., Bates, E., and Li, P. (1992) Sentence interpretation in bilingual speakers of English and Chinese. *Applied Psycholinguistics*, **133**, pp. 451–84.

Livia, A., and Hall, K. (1997) *Queerly phrased: language, gender, and sexuality.* Oxford: Oxford University Press.

LoCastro, V. (1987) Aizuchi: a Japanese conversational routine, in L. Smith (ed.) *Discourse across cultures.* New York: Prentice-Hall, pp. 101–13.

Long, D. (1990) What you don't know can't help you: an exploratory study of background knowledge and second language listening comprehension. *Studies in Second Language Listening,* **12**, pp. 65–80.

Long, M. (2009) Methodological principles for language teaching, in M. Long and C. Doughty (eds) *The Handbook of Language Teaching.* Oxford: Blackwell.

Long, M., and Robinson, P. (1998) Focus on form: theory, research, and practice, in C. Doughty and J. Williams (eds) *Focus on form in classroom second language acquisition.* Cambridge: Cambridge University Press.

Lonneker-Rodman, B., and Baker, C. (2009) The FrameNet model and its applications. *Natural Language Engineering,* **15**, pp. 415–53.

Lopez-Barroso, D., Diego-Balaguer, R., Cunillera, T., Camara, E., and Rodriguez-Fornells, A. (2009) Subcortical structures related to phonological loop in language learning: a DTI study. *NeuroImage,* **47**, Supplement 1, S96.

Lowerre, B. T. (1976) The Harpy Speech Recognition System. Ph.D. dissertation, Cambridge, MA: Harvard University.

Lowerre, B., and Reddy, R. (1980) The HARPY speech understanding system, in W. Lea (ed.) *Trends in speech recognition.* Voice I/O Applications Conference Proceedings. Palo Alto, CA: AVIOS.

Lozanov, G. (1971) *Suggestology and outlines of suggestopedy,* New York: Gordon & Breach.

Lund, R. (1991) A comparison of second language listening and reading comprehension. *Modern Language Journal,* **75** (2), pp. 197–204.

Lunzer, E. (2006) Some points of Piagetan theory in the light of experimental criticism. *Journal of Child Psychology and Psychiatry,* **1**, pp. 191–202.

Lutz, A., Lachaux, J., Matrinerie, J., and Varela, F. (2002) Guiding the study of brain dynamics by using first-person data: synchrony patterns correlate with ongoing conscious states during a simple visual task. *Proceedings of the National Academy of Science USA,* **99**, pp. 1586–91.

Lynch, T. (1996) *Communication in the language classroom.* Oxford: Oxford University Press.

Lynch, T. (2001) EAP learner independence: developing autonomy in a second language context, in J. Flowerdew and M. Peacock (eds) *Research perspectives on English for academic purposes.* Cambridge: Cambridge University Press.

Lynch, T. (2001) Seeing what they meant: transcribing as a route to noticing. *ELT Journal* 55 (2), pp. 124–32.

Lynch, T. (2006) Academic listening: marrying top and bottom, in E. Usó-Juan and A. Martínez-Flor (eds) *Current trends in the development and teaching of the four language skills.* The Hague: Mouton de Gruyter.

Lynch, T. (2009) Responding to learners' perceptions of feedback: the use of comparators in second language speaking courses. *Innovation in Language Learning and Teaching,* **3**, pp. 191–203.

Lyons, J. (1995) *Linguistic semantics: an introduction.* Cambridge: Cambridge University Press.

Maatman, R., Gratch, J., and Marsella, S. (2005) Natural behavior of a listening agent. *Lecture Notes in Computer Science: Intelligent Virtual Agents.* Berlin: Springer.

Macaro, E. 2005. Research on listening, in *Teaching and learning a second language: a review of recent research*. London: Continuum.

Mackey, A., and Abdul, R. (2005) Input and interaction, in C. Sanz (ed.) *Mind and context in adult second language acquisition: methods, theory, and practice*. Washington DC: Georgetown University Press.

MacWhinney, B. (1994) Implicit and explicit processes. *Studies in Second Language Acquisition*, **19**, pp. 277–81.

MacWhinney, B. (1995) Language-specific prediction in foreign language learning language testing, **12**, pp. 292–320.

MacWhinney, B. (2001) The competition model: the input, the context, and the brain, in P. Robinson (ed.) *Cognition and second language instruction*. New York: Cambridge University Press.

MacWhinney, B. (2002) The development of language and communication, in B. Hopkins (ed.) *Cambridge encyclopedia of child development*. Cambridge: Cambridge University Press.

MacWhinney, B. (2005a) A unified model of language acquisition, in J. F. Kroll and A. M. B. de Groot (eds) *Handbook of bilingualism: psycholinguistic approaches*. Oxford: Oxford University Press.

MacWhinny, B. (2005b) The emergence of grammar from perspective, in D. Pecher and R. Zwaan (eds) *Grounding cognition: the role of perception and action in memory, language, and thinking*. Cambridge: Cambridge University Press.

Madden, J. (2004) The Effect of Prior Knowledge on Listening Comprehension in ESL Class Discussions. Dissertation, University of Texas.

Magiste, E. (1985) Development of intra- and interlingual inference in bilinguals. *Journal of Psycholinguistic Research*, **14**, pp. 137–54.

Maingueneau, D., and Charaudeau, P. (2002) *Dictionnaire d'analyse du discours*. Paris: Le Seuil.

Maleki, A. (2007) Teachability of communication strategies: an Iranian experience. *System*, **35**, pp. 583–94.

Malinowski, B. (1923) The problem of meaning in primitive languages, in C. Ogden and I. Richards (eds) *The meaning of meaning*. London: Routledge.

Maltz, D., and Borker, R. (2007) A cultural approach to male–female miscommunication, in L. Monaghan and J. Goodman (eds) *A cultural approach to interpersonal communication: essential readings*. Oxford: Blackwell.

Mandler, J., and Johnson, N. (1977) Remembrance of things parsed: story structure and recall. *Cognitive Psychology*, **9**, pp. 111–51.

Manyozo, L. (2006) Manifesto for development communication: Nora C. Quebral and the Los Baños school of development communication. *Asian Journal of Communication*, **16** (1), pp. 79–99.

Manzotti, R. (2005) Consciousness and existence as a process, www.homepages. ucl.ac.uk/~uctytho/ManzottiPdf.pdf.

Mareschal, C. (2007) Student Perceptions of a Self-regulatory Approach to Second Language Listening Comprehension Development. Ph.D. dissertation, University of Ottawa.

Marrow, G. (1970) Teaching with *Voix et images de France*. *Audiovisual Language Journal*, **8** (2), pp. 75–83.

Marshall, C., and Rossman, G. (2006) *Designing qualitative research*. London: Sage.

Marslen-Wilson, W. (1984) Function and process in spoken word recognition, in H. Bouma and D. Bouwhis (eds) *Attention and performance*, X. Hillsdale, NJ: Erlbaum.

Martínez, A. (2009) A state-of-the-art review of background knowledge as one of the major factors that influence reading comprehension performance. *Elia*, **9**, pp. 31–57.

Martínez-Flor, A. (2006) The effectiveness of explicit and implicit treatments on EFL learners' confidence in recognizing appropriate suggestions, in K. Bardovi-Harlig, C. Félix-Brasdefer and A. Omar (eds) *Pragmatics and language learning*. Manoa: National Foreign Language Resource Center, University of Hawai'i.

Martín-Loeches, M., Schacht, A., Casado, P., Hohlfeld, A., Rahman, R., and Sommer, W. (2009) Rules and heuristics during sentence comprehension: evidence from a dual-task brain potential study. *Journal of Cognitive Neuroscience*, **21**, pp. 1365–79.

Massaro, D. (1994) A pattern recognition account of decision making. *Memory and Cognition*, **22** (5), pp. 616–27.

Massaro, D. (2001) Speech perception, in N. Smelser and P. Baltes (eds) and W. Kintsch (section ed.) *International encyclopedia of social and behavioral sciences* Amsterdam: Elsevier, pp. 14870–5.

Massaro, D. (2004) A framework for evaluating multimodal integration by humans and a role for embodied conversational agents. *Proceedings of the Sixth International Conference on Multimodal Interfaces*. State College, PA, pp. 24–31.

Mattys, S., Brooks, J., and Cooke, M. (2009) Recognizing speech under a processing load: dissociating energetic from informational factors. *Cognitive Psychology*, **59**, pp. 203–43.

May, L. (2009) Co-constructed interaction in a paired speaking test: the rater's perspective. *Language Testing*, **26** (3), pp. 397–421.

Maynard, S. (1997) *Japanese communication: language and thought in context*. Honolulu: University of Hawaii Press.

Maynard, S. (2002) *Linguistic emotivity: centrality of place, the topic–comment dynamic, and an ideology of pathos in Japanese discourse*. Amsterdam: Benjamins.

Maynard, S. (2005) *Expressive Japanese: a reference guide to sharing emotion and empathy*. Honolulu, HI: University of Hawaii Press.

Mayo, P. (1999) *Gramsci, Freire, and adult education: possibilities for transformative action*. London: Macmillan.

McCarthy, M., and Slade, D. (2006) Extending our understanding of spoken discourse, in J. Cummins and C. Davison (eds) *International handbook of English language teaching*. New York: Springer.

McClelland, J., and Ellman, J. (1986) The TRACE model of speech perception. *Cognitive Psychology*, **18**, pp. 1–86.

McClelland, J. L. and Rumelhart, D. E. (1981) An interactive activation model of context effects in letter perception, Part 1, An account of basic findings. *Psychological Review*, **88**, pp. 375–407.

McClelland, J., Mirman, D., and Holt, L. (2006) Are there interactive processes in speech perception? *Trends in Cognitive Sciences*, **10**, pp. 363–9.

McClelland, J., Rumelhart, D., and Hinton, G. (2004) The appeal of parallel distributed processing, in D. A. Balota and E. Marsh (eds) *Cognitive psychology: key readings*. London: Psychology Press.

McCornack, S. (1997) The generation of deceptive messages: laying the groundwork for a viable theory of interpersonal deception, in J. Greene (ed.) *Message production: advances in communication theory*. Mahwah, NJ: Erlbaum.

McGrath, I. (2002) *Materials evaluation and design for language teaching.* Edinburgh: Edinburgh University Press.

McGregor, G. (1986) Listening outside the participation framework, in G. McGregor and R. White (eds) *The art of listening.* Beckenham: Croom Helm.

McGurk, H., and MacDonald, J. (1976) Hearing lips and seeing voices. *Nature,* **264**, pp. 746–8.

McNamara, T., and Roever, C. (2006) *Language testing: the social dimension.* Oxford: Blackwell.

McQueen, J. (2005) Speech perception, in K. Lamberts and R. Goldstone (eds) *Handbook of cognition.* London: Sage.

McQueen, J. (2007) Eight questions about spoken word recognition, in M. G. Gaskell and G. Altman (eds) *The Oxford handbook of psycholinguistics.* Oxford: Oxford University Press.

McVeigh, J. (2010) Tips for establishing a self-access center. Personal web site, www.joemcveigh.org/materials-development/.

Meara, P., and Wolter, B. (2004) V_links: beyond vocabulary depth, in D. Albrechtsen, K. Haastrup and B. Henriksen (eds) *Writing and vocabulary in foreign language acquisition.* Copenhagen: Musuem Tusculanem Press.

Melby, A. K. (2003) Listening comprehension, laws and video, in *LACUS Forum XXIX: Linguistics and the Real World.* Houston, TX: LACUS.

Mendelsohn, D. (2002) The Lecture Buddy project: an experiment in EAP listening comprehension. *TESL Canada Journal,* **20**, pp. 64–73.

Mendelsohn, D. (2006) Learning how to listen using listening strategies, in E. Usó and M. Flores (eds) *Current trends in the development and teaching of the four language skills.* The Hague: Mouton.

Mercer, N. (2000) *Words and minds.* London: Routledge.

Messick, S. (1995) Validity of psychological assessment: validation of inferences from persons' responses and performances as scientific inquiry into score meaning. *American Psychologist,* **50**, pp. 741–9.

Miller, J. (2004). Identity and language use: the politics of speaking ESL in schools, in A. Pavlenko, A. Blackledge, I. Piller and M. Teutsch-Dwyer (eds) *Multilingualism, second language learning, and gender.* Berlin: Mouton de Gruyter.

Miller, L., Tsang, E., and Hopkins, M. (2007) Establishing a self-access centre in a secondary school. *ELT Journal,* **61**, pp. 220–7.

Minami, M. (2002) *Culture-specific language styles: the development of oral narrative and literacy.* Clevedon: Multilingual Matters.

Mingsheng, L. (1999) Discourse and Culture of Learning: Communication Challenges. Paper presented at the joint AARE–NZARE conference.

Mintz, T. (2003) Frequent frames as a cue for grammatical categories in child-directed speech. *Cognition,* **90**, pp. 1–117.

Mishan, F. (2004) *Designing authenticity into language learning materials.* Bristol: UKL Intellect Books.

Mislevy, R., and Risconscente, M. (2006) Evidence-centered assessment design, in S. Downing and T. Haladyna (eds) *Handbook of test development.* Oxford: Routledge.

Mitchell, R., and Myles, R. (1998) *Second language learning theories.* London: Arnold.

Mitkov, R., Evans, R., Orasan, C., Ha, L.-A., and Pekar, V. (2007) Anaphora resolution: to what extent does it help NLP applications? In *Lecture Notes in Computer Science.* Berlin: Springer.

Miyata, S., and Nisisawa, H. Y. (2007) The acquisition of Japanese backchanneling behavior: observing the emergence of *aizuchi* in a Japanese boy. *Journal of Pragmatics*, **39**, pp. 1255–74.

Moeschler, J. (2004) Intercultural pragmatics: a cognitive approach, *Intercultural Pragmatics*, **1**, pp. 49–70.

Monaghan, L., and Goodman, J. (2007) *A cultural approach to interpersonal communication: essential readings.* Oxford: Blackwell.

Mondala, L., and Doehler, S. (2005) Second language acquisition as situated practice: task accomplishment in the French second language classroom. *Canadian Modern Language Review*, **61**, pp. 1710–131.

Moore, B. (2004) *An introduction to the psychology of hearing*, 5th edn. Oxford: Elsevier.

Moore, R. (2007) Spoken language processing: piecing together the puzzle. *Speech Commuinication*, **49**, pp. 418–35.

Moore, V. (2004) An alternative account for the effects of age of acquisition, in P. Bonin (ed.) *Mental lexicon: some words to talk about words.* New York: Nova Science.

Morley, J. (1972) *Improving aural comprehension.* Ann Arbor, MI: University of Michigan Press.

Morley, J. (1984) *Listening and language learning in ESL: developing self-study activities for listening comprehension.* Orlando, FL: Harcourt.

Morrison, D., Wang, R., and DeSilva, L. (2007) Ensemble methods for spoken emotion recognition in call centres. *Speech Communication*, **49**, pp. 98–112.

Morton, J. (1969) Interaction of information in word recognition. *Psychological Review*, **76**, pp. 165–78.

Movellan, J., and McClelland, J. (2001) The Morton–Massaro law of information integration: implications for models of perception. *Psychological Review*, **108** (1), pp. 113–48.

Moyer, A. (2006) Language contact and confidence in second language listening comprehension: a pilot study of advanced learners of German. *Foreign Language Annals*, **39**, pp. 255–75.

Mozziconacci, S. (2001) Modeling emotion and attitude in speech by means of perceptually based parameter values. *User Modeling and User-adapted Interaction*, **11**, pp. 297–326.

Murchie, G. (1999) *The seven mysteries of life: an exploration of science and philosophy.* NY: Houghton Mifflin.

Murphey, T. (2000) Shadowing and summarizing. National Foreign Language Research Center video No. 11. Honolulu: Second Language Teaching and Curriculum Center, University of Hawai'i.

Murray, J., and Burke, K. (2003) Activation and encoding of predictive inferences: the role of reading skill. *Discourse Processes*, 1532–6950, **35** (2), pp. 81–102.

Musiek, F., and Baran, J. (2007) *The auditory system: anatomy, physiology and clinical correlates.* Boston, MA: Allyn & Bacon.

Nakatsuhara, F. (2008) Inter-interviewer variation in oral interview tests. *ELT Journal*, **62**, pp. 266–75.

Nassaji, H. (2003) L2 vocabulary learning from context: strategies, knowledge sources, and their relationship with success in L2 lexical inferencing. *TESOL Quarterly*, **37**, pp. 645–70.

Nation, K., Snowling, M., and Clarke, P. (2007) Dissecting the relationship between language skills and learning to read: semantic and phonological contributions to new vocabulary learning in children with poor reading comprehension. *International Journal of Speech–Language Pathology*, **9**, pp. 131–9.

Nation, P. (2006) Second language vocabulary, in K. Brown (ed.) *Encyclopaedia of Language and Linguistics*, 2nd edn, **13**. Oxford: Elsevier.

Nation, P. (2007) The four strands of innovation in language learning and teaching. *Innovations in Language Learning and Teaching*, **1**, pp. 2–13.

Nation, P., and Newton J. (2009) *Teaching ESL/EFL listening and speaking*. London: Routledge.

Newton, A., and de Villiers, J. (2007) Thinking while talking: adults fail nonverbal false-belief reasoning. *Psychological Science*, **18**, pp. 574–9.

Nichols, R. (1947) Listening: questions and problems. *Quarterly Journal of Speech*, **33**, pp. 83–6.

Nissan, S., de Vincenzi, F., and Tang, K. (1996) *Analysis of factors affecting the difficulty of dialogue items in TOEFL listening comprehension*. TOEFL Research Report No. RR-95-37. Princeton, NJ: Educational Testing Service.

Nitta, R., and Gardner, S. (2005) Consciousness-raising and practice in ELT course-books. *ELT Journal*, **59**, pp. 3–13.

Nix, D. (1983) Links: a teaching approach to developmental progress in children's reading comprehension and meta-comprehension, in J. Fine and R. Freedle (eds) *Developmental issues in discourse*. Norwood, NJ: Ablex.

Norman, D. (1982) *Learning and memory*. San Francisco, CA: Freeman.

Norman, D., and Shallice, T. (2000) Cognitive neuroscience: a reader, in M. Gazzaniga (ed.) *The New Cognitive Neurosciences*. Boston: MIT Press.

Norrick, N. (2000) *Conversational narrative: storytelling in everyday talk*. Amsterdam: Benjamins.

Norrick, N. (2005) The dark side of tellability. *Narrative Inquiry*, **15**, pp. 323–43.

Norrick, N. (2008) Negotiating the reception of stories in conversation: teller strategies for modulating response. *Narrative Inquiry*, **18** (1), pp. 131–51.

Norris, D., Cutler, A., McQueen J. and Butterfield, S. (2006) Phonological and conceptual activation in speech comprehension. *Cognitive Psychology*, **53** (2), pp. 146–93.

Norris, D., McQueen, J., and Cutler, A. (2000) Merging information in speech recognition: feedback is never necessary. *Behaviorial and Brain Sciences*, **23**, pp. 299–370.

Norris, J., and Ortega, L. (2000) Effectiveness of L2 instruction: a research synthesis and quantitative meta-analysis. *Language Learning*, **50**, pp. 417–528.

Nunan, D. (2002) Listening in language learning. Methodology in language teaching: an anthology of current practice, in J. Richards and W. Renandya (eds) *Methodology in language teaching*. Cambridge: Cambridge University Press.

Nunan, D. (2004) *Task-based language teaching*. Cambridge: Cambridge University Press.

Nuñez, J. (2009) Didactica de las grabaciones audiovisuals para desarrollar la comprension oral en el aula de lenguas extranjeras (Use of audiovisual technology in the teaching of oral comprehension of foreign languages). *MarcoELE: revista de didactica*, **8**, supplement.

O'Barr, W., and Atkins, B. (2009) 'Women's language' or 'powerless language'? in N. Coupland, and A. Jaworski, (eds) *The new sociolinguistics reader*. New York: Palgrave Macmillan.

O'Donnell, T., Tenenbaum, J., and Goodman, N. (2009) Fragment grammars: exploring computation and reuse in language. Computational Cognitive Science MIT

Computer Science and Artificial Intelligence Laboratory Technical Report Series, MIT-CSAIL-TR-2009-013.

O'Driscoll, J. (2007) Brown and Levinson's face: how it can – and can't – help us to understand interaction across cultures. *Intercultural Pragmatics*, **4**, pp. 463–92.

O'Loughlin, K. (2001) *The equivalence of direct and semi-direct speaking tests*. Cambridge: Cambridge University Press.

O'Malley, J. M., and Chamot, A. (1990) *Learning strategies in second language acquisition*. Cambridge: Cambridge University Press.

O'Malley, J. M., Chamot, A., and Kupper, L. (1989) Listening comprehension strategies in second language acquisition. *Applied Linguistics*, **10**, pp. 418–37.

O'Sullivan, B., Weir, C., and Saville, N. (2002) Using observation checklists to validate speaking-test tasks. *Language Testing*, **19**, pp. 33–56.

Ochs, E., and Schieffelin, B. (2009) Language acquisition and socialization: three development stories and their implications, in A. Duranti (ed.) *Linguistic anthropology: a reader*. New York: Wiley.

Ogle, D. (1986) KWL: a teaching model that develops active reading of expository text. *The Reading Teacher*, **39**, pp. 564–70.

Ohala, J. (1996) Ethological theory and the expression of emotion in the voice. *Spoken Language ICSLP 96: Proceedings*, Fourth International Conference, Philadelphia, PA.

Ohta, A. (2000) *Second language acquisition processes in the classroom*. Mahwah, NJ: Erlbaum.

Okamoto, S. (2008) An analysis of the usage of Japanese *biniku:* based on the communicative insincerity theory of irony. *Journal of Pragmatics*, **39**, pp. 1142–69.

Olsen, L., and Huckin, T. (1990) Point-driven understanding in engineering lecture comprehension. *English for Specific Purposes*, **9**, pp. 33–47.

Ontai, L., and Thompson, R. (2008) Attachment, parent–child discourse, and theory of mind development. *Social Development*, **17**, pp. 47–60.

Ortega, L. (2007) Meaningful L2 practice in foreign language classrooms, in R. DeKeyser (ed.) *Practice in a second language*. Cambridge: Cambridge University Press.

Osada, N. (2001) What strategy do less proficient learners employ in listening comprehension? A reappraisal of bottom-up and top-down processing. *Journal of the Pan-Pacific Association of Applied Linguistic*, **5** (1), pp. 73–90.

Osterhout, L., and Mobley, L. (1995) Event-related brain potentials elicited by failure to agree. *Journal of Memory and Language*, **34**, pp. 739–73.

Osterhout, L., and Nicol, J. (1999) On the distinctiveness, independence, and time course of the brain responses to syntactic and semantic anomalies, *Language and Cognitive Processes*, **14**, pp. 283–317.

Ouni, S., Cohen, M., Ishak, H., and Massaro, D. (2007) Visual contribution to speech perception: measuring the intelligibility of animated talking agents. *Journal of Audio, Speech, and Music Processing*, **1**, pp. 3–13.

Owens, R. (2007) *Language development*, 7th edn. Boston, MA: Allyn & Bacon.

Oxford, R. (2010) *Applied linguistics in action: teaching and researching learning strategies*, 2nd edn. Harlow: Longman.

Paivio, A. (1986) *Mental representation: a dual-coding approach*. Oxford: Oxford University Press.

Palinscar, A., and Brown, A. (1984) Reciprocal teaching of comprehension-fostering and comprehension-monitoring activities. *Cognition and Instruction*, **1**, pp. 117–75.

Palmer, M., Gildea, D., and Xue, N. (2010) *Semantic Role Labeling*. Synthesis Lectures on Human Language Technologies. San Rafael, CA: Morgan & Claypool.

Paradiso, M., Bear, M., and Connors, B. (2007) *Neuroscience: exploring the brain*. Hagerstown, MD: Lippincott Williams & Wilkins.

Paribakht, T. S. (2010) The effect of lexicalization in the native language on second language lexical inferencing: a cross-linguistic study, in R. Chacón-Beltrán, C. Abello-Contesse, M. Torreblanca-López and M. López-Jiménez (eds) *Further insights into non-native vocabulary teaching and learning*. Clevedon: Multilingual Matters.

Park, M. (2004) The Effects of Partial Captions on Korean EFL Learners' Listening Comprehension. Doctoral dissertation, University of Texas.

Pasupathi, M. (2001) The social construction of the personal past and its implications for adult development. *Psychological Bulletin*, **127**, pp. 651–72.

Pasupathi, M. (2003) Social remembering for emotion regulation: differences between emotions elicited during an event and emotions elicited when talking about it. *Memory*, **11**, pp. 151–63.

Pasupathi, M., and Rich, B. (2005) Inattentive listening undermines self-verification in conversation. *Journal of Personality*, **73**, pp. 1051–86.

Pasupathi, M., Henry, R., and Carstensen, L. (2002) Age and ethnicity differences in storytelling to young children: emotionality, relationality, and socialization. *Psychology and Aging*, **17**, pp. 610–21.

Pasupathi, M., Lucas, S., and Coombs, A. (2002) Conversational functions of auto-biographical remembering: long-married couples talk about conflicts and pleasant topics. *Discourse Processes*, **34**, pp. 163–92.

Paul, P. (2009) *Language and deafness*, 4th edn. London: Jones & Bartlett.

Pauls, A., and Klein, D. (2009) *Hierarchical search for parsing*. Proceedings of Human Language Technologies: the 2009 annual conference of the North American chapter of the Association for Computational Linguistics, Boulder, CO, pp. 557–65.

Pavlenko, A. (2006) Narrative competence in a second language, in H. Byrnes, H. Weger-Guntharp and K. Sprang (eds) *Educating for advanced foreign language capacities: constructs, curriculum, instruction, assessment*. Washington, DC: Georgetown University Press.

Pavlenko, A., and Norton, B. (2007) Imagined communities, identity, and English language teaching, in J. Cummins and C. Davison (eds) *International handbook of English language teaching*. New York: Springer.

Pellicer-Sánchez, A., and Schmitt, N. (2010) Incidental vocabulary acquisition from an authentic novel: do things fall apart? *Reading in a Foreign Language*, **22** (1), pp. 31–55.

Peng, K., and Nisbett, R. (1999) Culture, dialectics, and reasoning about contradiction. *American Psychologist*, **54** (9), pp. 741–54.

Penn-Edwards, S. (2004) Visual evidence in qualitative research: the role of video-recording. *Qualitative Report*, **9** (2), pp. 266–77.

Perrino, S. (2005) Participant transposition in Senegalese oral narrative. *Narrative Inquiry*, **15**, pp. 345–75.

Peters, A., and Boggs, S. (1986) Interactional routines as cultural influences on language acquisition, in B. Schieffelin and E. Ochs (eds) *Language socialization across cultures*. Cambridge: Cambridge University Press.

Peterson, C., and McCabe, A. (1983) *Developmental psycholinguistics: three ways of looking at a child's narrative*. New York: Plenum.

Petronio, S. (2002) *Boundaries of privacy: dialectics of disclosure* Albany, NY: State University of New York Press.

Piaget, J. (1951, 2007) *The child's conception of the world*. Plymouth: Rowman & Littlefield.

Pica, T. (2005) Classroom learning, teaching, and research: a task-based perspective. *Modern Language Journal*, **89**, pp. 339–52.

Pica, T., Doughty, C., and Young, R. (1987) The impact of interaction on comprehension. *TESOL Quarterly*, **21**, pp. 737–58.

Pickering, L. (2009) Intonation as a pragmatic resource in ELF interaction. *Intercultural Pragmatics*, **6**, pp. 235–55.

Pickett, J., and Morris, S. (2000) The acoustics of speech communication: fundamentals, speech perception theory, and technology. *Journal of the Acoustic Society of America*, **108**, pp. 1373–74.

Pienemann, M. (1999) *Language processing and second language development processes: processability theory*. Amsterdam: Benjamins.

Pienemann, M. (2005) *Cross-linguistic aspects of processability theory*. Amsterdam: Benjamins.

Plonka, L. (2007) *Walking your talk*. New York: Penguin.

Poeppel, D., Idsardi, W. J., and van Wassenhove, V. (2008) Speech perception at the interface of neurobiology and linguistics. *Philosophical Transactions of the Royal Society: Biological Sciences*, **363**, pp. 1071–86.

Poldrack, R. (2006) Can cognitive processes be inferred from neuroimaging data? *Trends in Cognitive Sciences*, **10**, pp. 59–63.

Poldrack, R., Halchenko, Y., and Hanson, S. (2009) Decoding the large-scale structure of brain function by classifying mental states across individuals. *Psychological Science*, **20**, pp. 1364–72.

Ponzetto, S., and Poesio, M. (2009) State-of-the-art NLP Approaches to Coreference Resolution: Theory and Practical Recipes. Annual meeting of the Association of Computational Linguistics, Suntec, Singapore.

Poulsen, R., Hastings, P., and Allbritton, D. (2007) Tutoring bilingual students with an automated reading tutor that listens. *Journal of Educational Computing Research*, **36**, pp. 191–221.

Prescott-Griffin, M. L., and Witherell, N. L. (2004) *Fluency in focus: comprehension strategies for all young readers*. Portsmouth, NH: Heinemann.

Puakpong, N. (2008) An evaluation of a listening comprehension program, in F. Zhang and B. Barber (eds) *Handbook of research on computer-enhanced language acquisition and learning*. London: IGI Global.

Quinn, A. (1999) Functions of nonverbal communication in teaching and learning a foreign language. *French Review*, **72**, pp. 469–80.

Rahimi, M. (2008) Using dictation to improve language proficiency. *Asian EFL Journal*, **10**, p. 1, www.asian-efl-journal.com/March_08_mr.php.

Rampton, B. (2006) *Language in late modernity: interaction in an urban school*. Cambridge: Cambridge University Press.

Raphael, T., and Wonnacott, C. (1985) Heightening fourth-grade students' sensitivity to sources of information for answering comprehension questions. *Reading Research Quarterly*, **20**, pp. 282–96.

Rayner, K., and Clifton, C. (2009) Language processing in reading and speech perception is fast and incremental: implications for event-related potential research. *Biological Psychology*, **8**, pp. 4–9.

Read, B. (2002) The use of interactive input in EAP listening assessment. *Journal of English for Academic Purposes*, **1**, 105–19.

Read, J. (2000) *Assessing vocabulary*. Cambridge: Cambridge University Press.

Reinders, H., and Lewis, M. (2006) An evaluative checklist for self-access materials. *ELT Journal*, **60**, pp. 272–8.

Reitbauer, M. (2006) Hypertextual information structures and their influence on reading comprehension: an empirical study. *Miscelanea: a Journal of English and American Studies*, **33**, pp. 65–87.

Renandya, W., and Farrell, T. (2010) 'Teacher, the tape is too fast!' Extensive listening in ELT. *ELT Journal*.

Renkema, J. (2004) *Introduction to discourse studies*. Amsterdam: Benjamins.

Rhea, P., Chawarska, K., Fowler, C., Cicchetti, D., and Volkmar, F. (2007) 'Listen, my children and you shall hear': auditory preferences in toddlers with autism spectrum disorders. *Journal of Speech, Language, and Hearing Research*, **50**, pp. 1350–64.

Rhodes, S. (1987) A study of effective and ineffective listening dyads using the systems theory principle of entropy. *Journal of the International Listening Association*, **1**, pp. 32–53.

Rhodes, S. (1993) Listening: a relational process, in A. Wolvin and C. Coakley (eds) *Perspectives on listening*. Westport, CT: Greenwood.

Richards, J. (2005) Second thoughts on teaching listening. *RELC Journal*, **36**, pp. 85–92.

Richards, J. (2008) *Teaching speaking and listening*. Cambridge: Cambridge University Press.

Richards, K. (2009) Trends in qualitative research in language teaching since 2000. *Language Teaching*, **42**, pp. 147–80.

Ricketts, J., Nation, K., and Bishop, D. (2007) Vocabulary is important for some, but not all, reading skills. *Scientific Studies of Reading*, **11** (3), pp. 235–57.

Rickford, J. (2004) Implicational scaling, in J. K. Chambers, P. Trudgill and N. Schilling-Estes (eds) *The handbook of language variation and change*. Oxford: Blackwell.

Riecken, T., Strong-Wilson, T., Conibear, F., Michel, C., and Riecken, J. (2005) Connecting, speaking, listening: toward an ethics of voice with/in participatory action. *Forum: Qualitative Social Research*, **6** (1), article 26.

Rinvolucri, M. (1981) Empathic listening, in *The teaching of listening comprehension*. London: British Council.

Risen, J., and Gilovitch, T. (2007) Informal logical fallacies, in R. Sternberg, H. Roediger and Diane F. Halpern (eds) *Critical thinking in psychology*. Cambridge: Cambridge University Press.

Roach, P. (2000) *English phonetics and phonology: a practical course*. Cambridge: Cambridge University Press.

Roach, P. (2000) Techniques for the phonetic description of emotional speech. *Proceedings of the ISCA Workshop on Speech and Emotion, 2000: a Conceptual Framework for Research*. Newcastle, NI, pp. 53–9.

Robb, C. (2006) 'This changes everything': the relational revolution in psychology. New York: Farrar Straus & Giroux.

Robbins, J. (1996) Between 'Hello' and 'See you later': Development Strategies for Interpersonal Communication. Ph.D. dissertation, Washington, DC: Georgetown University. (UMI 9634593.)

Roberts, C., and Sarangi, S. (2005) Theme-oriented discourse analysis of medical encounters. *Medical Education*, **39**, pp. 632–40.

Roberts, C., Davies, E., and Jupp, T. (1992) *Language and discrimination: a study of communication in multiethnic workplaces*. Harlow: Longman.

Roberts, C., Moss, B., Wass, V., and Jones, R. (2005) Misunderstandings: a qualitative study of primary care consultations in multilingual settings, and educational implications. *Medical Education*, **39**, pp. 465–75.

Rochat, P., and Striano, T. (1999) Social-cognitive development in the first year, in P. Rochat (ed.) *Early social cognition: understanding others in the first months of life*. Mahwah, NJ: Erlbaum.

Rocque, R. (2008) A Study of the Effectiveness of Annotation in improving the Listening Comprehension of Intermediate ESL Learners. M.A. thesis, Provo, UT: Brigham Young University.

Rodd, J., Davis, M., and Johnsrude, I. (2005) The neural mechanisms of speech comprehension: fMRI studies of semantic ambiguity. *Cerebral Cortex*, **15**, pp. 1261–9.

Rodman, R. (1988) Linguistics and computer speech recognition, in L. Hyman and T. Li (eds) *Language, speech and mind*. London: Routledge.

Rogers, C. R., and Freiberg, H. J. (1994) *Freedom to learn*, 3rd edn. Columbus, OH: Merrill/Macmillan.

Rogoff, B. (2003) *The cultural nature of human development*. New York: Oxford University Press.

Roland, D., Dick, F., and Elman, J. (2007) Frequency of basic English grammatical structures: a corpus analysis. *Journal of Memory and Language*, **57**, pp. 348–79.

Ronnberg, J., Rudner, M., Foo, C., and Lunne, T. (2008) Cognition counts: a working memory system for ease of language understanding (ELU). *International Journal of Audiology*, **47** (2), pp. S99–S105.

Rosch, E., Mervis, C., Gray, W., Johnson, D., and Boyes-Braem, P. (2004) Basic objects in natural categories, in D. Balota and E. Marsh (eds) *Cognitive psychology: key readings*. New York: Psychology Press.

Rose, K., and Kasper, G. (2001) *Pragmatics in language teaching*. Cambridge: Cambridge University Press.

Rost, M. (1990) *Listening in language learning*. London: Longman.

Rost, M. (2003) *Longman English interactive*, 1–4. White Plains, NY: Longman.

Rost, M. (2005) L2 listening, in E. Hinkel (ed.) *Handbook of research in second language teaching and learning*. Mahwah, NJ: Erlbaum.

Rost, M. (2006) Areas of research that influence L2 listening instruction, in E. Usó-Juan and A. Martínez-Flor (eds) *Current trends in the development and teaching of the four language skills*. Amsterdam: Mouton de Gruyter.

Rost, M. (2007) 'I'm only trying to help': a role for interventions in teaching listening. *Language learning and technology*, **11** (1), pp. 102–8.

Rost, M. (2009) *Teacher development interactive: listening*. White Plains, NY: Pearson Longman, www.teacherdevelopmentinteractivetdi.com/.

Rost, M., and Ross, S. (1991) Learner use of strategies in interaction: typology and teachability. *Language Learning*, **41**, pp. 235–73.

Rubin, A., Haridakis, P., and Piele, L. (2009) *Communication research: strategies and sources*. Florence, KY: Cengage.

Rubin, H., and Rubin, I. (2005) *Qualitative interviewing: the art of hearing data*. London: Sage.

Rubin, J. (1988) *Improving foreign language listening comprehension*. Report prepared for the International Research and Studies Program, Project No. 017AH70028. Washington, DC: US Department of Education.

Rubin, J., and Thompson, I. (1998) The communication process, in J. Rubin and I. Thompson (eds) *How to be a more successful language learner*, 2nd edn. Boston, MA: Heinle & Heinle.

Ruchkin, D., Grafman, J., Cameron, K., and Berndt, S. (2003) Working memory retention systems: a state of activated long-term memory. *Behavioral and Brain Sciences*, **26**, pp. 709–28.

Rumelhart, D., and Norman, D. (1981) Analogical processes in learning, in J. Anderson (ed.) *Cognitive skills and their acquisition*. Hillsdale, NJ: Erlbaum.

Sajavaara, K. (1986) Transfer and second language speech-processing, in E. Kellerman and M. Sharwood Smith (eds) *Crosslinguistic influence in second language acquisition*. New York: Pergamon.

Salahzadeh, J. (2005) *Academic listening strategies: a guide to understanding lectures*. Ann Arbor, MI: University of Michigan Press.

Salthouse, T. (1996) The processing-speed theory of adult age differences in cognition. *Psychological Review*, **103**, pp. 403–28.

Samuda, V., and Bygate, M. (2008) *Tasks in second language learning: research and practice in applied linguistics*. London: Palgrave Macmillan.

Sanchez-Casas, R., and Garcia-Albea, J. (2005) The representation of cognate and non-cognate words in bilingual memory, in J. Kroll and A. de Groot (eds) *Handbook of bilingualism: psycholinguistic approaches*. Oxford: Oxford University Press.

Sanders, T., and Gernsbacher, M. A., eds (2004) *Accessibility in text and discourse processing*. Mahwah, NJ: Erlbaum.

Santrock, J. (2008) *A topical approach to life-span development*. New York, NY: McGraw-Hill.

Sanz, C., ed. (2005) *Mind and context in adult second language acquisition: methods, theory, and practice*. Washington D.C.: Georgetown University Press.

Saraceni, M. (2009) Relocating English: towards a new paradigm for English in the world. *Language and Intercultural Communication*, **9**, pp. 175–86.

Sarangi, S. (2009) Accounting for mismatches in intercultural selection interviews. *Multilingua*, **13**, pp. 163–94.

Sarangi, S. (2009) Culture, in G. Senft, J. Östman and J. Verschueren (eds) *Culture and language use*. Amsterdam: Benjamins.

Sarangi, S., and Brookes-Howell, L. (2006) Recontextualising the familial life world in genetic counselling case notes, in M. Gotti and F. Salagar-Meyer (eds) *Advances in medical discourse analysis: oral and written contexts*. Berne: Peter Lang.

Sarangi, S., and Roberts, C. (2001) Discoursal (mis)alignments in professional gate-keeping encounters, in C. Kramsch (ed.) *Language acquisition and language socialization: ecological perspectives*. London: Continuum.

Sawaki, Y., and Nissan, S. (2009) *Criterion-related validity of the TOEFL iBT listening section*. TOEFL iBT Research Report RR-09-02. Princeton, NJ: Educational Testing Service.

Sawyer, R. (2006) *The Cambridge handbook of the learning sciences*. Cambridge: Cambridge University Press.

Saxton, T. (2009) The inevitability of child-directed speech, in S. Foster-Cohen (ed.) *Language acquisition*. London: Palgrave Macmillan.

Schacter, D. (2001) *The seven sins of memory*. New York: Houghton Mifflin.

Schank, R. (1980) Language and memory. *Cognitive Science*, **4**, pp. 243–84.

Schank, R. (1982) Reminding and memory organization, in W. Lenhert and M. Ringle (eds) *Strategies for natural language processing*. Hillsdale, NJ: Erlbaum.

Schank, R. (1986) What is AI, anyway? *AI Magazine*, **8**, pp. 59–65.

Schank, R. (1991) Where's the AI? *AI Magazine*, **12**, pp. 38–48.

Schank, R. (1999) *Dynamic memory revisited*. Cambridge: Cambridge University Press.

Schaub, A. (2009) *Digital hearing aids*. New York: Thieme.

Scheepers, R., and Smit, T. (2009) Listening Comprehension in Academic Lectures: a Focus on the Role of Discourse Markers. Doctoral thesis, Pretoria: University of South Africa.

Scherer, K. (2003) Vocal communication of emotion: a review of research paradigms. *Speech Communication*, **40** (1–2), pp. 227–56.

Schmidt, R. (1995) Consciousness and foreign language learning: a tutorial on the role of attention and awareness in learning, in R. Schmidt (ed.) *Attention and awareness in language learning*. Honolulu, HI: University of Hawaii Press.

Schmidt-Rinehart, B. (1994) The effects of topic familiarity on second language listening comprehension. *Modern Language Journal*, **18**, pp. 179–89.

Schmitt, N. (2008) Review article. Instructed second language vocabulary learning. *Language Teaching Research*, **12**, pp. 329–63.

Schneider, B., Daneman, M., and Pichora-Fuller, M. (2002) Listening in aging adults: from discourse comprehension to psychoacoustics. *Revue canadienne de psychologie expérimentale*, **56**, p. 152.

Schoepflin, T. (2009) On being degraded in public space: an autoethnography. *The Qualitative Report*, **14** (2), pp. 361–73, www.nova.edu/ssss/QR/QR14-2/schoepflin.pdf.

Schooler, J. W., and Fiore, S. M. (1997) Consciousness and the limits of language, in J. Cohen and J. Schooler (eds) *Scientific approaches to consciousness*. Hillsdale, NJ: Erlbaum.

Schuler, W., Abdel Rahman, S., Miller, T., and Schwartz, L. (2010) Broad-coverage parsing using human-like memory constraints. *Computational Linguistics*, **36**, pp. 1–30.

Scollon, R., and Scollon, S. (1995) *Intercultural communication: a discourse approach*. Oxford: Blackwell.

Scollon, S. (2006) Not to waste words or students: Confucian and Socratic discourse in the tertiary classroom, in E. Hinkel (ed.) *Culture in second language teaching and learning*. Cambridge: Cambridge University Press.

Searle, J. (1969) *Speech acts: an essay on the philosophy of language*. Cambridge: Cambridge University Press.

Searle, J. (1975) A taxonomy of illocutionary acts. *Language and Society*, **5**, pp. 1–23.

Segalowitz, N., Trofimovich, P., Gatbonton, E., and Sokolovskaya, A. (2008) Feeling affect in a second language: the role of word recognition automaticity. *Mental Lexicon*, **3**, pp. 47–71.

Segalowitz, S., Segalowitz, N., and Wood, A. (1998) Assessing the development of automaticity in second language word recognition. *Applied Psycholinguistics*, **19**, pp. 53–67.

Sercu, L. (2004) Assessing intercultural competence: a framework for systematic test development in foreign language education and beyond. *Intercultural Education*, **15**, pp. 73–89.

Shao, A., and Morgan, C. (2005) Consideration of age in L2 attainment: children, adolescents and adults. *Asian EFL Journal*, **6**, article 11.

Shaules, J. (2008) *Deep culture*. Clevedon: Multilingual Matters.

Shaules, J. (2009) *A beginner's guide to the deep culture experience: beneath the surface*. Boston, MA: Intercultural Press.

Shea, D. (1995) Perspective and production: structuring conversational participation across cultural borders. *Journal of Pragmatics*, **4**, pp. 357–89.

Sherer, K. (2003) Vocal communication of emotion: a review of research paradigms. *Speech Communication*, **40**, pp. 227–56.

Shohamy, E. (2001) *The power of tests: a critical perspective on the uses of language tests.* Harlow: Pearson.

Shohamy, E., and Inbar, O. (1991) Validation of listening comprehension tests: the effect of text and question type. *Language Testing*, **8**, pp. 23–40.

Simard, D., and Wong, W. (2001) Alertness, orientation, and detection. *Studies in Second Language Acquisition*, **23** (1), pp. 103–24.

Sindrey, D. (2002) *Listening games for littles.* London, Ont.: WordPlay.

Singer, M. (2007) Inference processing in discourse comprehension, in M. Gaskell and G. Altmann (eds) *The Oxford handbook of psycholinguistics*. Oxford: Oxford University Press.

Singhal, A., Cody, M., Rogers, E., and Sabido, M. (2004) *Entertainment-education and social change: history, research, and practice.* Mahwah, NJ: Erlbaum.

Singleton, D. (1995) A critical look at the critical period hypothesis in second language acquisition research, in D. Singleton and Z. Lengyel (eds) *The age factor in second language acquisition*. Clevedon: Multilingual Matters.

Singleton, D., and Lengyel, Z. (1995) *The age factor in second language acquisition.* Clevedon: Multilingual Matters.

Skierso, A. (1991) Textbook selection and evaluation, in M. Celce-Murcia (ed.) *Teaching English as a second or foreign language*. Berkeley and Los Angeles: University of California Press.

Skierso, A. (1991) Textbook selection, in M. Celce-Murcia (ed.) *Teaching English as a second or foreign language*. Boston, MA: Heinle & Heinle.

Skutnabb-Kangas, T. (2008) Human rights and language policy in education, in J. Cummins and N. Hornberger (eds) *Encyclopedia of language and education*, 2nd edn. New York: Springer.

Skutnabb-Kangas, T., and McCarty, T. (2008) Clarification, ideological/epistemological underpinnings and implications of some concepts in bilingual education, in J. Cummins and N. Hornberger (eds) *Encyclopedia of language and education*, 2nd edn. New York: Springer.

Slobin, D. (2004) Cognitive prerequisites for the development of grammar, in B. Lust and C. Foley (eds) *First language acquisition: the essential readings*. Oxford: Blackwell.

Snow, C. (1994) Beginning from baby talk: twenty years of research on input and interaction, in C. Gallaway and B. Richards (eds) *Input and interaction in language acquisition*. Cambridge: Cambridge University Press.

Soaves, C., and Grosjean, F. (1984) Bilingual in a monolingual and bilingual speech mode: the effect on lexical access. *Memory and Cognition*, **12**, pp. 380–6.

Sollier, P. (2005) *Listening for wellness: an introduction to the Tomatis method.* Walnut Creek, CA: Mozart Center Press.

Song, W., Liu, W., Gu, N., Quan, X., and Hao, T. (2010) Automatic categorization of questions for user-interactive question answering. *Information Processing and Management*, 6 March. DOI 10.1016/j.ipm.2010.03.002.

Spector, J. (2008) *Handbook of research on educational communications and technology.* Mahwah, NJ: Erlbaum.

Spencer-Oatey, H., and Franklin, P. (2009) *Intercultural interaction: a multidisciplinary approach to intercultural communication*. Basingstoke: Palgrave Macmillan.

Sperber, D., and Wilson, D. (1995) *Relevance: communication and cognition*, 2nd edn. Oxford: Blackwell.

Sperber, Dan, and Wilson, Deirdre (2004) Relevance theory, in G. Ward and L. Horn (eds) *Handbook of Pragmatics*. Oxford: Blackwell.

Steil, L., Barker, L. and Watson, K. (1983) *Effective listening: key to your success*. Reading, MA: Addison-Wesley.

Stephenson, J. (2004) A teacher's guide to controversial practices. *Special Education Perspectives*, **13**, pp. 66–74.

Stern, D. (1999) Vitality contours: the temporal contour of feelings as a basic unit for constructing the infant's social experience, in P. Rochat (ed.) *Early social cognition*. Mahwah, NJ: Erlbaum.

Stone, D., Patton, B., and Heen, S. (1999) *Difficult conversations*. New York: Viking Penguin.

Stoness, S. C., Allen, J., Aist, G., and Swift, M. (2005) Using Real-world Reference to improve Spoken Language Understanding. AAAI Workshop on Spoken Language Understanding, Pittsburgh, PA, pp. 38–45.

Stork, D., and Hennecke, M., eds (1995) *Speechreading by humans and machines: proceedings of the NATO Advanced Study Institute on Speechreading by Man and Machine, Computer and Systems Sciences*, Vol. 150. New York: Springer.

Strange, W., and Schaefer, V. (2008) Speech perception in second language learners: the re-education of selective perception, in J. Edwards and M. Zampini (eds) *Phonology and second language acquisition*. Amsterdam: Benjamins.

Stringer, E. (2007) *Action research*. London: Sage.

Strodt-Lopez, B. (1996) Using stories to develop interpretive processes. *ELT Journal*, **50**, pp. 35–42.

Stubbe, M. (1998) Are you listening? Cultural influences on the use of supportive verbal feedback in conversation. *Journal of Pragmatics*, **29**, pp. 257–89.

Sullivan, K. (2007) Pros and cons of class podcast projects: evaluating a classroom innovation, in K. Bradford-Watts (ed.) *JALT2006: Conference Proceedings*. Tokyo: JALT.

Sunderland, J. (2006) *Language and gender*. Abingdon: Routledge.

Suvorov, R. (2008) Context Visuals in L2 Listening Tests: the Effectiveness of Photographs and Video vs. Audio-only Format. M.A. thesis, Ames, IA: Iowa State University.

Swain, M. (1985) Communicative competence: some roles of comprehensible input and comprehensible output in its development, in S. Gass and C. Madden (eds) *Input in second language acquisition*. Boston, MA: Newbury House.

Swain, M. (1995) Three functions of output in second language learning, in G. Cook and B. Seidlhofer (eds) *Principles and practice in applied linguistics*. Oxford: Oxford University Press.

Swain, M. (2000) The output hypothesis and beyond: mediating acquisition through collaborative dialogue, in J. Lantolf (ed.) *Sociocultural theory and second language learning*. Oxford: Oxford University Press.

Swain, M., and Lapkin, S. (1999) *Sociocultural theory and second language learning*. Oxford: Oxford University Press.

Swales, J. (1990) *Genre analysis*. Cambridge: Cambridge University Press.

Szabo, Csilla (2006) Language choice in note-taking for consecutive interpreting. *Interpreting*, **8**, pp. 129–47.

Szymanski, M. (1999) Re-engaging and dis-engaging talk in activity. *Language in Society*, **28**, pp. 1–23.

Taguchi, N. (2009) Comprehension of indirect opinions and refusals in L2 Japanese, in N. Taguchi (ed.) *Pragmatic competence*. The Hague: Mouton de Gruyter.

Tanaka, H. (2001) Adverbials for turn projection in Japanese: toward a demystification of the 'telepathic' mode of communication. *Language in Society*, **30** (4), pp. 559–87.

Tanenhaus, M. K., Spivey-Knowlton, M. J., Eberhard, K. M., and Sedivy, J. (1995) Integration of visual and linguistic information in spoken language comprehension. *Science*, **268**, pp. 1632–4.

Tanenhaus, M., and Trueswell, J. (2006) Eye movements and spoken language comprehension, in M. Traxler and M. Gernsbacher (eds) *Handbook of Psycholinguistics*, 2nd edn. Oxford: Elsevier.

Tanenhaus, M., Chambers, C., and Hanna, J. (2004) Referential domains in spoken language comprehension: using eye movements to bridge the product and action traditions, in *The interface of language, vision, and action: eye movements and the visual the visual world*. New York: Psychology Press.

Tannen, D. (1990) *You just don't understand: women and men in conversation*. New York: Morrow.

Tannen, D. (2006) Intertextuality in interaction: reframing family arguments in public and private. *Text and Talk: an Interdisciplinary Journal of Language, Discourse Communication Studies*, **26**, pp. 597–617.

Tannen, D. (2007) 'Put down that paper and talk to me': rapport-talk and report-talk, in L. Monaghan and J. Goodman (eds) *A cultural approach to interpersonal communication: essential readings*. New York: Wiley.

Tatsuoka, K. (2009) *Cognitive assessment: an introduction to the rule space method*. New York: Taylor & Francis.

Tauroza, S., and Allison, D. (1994) Expectation-driven understanding in information systems lecture comprehension, in J. Flowerdew (ed.) *Academic listening: research perspectives*. Cambridge: Cambridge University Press.

Taylor, A., Stevens, J., and Asher, J. (2006) The effects of explicit reading strategy training on L2 reading comprehension, in J. Norris and L. Ortega (eds) *Synthesizing research on language learning and teaching*. Amsterdam: Benjamins.

Taylor, D. (1994) Inauthentic authenticity or authentic inauthenticity? *TESL-L*, **1** (2), http://tesl-ej.org/ej02/a.1.html.

Taylor, G. (2005) Perceived processing strategies of students watching captioned video. *Foreign Language Annals*, **38**, pp. 422–7.

Thein, N. (2006) Evaluating the Suitability and Effectiveness of three English Coursebooks at Myanmar Institute of Technology. M.A. thesis, University of Thailand.

Thibault, P. (2004) *Brain, mind and the signifying body: an ecosocial semiotic theory*. New York: Continuum.

Thibault, P. (2006) Agency, individuation and meaning-making, in G. Williams and A. Lukin (eds) *The development of language: functional perspectives on species and individuals*. London: Continuum.

Thomas, J. (2006) Cross-cultural pragmatic failure, in K. Bolton and B. Kachru (eds) *World Englishes: critical concepts in linguistics*. London: Taylor & Francis.

Thomas, S., and Pollio, H. (2002) *Listening to patients: a phenomenological approach to nursing research and practice*. New York: Springer.

Tomasello, Michael (2003) *Constructing a language: a usage-based theory of language acquisition*. Cambridge, MA: Harvard University Press.

Tomatis, A. (1991) *The conscious ear: my life of transformation through listening*. Barrytown, NY: Station Hill Press.

Tomlinson, B., ed. (2003) *Developing materials for language teaching*. London: Continuum.

Tosi, A. (1984) *Immigration and bilingual education: a case of study of movement of population, language change, and education within the EEC*. London: Pergamon.

Toulmin, S. (1987) *An introduction to reasoning*, 2nd edn. New York: Macmillan.

Traat, M. (2006) Information Structure in Discourse. Ph.D. thesis, University of Edinburgh.

Trabasso, T., and Magliano, J. (1996) Conscious understanding during comprehension. *Discourse Processes*, 21, pp. 255–87.

Trabasso, T., and Sperry, L. (1985) Causal relatedness and importance of story events. *Journal of Memory and Language*, 24, pp. 595–611.

Treisman, A. (2003) Consciousness and perceptual binding, in A. Cleeremans (ed.) *The unity of consciousness: binding, integration, dissociation*. Oxford: Oxford University Press.

Trites, L., and McGroarty, M. (2005) Reading to learn and reading to integrate: new tasks for reading comprehension tests. *Language Testing*, 22, pp. 174–20.

Trochim, William M. (2006) Likert scaling. *Research methods knowledge base*, 2nd edn, www.socialresearchmethods.net/kb/scallik.php.

Truax, C., and Carkhuff, R. (2007) *Toward effective counseling and psychotherapy: training and practice*. New Brunswick, NJ: Transaction.

Trueswell, J., and Gleitman, L. (2004) Children's eye movements during listening: developmental evidence for a constraints-based theory of sentence processing, in J. Henderson and F. Ferreira (eds) *The interface of language, vision, and action*. New York: Psychology Press.

Tseng, W., and Schmitt, N. (2008) Toward a model of motivated vocabulary learning: a structural equation modeling approach. *Language Learning*, 58, pp. 357–400.

Tsui, A. (1994) *English conversation*. Oxford: Oxford University Press.

Tsui, A., and Fullilove, J. (1998) Bottom-up or top-down processing as a discriminator of L2 listening performance. *Applied Linguistics*, 19, pp. 432–451.

Tudge, J., and Rogoff, B. (1999) Peer influence on cognitive development: Piagetan and Vygotskian perspectives, in P. Lloyd and C. Fernyhough (eds) *Lev Vygotsky: critical assessments: the zone of proximal development*, Vol. III. London: Taylor & Francis.

Tuzi, F., Mori, K., and Young, A. (2008) Using TV commercials in ESL/EFL classes. *Internet TESL Journal*, 14 (5), http://iteslj.org/Techniques/Tuzi-TVCommercials. html.

Tyler, A. (1995) The co-construction of cross-cultural miscommunication: conflicts in perception, negotiation, and enhancement of participant role and status. *Studies in Second Language Acquisition*, 17, pp. 129–52.

Umino, T. (2006) Learning a second language through audiovisual media: a longitudinal investigation of strategy use and development, in Y. Asako, T. Umino and M. Negishi (eds) *Readings in second language pedagogy and second language acquisition*. Amsterdam: Benjamins.

Ushioda, E. (2008) Motivation and language, in J. Verschueren, J. Östman and E. Versluys (eds) *Handbook of pragmatics* 4. Amsterdam: Benjamins.

Valett, R. (1977) *Humanistic education*. St Louis, MO: Mosby.

Van den Broek, P., Rapp, D., and Kendeou, P. (2005) Integrating memory-based and constructionist processes in accounts of reading. *Discourse Processes*, **39**, pp. 299–316.

Van Den Noort, M., Bosch, P., Hadzibeganovic, T., Mondt, K., Haverkort, M., and Hugdahl, K. (2010). Identifying the neural substrates of second language acquisition, in J. Arabski and A. Wojtaszek (eds) *Neurolinguistic and psycholinguistic perspectives on SLA*. Clevedon: Multilingual Matters.

Van der Veer, R. (2007) *Lev Vygotsky*. Continuum Library of Educational Thought. London: Continuum.

Van Heuven, W., and Dijkstra, T. (2010) Language comprehension in the bilingual brain: fMRI and ERP support for psycholinguistic models. *Brain Research*, 3.

Vandergrift, L. (2005) Relationships among motivation orientations, metacognitive awareness and proficiency in L2 listening. *Applied Linguistics*, **26**, pp. 70–89.

Vandergrift, L. (1997) The comprehension strategies of second language (French) listeners: a descriptive study. *Foreign Language Annals*, **30**, pp. 387–409.

Vandergrift, L. (1998) Successful and less successful listeners in French: What are the strategy differences? *French Review*, **71**, pp. 370–95.

Vandergrift, L. (1999) Facilitating second language listening comprehension: acquiring successful strategies. *ELT Journal*, **53** (4), pp. 73–8.

Vandergrift, L. (2007) Recent developments in second and foreign language listening comprehension research. *Language Teaching*, **40**, pp. 191–210.

Vandergrift, L., and Goh, C. (2009) Teaching and testing listening comprehension, in M. Long and C. Doughty (eds) *The handbook of language teaching*. Oxford: Blackwell.

Vandergrift, L., Goh, C., Mareschal, C. and Tafaghodtari, M. (2006) The metacognitive awareness listening questionnaire: development and validation. *Language Learning*, **56**, pp. 431–62.

VanPatten, B. (1996) *Input processing and grammar instruction in second language acquisition*. Norwood, NJ: Ablex.

VanPatten, B. (2005) Processing instruction, in C. Sanz (ed.) *Mind and context in adult second language acquisition: methods, theory, and practice*. Washington, DC: Georgetown University Press.

VanPatten, B., Inclezan, D., Salazar, H., and Farley, A. (2009) Processing instruction and dictogloss: a study on object pronouns and word order. *Spanish Foreign Language Annals*, **42**, pp. 557–75.

VanPatten, C., Coulson, S., Rubin, S., Plante, E., and Parks, M. (1999) Time course of word identification and semantic integration in spoken language. *Journal of Experimental Pyschology: Learning, Memory, and Cognition*, **25**, pp. 394–417.

Varela, F., and Shear, J. (2001) *The view from within: first-person methodologies*. Exeter: Imprint Academic.

Vendrame, M., Cutica, I., and Bucciarelli, M. (2010) 'I see what you mean': oral deaf individuals benefit from speaker's gesturing. *European Journal of Cognitive Psychology*, **1**, pp. 38–52.

Verschueren, J. (1999) *Understanding pragmatics*. London: Arnold.

Verschueren, J. (2009) The pragmatic perspective, in J. Verschueren and J. Östman (eds) *Key notions for pragmatics*. Amsterdam: Benjamins.

Vidal, K. (2003) Academic listening: a source of vocabulary acquisition? *Applied Linguistics*, **24**, pp. 56–89.

Vihman, M., and Croft, W. (2008) Phonological development: toward a 'radical' templatic phonology. *Linguistics*, **45** (4), pp. 683–725.

Villaume, W., and Bodie, G. (2007) Discovering the listener within us: the impact of trait-like personality variables and communicator styles on preferences for listening style. *International Journal of Listening*, **21**, pp. 102–23.

Vitevitch, M. (2007) The spread of the phonological neighborhood influences spoken word recognition. *Memory and Cognition*, **35** (1), pp. 166–75.

Vogely, A. (1995) Perceived strategy use during performance on three authentic listening comprehension tasks. *Modern Language Journal*, **79** (1), pp. 41–56.

Vouloumanos, A., and Werker, J. (2007) Listening to language at birth: evidence for a bias for speech in neonates. *Developmental Science*, **10**, pp. 159–71.

Vygotsky, L. (1978) *Mind in society: the development of higher psychological processes.* Cambridge, MA: Harvard University Press.

Wagner, E. (2010) The effect of the use of video texts on ESL listening test-taker performance. *Language Testing*.

Wajnryb, R. (1990) *Grammar dictation.* Oxford: Oxford University Press.

Walters, S. (2009) A conversation analysis-informed test of L2 aural pragmatic comprehension. *TESOL Quarterly*, **43**, pp. 29–54.

Waring, R. (2010). Starting extensive listening, www.robwaring.org/er/ER_info/starting_extensive_listening.htm.

Waring, R., and Nation, P. (2004) Vocabulary size, text coverage, and word lists, in D. Albrechtsen, K. Haastrup and B. Henriksen (eds) *Angles on the English-speaking world: writing and vocabulary in foreign language acquisition.* Copenhagen: Museum Tusculanum Press, University of Copenhagen.

Watanabe, Y., and Swain, M. (2007) Effects of proficiency differences and patterns of pair interaction on second language learning: collaborative dialogue between adult ESL learners. *Language Teaching Research*, **11**, pp. 121–42.

Weir, C. (2005) Limitations of the Common European Framework for developing comparable examinations and tests. *Language Testing*, **22**, pp. 281–300.

Weizenbaum, J. (1966) ELIZA: a computer program for the study of natural language. *Communication of the Association for Computing Machinery*, **9**, pp. 36–45.

Weller, G. (1991) The influence of comprehension input on simultaneous interpreter's output. *Proceedings of the Twelfth World Congress of FIT.* Amsterdam, Benjamins.

Wells, G. (2009) *The meaning makers: learning to talk and talking to learn.* Bristol: Multilingual Matters.

Wenner, J., Burch, M., Lynch, J., and Bauer, P. (2008) Becoming a teller of tales: associations between children's fictional narratives and parent–child reminiscence narratives. *Journal of Experimental Child Psychology*, **101**, pp. 1–19.

Werker, J. F. (1991) The ontogeny of speech perception, in G. Mattingly and M. Studdert-Kennedy (eds) *Modularity and the motor theory of speech perception.* Hillsdale, NJ: Erlbaum.

Werker, J., and. Tees, R. (2002) Cross-language speech perception: evidence for perceptual reorganization during the first year of life. *Infant Behavior and Development*, **25**, pp. 121–33.

Wesche, M., and Paribakht, T. (2010) *Lexical inferencing in a first and second language: cross-linguistic dimensions.* Clevedon: Multilingual Matters.

Wetzels, S. (2009) Individualised Strategies for Prior Knowledge Activation. Doctoral thesis, Heerlen: Open Universiteit Nederland.

Whaley, B. and Samter, W. (eds) (2007) *Explaining communication: contemporary theories and examples*. Mawah, NJ: Erlbaum.

White, C., and Burgoon, J. (2006) Adaptation and communicative design: patterns of interaction in truthful and deceptive conversations. *Human Communication Research*, **27**, pp. 9–37.

White, G. (1998) *Listening*, Oxford: Oxford University Press.

White, G. (2008) Listening and the good language learner, in C. Griffiths (ed.) *Lessons from good language learners: insights for teachers and learners: a tribute to Joan Rubin*. Cambridge: Cambridge University Press.

Wicks, P., Reason, P., and Bradbury, H. (2008) Living inquiry: personal, political and philosophical grounding in action research practice, in P. Reason and H. Bradbury (eds) *The Sage handbook of action research: participative inquiry and practice*. London: Sage.

Widdowson, H. (2007) Un-applied linguistics and communicative language teaching. *International Journal of Applied Linguistics*, http://ciilibrary.org:8000/ciil/}Fulltext/International_Journal_of_Applied_Linguistics/2007/Vol_17_2_2007/Article_4.pdf.

Wiegrebe, L., and Krumbolz, K. (1999) Temporal resolution and temporal masking properties of transient stimuli: data and an auditory model. *Journal of the Acoustic Society of America*, **105**, pp. 2746–56.

Wilce, J. (2009) Medical discourse. *Annual Review of Anthropology*, **8**, pp. 199–215.

Wilensky, R. (1981) PAM, in R. Schank and C. Riesbeck (eds) *Inside computer understanding: five programs plus miniatures*. Hillsdale, NJ: Erlbaum.

Wilensky, R. (1981) Cognitive science meta-planning: representing and using knowledge about planning in problem solving and natural language understanding. *Cognitive Science*, **5**, pp. 197–233.

Willard, G., and Gramzow, R. (2008) Exaggeration in memory: systematic distortion of self-evaluative information under reduced accessibility. *Journal of Experimental Social Psychology*, **44**, pp. 246–59.

Willems, R., and Hagoort, P. (1999) Neural evidence for the interplay between language, gesture, and action: a review. *Brain and Language*, **101**, pp. 3278–89.

Williams, Brian (2006) The Listening Behaviors of Managers in the Workplace. Ed.D. dissertation. Washington, DC: George Washington University.

Willingham, Daniel T. (2007) Critical thinking: why is it so hard to teach? *American Educator*, summer **8–19**, http://mres.gmu.edu/pmwiki/uploads/Main/CritThink.pdf.

Willis, A. (2009) Edupolitical research: reading between the lines. *Educational Researcher*, **38**, pp. 528–36.

Wilson, JJ (2008) *How to teach listening*. London: Pearson.

Wimmer, R., and Dominick, J. (2005) *Mass media research: an introduction*. Belmont. CA: Thomson.

Wiseman, C. (2004) Review of D. Boxer and A. D. Cohen (eds) *Studying speaking to inform second language learning*. Clevedon: Multilingual Matters.

Wodak, R. (1996) *Disorders of discourse*. London: Longman.

Wodak, R., ed. (1997) *Gender and discourse*. London: Sage.

Wodak, R. (2009) *The discourse of politics in action*. London: Palgrave Macmillan.

Wode, H. *et al.* (1992) L1, L2, L3: continuity vs. discontinuity in lexical acquisition, in P. Arnaud and H. Béjoint (eds) *Vocabulary and applied linguistics*. London: Macmillan.

Wong-Fillmore, L. (1991) Second language learning in children: a model of language learning in social context, in E. Bialystok (ed.) *Language processing in bilingual children*. Cambridge: Cambridge University Press.

Wood, J., and Eriksen, E. (2005/2008) The effects of simultaneous paring of auditory and visual stimuli in short-term memory. *University of Wisconsin Journal of Student Research*, www.uwstout.edu/rs/2005/2005contents.htm.

Wray, A. (2009). Identifying formulaic language: persistent challenges and new opportunities, in G. Corrigan, E. Moravcsik and H. Ouali (eds) *Formulaic language*, Vol. I. Amsterdam: Benjamins.

Wray, A., and Perkins, M. (2000) The functions of formulaic language: an integrated model. *Language and Communication*, **20**, pp. 1–28.

Yanagawa, K. and Green, A. (2008) To show or not to show: the effects of item stems and answer options on performance on a multiple-choice listening comprehension test. *System*, **36**, pp. 107–22.

Yang, R.-L. (1993) A study of the communicative anxiety and self-esteem of Chinese students in relation to their oral and listening proficiency in English. Doctoral dissertation, Atlanta, GA: University of Georgia. *Dissertation Abstracts International*, **54**, p. 2132A.

Yanushevskaya, I., Gobl C., and Chasaide A. (2008) Voice quality and loudness in affect perception. *Conference Proceedings*, *Speech Prosody*, Campinas, Brazil.

Yepes, J. (2001) Using Analysis of Retrospective Interviews following a TOEFL Listening Task to refine a Model of L2 Listening Comprehension. Paper presented at the AAAL conference, St Louis, MO.

Yuen, I., Davis, M., Brysbaert, M., and Kath Rastle, K. (2010) Activation of articulatory information in speech perception. *Proceedings of the National Academy of Sciences*, **107**, pp. 592–7.

Zadeh, L. (1965) Fuzzy sets. *Information and Control*, **8**, pp. 338–53.

Zatorre, R., Belin, P., and Penhune, V. (2002) Structure and function of auditory cortex: music and speech. *Trends in Cognitive Sciences*, **6**, pp. 37–46.

Zhang, Y. (2009) An experimental study of the effects of listening on speaking for college students. *English Language Teaching*, **3**, pp. 194–204.

Zhang, Y., Kuhl· P., Imada, T., Kotani, M., and Tohkura, Y. (2005) Effects of language experience: neural commitment to language-specific auditory patterns. *NeuroImage*, **26**, pp. 703–20.

Zipf, H. (1949) *Human behavior and the principle of least effort*. New York: Addison-Wesley.

Zubizarreta, M. L. (1998) *Prosody, focus and word order*. Cambridge, MA: MIT Press.

Zwaan, R. (2004) The immersed experiencer: embodied theory of language comprehension, in B. Ross (ed.) *The psychology of learning and motivation: advances in research and theory*. Oxford: Elsevier.

Zwaan, R. (2006) The construction of situation models in narrative comprehension: an event-indexing model. *Psychological Science*, **6** (5), pp. 292–297.

Zwaan, R. A., Kaup, B., Stanfield, R. A., and Madden, C. J. (2000) Language comprehension as guided experience, http://cogprints.org/949/00/lc_as_guided-exp.

Zwaan, R., Stanfield, R., and Yaxley, R. (2002) Language comprehenders mentally represent the shapes of objects. *Psychological Science*, **13**, pp. 168–71.

Index

The index is in word by word order. Figures are prefixed with *f* and tables are prefixed with *t*.
An example is: voice modulations 33*t*2.2